CORPORATE CRIME AND ACCOUNTABILITY IN CANADA:
FROM PROSECUTIONS TO CORPORATE SOCIAL RESPONSIBILITY

Norm Keith, B.A., J.D., LL.M., CRSP

LexisNexis

Corporate Crime and Accountability in Canada: From Prosecutions to Corporate Social Responsibility

Library and Archives Canada Cataloguing in Publication

Keith, Norman, 1956-
  Corporate crime and accountability in Canada : from prosecutions to corporate social responsibility / Norman (Norm) Keith.

Includes bibliographical references and index.
ISBN 978-0-433-46880-6

  1. Commercial crimes--Canada. 2. Criminal liability of juristic persons-- Canada. 3. Corporation law--Canada--Criminal provisions. I. Title.

KE8958.K43 2011   345.71'0268   C2011-903575-8
KF9350.K43 2011

Published by LexisNexis Canada, a member of the LexisNexis Group
LexisNexis Canada Inc.
123 Commerce Valley Dr. E., Suite 700
Markham, Ontario
L3T 7W8

Customer Service
Telephone: (905) 479-2665 • Fax: (905) 479-2826
Toll-Free Phone: 1-800-668-6481 • Toll-Free Fax: 1-800-461-3275
Email: customerservice@lexisnexis.ca
Web Site: www.lexisnexis.ca

Printed and bound in Canada.

ABOUT THE AUTHOR

Norm Keith, B.A., J.D., LL.M., CRSP, is a partner at Gowling Lafleur Henderson LLP, and has over 28 years experience in advising, representing and defending corporate and individual defendants in a variety of regulatory and criminal prosecutions. Mr. Keith has authored a number of publications, including, but not limited to, *Workplace Health and Safety Crimes* and the Halsbury's Laws of Canada *"Workplace Health and Safety"*. Mr. Keith completed his Masters of Law Degree from Osgoode Hall Law School in 2010; his thesis addressed the application of the *Charter of Rights and Freedoms* to corporations in Canada. He has successfully defended over 1,000 regulatory and criminal charges. Mr. Keith has given presentations to many professional associations boards of directors, and multi-national corporations on corporate risk management, emergency response planning, environmental, health and safety due diligence, managing regulatory and criminal investigations, foreign corruption and corporate social responsibility. Mr. Keith is based in Toronto and practices throughout Canada and internationally.

PREFACE

Corporate Crime and Accountability in Canada: From Prosecutions to Corporate Social Responsibility was written to provide a thoughtful, practical guide to the law of corporate crime and regulatory offences in Canada. There has been little review of corporate criminal liability in Canadian law. This book is intended to help corporations, their legal advisors, lawyers, boards of directors, senior managers and risk managers understand corporate criminal liability and accountability. This book is also intended to assist policy makers, regulators and prosecutors in understanding the subject of Corporate Crime and Accountability. This book addresses both criminal and regulatory laws and offences that apply to corporations in Canada.

This book provides a summary of the evolution of corporate accountability, corporate decision making and corporate liability. The book reviews the different types of offences that corporations may face. In the chapter "The Game Changer", I provide a detailed review of Bill C-45 and how it has changed criminal law for corporations in Canada. It is hard to overstate the significance of the change that Bill C-45 brought to criminal law in Canada. It established a new offence of occupational health and safety criminal negligence but it is much more than that. It also provides a new formula for all charges under the *Criminal Code* and other criminal statutes, against corporations, and organizations more broadly.

I have also used a risk management assessment approach to catalogue crimes and offences in Canadian law. Using an innovative "victim vulnerability-harm matrix", the efficacy of various enforcement systems will be analyzed. I then go on to discuss the criminal justice system and how corporations are impacted by prosecutions in our criminal courts.

I then review the rights of corporations under the *Charter of Rights and Freedoms.* This chapter is partly based on the thesis for my Masters of Law degree that I completed in 2010 at Osgoode Hall Law School. The jurisprudence of Charter cases and their application to corporations is an important area covered by this work. Since corporations are being treated more and more like individuals in criminal prosecution, corporations' rights under the Charter are becoming more important. The draconian nature of criminal prosecution for individuals is balanced in our legal system by the Charter. It is argued that corporations ought not to be afforded similar rights as individual defendants when facing criminal or regulatory charges.

I then review the various defences to criminal and strict liability offences. They are much more limited for corporations than for individuals. In strict liability charges, the defence of due diligence is available to the corporate accused and is extensively reviewed. That defence is particularly important to responsible corporations who have a management system in place to minimize legal risk.

If a corporation is convicted of an offence, then there is a sentencing and probationary process. Sentencing, on the one hand, is intended to punish, by way of deterrence, retributive penalties, and denunciation of the criminal or regulatory offence that has been committed. Probation, on the other hand, is fundamentally a rehabilitative concept that hopes to reintegrate the offender back into society. There are particular challenges with corporations being sentenced and put on probation. The important role of corporations in society as both primary employers, providers and generators of wealth and sustainers of our economic system, complicate the problem of punishing, sentencing and rehabilitating the corporate offender.

Administrative Monetary Penalties ("AMPs") are growing in popularity and introduction by new regulatory initiatives across Canada. Government policy makers are attracted to AMPs for their practicality and because they provide a more direct source of corporate accountability than prosecution. The review of AMPs in the book is critical to understanding how regulators and public policy is moving in the direction of corporate accountability.

In the last chapter I address the important subject of corporate social responsibility ("CSR"). There is a growing international consensus on the viability of CSR for improved interaction and accountability of corporations. CSR is finding a way into legislative proposals, private member bills, standards for international behaviour and its related application to corporate sustainability and environmental sustainability. The rejection of Bill C-300 by federal parliament, was not necessarily a rejection of the growing importance of CSR. The review of Bill C-300 in this work is useful to highlight the significance of the growing CSR movement. Although CSR is not likely to replace criminal and regulatory prosecution of corporations, it does provide new directions in corporate accountability.

Throughout this book, the reader may be tempted to say "what about accountability of directors, officers and senior executives of corporations"? Certainly, that is a broad and important subject in the area of the management of organizations and corporations. However, it is beyond the scope of this book to focus on the individual behaviour, management style and individual criminal and regulatory contraventions. By focusing on corporate crime and accountability, this book seeks to consider the history, evolution, theories, legal standards and practice of corporate crime and accountability. Perhaps individual accountability of directors, officers and senior executives and their personal liability and accountability may be the subject of another work.

Norm Keith, Toronto, September 2011.

TABLE OF CONTENTS

Chapter 1

INTRODUCTION TO CORPORATE CRIME AND ACCOUNTABILITY

1.1 INTRODUCTION TO CORPORATE CRIME

Corporate crime and accountability is an important subject for policy makers, businesses, workers, government, investors, stakeholders, trade unions, regulators and the public in Canada. Leaders of corporations have fiduciary duties to act in a responsible manner. However, corporations are responsible for some of the worst man-made disasters of human suffering over the years. Corporate criminals have been described as the scourge of the 21st century. The advent of technology, sophisticated organized criminal organizations, and potential harm to individuals and society, makes this an important subject indeed.

In a complex, modern, liberal democracy, the setting and enforcing standards for corporations is essential. The safety, well-being and confidence in the democratic process makes corporate accountability essential. Corporate criminals are often portrayed in the media as shadowy businessmen seeking to make profits by exploiting vulnerable members of society at any cost. Yet the role of corporations in society is integral to the economic and practical functioning of Canadian society. The subject of corporate crime and accountability deserves a more comprehensive and thorough review than media sound bites or ideological stereotypes. That is the purpose of this book.

Corporate accountability through prosecution and punishment of corporate offenders is an important but often overlooked subject in the administration of criminal justice. The evolution of the corporation, as a separate legal person and as a criminal defendant, impacts the public interest and social justice. The accountability of corporations, regarding their activities in the marketplace and their impact on individuals and society is especially critical to address in this era of growing globalization. Corporate and economic globalization has been argued to materially affect individuals, society and social justice.[1]

The development of the corporation, as a separate legal person, was in part to protect investors or those supporting the organization. In the classic

---

[1] Jock Young, *The Vertigo of Late Modernity* (Los Angeles: Sage Publishing, 2007) at 38-40.

decision of *Salomon v. Salomon & Co.*,[2] the English House of Lords held, in a civil action, that the limited liability of shareholders reduced the financial exposure of the shareholders to the extent that the company had assets. In this classic judicial decision identifying the limited liability of shareholders, it held that the individual behind the corporation, had a separate legal status as a person from that of the corporation. Similarly, in criminal prosecutions, this separate legal identity of the corporation gave rise to the legal prospect of the prosecution of the corporation as a separate legal entity.

Prosecuting corporate offenders to achieve accountability first requires a reliable theory of corporate criminal liability. The law struggled with the application of criminal law to the legal entity of the corporation. Punishing corporate offenders, for example, is only briefly addressed in the traditional criminal law sentencing literature.[3] Deterrents have been the central theory for sentencing individuals and corporations, but there has not been an extensive review of this sentencing theory for corporate offenders.[4] In short, there is a compelling need to review the evolution of corporations, their accountability by prosecution and review other means to thwart their illegal activities. It is also important to address the purpose and social utility of prosecuting corporations in the new millennium.

The Supreme Court has recognized the important role that corporations play in society and in the administration of criminal law. In the now infamous Hamilton drudging scandal, Supreme Court Justice Estey commented on the role of corporations in Canadian society, in the mid-1980s:

> The corporate vehicle now occupies such a large portion of the industrial, commercial and sociological sectors that amenability of the corporation to our criminal law is as essential in the case of the corporation as in the case of the natural person.[5]

This book will briefly consider the history of corporations and theories of corporate accountability. It will review the effect of moral panic on the development of legal standards and prosecutions to enforce those standards against corporations. It will be argued that laws establishing offences against corporations have been significantly influenced by moral panic. Moral panic has been associated with a social, media and political response to real issues that have been escalated with surreal overreactions. New offences have been established against corporations, under the influence of moral panic, with harsh monetary penalties. This political response to a social problem is not always done in the most thoughtful and effective manner.

---

[2]   [1897] A.C. 22 (H.L.).

[3]   For example, Clayton C. Ruby, *Sentencing*, 7th ed. (Markham, ON: LexisNexis Canada, 2008) is one of the few criminal law texts that has a chapter on the subject of sentencing the corporate offender, however, the chapter only devotes a brief 11 pages out of 1138 to sentencing corporate offenders; see pp. 478-89.

[4]   A.N. Doob & C.M. Webster, "Sentence Severity and Crime: Accepting the Null Hypothesis" (2003) 30 Crime and Justice: A Review of Research 143.

[5]   *R. v. Canadian Dredge & Dock Co.*, [1985] S.C.J. No. 28, [1985] 1 S.C.R. 662 at 92 (S.C.C.).

The role of the corporation in Canadian society is not just one of "for profit" businesses. Incorporated entities, both "for-profit" and "not-for-profit" corporations permeate and largely sustain Canadian society. Indeed, churches, synagogues and mosques are now generally incorporated. The same applies to local athletic facilities, universities, boys and girls community groups and registered charities doing all manner of good work for the benefit of many deserving and disadvantaged Canadians.

The issue of whether or not charitable corporations should be subject to the same laws as publicly traded, profit motivated multi-national corporations, listed on a public stock exchange has been considered by the courts. The Court of Appeal for Ontario made some comments with respect to this issue in the *R. v. Church of Scientology*[6] decision. It was argued in that case, by the religious organization, a corporate defendant, that since there were no shareholders of the corporation and that it was not engaged in commerce or the pursuit of profit, that the traditional rules of corporate criminal liability should not apply, or at least not to the same extent. The court said:

> The evidence in this case bears out the important role of the non-profit corporation in modern society. The latest figures available at the time of trial indicated that there were over 25,000 corporations without share capital in Ontario; that there were approximately 65,000 registered charities in Canada, and that almost 30,000 of these carry out religious activities; and that Canadian taxpayers donated about 3 billion to charities. To leave these organizations outside the purview of the criminal law would be intolerable. Some of the most important activities undertaken in society are performed under the umbrella of the corporate vehicle. *I can see no rational basis for adopting a different test for criminal liability than the case of non-profit corporations solely because they do not have shareholders or because any profits are used to promote the objects of the corporation rather than to enrich the shareholders personally.* The need for regulation of the conduct of the corporation through the criminal law is the same.[7]

Establishing more corporate crimes, offences and higher fines, however, does not appear to be improving corporate accountability. Scholarly study has seriously challenged the prosecution of corporations as an effective means of corporation accountability. For example, the validity of Khanna's "substitution thesis" — that corporations actually prefer fines that they pass on to customers and end users — does not necessarily promote social accountability.[8] It will be argued that the prosecution of corporate offenders in the traditional criminal justice system is not a panacea to improved corporate conduct. This book will provide an academic and practical opportunity to consider the broader impact that corporations have on society

---

[6] [1997] O.J. No. 1548, 33 O.R. (3d) 65 (Ont. C.A.), leave to appeal refused [1997] S.C.C.A. No. 683 (S.C.C.).

[7] *Ibid.*, at para. 181 [emphasis added].

[8] V.S. Khanna, "Corporate Crime Legislation: a Political Economy Analysis" (2004) 82 Wash. U.L.Q. 95.

as a whole and how to achieve corporate accountability. Support for a principled approach to prosecuting and sentencing corporate offenders may be found in the application of Alternative Dispute Resolution ("ADR") principles, a move away from monetary deterrents, and a move towards a rehabilitative model of criminal justice. It will be suggested that to achieve corporate accountability, regulators must move away from moral panic, the traditional criminal justice system and engage the concept of Corporate Social Responsibility ("CSR").[9]

Arguments in favour and against prosecuting corporations as criminals, with either criminal or regulatory offences, has been reviewed and debated in legal and policy literature in the United States, but less so in Canada. Although this book focuses on corporate crime and accountability in Canada, the debate about the rationale for treating corporations as criminals and using the traditional criminal law prosecution process, to enforce public policy, is well reviewed in American literature. In a classic *Harvard Law Review* paper, Khanna drives the trend towards increased prosecution of corporations and then calls it into serious question. He states:

> Corporate criminal liability under environmental, antitrust, securities, and other laws has grown rapidly over the last two decades in both the United States and overseas. Although the imposition of criminal liability on corporations, as opposed to managers or employees, has generated considerable debate, commentators have not comprehensively analyzed *why* corporate criminal liability exists. After all, corporations cannot be imprisoned. Furthermore, it is not clear that corporate criminal liability is the best way to influence corporate behaviour. This article compares the costs and benefits of corporate criminal liability with the costs and benefits of other possible liability strategies, including various forms of civil liability, managers' personal liability, third-party liability, and administrative sanctions, in an effort to determine the best strategy or mix of strategies for society.
>
> .....
>
> This Article concludes that the circumstances in which substantially all of the traits of corporate criminal liability are socially desirable are nearly nonexistent. Corporate criminal liability is socially desirable when corporate liability is optimal, when detection and prosecution are difficult, when sanctions on corporations need to be extremely high to maintain deterrence (yet not so high that parties other than the corporation should be sanctioned as well) and when these extremely high sanctions chill desirable behavior or there are a large number of false convictions compared to false acquittals that cannot be efficiently remedied other than through the protection of criminal procedure. All of these events must occur at about the same time that we want to send messages to society about the propriety of certain

---

[9]   Corporate social responsibility does not have a universal definition, but is generally understood as a corporate entity's system of integrating economic, social, environmental and human rights activities and responsibilities. Corporate social responsibility frequently involves creating innovative and proactive solutions to societal problems, while at the same time engaging in sustainable and profitable economic activity.

activities. This analysis suggests that corporate criminal liability would only be socially desirable in the rarest of circumstances. Therefore, pursuing corporate criminal liability results in society bearing the higher sanctioning costs of stigma, penalties and the increased cost of deterring corporate misbehavior created by the procedural protections of criminal law.[10]

Although Khanna's legal, economic and policy analysis has been widely respected by academics and scholars, it has not been embraced by policy makers, politicians and law enforcement officials in the United States or in Canada. His article starts by simply asking the question "why" corporations are subject to criminal prosecution. It may appear provocative or audacious, but it is simply rational and practical. Interestingly, the debate about the formation of the *Charter of Rights and Freedoms*[11] that was passed in April, 1982, significantly ignored the debate about whether the rights of criminals accused would include corporations. The subject of the rights of corporations under the Charter is dealt with extensively in Chapter 7. However, Khanna's thesis is that the procedural and constitutional rights guaranteed for any accused, either individual or corporate, are a significant impediment to effectively, efficiently and expeditiously addressing corporate misconduct. In other words, he suggests that there is a better way to achieve corporate accountability than the traditional criminal justice solution of prosecution, conviction and sentencing.

The thesis of Khanna is not the mainstream thinking of political or policy makers in Canada today. The trend has been towards establishing more corporate standards that are enforced through prosecution. A number of the arguments in favour of corporate crime and punishment, through a traditional criminal justice prosecution model, is set out by Beale, as follows:

First, imposing criminal liability on corporations makes sense, because corporations are not, fundamentally, fictional entities. Rather, they are very real and enormously powerful actors whose conduct often causes very significant harm both to individuals and to society as a whole. Second, many of the problems with corporate liability are endemic to U.S. criminal law, rather than unique. ... Third, a comparative review reveals something that may come as a surprise: in other countries, the focus in the past several decades has been on the creation of corporate criminal liability in jurisdictions in which it did not exist, and where such liability already existed the modern reforms included modifications intended to make it easier, rather than harder, to prosecute corporations criminally. ... Accordingly, if the reform of corporate criminal liability is to be made a priority, we should be asking about not only the need for restrictions, but also whether there is a need to expand liability or enforce existing offenses more vigorously. Finally, I will address the possible collateral consequences of a corporation's criminal conviction, such as debarment from government contracting. The key point

---

[10]   V.S. Khanna, "Corporate Criminal Liability: What Purpose Does it Serve?" (May 1996) 109:7 Harv. L. Rev. at 1477-78 and 1532-33.

[11]   Part I of the *Constitution Act, 1982*, being Schedule B to the *Canada Act, 1982* (U.K.), 1982, c. 11 [hereinafter the "Charter"].

is that these consequences are not intrinsically tied to criminal liability, nor are they limited to corporations. Accordingly, they should be considered by prosecutors on a case by case basis, but should not affect the policy questions addressed here.[12]

1.2   THE CORPORATION AS AN ACCUSED

A corporation doing business in Canada may be a legal fiction; however, it has a real impact on the society in which it operates. The corporation is a legal entity that exists for the purpose of achieving its intended, lawful activities. However, its impact goes well beyond its own interests and activities and occasionally may cross the line into illegal activities. The corporation as the primary means of conducting business, employs the vast majority of workers, produces most of the economy's goods and services, purchases many goods and services itself, and supports government and a multitude of social services. Whether the corporation is a for-profit or not-for-profit organization, it exists to facilitate the purposes of the organization. In short, corporations have a critical role to play in modern society. However, if corporations commit crimes or other offences in the course of their activities they may be prosecuted and convicted just like an individual. Criminal law sentencing literature primarily focuses on the individual and not corporations. This is understandable given the historical religious, social and moral ethos of criminal law.[13] However, when it comes to enforcing socially responsible and moral behaviour for a corporation, it is problematic that a corporation has no soul to be punished or body to be imprisoned.

Some of the literature with respect to the role of a corporation as an accused describes the struggle to prosecute corporations as one of an ideological or power struggle. This approach would tend to ignore the social benefits and practical importance of the role of a corporation, and its extension of collective decision making, but rather as a capitalism versus socialism struggle. This view has been expressed as follows:

> Thus, a series of assumptions that current forms of corporate capitalism are an essential component of Canadian society, and that corporations and their actors are inherently good *i.e.*, not profit maximising opportunist, permeated Committee hearings. Corporate crimes were overwhelmingly represented as different from "criminal" offences. This underlines the ubiquity of the ideology based perception that corporate crimes are not serious, that they are *mala prohibita* offences, not *mala in se* (that is, wrong because prohibited by government, not intrinsically evil) ... it also stands as a reminder that, while the state is not the only site where power is realized, it still plays an

---

[12]   S.S. Beale, "A Response to the Critics of Corporate Criminal Liability" (2009) 46 Am. Crim. L. Rev. 1481 at 1482.

[13]   For an interesting review of the origins of criminal law in England, which includes quotes from the Holy Bible and excerpts from history, see William Blackstone's *Commentaries on the Laws of England*, Volume IV, "Of Public Wrongs" (1769) (Chicago: University of Chicago Press, 1979) at 1-20.

important role ... ignoring this fact is empirically incorrect as well as theoretically blind.[14]

The simple truth is that criminal law is largely a reflection of moral standards imposed by various means of social control in individuals. Historically, organizations including corporations have rarely been the subject of drafting or enforcement of criminal law. The very notion that a separate legal entity known as a corporation could be held responsible for an immoral act that has been identified as a crime, is a very recent development. Certainly, directors, officers and employees of corporations and organizations have been held responsible for illegal acts that amount to crimes or regulatory offences. The idea that the organization itself, as a separate legal entity, could be an accused in a criminal or regulatory prosecution, is a recent and almost novel concept in the history of law. Further, the idea of blaming the corporation, rather than its individual decision makers, managers or employees, has a vague notion of avoiding responsibility on the part of those individuals who make decisions within the corporation. In other words, why not blame the faceless, soulless corporation, rather than the individuals who have made the decisions that result in corporate activity that causes harm to others.

The means by which a corporation may commit a crime or regulatory offence has been based on various theories of how a corporation makes decisions. The dominant theory of which was the identification theory.[15] The identification theory was recognized and affirmed by the Supreme Court of Canada in *R. v. Canadian Dredge & Dock Co.*[16] That prosecution involved bid-rigging allegations involving contracts to dredge Hamilton Harbour. The charges alleged that companies were in price collusion and bid-rigging activities were used to inflate the prices in the government contracts. The corporate defendants denied any knowledge that their representatives were acting fraudulently. The Supreme Court held that under the identification theory of corporate criminal liability, only the Board of Directors, officers and senior managers would have the necessary mental intent or *mens rea* to bind the corporation. The identification theory, therefore, had the effect of reducing the likelihood of corporations being held criminally responsible for the offences committed by lower level managers and mere representatives of the corporation. This theory of corporate criminal liability was in contrast to strict liability offences where the mere establishment of the *actus reus* of the

---

[14]   Steven Bittle & Laureen Snider, "From Manslaughter to Preventable Accident: Shaping Corporate Criminal Liability" (October 2006) 28:4 Law & Pol'y 470 at 488.

[15]   The identification theory holds a corporation liable for the acts and omissions of the senior officials and directing minds of the corporation. Depending on the size, structure and hierarchy of authority within the corporation, case law generally struggled to determine, on a case-by-case basis, what level of managerial authority and position amounted to a person whose acts and omissions were also those of the corporation.

[16]   [1985] S.C.J. No. 28, [1985] 1 S.C.R. 662 at 92 (S.C.C.).

offence would *prima facie* import guilt, subject to the defence of due diligence.[17]

The differences between *mens rea* and strict liability offences for corporations were effectively diminished in Canadian law with the introduction of statutory corporate *actus reus* and *mens rea* on March 31, 2004. The Bill C-45 amendments to the *Criminal Code*,[18] referred to at the time as the "Westray Amendments to the *Code*" introduced a statutory framework by which organizations, including corporations, may now be held criminally liable.[19] The Bill C-45 amendments were intended, among other purposes, to modernize the law and lower the threshold for establishing criminal liability for a corporation. Sections 22.1 and 22.2 of the Code, for the first time, provided a statutory formula for *mens rea* and for guilt for organizations, including corporations. Those provisions are strikingly similar to the language of many strict liability-regulatory offences.

Section 22.1 applies with respect to offences under the Code where the prosecution is required to prove negligence. Section 22.2 applies to offences under the Code where the prosecution is required to prove fault, or *mens rea*, other than negligence. Both provisions significantly redefined how an organization, including a corporation, may be proven to have committed an offence.[20]

These changes significantly lowered the threshold for the identification theory from the conduct of senior executives to the conduct of all representatives of the corporation, including employees, agents and contractors, and placed special legal responsibility on senior officers to ensure compliance with the Code, failure of which will result in criminal liability.[21] Although both provisions stop short of establishing a reverse onus on an organization that is charged with an offence under the Code, as in a strict liability offence, the language of sections 22.1 and 22.2 focuses on the nature of activity within the organization and the responsibility for establishing and maintaining management systems to ensure legal compliance by the corporation. Bill

---

[17] For a more complete discussion of the four models of Corporate Liability, see Paul Dusome, "Criminal Liability under Bill C-45: Paradigms, Prosecutor, Predicaments" (2007) 53:1 Crim. L.Q. 98.

[18] R.S.C. 1985, c. C-46 [hereinafter the "Code"].

[19] This referred to the Westray Mine disaster in Pictou County, Nova Scotia when 26 miners were killed in a series of explosions and fire on May 9, 1992. Recommendation 73 of the Report of the Public Inquiry, *The Westray Story: A Predictable Path to Disaster* (Nova Scotia: Lieutenant Governor in Council by the Westray Mine Public Inquiry, 1997) K.P. Richard, Commissioner, recommended amendments to establish criminal law accountability of officers and directors for workplace safety.

[20] Bill C-45 replaced the term "corporation" with "organization" in the *Criminal Code*, R.S.C. 1985, c. C-46. The term "organization" is now defined in the Code as follows: "'organization' means (a) a public body, body corporate, society, company, firm, partnership, trade union or municipality, or (b) an association of persons that (i) is created for a common purpose, (ii) has an operational structure, and (iii) holds itself out to the public as an association of persons".

[21] Paul Dusome, "Criminal Liability under Bill C-45: Paradigms, Prosecutor, Predicaments" (2007) 53:1 Crim. L.Q. 98, argues on Bill C-45 that it did not lower the threshold enough.

C-45 also dramatically impacted sentencing under the Code, but only for organizations, including corporations, which were convicted of a *mens rea* offence.[22] In short, corporations that are charged with criminal offences now have more in common with strict liability offences than they do with individuals charged with criminal offences.

1.3   SETTING STANDARDS FOR MODERN CORPORATION

The safety and security of individuals, the consumer goods marketplace, the financial marketplace, the environment and the public generally are the primary purposes for establishing offences against corporations. Public welfare statutes have grown to be more important than the Code in regulating the conduct of corporations in our modern, complex society. The expansion of public expectations in the areas of environmental, occupational and public safety are the subjects of media coverage and interest group advocacy almost on a daily basis. Public pressure to regulate corporations and their activities is demonstrated by legislatures passing more statutes and more regulatory standards to respond to new technologies and evolving public expectations. Compelling public interest for the regulation of the modern corporation is found in the consequences that organizations, including corporations, cause for individuals as well as society as a whole. However, from a legal perspective, there must be a basis to regulate the modern corporation within the established theory of criminal liability. As one author notes: "the theoretical basis for criminal liability of a group has historically rested on the acts and mental states of individual human beings involved in the group ... then attributed to the group."[23]

Conservative political movements and their policies of free markets and deregulation are generally out of favour in Western democracies and Canada, in particular, in the new Millennium. There is increased fear[24] of terrorism, pandemics, financial industry collapse and environmental disasters together with increased public expectations that government needs to protect its citizens in the post 9/11 world.[25] This often results in corporations being targeted for new laws and offences to hold them accountable to address these public fears and expectations. The legislative response and government prosecution of corporations to meet these expectations may be good

---

[22]   J.W. Roberts & A. Von Hirsch, "Legislating the Purpose and Principles of Sentencing" in D.P. Cole & J.V. Roberts, eds., *Making Sense of Sentencing* (Toronto: University of Toronto Press, 1999) Chapter 3.

[23]   Paul Dusome, "Criminal Liability under Bill C-45: Paradigms, Prosecutor, Predicaments" (2007) 53:1 Crim. L.Q. 98 at 110.

[24]   For a well researched and provocative commentary on the use of fear to promote the environmental-political agenda, see Michael Crichton, *State of Fear* (New York: Harper Collins, 2004).

[25]   For an excellent, early commentary of the impact of 9/11 on Canadian society and the Canadian legal system, see Kent Roach, *September 11: Consequences for Canada* (Montreal: McGill – Queen's University Press, 2003).

politics, but unfortunately it has also resulted in an oversimplified, punitive and even anti-societal approach to prosecuting and sentencing the corporate offender. This trend using more prosecutions and increasing severe fines as deterrence, however, is not always appropriate or even desirable for corporate offenders.

The aggressive prosecution of criminal and strict liability offences against corporations is problematic. On the one hand, charges against corporate offenders enhance the importance of financial stability, security, environmental, occupational and public safety in a complex society; penal enforcement seems well justified and in the public interest. On the other hand, enforcement of these laws by prosecuting corporations often results in considerable state resources being used by corporate defendants to advance traditional criminal law strategies and defences and the charges are vigorously defended; corporations naturally want to avoid the adverse effect of a conviction on business finances, reputation and viability.

A corporation charged with an offence will necessarily act in a rational manner for its best interest that may not, however, result in positive change that benefits society. Strict liability offences, like criminal charges, place legal blame on corporate offenders. The trial and prosecution process is generally retributive not restorative and does not provide a process for creative solutions in the sentencing process.[26] The prosecution process may be effective for factual and fault finding. However, by convicting and then sentencing a corporate offender with a high fine as a deterrent, there may be a failure to address broader social objectives of public welfare statutes and the Code.

There is often a policy choice to be made by politicians and regulators, regarding the setting of standards and regulation of the modern corporation. Is it better to establish a legal duty in the Code or a regulatory statute? Or, to put it another way, is it better to establish a crime or a strict liability offence to deter inappropriate corporate conduct? The view expressed by one influential prosecutor, Murray D. Segal, is interesting:

> Regulatory prosecution can also be an effective answer to corporate misconduct. Strict-liability offences can be less onerous to prove than criminal charges, where all the essential elements have to be proved beyond a reasonable doubt. Often regulatory regimes provide for enhanced evidence-gathering tools and for trial before a judge alone. Most regulatory legislation seeks to prevent harm by setting out detailed and precise regulation, whereas criminal legislation employs general terminology and tends to focus on harm after it has been caused. There is undoubtedly a role for the criminal law prosecutor to play in responding to corporate misconduct, but there are

---

[26] The leading case, for example, in sentencing for strict liability offences in Ontario is *R. v. Cotton Felts Ltd.*, [1982] O.J. No. 178, 2 C.C.C. (3d) 287 (Ont. C.A.) where the criteria for sentencing focuses primarily on specific and general deterrents.

also important roles to be played by the Ontario Securities Commission as well as environmental and workplace health and safety prosecutors.[27]

Strict liability offences now regulate corporate conduct more significantly than crimes under the Code. From *Highway Traffic Act*[28] offences to product liability regulations, from environmental protection to occupational health and safety standards, from securities legislation to consumer product regulations, corporations are subject to significant public standards, regulation and accountability. Many public welfare statutes and regulations are a political reaction to public crisis, resulting in substantial government intervention. However, the literature indicates that this rights-based approach enforcement model does not work well for meaningful resolving of complex societal disputes.[29]

One tragic incident that is an example of how the regulation of corporations evolves and where both regulatory and criminal law enforcement overlapped is Walkerton. The incident occurred in May 2000, in the small Ontario Town of Walkerton. It had a severe problem in the quality of its drinking water. Seven people died and more than 500 persons became ill as a direct result of bad drinking water.[30] Justice O'Connor, in the public inquiry that followed, noted the public's concern in his report from the Walkerton Inquiry that, "there were widespread feelings of frustration, anger and insecurity".[31] There were two direct legal responses to the Walkerton incident, in addition to the public inquiry.

The first was to establish more strict liability offences, with higher penalties. The Provincial Legislation passed stringent new standards for water testing in Ontario under the *Safe Drinking Water Act, 2002.*[32] Ontario's *Environmental Protection Act*[33] was also amended to increase the penalties on individual directors and officers of corporations when they were found guilty of a contravention of the statute, which regulates air, water or ground pollution. The *Environmental Protection Act*, provides for individuals to be imprisoned for up to one year, or a fine up to $50,000 per day for an offence on a first conviction and up to $100,000 per day for a subsequent offence, or

---

[27]   Murray D. Segal, "Responding to Misconduct in the Corporate World" (Summer 2007) 26:1 Advocates' Soc. J. 12 at para. 26.

[28]   R.S.O. 1990, c. H.8.

[29]   Julie McFarlane, *Dispute Resolution: Readings and Case Studies* (Toronto: Emond Montgomery Publications, 2003).

[30]   See the Honourable D.R. O'Connor, *Report of the Walkerton Inquiry: The Events of May 2000 and Related Issues* (Toronto: Queen's Printer for Ontario, 2002).

[31]   *Ibid.*, at 2. The public and the media's criticism of Premier Mike Harris and his Conservative government was much stronger than of Stan Koebel's failure to notify the government of the E. coli contamination which resulted in criminal liability in failing to perform their duties in testing the water quality in Walkerton that caused the death of seven residents.

[32]   S.O. 2002, c. 32. Section 1(1) of the Act states: "… the people of Ontario are entitled to expect their drinking water to be safe". Under ss. 141 and 142 of the Act, individuals may be imprisoned for a year and fined up to $100,000 per day, or both.

[33]   R.S.O. 1990, c. E.19, as amended.

both a fine and imprisonment.[34] Individuals may be fined up to $6,000,000 in certain circumstances.[35] Corporations are subject to a maximum fine of $10,000,000 upon a conviction.[36] These escalating fines may intimidate some potential corporate offenders to change behaviour, but generally fail to address or prevent the root causes of regulatory non-compliance.[37]

The second legal response to Walkerton was to prosecute two individuals criminally under the Code. There was a prosecution and eventually a guilty plea by the Koebel brothers, Frank and Stan, for the criminal offences causing the death and injury of the citizens of Walkerton.[38] These two employees of the Town of Walkerton were held criminally responsible for the failure to manage and monitor the Town's water quality. The Koebel brothers criminal responsibility was given much less media and political attention than the blame directed towards the Premier of the day, Mike Harris, and the alleged failure of the provincial regulatory system. The municipal corporation, which employed and supervised Frank and Stan Koebel, was never charged or held directly legally accountable. Municipal corporations and their employees clearly are part of the broader corporate community that needs regulation and accountability. However, the provincial government response was to introduce a harsher financial deterrent, not more effective sentencing provisions for provincial offences.

In summary, Walkerton is an example of a serious environmental and public health incident causing death, widespread fear and resulting in public expectations for action in the form of legislation with more severe fines. However well intentioned, enforcement of these community reactions, expectations and legislation to establish new strict liability offences has not always been effective and more effective regulatory models are available.[39]

1.4   CRIMINAL AND STRICT LIABILITY OFFENCES COMPARED

An important aspect of this introductory chapter is to gain an understanding of both criminal and strict liability offences. A brief review of the differences and similarities between *mens rea* and strict liability offences is appropriate before reviewing the law for corporate offenders in both types of legal systems. True crimes require proof of intention, *mens rea* and the action, *actus reus*, of breaking the law. Strict liability offences, a phrase

---

[34]   *Ibid.*, s. 187(1).

[35]   *Ibid.*, s. 187(5).

[36]   *Ibid.*, s. 187(4).

[37]   See Julie McFarlane, *Dispute Resolution: Readings and Case Studies* (Toronto: Emond Montgomery Publications, 2003) at 17-28 for a helpful discussion of the root causes of conflict based on an understanding of human and organizational needs by B. Mayer.

[38]   *R. v. Koebel*, [2004] O.J. No. 5199, 25 C.R. (6th) 231 (Ont. S.C.J.).

[39]   Gary T. Furlong, *The Conflict Resolution Toolbox* (Toronto: John Wiley & Sons Canada, 2005).

adopted by the Supreme Court in *R. v. Sault Ste. Marie (City)*,[40] is an offence where guilt follows proof of the *actus reus*. The accused is then able to raise either of the two branches of the due diligence defence; namely, the mistake of fact branch or the reasonable precautions branch. The onus of proof is on the corporate defendant to prove the defence.[41] Strict liability offences are often identified as public welfare, regulatory or *quasi*-criminal offences. Strict liability offences include, but are not limited to, environmental, occupational health and safety, public safety, transportation safety, highway safety, food safety, false advertising and product safety offences. These offences are primarily committed by corporations and *mens rea* offences are predominantly committed by individuals.

Both criminal and strict liability offences are prosecuted by way of a trial. Although there are some evidentiary differences, which will be discussed in Chapter 3, both proceedings may result in a lengthy and complex trial. One prosecutor's perspective called the prosecution of a criminal charge a "blunt and expensive instrument".[42] Therefore, one of the similarities between criminal and strict liability offences is that they are both prosecuted in courts, proof of facts are determined by evidence, and they often result in lengthy and expensive trials. Expensive for the prosecution and the state, and ultimately taxpayers. Also, very expensive for the corporate defendants, even if they win and have the charges dismissed, cannot normally recover the legal costs and other expenses associated with preparation for and defending a case in a criminal or strict liability trial.

The Supreme Court has held that strict liability offences as well as *mens rea* charges are both "offences" for the purpose of at least some legal rights under the Charter.[43] The prosecution and trial process provides corporate and individual accused with due process rights and fairness. For example, the right to full disclosure before trial, as established in *R. v. Stinchcombe*[44] and other legal rights of the defendants apply to strict liability offences as well as *mens rea* offences.

The initial legal characterization of strict liability offences by the Court in *Sault Ste. Marie* was in the pre-Charter era. The Charter has defined the rights of both individuals and corporate defendants charged with crimes and strict liability offences. The status of strict liability offences was specifically considered in the Charter by the Court in *Reference re Motor Vehicle Act (British Columbia) s. 94(2)* ("*MVR*").[45] In *MVR*, the Court held that any offence that results in a term of incarceration must, at minimum, be a strict liability offence. *MVR* did not, however, address the constitutionality of the

---

[40]   [1978] S.C.J. No. 59, [1978] 2 S.C.R. 1299 (S.C.C.).
[41]   *Ibid.*, at 1326 (S.C.R.).
[42]   Murray D. Segal, "Responding to Misconduct in the Corporate World" (Summer 2007) 26:1 Advocates' Soc. J. 12 at para. 27.
[43]   *R. v. Wigglesworth*, [1987] S.C.J. No. 71, [1987] 2 S.C.R. 541 (S.C.C.).
[44]   [1991] S.C.J. No. 83, [1991] 3 S.C.R. 326 (S.C.C.).
[45]   [1985] S.C.J. No. 73, [1985] 2 S.C.R. 486 (S.C.C.).

reverse onus of the defence of due diligence in strict liability offences. That issue is addressed in the next section of this chapter.

The Court of Appeal for Ontario applied *MVR* in *R. v. Cancoil Thermal Corp.*,[46] and held that all charges under the Ontario *Occupational Health and Safety Act*,[47] which has a maximum penalty for individuals of 12 months in jail or a fine of $25,000, or both, were at minimum strict liability offences. With significant penalties available in strict liability offences and some Charter rights applying to "offences" and not just "crimes", there is little distinction especially for corporate offenders. The *Provincial Offences Act*,[48] the procedural statute that governs prosecutions of provincial offences in Ontario, is less detailed on the subject of sentencing principles of strict liability defendants, including corporations, than is the Code. Interestingly, the less serious offences, strict liability offences, have less extensive and effective means of enforcing their purpose against corporations. Criminal and regulatory offences are otherwise very similar when they are applied to corporations.

1.5   LICENSING AND SOCIAL VULNERABILITY ARGUMENTS

The need for corporate accountability flows from the vulnerability of members of society that may be victims of the activities of corporations. The arguments in favour of treating corporate offenders with the same principles for both *mens rea* and strict liability offences have both a practical and legal foundation when dealing with corporations. Similarities between *mens rea* and strict liability offences are somewhat ironically found in the Court's justification of the reverse onus on a defendant charged with a strict liability offence. These are found in the corporate licensing and social vulnerability arguments that reflect the establishment and potential adverse social judgment of corporations. In *Sault Ste Marie*, the strict liability offence category of offences removed the *mens rea* requirement but provided a defence of due diligence. Once the prosecution has proven the *actus reus*, beyond a reasonable doubt, the onus shifts to the accused to prove due diligence, on a balance of probabilities. The defendant has the opportunity to demonstrate a reasonable belief in a mistaken set of facts which if true would render the act or omission innocent, or, that the accused took all reasonable precautions to avoid commission of the particular offence.

This reverse onus on the defendant was challenged as a contravention of the section 11(d) Charter right of the presumption of innocence of the corporate defendant. The right to be presumed innocent under section 11(d), it was argued, applied to defences as well as proof of the offence. This was

---

[46]   [1986] O.J. No. 290, 27 C.C.C. (3d) 295 (Ont. C.A.).
[47]   R.S.O. 1990, c. O.1.
[48]   R.S.O. 1990, c. P.33.

the central issue raised in *R. v. Wholesale Travel Group Inc.*[49] The Court of Appeal for Ontario held that a statutory provision in the federal *Competition Act*[50] which required the accused to bear the onus of proving statutory due diligence was contrary to section 11(d) of the Charter. The same Court in *R. v. Ellis-Don Ltd.*,[51] a similar case, quashed and set aside the reverse onus on an accused charged under the *Occupational Health and Safety Act*,[52] to prove the defence of due diligence, since that was in contravention of section 11(d) of the Charter.

The Crown appealed both *Wholesale Travel Group Inc.* and *Ellis-Don Ltd.* to the Supreme Court. The former was heard and decided first. The Court reversed the Court of Appeal and held that the statutory and common law reverse onus provisions of the due diligence defence did not offend the Charter. The Court was divided on the question of whether the reverse onus was a contravention of section 11(d) of the Charter and whether, if this was the case, the infringement was justified by section 1 of the Charter.[53] The arguments that ultimately justified the reverse onus on the accused in a strict liability offence, and the diminished presumption of innocence under section 11(d) of the Charter, were the corporate licensing and social vulnerability arguments.

Justice Cory identified a corporate licensing and vulnerability justification for the denial of the presumption of innocence for defences in a strict liability offence. He did not find a section 11(d) contravention, but if there was, he held it was justified under section 1 of the Charter. He said:

> The licensing argument is directed to this question of choice. Thus, while in the criminal context, the essential question to be determined is whether the accused has made the choice to act in the manner alleged in the indictment, the regulated defendant is, by virtue of the licensing argument, assumed to have made the choice to engage in the regulated activity. The question then becomes not whether the defendant chose to enter the regulated sphere but whether, having done so, the defendant has fulfilled the responsibilities attending that decision.
>
> The realities and complexities of a modern industrial society coupled with the very real need to protect all of society and particularly its vulnerable members, emphasize the critical importance of regulatory offences in Canada today. Our country simply could not function without extensive regulatory legislation. The protection provided by such measures constitutes a

---

[49]   [1991] S.C.J. No. 79, [1991] 3 S.C.R. 154 (S.C.C.).

[50]   R.S.C. 1970, c. C-23.

[51]   [1990] O.J. No. 2208, 1 O.R. (3d) 193 (Ont. C.A.), revd [1992] S.C.J. No. 33, [1992] 1 S.C.R. 840 (S.C.C.).

[52]   R.S.O. 1980, c. 321.

[53]   In a very complex series of reasons for judgment by four justices, Chief Justice Lamer along with Justices La Forest, Sopinka, Gonthier, McLachlin, Stevenson and Iacobucci held that there was an infringement of s. 11(d) and Justices Gonthier, Stevenson, Iacobucci, L'Heureux-Dubé and Cory held that the infringement was justified under s. 1 of the Charter.

second justification for the differential treatment, for *Charter* purposes, of regulatory and criminal offences.[54]

The corporate licensing and social vulnerability arguments have applications to both strict liability and *mens rea* offences committed by a corporation. The objectives of regulating corporate conduct in the Code are essentially the same as in the *Wholesale Travel* decision. They include the management of corporate ethics and prevention of corporate misconduct that is within their control. It is suggested that the corporate licensing and social vulnerability arguments also apply to sentencing of the corporate offender, regardless of the type of offence. Since the corporate offender has no soul to be damned or no body to be kicked, or more practically speaking, no ability to be incarcerated for an offence, the similarities between both types of corporate offences are both legal and practical. However, that same aspect of a corporation makes it easier to blame, prosecute and punish by way of prosecution.

To some extent, the law has already categorized the legal status of corporations, where *mens rea* or strict liability offences, are the same when it comes to Charter rights. This is primarily based on the inability of a corporation, to be incarcerated or deprived of liberty. In *Irwin Toy Ltd. v. Quebec (A.G.)*,[55] the Supreme Court held that section 7 of the Charter could not be invoked by a corporation in an attempt to challenge provincial legislation that prohibited commercial advertising directed at persons under 13 years of age. The toy company sought a declaration that such a prohibition under the Quebec *Consumer Protection Act*[56] was, *inter alia*, contrary to section 7 of the Charter. The Court concluded that since the term "everyone", when read in light of the rest of the section, excludes corporations and other artificial entities incapable of enjoying life, liberty and security of the person, section 7 only applies to human beings. Corporations have only been permitted to raise section 7 Charter rights that would normally be exclusive purview of individual defendants when a corporation is challenging a statute which may infringe the rights of an individual.[57] This consistent treatment of corporations charged with *mens rea* and strict liability offences under the Charter demonstrates the similarities of both offences when enforced against corporations.

The *Irwin Toy* decision of the Supreme Court was the subject of considerable criticism by anti-corporate advocates. In that case, the corporate accused invoked rights found in the Charter, not only section 7, but also section 2(b) of the Charter with respect to freedom of expression. One of the most strident critics of corporations, and leveraging the emotional issue of

---

[54]   *R. v. Wholesale Travel Group Inc.*, [1991] S.C.J. No. 79 at paras. 157, 169, [1991] 3 S.C.R. 154 (S.C.C.).

[55]   [1989] S.C.J. No. 36, [1989] 1 S.C.R. 927 (S.C.C.).

[56]   R.S.Q. c. P-40.1.

[57]   *R. v. Big M Drug Mart Ltd.*, [1985] S.C.J. No. 17, [1985] 1 S.C.R. 295 (S.C.C.).

advertising to pre-teens, uses the *Irwin Toy* case to emphasize this point as follows:

> In 1978, worried about the impact of advertising on children, the Quebec government passed legislation to ban, in the province, all advertising directed at persons under 13 years of age. Irwin Toy corporation objected to this legislation, and the reason for its objection were obvious. The toy manufacturer advertised its products heavily on Saturday morning television, and it wanted to continue building the market for its products. It wanted to pursue the only meaningful goal that any red-blooded corporation has: To make money. Of course, when it went to a court to ask it to strike down the advertising-limited legislation, Irwin Toy did not say anything as crass as that. Rather, it swaddled itself in the clothes of a civil libertarian advocate. It argued that the Quebec government was attacking the freedom of expression as guaranteed to all Canadians by Canada's Charter of Rights and Freedoms – that is a right guaranteed to us, the people by *our* Constitution.[58]

This criticism of corporations who raise the same fairness and due process rights as individuals has been used to deny rights under the Charter. Therefore, the licensing and social vulnerability arguments have been used to deny a corporate accused the right to be presumed innocent in a strict liability offence, once the prosecution has proved the prohibited act. The distinction between a strict liability and a true criminal offence, has also been accepted as a justification to compromise an essential element of the English-Canadian common law prosecutorial system, the presumption of innocence. It has also been used to deny corporate defendants, charged with both criminal and strict liability offences, with the full rights of the law as now enshrined in the Constitution by way of the Charter. The full extent of the application of the Charter to corporations will be considered in detail in Chapter 7. The need of the state to license corporate activity and protect the vulnerable in society from corporate misconduct have been central themes in the law of corporate accountability in Canada.

---

[58]   Harry Glasbeek, *Wealth by Stealth: Corporate Crime, Corporate Law and their Perversion of Democracy* (Toronto: Between the Lines, 2002) at 90.

Chapter 2

THE EVOLUTION OF CORPORATE ACCOUNTABILITY

2.1 A BRIEF HISTORY OF CORPORATIONS

To understand the role of the corporation in modern Canadian society, as a precursor to reviewing corporate accountability, one needs to understand the history of the corporation. The corporation, as a separate legal person, has existed longer than Canada has been a nation. Although the prevalence of incorporation statutes was largely a 19th century phenomenon, corporations were known to exist in ancient Roman law.[1] English law, up until the last 200 years, saw the establishment of the corporation as a privilege granted by the Crown. Corporations did not originally have a statutory origin. The ability that exists today to incorporate a business without specific Crown approval, is a relatively recent development.[2] One of the first kind of organizations to be recognized as a separate legal entity was the ecclesiastical offices of bishops. They were given charters by the Crown and were recognized as separate legal persons. Therefore, as separate legal entities, ecclesiastical offices could own land, execute deeds and enter into contracts. Ecclesiastical bodies were not, however, established in order to conduct business like the modern profit motivated corporation. Rather, they were established to facilitate charitable activities. The positive experience of the incorporation of ecclesiastical offices was one catalyst of the modern form of corporation that exists as a separate person under the law today.[3]

The Crown also recognized merchant guilds as separate legal entities in medieval times. Merchants established industry practices and standards for trading that were approved and regulated by the guild. Trading missions were run on a joint stock basis.[4] The merchant guilds eventually gave way to charters being issued by the Crown to some of the first business

---

[1] D.L. Perrott, "Changes in Attitude to Limited Liability: the Europe Experience" in T. Orhnial, ed., *Limited Liability and The Corporation* (London: Croon Helm, 1982) at 81 and 86.

[2] Bruce Welling *et al.*, *Canadian Corporate Law: Cases, Notes and Materials* (Toronto: Butterworths Canada, 1996) at xxiii.

[3] Mark Gillen, Notes on Business Associations, "Chapter 11: History of the Corporation in England and Canada" online: <http://www.law.uvic.ca/mgillen/315/documents/Ch11-History.pdf> at 137.

[4] Joint Stock Basis meant that people would invest in the trade voyage by paying money to the company which would be used to buy goods for the voyage. Those goods would then be traded, and any profit made would be divided up amongst the original investors.

corporations. A classic Canadian example of royal prerogative establishing a corporation is the Hudson's Bay Company. The Hudson's Bay Company remains Canada's oldest existing corporation, having been granted royal charter by King Charles II in 1670. Corporations were often given charters to conduct business by the Crown and also for political reasons that benefited the Crown. European colonialism was made possible, in part, by the granting of corporate charters to business enterprises. A corporation that supported British colonialism for several centuries, the East Trading Company, was given its royal charter by Elizabeth I in 1600.[5]

The role of Crown charters establishing corporations continued into the 1700s and earlier 1800s. In 1765, Blackstone released volume one of his celebrated *Commentaries on the Laws of England*, and addressed the issue of the legal process of establishing a corporation in English law. Blackstone said:

> the King's consent is absolutely necessary to the erection of any corporation, either impliedly or expressly given. The King's implied consent is to be found in corporations which exist by force of the *common law* to which our former kings are supposed to have given their concurrent; common law being nothing else but custom, arising from the universal agreement of the whole community ... The King's consent is presumed, is as to all corporations by prescription, such as the city of London, and many others, which have existed as corporations, time whereof the memory of man runneth not to the contrary; and therefore are looked upon in law to be well created.[6]

With the growing influence of the corporation in society over the last 200 years, issues of corporate governance, shareholder rights, product liability, investor confidence, environmental impact and legal accountability have become a growing subject of public concern. However, the regulation and criminalization of corporate activity has, for the most part, been historically a more recent development and largely reactive process arising from specific crisis. For example, in 1720, the English Parliament outlawed some types of corporations in response to the infamous "South Sea Bubble".[7] The South Sea Bubble involved the exploits of a corporation called the South Sea Company. This company was a British joint stock company that was awarded exclusive trade in the Spanish colonies of South America by the Crown. The directors of the South Sea Company promised fabulous profits, gold and silver in exchange for common British exports such as cheese and pickles.[8] These promises by the directors, fuelled by investor greed,

---

[5]   Peter Marshall, "The British Presence in India in the 18th Century" *British Broadcasting Corporation* (May 1, 2001) online: <http:www.bbc.co.uk/history/british/empire_seapower/east_india_01.shtml>.

[6]   William Blackstone, *Commentaries on the Laws of England*, Volume I, "Of The Rights of Persons" (1765), with introduction by Stanley N. Katz (Chicago and London: University of Chicago Press, 1979) at 460-61.

[7]   Joel Bakan, *The Corporation: The Pathological Pursuit of Profit and Power* (Toronto: Viking Canada, 2004) at 6.

[8]   John Carswell, *The South Sea Bubble* (London: Cresset Press, 1960) at 55.

increased demand and stock prices rose to six times their original value in one year. However, when the promises were not fulfilled and shareholders came to realize that the company was essentially worthless, the stock value plummeted and shareholders faced huge losses. The South Sea Company ultimately collapsed in 1720.[9] The directors were brought before Parliament to explain their actions. Every director was fined and some were jailed.[10] The result of the collapse led the British Parliament to enact the *Bubble Act*, which abolished the issuance of stocks without the authority of an Act of Parliament or Royal Charter.[11]

Corporate legislative reform and accountability in England began in earnest after the *Bubble Act* was repealed and the subsequent introduction the *Joint Stock Companies Act*[12] (the "JSA") in 1844. The introduction of the *Companies Act* of 1862 (the "CA") broadened the legislative control over the establishment of corporations. Much of Canadian corporate law evolved from and was influenced by this English legislation.[13]

The JSA, the earlier of the two above mentioned statutes, provided for the incorporation process by registration and made those documents completely public.[14] For the first time, all that was required to form a business corporation was to register; there was no need for special act of parliament or royal prerogative to establish a corporation. However, at this time personal liability of shareholders still existed and therefore, the modern corporation was not yet fully developed.[15]

The CA has been referred to as the single most important event in the history of capitalism.[16] The CA gave birth to what is now the modern form of incorporation legislation with limited liability of shareholders. No longer was royal prerogative or special statute required, but rather the government granted authority to any individual or group of investors to incorporate a joint stock company at any time and for any lawful purpose as long as it met the statutory requirements. This harmonized the three core principles of the modern corporation. First, that it could be a distinct legal entity able to conduct business like any natural person. Second, it was able to issue shares to investors to raise capital. Third, those investors had limited liability in the

---

[9]   Mark Gillen, Notes on Business Associations, "Chapter 11: History of the Corporation in England and Canada" online: <http://www.law.uvic.ca/mgillen/315/documents/Ch11-History.pdf> at 137.

[10]   *Ibid.*

[11]   Ron Harris, "The Bubble Act: Its Passage and its Effects on Business Organization" (September 1994) 54:3 The Journal of Economic History 610.

[12]   7&8 Vict., ch. 110&111 (1844) (Engl.).

[13]   However, it should be noted that in more recent trends, the United States policies on corporate governance have blazed the trail for Canada.

[14]   Mark Gillen, Notes on Business Associations, "Chapter 11: History of the Corporation in England and Canada" online: <http://www.law.uvic.ca/mgillen/315/documents/Ch11-History.pdf> at 143.

[15]   This changed in 1855 and 1856 with the introduction of the *Limited Liability Act* and a revised JSA respectively.

[16]   Wesley B. Truitt, *The Corporation* (Westport, CT: Greenwood Press, 2006) at 7.

company and thus would only lose what they invested in the corporation.[17] The only requirements in the CA for incorporation were that seven or more people had to sign a memorandum of association, register that document with the government, and have the word limited in the company's title to warn creditors that they would have no recourse to the company's shareholders.[18] This development coincided with many technological innovations and to some extent was fuelled by the Industrial Revolution.[19]

One commentator, a criminal prosecutor, suggests that the consequences of the industrial revolution were a justification for corporate criminal liability:

> The industrial revolution of the late 18th and early 19th centuries brought a new view. Unregulated business enterprises devastated communities, destroyed families and tore up the countryside. The railways, in particular, created unprecedented havoc. In response to these new forms of misconduct, the courts began to recognize that corporations could render themselves amenable to the criminal law for the acts resulting in serious damage.[20]

In 1849, statutes were passed in both Upper (Ontario) and Lower (Quebec) Canada that provided for the incorporation of companies for the purpose of building roads and bridges.[21] This legislation was followed in 1850 with the enactment, by the United Provinces of Canada, of a general statute for incorporation. This statute allowed for the incorporation of mining, shipbuilding, manufacturing and chemical businesses through a more expedited process that was no longer tethered to royal prerogative.[22] The general incorporation statute provided for a separate legal identity and limited liability to the shareholders of the corporations incorporated under it. Effectively, this legislation established the modern law of corporations in Canada.

Throughout this period of the development of corporations, which were essential for the organization of society, and the development of early Canada, the thought that corporations could be charged with a crime was virtually unknown. There was a prevailing belief in common law countries that criminal offences, based on tradition and rules of the clergy, did not apply to an artificial legal entity such as a corporation. As noted by one scholar:

---

[17] John Micklethwait & Adrian Wooldridge, *The Company: A short History of a Revolutionary Idea* (New York: Modern Library, 2003) at xvii.

[18] Wesley B. Truitt, *The Corporation* (Westport, CT: Greenwood Press, 2006) at 7.

[19] *Ibid.*

[20] Murray D. Segal, "Responding to Misconduct in the Corporate World" (Summer 2007) 26:1 Advocates' Soc. J. 12 at para. 7.

[21] Anthony VanDuzer, *The Law of Partnerships and Corporations* (Canada: Irwin Law, 2003) at 80. See for example *An Act to Authorize the Formation of Joint Stock Companies in Lower Canada for the Constructions of Macadamized Roads, and of Bridges and Other Works of Like Nature*, S.C. 1849, c. 56.

[22] *Ibid.*

In the early 1700s, corporate criminal liability faced at least four obstacles. The first obstacle was attributing acts of a jurisdic fiction, the corporation. Eighteenth-century courts and legal thinkers approached corporate liability with an obsessive focus on theories of corporate personality; a more pragmatic approach was not developed until the twentieth century. The second obstacle was that legal thinkers did not believe corporations could possess the moral blameworthiness necessary to commit crimes of intent. The third obstacle was the ultra vires doctrine, under which courts would not hold corporations accountable for acts, such as crimes, that were not provided for in their charters. Finally, the fourth obstacle was courts' literal understanding of criminal procedures. For example, judges required the accused to be brought physically before the court. The following discussion of the historical development of corporate criminal liability emphasizes the first two obstacles – imputing acts and criminal intentions – because they were the most difficult for courts to overcome.[23]

The historical development of corporations in Canadian law is inextricably linked to the role of the Crown, the need for capital to finance nation-building and the public interest. The corporation was a legal means to an end in a society based on the rule of law. Social improvements, economic development and political interests were as much a reason for the development of the corporation as the pursuit of capitalist profits.

2.2   EVOLVING THEORIES OF CORPORATE ACCOUNTABILITY

A corporation, given its separate legal existence from those of its individual officers, directors, employees and investors, is a legal fiction with a very real impact on the society in which it operates. The corporation is now the primary means of conducting business, employing the vast majority of workers, producing most of the economy's goods and services, purchases many goods and services itself, and by paying taxes supports a multitude of social and governmental services. Corporations are, however, synonymous with business and capitalism. Most registered charities are corporations. Corporations have most of the rights and responsibilities of individuals in society. If corporations are determined to have committed crimes and other offences in the course of their activities, they may be prosecuted and convicted like an individual. However, the law has struggled to articulate a consistent theory of corporate criminal liability. Since criminal law is an extension of social values and enforces those values through social control, it may also be used to control corporations. This is understandable given the historical, religious, social and moral ethos of criminal law.[24] Social control and behaviour accountability for

---

[23]   V.S. Khanna, "Corporate Criminal Liability: What Purpose Does it Serve?" (May 1996) 109:7 Harv. L. Rev. at 1479-80.

[24]   For an interesting review of the origins of criminal law in England, which includes reliance on the Holy Bible and excerpts from history, see William Blackstone's *Commentaries on the Laws*

a corporation, however, is problematic since it has "no soul to damn or body to kick".[25]

The early concerns with respect to how to hold corporations criminally liable, assuming that policy was to be pursued, came long after the development of corporation statutes. In the United States, as one scholar notes, there were four historical developments that helped define and accelerate the identification of corporations as targets of criminal liability. They were:

1.   objection by U.S. federal courts of the European Model Penal Code approach to standards of criminal liability;

2.   U.S. congress started enacting legislation authorizing the prosecution of corporations for criminal liability for their actions;

3.   expansion of the U.S. civil service provided more resources to enforce the laws of the U.S. congress by including corporate criminal prosecutions; and

4.   development of federal sentencing guidelines for crimes committed by organizations.[26]

Four classic theories have evolved to establish corporate legal liability of crimes or *mens rea* offences. They are: the identification theory, the vicarious liability theory, the aggregation of individual fault theory and the general corporate fault mode. These four theories are reviewed in detail in Chapter 3. However, the dominant theory in Canadian jurisprudence was the identification theory.[27]

The identification theory evolved from English common law. As one commentator described it, the identification theory was a set of handcuffs on prosecutors:

> ... early in the 20th century, the ambit of corporate criminal liability in England was restricted by the development of the identification theory, under which a corporation can only be successfully prosecuted for a *mens rea* crime if it can be shown that the directing mind of the corporation was involved in the criminality.[28]

In spite of these restrictive elements of the identification theory, the Supreme Court upheld the conviction in the *R. v. Union Colliery Co. of British*

---

of England, Volume IV, "Of Public Wrongs" (1769) (Chicago: University of Chicago Press, 1979) at 1-20.

[25]   Lord Chancellor (Edward) Thurlow of England's famous 17th century quote referenced in J.C. Coffee, Jr., "'No Soul to Damn: No Body to Kick': An Unscandalized Inquiry into the Problem of Corporate Punishment" (1981) 79 Mich. L. Rev. 386 at 386.

[26]   V.S. Khanna, "Corporate Criminal Liability: What Purpose Does it Serve?" (May 1996) 109:7 Harv. L. Rev. at 1487-88.

[27]   The identification theory holds a corporation liable for the acts and omissions of the senior officials and directing minds of the corporation. Depending on the size, structure and hierarchy of authority within the corporation, case law generally struggled to determine, on a case-by-case basis, what level of managerial authority and position amounted to a person whose acts and omissions were also those of the corporation.

[28]   Murray D. Segal, "Responding to Misconduct in the Corporate World" (Summer 2007) 26:1 Advocates' Soc. J. 12 at para. 9.

Columbia[29] where a company was negligent in maintaining a railway bridge, resulting in an incident that caused six fatalities.

The identification theory was affirmed and restated in 1985 by the Supreme Court in *R. v. Canadian Dredge & Dock Co.*[30] The charges alleged that companies were involved in bid-rigging activities to inflate the prices of government contracts. The Court held that under the identification theory of corporate criminal liability, only the Board of Directors, officers and senior managers would have the *mens rea* to hold the corporation criminally liable. The identification theory had the effect of reducing the likelihood of corporations being held criminally responsible for the offences committed by lower level managers and mere representatives of the corporation. This theory of corporate criminal liability was in contrast to strict liability offences where the mere establishment of the *actus reus* of the offence would *prima facie* import guilt, subject to the defence of due diligence.[31]

Corporations are subject to accountability under both criminal and *quasi*-criminal regulatory laws. The differences between *mens rea* and strict liability offences for corporations, were substantially diminished with the introduction of statutory corporate *mens rea* on March 31, 2004. The Bill C-45 amendments to the *Criminal Code*,[32] referred to at the time as the "Westray Amendments to the *Code*" introduced a statutory framework by which organizations, including corporations, may now be held criminally liable.[33] The role of moral panic in the promulgation and passage of Bill C-45 is reviewed later in Chapter 4. Bill C-45 was intended, among other objectives, to modernize the law of establishing criminal liability for a corporation.

Sections 22.1 and 22.2 of the Code, for the first time, provided a statutory framework for the *mens rea* and *actus reus* of organizations, including corporations, charged with criminal offences. Those provisions are strikingly similar to the language of many regulatory, strict liability-regulatory offences. Both provisions significantly redefined how an organization, including a corporation, may be proven to have committed an offence.[34] These

---

[29]   [1900] S.C.J. No. 64, 31 S.C.R. 81 (S.C.C.).

[30]   [1985] S.C.J. No. 28, [1985] 1 S.C.R. 662 (S.C.C.).

[31]   For a more complete discussion of the four models of Corporate Liability see Paul Dusome "Criminal Liability under Bill C-45: Paradigms, Prosecutor, Predicaments" (2008) 53:1 Crim. L.Q. 98.

[32]   R.S.C. 1985, c. C-46 [hereinafter the "Code"].

[33]   This referred to the Westray Mine disaster in Pictou County, Nova Scotia when 26 miners were killed in a series of explosions and fire on May 9, 1992. Recommendation 73 of the Report of the Public Inquiry, *The Westray Story: A Predictable Path to Disaster* (Nova Scotia: Lieutenant Governor in Council by the Westray Mine Public Inquiry, 1997) K.P. Richard, Commissioner, recommended amendments to establish criminal law accountability of officers and directors for workplace safety.

[34]   Bill C-45 replaced the term "corporation" with "organization" in the *Criminal Code*, R.S.C. 1985 c. C-46. The term "organization" is now defined in the Code as follows: "'organization' means (a) a public body, body corporate, society, company, firm, partnership, trade union or municipality, or (b) an association of persons that (i) is created for a common purpose, (ii) has an operational structure, and (iii) holds itself out to the public at an association of persons."

changes lowered the *mens rea* threshold from the identification theory of senior executives to the conduct of all representatives of the corporation. Bill C-45 also impacted sentencing under the Code for organizations, including corporations, which were convicted of a *mens rea* offence.[35] It is submitted that this evolution means that criminal offences against corporations now have more in common with strict liability offences than they do with individuals charged with criminal offences. As a result, the process, rights of accused, defences, sentencing and accountability ought to be considered together.

2.3   REGULATION OF THE MODERN CORPORATION

The role of the corporation has evolved in modern society. The regulation of the modern corporation has been through both criminal and regulatory laws. More than new crimes for corporations, regulatory laws have become the primary choice for controlling the conduct of corporations. The safety and security of individuals, financial markets, consumer products, the environment and the public are the primary purposes of corporate accountability. Public welfare statutes have evolved to become more important than the Code in regulating the conduct of corporations in our modern, complex society. The increase in public expectations in the areas of environmental, occupational safety, public security and financial markets stability are the subjects of media coverage, interest group advocacy, political debate and public moral outrage. Public pressure to regulate corporations and their activities is demonstrated by government passing more statutes and more regulatory standards to respond to new technologies and evolving public expectations. In short, modern corporations are subject to increased standards through regulatory laws. However, regulatory laws have been enforced through criminal law means, namely prosecutions. The legislative response and government prosecution of corporations is not only good politics, it offers an oversimplified approach to the complex subject of the role of corporations in society and corporate accountability.

Vast influence that is wielded by the modern, multi-national corporation, is impressive if not staggering. Public interests must be protected through corporate accountability. However, a presumption in favour of prosecution and corporate criminal liability ought to be balanced with reasonable rights of the accused. The question for the legal policy maker is whether or not this responsibility needs to be recognized and enforced in law by means of criminal or regulatory prosecutions. As one commentator has said: "Modern corporations not only wield virtually unprecedented power, but they do so in a fashion that often causes serious harm to both individuals and to society as a whole. In some recent cases, corporate misconduct and malfeasance destabilized the stock market and led to the loss of billions in

---

[35]   *Criminal Code*, ss. 718.21 and 732.1.

shareholder equity and the loss of tens (or perhaps even hundreds) of thousands of jobs."[36]

One commentator, unsympathetic to critics of corporate criminal liability, makes an interesting comparison between a corporate and an individual criminal defendant. "[C]orporations are constructs of law; they are not natural phenomena. No one has ever seen a corporation, smelled a corporation, touched a corporation, lifted a corporation, or made love to a corporation."[37]

However accurate these observations may be, they ignore the fact that the state, through corporation statutes, have established corporations as a separate legal entity or person. Therefore, when the state passes accountability laws for individuals and corporations, the safeguards and protections given to individuals ought to also be available to other legal persons, such as corporations.

Corporate accountability through prosecution is more complex than it might first appear. The modern trend of regulating corporations by the prosecution of both strict liability and criminal offences against corporations is problematic. On the one hand, charges against corporate offenders enhance the importance of financial, environmental, occupational safety and public security laws in society; penal enforcement seems well justified to protect the public interest. On the other hand, prosecutorial enforcement of these laws against corporations often results in considerable public resources being used and in response, traditional criminal law defence strategies are employed by corporations to vigorously defend charges in court. Corporations naturally want to avoid the stigma and adverse effect of a conviction on business finances and reputation. Accountability can focus on improving corporate conduct or it can focus on truth telling for the purpose of a trial in court. However, it has been widely acknowledged that the truth is only a by-product of the adversarial trial.[38] Prosecution of corporations for crimes and regulatory offences is always a retrospective means of corporation accountability. The truth telling through evidence tendered at trials is always a retrospective attempt to deal with an incident after it happens. The adversary nature of a trial lacks a process for creative solutions in the sentencing process and relies primarily on the blunt theory of deterrence and monetary penalties.[39]

The evolution of corporate accountability has resulted in a plethora of regulatory strict liability offences which now regulate corporate conduct more than the Code. From public safety to product safety, from airplane

---

[36] S.S. Beale, "A Response to the Critics of Corporate Criminal Liability" (2009) 46 Am. Crim. L. Rev. 1481 at 1483.

[37] Harry Glasbeek, *Wealth by Stealth: Corporate Crime, Corporate Law and their Perversion of Democracy* (Toronto: Between the Lines, 2002) at 7.

[38] John H. Langbein, *The Origins of Adversary Criminal Trial* (London: Oxford University Press, 2003) at 331-33.

[39] The leading case, for example, in sentencing for strict liability offences in Ontario is *R. v. Cotton Felts*, [1982] O.J. No. 178, 2 C.C.C. (3d) 287 (Ont. C.A.) where the criteria for sentencing focuses primarily on specific and general deterrents.

safety to road safety under the *Highway Traffic Act*[40] corporations are subject to significant public regulation. Regulatory statutes and fines for their
contravention, often are a political reaction to public crisis, media campaigns
and momentary moral outrage resulting in substantial government legislative
intervention. New laws, with rights and responsibilities, can result in more
prosecutions of corporations. However, the literature indicates that this
prosecution-blame approach does not work well to meaningful resolving of
complex societal problems.[41]

What often has impacted the impetus to regulate and criminalize actions of the modern corporation is the potential for misuse of corporate resources and power. However, the mere existence of a large, multi-national
corporation, with large economic power, does not necessarily justify criminalized prosecution of corporations as the most effective means to manage,
regulate, or control such economic power. In other words, the *method* of
accountability, as well as the obvious *need* for corporate accountability,
must be carefully considered. Otherwise the mere size and enormity of the
economic influence that corporations in the modern world have, may be
used by all manner of interests, not the least of which are changing political
interests, to justify new and more aggressive criminalized laws against corporations. Although this might make for a good 30-second sound bite on the
evening news, it clearly does not make for good public policy. Criminalization of corporate activity may in fact work against society's interest of regulating and controlling economic power of multi-national corporations.

However, the risk that public manipulation and moral outrage may be
used to further justify the criminalization of corporate behaviour and increase numbers of prosecutions of corporations is easily understood when
the enormity of economic power of some, large multi-national corporations
is understood. One author, promoting the increased use of corporate criminal
liability, makes her argument based as follows:

> Moreover, the power now wielded by corporations is both enormous and
> unprecedented in human history. It misses a lot to compare corporations like
> Exxon Mobil, Microsoft, or AGI to a horse or a cart that was treated as a
> deodand under ancient English law. The wealth of the top Fortune 500 cor-
> porations is one measure of corporate power. In 2008, annual revenues from
> the top ten revenue-producing corporations in the U.S. were more than $2.1
> trillion; the profits from the ten most profitable U.S. corporations were more
> than $176 billion. Exxon Mobil topped both lists, recording almost $445 bil-
> lion in revenue and over $45 billion in profit. Corporations also wield power
> more directly via their lobbying efforts. Since 1998 Exxon Mobil has spent
> over $120 million on lobbying, including 29 million in 2009. The U.S.
> Chamber of Commerce has spent over $477 million since 1998, more than
> twice the amount of any other corporation or industry group. Other industry

---

[40] R.S.O. 1990, c. H.8.

[41] Julie McFarlane, *Dispute Resolution Readings and Case Studies* (Toronto: Emond Montgomery
Publications, 2003).

groups, like the Pharmaceutical Research and Manufacturers of America, spent hundreds of millions of dollars in the last ten years of lobbying on behalf of multiple corporations.[42]

2.4   MORAL PANIC AND CORPORATE ACCOUNTABILITY

The evolution of corporate criminal liability has been clearly influenced by social crisis, tragic events and political reaction to them. Sociologists refer to this phenomenon as moral panic. Moral panic has been discussed in the literature from both a sociological and a criminal justice perspective.[43] Moral panic is typified by an incident or series of incidents, with strong media coverage reaction or distortion, and a dramaturgical characterization of the activity or social actors being out of social control. Often the social drama has victims. Moral outrage at a high profile incident that is then exploited by interested parties leads to moral panic. The unacceptable and anti-social behaviour of an individual or group is then identified or named as deviant and socially unacceptable. Legislators, persons in authority, and law enforcement officials then play their role in this social drama. They often seek, then are granted broad, new enforcement powers to deal with the purported moral crisis.

The sociological theory of moral panic has roots in literature dealing with social control. The application of moral panic to corporate criminal law can take many forms. Cohen argues that the phenomena of moral panic occurs, from time to time, in most societies. The nature and cause of the moral panic may vary but the traits of moral panic are consistent regardless of the object of the panic. He states:

> Sometimes the object of the panic is quite novel and at other times it is something which has been in existence long enough, but suddenly appears in the limelight. Sometimes the panic passes over and is forgotten, except in folk-lore and collective memory; at other times it has more serious and long lasting repercussions and might produce such changes as those in society and social policy or even in the way the society conceives itself.[44]

Manning's contribution to the literature on the effect of moral panic on criminal law focuses on organizational performances and the structural meaning from the roles that organizations play. Although the application of a moral panic to corporate criminal accountability is not specifically included in his examples, Manning's theory that teamwork and coordination of

---

[42]   S.S. Beale, "A Response to the Critics of Corporate Criminal Liability" (2009) 46 Am. Crim. L. Rev. 1481 at 1483.

[43]   David Garland, *The Culture of Control* (Chicago: University of Chicago Press, 2001) see Chapters 1, 4 and 8.

[44]   Stanley Cohen, *Folk Devils and Moral Panics: The Creation of the Mods and Rockers*, 2d ed., (London: Basil Blackwell, 1987).

the various actors in the moral panic, potentially has strong application to corporate offenders.[45]

The key elements in a moral panic may involve very significant social values such as: safe drinking water, healthy workplaces and the stability of the financial system. Cohen argues that there is a need to label the individual, the criminal organization or the phenomena in particularly heinous terms to secure social, media and political support for response. This is often rooted in social, religious and cultural norms that define what behaviour is appropriate and acceptable and that which is not. Labelling corporate conduct as criminal is available at every level that a corporation may impact society. By using this labelling approach to corporate activity, the actors involved in a staging of the moral panic, knowingly or otherwise, garner support to establish strong legislative and reactive law enforcement activity. It is suggested that moral panic has had significant influence on the development of corporate crime and accountability.

A further means by which moral panic may insight the passage of new laws of corporate criminal accountability, and increase state resources to enforce such laws, is found in labelling the corporation as an instrument of class division or even class exploitation. Labelled the separate legal person of a corporation, as exclusively a tool of the rich to get richer, to exploit the poor and needy, is an inflammatory, inaccurate labelling process. It casts all corporations in the same light, be it a non-profit charitable corporation, as well as a multi-national oil and gas producer that may have caused severe environmental damage. This labelling is seen by one author who seeks to turn sympathies against corporations and label them as a means by which the rich can exploit the poor. One commentator put it this way: "… corporations are the primary, permanent, and very concrete tools that wealthy-owners use to satisfy their never-ending drive to accumulate more riches and power at the expense of the rest of us, the majority."[46]

The more visible and well publicized the incident the easier it is to classify the rebated corporate conduct as criminal. The more tragic the event, the easier it is to secure media attention, social support and political will for new law enforcement action. At first blush, this aspect of a moral panic may not appear to be as effective with corporate crime as with individuals. However, since the corporation has no "soul", or similar, sympathetic human attributes, that increases the vulnerability of corporations to moral panic to justify greater corporate criminal liability.

---

[45]   Peter K. Manning, *Police Work: The Social Organization of Policing* (Illinois: Waveland Press, 1997).

[46]   Harry Glasbeek, *Wealth by Stealth: Corporate Crime, Corporate Law and their Perversion of Democracy* (Toronto: Between the Lines, 2002) at 7.

2.5 MORAL PANIC AND CORPORATE TARGETING

Moral panic may lead to the naming, blaming and targeting of corporations for all manner of social problems. The media has the power to target a corporation, and its alleged greed for all sorts of events and social ills. Socialist politicians and political parties often do the same. It is respectfully suggested that corporations, especially large, publicly traded corporations, are easy targets of moral panic. Moral panic can lead to corporate targeting and more severe laws, aggressive enforcement and stringent punishment. When organizations rather than individuals are blamed for unsafe drinking water, financial crisis, workplace deaths and loss of one's life-savings, strong legislation and enforcement is demanded by the media and the public. Since a corporation, apart from individual directors, officers and employees, cannot be incarcerated for crimes, the public and media are tempted to mischaracterize the corporation as either above or beyond the law. However convenient this response is, unfair and unjustified targeting of corporations contributes to moral panic. This may lead to a general disdain for the corporate entity itself. The corporation, as a separate legal entity, has tremendous economic, social and public importance and benefit to modern society. But its lack of human existence makes it a subject of marginalization blaming and subsequent targeting.

The process of labelling a corporation as powerful, unaccountable and socially irresponsible fuels media, public and political outrage and action to prosecute corporations. When the rhetoric of social panic threatens perceived interests or order in modern society, strong political reaction often follows. Silver discusses the demand for order in the civil society and the use of naming and fear to achieve that end. His comments have applicability in the evolution of corporate accountability under the influence of corporations as an undesirable class.

> It was much more than a question of annoyance, indignation or personal insecurity; the social order itself was threatened by an entity whose characteristic name reflects the fears of the time – the 'dangerous classes'. ... One of an unmanageable, volatile, and convulsively criminal class at the base of society.[47]

There are at least three arguments suggesting that corporations are vulnerable to moral panic. First, the corporation has no soul or human face that would insulate it from irrational, unjustified and implausible moral panic. The absence of a human face and human identity of a corporation, ironically makes it more vulnerable to criticism, blame and moral panic. Even though many modern, large corporations have media relations personnel, the media are often free to criticize corporations for their mistakes and adverse effects on society. The very nature of the legal entity itself, makes a corporation

---

[47] Allan Silver, "The Demand for Order in Civil Society: A Review of Some Themes in the History of Urban Crime, Police and Riot" in David J. Bordua, ed., *The Police: Six Sociological Essays* (New York: John Wiley and Sons, 1967).

vulnerable to moral panic when individuals, groups or the public are adversely impacted by the actions of a corporation.

However, when a corporation is attributed to have a human identity or "face", it is often the face of a particularly vilified or despised member of society. A socialist view of leaders of Canadian corporations, seeks to put a human "face" to the corporation, in an attempt to criticize the separate legal entity that a corporation has, rather than "humanize" the corporation.

> Conrad Black has an invisible friend. So does Lord Thomson of Fleet, and so do Wallace and Harrison McCain, Kenneth Irving, Paul Desmarais, Frank Stronach, Galen Weston – as do all other captains of Canadian industry, finance, retail and everything else. But, unlike our little kid, they are not asked to shoulder the responsibility for any havoc they may cause.[48]

Second, the management of corporations, especially large corporate organizations, is not well understood by society generally, and the law in particular. Decision making process in a large organization may be complex and may vary from corporation to corporation. The extent of both external regulatory standards, be they financial, environmental, occupational or public safety, must be addressed at various levels within a large corporate organization. However, there is a broad range of management decision making models available to corporations. Therefore, what may seem as a reasonable and plausible management decision within the organization, may be misunderstood or even vilified by society, the media and legislators. The review of theories of corporate legal liability, illustrates the legal difficulties regarding how corporate decisions are made. When there is a breakdown in the decision making process, even with a small element within the corporation resulting in illegal activity, the corporation as a whole is vulnerable to criticism and prosecution. Therefore, the lack of knowledge of the management structure and decision making process of the corporation makes it easier to criticize the corporation as being socially irresponsible and in need of stronger punitive laws and legal enforcement. An oversimplified or misunderstanding of corporate decision making can lead to a generalization that attempts to justify corporate criminal liability. As one author said: "Every sane, non-bankrupt adult has the right to form a corporation by meeting a few minor procedural requirements to the satisfaction of a government bureaucracy. Evidently, the law is eager to help us create corporations."[49]

Third, corporations are an easy target for blame from politicians, policy makers and pundits when social and economic political policy goes awry. Corporations operate *prima facie* in accordance with the social and economic structure mandated by corporate, regulatory, securities and tax laws in modern society. However, during a period of economic instability or recession, it is much easier for a politician to blame "corporate greed" and

---

[48] Harry Glasbeek, *Wealth by Stealth: Corporate Crime, Corporate Law and their Perversion of Democracy* (Toronto: Between the Lines, 2002) at 6.

[49] *Ibid.*, at 7.

"mismanagement" by the corporation, than a lack of regulatory oversight or misconceived or poorly executed government economic policy. Corporations operate within a highly regulated society that encourages globalization. Yet government policy regarding corporate conduct has social impact. Young argues that globalization has led to underemployment and insecurity in the middle class and working poor in North America.[50] This aspect of late modernity is fertile soil for the politics of moral panic. Corporations are targeted and vulnerable to moral panic because they are non-human legal entities, with complex management structures that often are easy to blame for public policy and political decisions that contributed to economic and social problems.

Concerns about globalization, that incited many riots of various G20 summits, including the Toronto 2007 summit, is used to justify violence, property damage, looting and other criminal behaviour. Inciting such anti-social, criminal behaviour, is moral panic that blames complex, international issues on corporations. As one author said:

> Capitalists no longer need to rely directly on the military and economic might of their own nation-states. The traditional uses of national power, namely to protect capitalists from rivals from another country and to help them subjugate local populations, are no longer necessary. A worldwide commitment to the free movement of goods and people is rapidly emerging and eventually this phenomenon will turn the world into one integrated market. ... It will be a world in which the neutral market, rather than political power with its potential for tyranny, will determine people's well-being, even if this well-being seems a little out of reach just now.[51]

2.6   MORAL PANIC AND NEW CORPORATE OFFENCES

Moral panic has been used to establish new crimes and offences to improve corporate accountability. This section provides three examples of significant new legislation and increased fines all in the name of improved corporate accountability in Canada. All examples arise from serious incidents that relate to important social issues. These incidents all triggered investigations, media events, public inquiries and resulted in legislative change. These examples support the argument that corporate activity that results in public harm may result in a moral panic which in turn results in increased corporate criminality and law enforcement. The important social values of workplace and environmental safety and financial and market stability all loom large in these examples. The response of policy makers, in all cases, was to create new offences, increase corporate penalties, and promise greater enforcement of the new offences. All three examples illustrate the application of the principles of moral panic to corporate crime and accountability.

---

[50]   Jock Young, *The Vertigo of Late Modernity* (Los Angeles: Sage Publishing, 2007) at 100.

[51]   Harry Glasbeek, *Wealth by Stealth: Corporate Crime, Corporate Law and their Perversion of Democracy* (Toronto: Between the Lines, 2002) at 3.

2.6.1 Workplace Safety

On May 9, 1992, 26 miners died in an explosion and fire that ripped through the Westray Mine in Plymouth, Pictou County, Nova Scotia. Only 15 of the 26 miners' bodies were ever recovered. After a failed criminal prosecution of two mine managers and the corporation under the Code a public inquiry was conducted. The Royal Canadian Mounted Police and the provincial prosecutors in Nova Scotia decided that there was not sufficient evidence to hold a second trial after the first trial had been stayed for prosecutorial misconduct and failure to provide full disclosure to the defence. Justice K.P. Richard, the Commissioner appointed to hold the public inquiry, stated in his final report that there was a "complex mosaic of actions, omissions, mistakes, incompetence, apathy, cynicism, stupidity and neglect" ... that contributed to the disaster.[52]

Tragically, the Westray Mine disaster was not the worst coal mine disaster in the history of Nova Scotia. In 1873, an explosion and fire killed 60 workers at the Drummond Mine in Westville, Nova Scotia; in 1880, an explosion resulted in the death of 44 miners at the Foord Pit; in 1918, there was an explosion and fire at the Alan Shaft Mine that resulted in the death of 88 miners.[53]

The Westray Mine disaster and the subsequent scathing report by Justice Richard, the public inquiry Commissioner, resulted in many calls for stricter occupational health and safety and criminal law sanctions for corporations, and their executives that failed to provide a safe workplace. The province of Nova Scotia reacted quickly in amending its *Occupational Health and Safety Act*.[54] These amendments increased responsibility of all workplace parties, especially employers, and increased fines for employer corporations who contravene the legislation. However, no specific director and officer duties or liability provisions were added to the Nova Scotia health and safety legislation.

Commissioner Richard, in his report on the Westray disaster, made 74 recommendations; number 73 read as follows: "The Government of Canada through the Department of Justice, should institute a study of the accountability of corporate executives and directors for the wrongful or negligent acts of the corporation and should introduce in the parliament of Canada such amendments to legislation as are necessary to ensure that corporate executives and directors are held properly accountable for workplace safety".[55] The result was the eventual introduction of Bill C-45, an act to amend the Code. When introducing the Bill, the Justice Minister, the Honourable Martin

---

[52]   K.P. Richard, Commissioner, *The Westray Story: A Predictable Path to Disaster* (Nova Scotia: Lieutenant Governor in Council by the Westray Mine Public Inquiry, 1997) an Executive Summary at vii.

[53]   Shaun Comish, *Westray Tragedy: A Miners' Story* (Halifax: Fernwood Publishing, 1993) at 2.

[54]   S.N.S. 1996, c. 7, as amended.

[55]   K.P. Richard, Commissioner, *The Westray Story: A Predictable Path to Disaster* (Nova Scotia: Lieutenant Governor in Council by the Westray Mine Public Inquiry, 1997) at 57.

Cauchon, said "employers must fully recognize their responsibility in providing a safe work environment. Failure to do so in a manner that endangers employee and public safety must be appropriately dealt with through our criminal laws. I am pleased to introduce measures today that will effectively modernize the law on corporate liability."[56]

Bill C-45 attracted attention both within and outside Canada. It is interesting to note how foreign academics and commentators have viewed the passage of Bill C-45. For example, Professor Beale, of Duke Law School stated:

> The developments in Canadian law were also a response to perception that it was too difficult to obtain corporate convictions. A government explanation of Bill C-45 refers to it as the Westray Bill, and identifies it as a response to a 1992 explosion in the Westray coal mine that left 26 miners dead. After an unsuccessful attempt to prosecute either the company or three of its employees, a Royal Commission was established to make recommendations, including the recommendation that led to the enactment of Bill C-45.[57]

What is interesting about this foreign commentary on Bill C-45, is that it clearly acknowledged the "perception" that Canadian criminal law, prior to Bill C-45, was inadequate; and this was as a result of a failure to obtain a conviction in the Westray tragedy. This is a classic example of moral outrage, with media misinformation on the reason why there was no conviction, which in form lead to public and political pressure to change the law. The state of the law at the time of the Westray disaster had very little to do with the real reasons why the Westray prosecution failed.[58]

Bill C-45 was passed into law on March 31, 2004, and it provided that corporations could receive unlimited fines. The only corporation prosecuted under Bill C-45 that has been resolved to date is *R. c. Transpavé Inc.*,[59] a Quebec corporation that pleaded guilty to criminal negligence causing death of an employee arising from a workplace fatality. The court in the *Transpavé* prosecution considered the new sentencing provisions of the Code for corporations in determining the appropriate fine. Justice Chevalier, said:

> Transpavé is not a multinational but a family corporation. It employs up to one hundred employees during production period. It has never paid dividends to its owners-shareholders, reinvesting year after year its profits in order to modernize and remain competitive. Its owners have also been very marked by this accident. They had called the next day a psychologist to help the employees. They had personally called every employee to inform them

---

[56]   Department of Justice Canada, News Release, "Justice Minister Introduces Measures to Protect Workplace Safety in Modernized Corporate Liability" (June 12, 2003).

[57]   S.S. Beale, "A Response to the Critics of Corporate Criminal Liability" (2009) 46 Am. Crim. L. Rev. 1481 at 1497.

[58]   For a complete review of the legal history of the proceedings involving the prosecution of Durragh Inc. and the two individuals prosecuted, see: Norman Keith, *Workplace Health and Safety Crimes*, 2d ed. (Markham, ON: LexisNexis Canada, 2009) and in particular, the detailed chronology of the legal proceedings that followed the Westray mine disaster in Appendix B.

[59]   [2008] J.Q. No. 1857 (Que. Ct.).

of the place and date of the funerals of their colleague. They went to the fu-
neral home to offer their sympathy to Mr. L'Écuyer's family and had reiterated their condolences at the hearing through their attorney. It is therefore
not an incentive corporation ... with regards to the factor analysis to take
into account, it must be noted that Transpavé has derived no advantage from
the perpetration of this offence ...[60]

Bill C-45 was passed, *inter alia*, to hold corporations accountable for workplace safety. Over seven years later, at the time of writing, only one corporation has been successfully prosecuted. The promise of severe fines to deter
corporate criminal negligence relating to workplace safety has not occurred.

2.6.2 Public Safety

The twin issues of public safety and environmental security arose in the
Walkerton incident. In June 2000, the small Town of Walkerton, Ontario
had a severe problem in the quality of its drinking water. E. coli from cow
manure seeped into the ground water and wells that supplied drinking water
to the residents of Walkerton. Seven people died and more than 500 persons
became ill as a result of bad drinking water.[61] Following the Walkerton incident, a public inquiry was called to address the problem and its moral panic.
Justice O'Connor, appointed to preside over the public inquiry, noted the
public's concern in his report from the Walkerton Inquiry that, "there were
widespread feelings of frustration, anger and insecurity".[62] There were two
primary legal responses to the Walkerton incident and public inquiry. The
media focused on the first more than the second. The first was to establish
more strict liability offences, with higher penalties. The Provincial Legislature passed stringent new standards for water testing in Ontario under the
Safe Drinking Water Act, 2002.[63] Ontario's *Environmental Protection Act*[64]
was also amended to increase the penalties on individual directors and officers of corporations when they were found guilty of a contravention of the
statute, which regulates air, water or ground pollution. The *Environmental
Protection Act*, provides for individuals to be imprisoned for up to one year, or
a fine up to $50,000 per day for an offence on a first conviction and up to
$100,000 per day for a subsequent offence, or both a fine and imprisonment.
Individuals may be fined up to $6,000,000 in certain circumstances.[65] Corp-

---

[60] *Ibid.*, at paras. 11 and 12.

[61] See the Honourable D.R. O'Connor, *Report of the Walkerton Inquiry: The Events of May 2000
and Related Issues* (Toronto: Queen's Printer for Ontario, 2002).

[62] *Ibid.*, at 2. The public and the media's criticism of Premier Mike Harris and his Conservative
government was much stronger than that of Stan Koebel's failure to notify the government of
the E. coli contamination which resulted in criminal liability in failing to perform their duties in
testing the water quality in Walkerton that caused the death of 7 residents.

[63] S.O. 2002, c. 32. Section 1(1) of the Act states: "... the people of Ontario are entitled to expect
their drinking water to be safe". Under ss. 141 and 142 of the Act, individuals may be imprisoned for a year and fined up to $100,000 per day or both.

[64] R.S.O. 1990, c. E.19, as amended.

[65] *Ibid.*, s. 187(5).

orations are now subject to a maximum fine of $10,000,000, upon a conviction.[66] These escalating fines may intimidate some potential offenders to change behaviour but generally fail to address the root causes of regulatory non-compliance.

The lesser publicized legal response to Walkerton was the arrest, prosecution and conviction of two individuals under the Code. There was a prosecution and guilty plea of the Koebel brothers, Frank and Stan, for criminal offences causing the death and injury of the citizens of Walkerton.[67] These two employees of the Town of Walkerton, who were held criminally responsible for the failure to manage and monitor the Town's water quality, were given much less media attention than the blame directed towards an unpopular Premier and the alleged failure of the provincial regulatory system.

Walkerton was an example of a serious environmental incident raising critical public health concerns. The incident caused widespread fear as a result of extensive media coverage. The Walkerton incident resulted in a call for action in the form of legislation regulating municipal corporations and private corporations with severe fines. Walkerton was exploited by political opponents of the presiding provincial government. The enforcement of these community expectations by the new strict liability offences ignored more effective dispute resolution models available.[68] Political expedience drove legislative action, new offences, higher fines and promised more aggressive enforcement.

2.6.3 Financial Security

Financial and market stability is a critical issue for personal and corporate economic decisions and prosperity in society. The recent Canadian legislative reaction to financial markets manipulation, dishonesty and fraud had its origins in the financial crisis of the United States. The Enron case provides a helpful example of financial instability and moral panic in the financial markets. Enron opened its doors in 1985 as a small energy company based out of Houston, Texas. Enron was the result of a merger between Houston Natural Gas and InterNorth.[69] By the 1990s Enron became one of the largest corporations in the energy market in the country, controlling 25 per cent of all gas business.[70] Expanding quickly, by late 2000 Enron's share price reached an all time high of over $90 per share reporting global revenues in excess of $100 billion.[71] Around this time, however, concerns began to surface regard-

---

[66] *Ibid.*, s. 187(4).

[67] *R. v. Koebel*, [2004] O.J. No. 5199, 25 C.R. (6th) 231 (Ont. S.C.J.).

[68] Gary T. Furlong, *The Conflict Resolution Toolbox* (Toronto: John Wiley & Sons Canada, 2005).

[69] BBC News, "Enron: Timeline" online: <http://news.bbc.co.uk/hi/english/static/in_depth/business/2002/enron/timeline/1.stm> at tab 1.

[70] *Ibid.*, at tab 4.

[71] *Ibid.*, at tab 7.

ing the sustainability of the stock price as well as the accuracy of the numbers being reported.

Confirming these concerns, then CEO of Enron, Jeff Skilling resigned on August 14, 2001. This sent shockwaves through the investor community and as a result, millions of shares in Enron dropped below $40 per share.[72] Realizing that they were likely facing serious trouble, the shredding of accounting documents began.[73] On November 8, 2001, the company restated their earnings for the past four years effectively admitting it had inflated its profits over that time. Enron filed for bankruptcy on December 2, 2001, with its share price below $1 per share.[74] The fall of Enron led to a public inquiry headed by William Powers Jr.[75] who laid the blame for the financial collapse at management. In his address to Congress, Mr. Powers stated that his report "found a systematic and pervasive attempt by Enron's Management to misrepresent the Company's financial conditions".[76]

Enron's collapse together with that of WorldCom led the United States Congress to pass the *Sarbanes-Oxley Act* of 2002 ("SOX").[77] The WorldCom collapse also resulted in a special inquiry and report listing 78 specific recommendations regarding corporate governance procedures.[78] SOX has been criticized for establishing regulatory overreaction that significantly increases the costs of managing public corporations with little benefits to shareholders.

The Canadian response to this financial crisis and economic instability in financial markets was the enactment of Bill C-13.[79] The overall purpose of the Bill was aimed at "strengthening measures to investigate, prosecute and deter capital markets fraud".[80] In order to achieve this goal, the Bill implemented five new principal provisions under the Code:

    1.   it created a new criminal offence of improper "insider trading";

---

[72] *Ibid.*, at tab 9.

[73] *Ibid.*, at tab 10.

[74] *Ibid.*, at tab 12.

[75] William Powers Jr. was a member of the Enron board of directors, as well as the chairman of the Special Investigation Committee.

[76] William Powers Jr., "The findings of Enron's special investigative committee with respect to certain transactions between Enron and certain of its current and former officers and employees" (Address given to Subcommittee on Oversight and Investigations, 5 February 2002) *Committee on Energy and Commerce* online: <http://archives.energycommerce.house.gov/reparchives/107/hearings/02052002Hearing481/Powers781.htm>.

[77] 15 U.S.C. 7201 *et al.* After numerous failed attempts, SOX was almost unanimously passed at this point.

[78] Richard Breeden, "Restoring Trust, Report to the Hon. Jed S. Rakoff, The United States District Court for the Southern District of New York" (August 2003) *Southern District of New York* online: <http://www.nysd.uscourts.gov/ruling/02cv4963082603.pdf>.

[79] Bill C-13, *An Act to amend the Criminal Code (Capital Markets Fraud and Evidence Gathering)*, 1st. Sess., 38th Parl., 2004.

[80] Robin MacKay & Margaret Smith, "Bill C-13: An Act to Amend the Criminal Code (Capital Markets Fraud and Evidence Gathering)" (Legislative Summary) *Library of Parliament* (16 February 2004) online: <http://www2.parl.gc.ca/Content%5CLOP%5CLegislativeSummaries%5C37/3/c13-e.pdf> (the "Summary").

2.   it provided whistleblower protection to employees who report unlawful conduct;

3.   it increased the maximum sentences for existing fraud offences and established a list of aggravating factors to aid the courts in sentencing;

4.   it allowed the courts to issue production orders to obtain data and documents from persons not under investigation; and

5.   it established concurrent federal jurisdiction to prosecute certain capital market fraud cases.[81]

The two most important additions to the Code were the creation of the criminal offence for insider trading and the protection of whistleblowers. Both these provisions assist the government and securities regulator to keep companies from misbehaving, in the capital markets and in improving corporate governance. The other significant changes made by the Bill include the ability for investigators to obtain production orders to compel those who are not under investigation to produce documentation deemed to be relevant to the commission of an alleged offence under section 487.012. In order to issue an order, the court must be satisfied that reasonable grounds exist to suspect that:

1.   an offence against this Act or any other Act of Parliament has been or is suspected to have been committed;

2.   the documents or data will afford evidence respecting the commission of the offence; and

3.   the person who is subject to the order has possession or control of the documents or data.[82]

Bill C-13 added new crimes and severe penalties in the Code for capital market crimes. However, there has been virtually no prosecutions under this amendment. Markets are no more secure than before the Bill. More importantly, there is no evidence that corporations, and their directors and officers have significantly changed behaviour in financial markets as a result of Bill C-13. Higher penalties, in and of themselves, have not proven to have a constructive, positive change in corporate accountability. Stan Grmovsek, a Toronto lawyer, was the first person convicted under this new insider trading crime in the Code and received a 39-month prison term.

2.7   EVOLUTION OF CORPORATE CRIME AND ACCOUNTABILITY

As indicated earlier in this chapter, corporations have evolved to become an essential part of modern Canadian society. Organizations, including corpora-

---

[81]   *Criminal Code*, R.S.C. 1985, c. C-46.

[82]   *Ibid.*, s. 487.012(3)(a)-(c).

tions, establish and manage most of the private-sector and much of the broader public-sector activities in Canada. Corporations are efficient, convenient and practical legal mechanisms to facilitate economic, charitable and socially desirable activity. The question remains, is it in the broader public interest to continue to increase the number and vigorous enforcement of crimes and regulatory offences for corporations, or is there a better way to achieve corporate accountability? Establishing and enforcing offences through prosecution has a certain political and media appeal. Prosecution is a blunt and expensive instrument for corporate accountability. However, the more important question is whether or not it will actually achieve the broader public interest of holding corporations to high standards of accountability in society, worker health and safety, environmental compliance, financial integrity, product liability, the protection of intellectual and other property rights in society.

It is hard to separate the concepts of corporate crime and accountability from the continuing and important role that corporations have in society. A balancing of interests is necessary to develop effective public policy. Moral panic does not facilitate such a balanced approach. Moral panic and purely reactive legal and policy initiatives generally ignore the broader role that corporations have in society. Therefore, the means of corporate accountability and the model of liability are a critical public policy issue. The next chapter of this book deals with methods of corporate decision making, criminal and strict liability prosecutions, and the process of accountability. The future of corporate accountability is extensively addressed in the last chapter of this book.

Chapter 3

MODELS OF CORPORATE LIABILITY AND CATEGORIES OF OFFENCES

3.1 INTRODUCTION TO CORPORATE OFFENCES

To understand how the law conceptualizes a legal fiction committing an offence, we must understand the theory behind corporate criminal liability. First, it is critical to understand that corporate criminal liability has never been a major focus of the *Criminal Code*.[1] The Code is primarily focused on individual morality and criminal conduct that is prohibited by law. That may explain the lack of Canadian literature on the subject of models of corporate criminal liability. As discussed in Chapter 2, Bills C-45 and C-13 have changed that focus in criminal law, but there has not yet been a great deal of enforcement of those provisions to date. Corporate criminal liability is problematic not only because of legal challenges of prosecuting a "legal fiction" but also since it competes with other priorities like the "war on drugs" and the "war on terror".

In the previous chapter we looked at the history of corporations and the evolution of corporate accountability. In this chapter we look at models of corporate liability and categories of offences that may be committed by corporations. As the existence of a corporate entity is established by statute, the law has to conceptualize the nature of offences against a corporation. It is easier to conceptualize offences against corporate decision makers than offences against the corporation. Directors and officers have responsibility for the legal operation of a corporation. Increasingly, both in the United States and Canada, criminal and regulatory investigations have investigated and prosecuted officers and directors of corporations. Both category of individual, whether an employee or outside director, have been held to have fiduciary duties towards the corporation, investors and stakeholders, as well as a duty to act in good faith towards the owners of the corporation, the shareholders. It is somewhat easier to identify the acts or omissions of individuals, such as officers and directors, than those of the corporation. Therefore, this chapter will look at the models and theories of corporate criminal liability and categories of offences in Canadian law that may apply to corporations.

---

[1] R.S.C. 1985, c. C-46 [hereinafter the "Code"].

Developments in the area of the accountability of corporations has looked for an appropriate theory regarding how a corporation could be held criminally liable. Since the corporation is not a human person, but rather a legal fiction established by statute to achieve commercial or other organization purposes, it engenders less sympathy and empathy than individual offenders. No corporations can argue, it had a bad childhood, divorced parents or deprived social economic upbringing as a child. Since the Code provided only limited direction on how to establish corporate criminal liability, this issue is one the Canadian legal system and courts has struggled with for some time.

Corporations have been held criminally liable for acts that have been specifically authorized by the directing mind of the corporation. The corporation could not insulate itself from liability for crimes committed by senior officers or boards of directors of the corporation. This principle developed from the identification theory. Canadian courts developed the identification theory of corporate criminal liability to hold a corporation responsible for the acts and omissions of senior officers or directing minds of the corporation. The origins of the directing mind theory pre-dates Canadian jurisprudence.

An early English House of Lords decision described the "directing mind and will" of a corporation as, "the very ego and centre of the personality of the corporation".[2] In the Canadian case of *R. v. Union Colliery Co. of British Columbia*,[3] the company was indicted for unlawfully causing the death of six persons by neglecting to properly maintain a bridge over which trains passed. The company was convicted of unlawfully neglecting, without lawful excuse, to take reasonable precautions and to use reasonable care in maintaining the trust bridge in question. A locomotive engine and several passenger cars broke through the bridge and fell into the valley of the Trent River, resulting in six deaths. The corporation was convicted at trial and eventually appealed to the Supreme Court. The Supreme Court established in that landmark case that "a corporation can render itself amenable to the criminal law for acts resulting in damage to numbers of people, or which are invasions of the rights or privileges of the public at large, or detrimental to the general well being or interests of the state."[4] Notwithstanding this acknowledgement, the question remained as to the theory or model that was appropriate to establish corporate criminal liability.

Since the initial recognition of corporate criminal liability, the common law has evolved to embrace a broader concept of corporate responsibility in the marketplace and society. Justice Schroeder in *R. v. St. Lawrence Corp.*[5] attributed this trend to the fact that, "corporations are at once more

---

2   *Lennard's Carrying Co. v. Asiatic Petroleum Co.*, [1915] A.C. 705 at 713 (H.L.).
3   [1900] S.C.J. No. 64, 31 S.C.R. 81 (S.C.C.).
4   *Ibid.*, at 84 (S.C.R.).
5   [1969] O.J. No. 1326, [1969] 3 C.C.C. 263 (Ont. C.A.).

powerful and more materially endowed and equipped than are individuals and, if allowed to roam unchecked in the field of industry and commerce, they are potentially more dangerous and can inflict greater harm upon the public than can their weaker competitors."[6] In light of Bill C-45, it is clear that this principle will continue to expand, specifically in relation to the corporation's liability for *any* employee's actions that are covered by all charges under the Code and the new Occupational Health and Safety ("OHS") legal duty added to the Code.

Interestingly, the term corporation was not defined in the Code. Therefore, the definition of a corporation would be found in the applicable corporate law statutes under federal or provincial legislation. Bill C-45 has the replacement of the word "corporation" with "organization" in the Code. The detailed analysis of this change and Bill C-45 can be found, in Chapter 4 of this book. Therefore, in the post-Bill C-45 era of the Code, it may be more accurate, legally speaking, to discuss organizational criminal liability rather than corporate criminal liability. However, corporate criminal liability will remain the popular usage term throughout this book.

3.2 THEORIES OF CORPORATE IDENTITY

The law of corporate criminal liability is inextricably linked to the nature of the corporation as a separate legal person. The manner in which the law and the courts view corporate decision-making materially affects the manner in which corporate accountability is exercised by the state. Policy makers and legislators make and pass laws regarding corporate crime and corporate accountability based on their theory of the nature and identity of the corporation. Over time, political and legal theorists have developed three primary theories of the corporation. These have been extensively reviewed by Tollefson and will only be summarized here.[7]

The concession theory of the corporation postulates that the state provides for the establishment of an artificial or legal fiction pursuant to various terms and conditions granted by the state. The concession theory inherently supports a fundamental public interest in the existence and operational success of the corporation. A corporation may exist to make money for its shareholders, but it must also exist to serve the public interest. As Tollefson remarks:

> the corporations which did exist tended to be engaged in trade or public
> works under special state charters which imposed explicit restrictions on
> capitalization, lawful activities, corporate lifespan, and share ownership
> ... the common law exempt corporations from criminal and some forms of

---

[6] *Ibid.*, para. 24.

[7] Chris Tollefson, "Corporate Constitutional Rights and the Supreme Court of Canada" (1993–1994) 19 Queen's L.J. 309.

tortious liability on the basis that, due to their artificial nature, they lacked the capacity to form the requisite intent.[8]

The second theory of the corporation is known as the contractualist theory. This approach to identifying corporate relationship and decision making is based on the human individuals who developed and promoted the corporate organizational activity by entrepreneurial initiative. The state and the public interest are not central to the contractualist theory of the corporation and, as the title of this theory suggests, it is primarily based on the concept of the freedom of contract. The contractualist theory permitted an integration of other private law systems, both contract law and the law of torts, in respect of the conduct of a corporation. This permitted a developing theory of corporate tortious liability and also potential criminal liability.[9] Contractualist theory of the corporation suggests that corporations exist to pursue the interests of the contracting parties, investors, managers and employees.

The third theory, the natural entity theory, is somewhat similar to the contractualist theory. It suggests that a corporation had a legal existence independent of state initiated positive law or the evolution of traditional private law concepts such as contract and torts. The metaphor used by natural entity theorists was that of the body, complete with various skeletal structures, systems and organs that made up the corporate "body". As Tollefson observes, "the natural entity theory advances a highly privatized notion of the corporation at once resistant to state regulation and yet capable of facilitating the doctrinal assimilation of the corporation within the broader legal system."[10] In other words, a corporation had a right to exist in law without state authorization or other legal constructs.

Each of these theories of corporate identity may influence the outlook of the state, and specific state regulatory agencies, on the manner in which corporate accountability is to be best achieved. Whether a corporation is primarily an extension of the state and its objectives, or only represents private interests, including investors and entrepreneurs, will significantly affect the method of establishing corporate crime and accountability in law. The identity of the corporation explicitly or implicitly affects the purpose of corporate accountability. However, the problem with all of these theories is that they tend to provide a two dimensional view of the modern corporation. None of these theories is necessarily representative of all corporations, large or small in modern Canadian society. None of these theories spans the full range of interests that corporations represent or activities that they facilitate.

Corporations that are established by business corporation statutes may have one shareholder and employee, or tens of thousands of shareholders and employees. Corporations may own and operate vast industrial

---

[8]   *Ibid.*, at 314.
[9]   *Ibid.*, at 317.
[10] *Ibid.*, at 319.

and extraction industries. Religious orders and charitable organizations are often incorporated. Corporations may also represent an individual personal service corporation embodied by a butcher, baker or candlestick maker.

Therefore, the search for a comprehensive theory of how and why corporations exist in society, how they are governed, how they make decisions, and ultimately, how they ought to be held accountable, may be futile. Corporations are as varied as the individuals that make up our multicultural society. Individuals may have an entrepreneurial, profit motive as their reason for being, while at the same time be highly motivated by environmental responsibility. For profit corporations may value the ethical treatment of employees and embrace corporate social responsibility principles. It is respectfully suggested that theories of corporations and their decision making methods and motives, is as diverse as the individuals who incorporate, direct, manage and are employed by them.

As Tollefson indicates, reliance on a corporate identity theory may predispose the state, and its regulators, to its predetermined and pre-conceded view of how certain social and political objectives may be achieved. For example "natural entity theory and contractualism, it is suggested, fundamentally picture the corporation as serving private interests and thus are sceptical of, if not openly hostile to, state regulation."[11] This appears to be the conclusion that state authorities and regulators take when calling for corporate accountability and liability.

3.3   MODELS OF CORPORATE CRIMINAL LIABILITY

After looking at theories of corporate decision making and identity, we now will consider models of corporate liability. The key issue that the various models of corporate criminal liability attempt to address is how to identify the individuals in a corporation whose actions will result in liability for the corporation. It is also critical to set out the process by which corporate criminal liability is established. Different countries and jurisdictions have approached corporate liability through a variety of theories or models. Canadian courts have, in the past, primarily adopted the identification theory, whereas the vicarious liability model or *respondent superior* model is used in the United States. Australia has established the corporate culture model, and corporate killing legislation is currently being discussed in the United Kingdom. Various models were considered in the public policy and political review process that ultimately culminated in Bill C-45. Each model will be briefly discussed below.

3.3.1   Identification Theory

The prevailing, pre-Bill C-45, model of corporate criminal liability in Canadian criminal jurisprudence is the identification theory. This theory holds

---

[11]   *Ibid.*, at 320.

corporations liable for the acts and omissions of senior officials and directing minds of the corporation. In the modern corporation there is some difficulty in establishing who is a senior official or a directing mind that will bind the corporation for the purposes of criminal liability. The directing mind normally must be held to have executive level authority in the corporation. However, depending on the size, structure and hierarchy of the corporation that is not always an easy level of authority to identify. The identification theory has come under criticism, for a number of years, for placing too many limits on who might be considered the corporation's directing mind. Since criminal law is restrictively applied in order to safeguard the rights of the accused, a growing consensus determined that the identification theory was inadequate to address the modern, complex corporation.

The identification theory was recognized and affirmed in Canadian law in *R. v. Canadian Dredge & Dock Co.*[12] This criminal prosecution related to alleged bid-rigging for the dredging of the Hamilton harbour. Several charges in the indictments related to contracts between public authorities and the accused where the bids were alleged to have been tendered on a collusive basis, with the low bidders arranging to compensate high bidders or non-bidders in order to secure the contract. Each company had a manager who conducted the business of the company relating to the submission of bids for tender. The accused denied any criminal involvement and maintained that the managers were acting fraudulently against their own employers, were acting on their own behalf, and were acting contrary to instructions given to them.

The identification theory focuses on the actions of the directing mind of the corporation and merges individual and corporate persons in order to assign criminal liability. The Supreme Court expanded the directing mind in *Canadian Dredge & Dock Co.* to include "the board of directors, the managing director, the superintendent, the manager or anyone else delegated by the board of directors to whom is delegated the governing executive authority of the corporation".[13] According to the Supreme Court, the identification doctrine operates, and thus imposes criminal liability on the corporation, where the Crown can demonstrate that the action taken by the directing mind (a) was within the field of operation assigned to him; (b) was not totally in fraud of the corporation; and (c) was by design or result partly for the benefit of the company.[14] Prior to *Canadian Dredge & Dock Co.*, the target group for establishing corporate criminal liability under the identification theory in the common law was defined more narrowly, including only the board of directors, the managing director and other highly placed managers.[15]

---

[12]   [1985] S.C.J. No. 28, [1985] 1 S.C.R. 662 (S.C.C).
[13]   *Ibid.*, at para. 32.
[14]   *Ibid.*, at para. 66.
[15]   *Ibid.*, at para. 32.

The identification theory is also referenced in the court decision in *R. v. Waterloo Mercury Sales Ltd.*[16] In that case, an Alberta car dealer company was prosecuted for rolling back odometers and fraudulently representing to potential customers lower mileage of various motor vehicles. The manager of the used car lot was held to be the corporation's directing mind for the purposes of determining whether it had committed criminal fraud. The president of the corporation was found to have had no knowledge of the conduct by the manager of the used car lot part of the business. The evidence at trial indicated that the president of the company had circulated written instructions prohibiting the rollback of odometers on used vehicles offered for sale. The court held that the manager was acting as the corporation's directing mind within the field of operation assigned to him, the sale of used cars, based on his power to incur debts and approve all invoices relating to the used car portion of the business. However, it appears that an employee with lesser responsibility, such as a used car salesperson or a mechanic committing the same fraudulent act of rolling back odometers, may not have been held by the court to be a directing mind of the corporation under the identification theory.

3.3.2 Vicarious Liability Model

Vicarious liability, which is prevalent in tort law, may also be a theory of corporate criminal liability. Vicarious liability is the attribution of liability to the corporation of a civil wrong by a representative of the corporation. Vicarious liability may occur when the acts or omissions of another person, such as a representative of the corporation, are held to be the acts or omissions of the corporation. The general rule in criminal law was that courts had a presumption against vicarious liability unless there was clear legislative intention to establish criminal acts by vicarious liability. In Canadian criminal law, vicarious liability has three specific requirements. First, it must be established that the employee committed the crime with the requisite fault element, and if established it is imputed to the corporation. The fault element may also be established on the collective knowledge of the employees as a group. Second, the employee must have acted within the scope of his or her employment. Third, the employee must have intended to benefit the corporation in some way. The final two requirements have been criticized for being extremely broad and easily met, thereby imposing liability without significant restriction.[17]

The vicarious liability model has been considered and rejected in both Canada and the United Kingdom. However, the Government of Canada recognized that the differences between the identification theory and the vicarious model were not that significant. In its response to the Fifteenth Report of

---

[16] [1974] A.J. No. 135, 18 C.C.C. (2d) 248 (Alta. Dist. Ct.).

[17] Dean Jobb, *Calculated Risk—Greed, Politics, and The Westray Tragedy* (Halifax: Nimbus Publishing, 1994) at 3.

the Standing Committee on Justice and Human Rights, the federal government quoted Professor Healy to explain its position: "The identification doctrine is vicarious liability. It's just at a very focused, narrow level, whereas you can have a wider range of people engaging the liability of the corporation under the American approach."[18]

Despite the appearance of a similarity between the vicarious liability model and the identification theory, Canada has been reluctant to go as far as the United States has in adapting the vicarious liability model, due to issues involving the *Charter of Rights and Freedoms*.[19] Specifically, the concern was that an absolute liability offence would be created if the net was cast too broadly, and that the Charter would not allow that result. This concern was addressed in the United Steelworkers of America's presentation to the Committee in their Bill C-45 submissions: "… things could be going on that people don't know anything about in the corporation, that, in fact, aren't even authorized by the corporation. In some jurisdictions in the U.S. that's still sufficient to warrant a conviction for the corporation. That … would run into a considerable number of Charter challenges, as well as not accomplishing the purpose."[20]

3.3.3   Corporate Culture Model

Another model of corporate criminal liability is the business or corporate culture theory. This model suggests that a corporation may commit crimes by developing a culture that promotes or tolerates criminal conduct. Bill C-284, a private members bill proposed in the post-Westray disaster response, discussed in Chapter 2, proposed a model of corporate culture criminal liability. While the federal government did not ultimately follow this direction, Australia has adopted the corporate culture model of criminal liability. That model has four alternative elements:

   (i)   the board of directors intentionally, knowingly or recklessly carried out the relevant conduct, or expressly, tacitly or impliedly authorized or permitted the commission of the offence; or

  (ii) a high managerial agent intentionally, knowingly or recklessly engaged in the relevant conduct, or expressly, tacitly or impliedly authorized or permitted the commission of the offence; or

---

[18] Canada, Department of Justice, *Government Response to the Fifteenth Report of the Standing Committee on Justice and Human Rights* (Ottawa: Department of Justice, 2002) at 9, online: <http://canada.justice.gc.ca/eng/dept-min/pub/jhr-jdp/hear-aud.html>. For Professor Healy's original comments in context, see the *Minutes of Proceedings*, at 1205, online: <http://cmte.parl.gc.ca/cmte/CommitteePublication.aspx?COM=0&SourceId=46768&SwitchLanguage=1>.

[19] Part I of the *Constitution Act, 1982*, being Schedule B to the *Canada Act, 1982* (U.K.), 1982, c. 11 [hereinafter the "Charter"].

[20] From the testimony of Andrew King, Department Leader for Health, Safety and the Environment for the United States of America, online: <http://cmte.parl.gc.ca/cmte/CommitteePublication.aspx?SourceId=46633&Lang=1&PARLSES=371&JNT=0&COM=222>.

(iii) a corporate culture existed within the corporation that directed, encouraged, tolerated or led to non-compliance with the relevant provision; or

(iv) the corporation failed to create and maintain a corporate culture that required compliance with the relevant position.[21]

Canada's pre-Bill C-45 criminal law standard for corporations was represented by the first two elements of the model. The final two points represent a divergence from Canadian corporate criminal liability rules. By establishing corporate culture criminal liability Bill C-284 would have controlled management's activities if it:

(i) tolerated, condoned or encouraged the act by the policies or practices it permitted,

(ii) was wilfully blind to the act or omission,

(iii) had allowed the development of a culture among its officers and employees that encouraged them to believe that the act or omission would be tolerated, or

(iv) failed to take steps that a reasonable corporation should take to ensure its employees knew the act or omission was unlawful or forbidden by the corporation.[22]

While some witnesses at the Committee hearings were in favour of a corporate culture model, the Canadian government decided that the model would not necessarily achieve its intended results. Furthermore, the Australian model had not yet been applied in any criminal cases. Therefore in the Canadian government's view the law remained an untested basis for criminal liability. The government response to the Committee report said:

> The Government is conscious of the need for clarity in the law and considers that "corporate culture" is too vague to constitute the necessary corporate *mens rea*. Any changes to the criminal law should be simpler and depart less from general principles than the corporate culture model.[23]

One of the most significant detractions of this model seems to be that it would be possible for a corporation to be held criminally liable without there being a requirement for an individual within the corporation to be found guilty of an offence. The federal government was not prepared to adopt this broad a collective responsibility approach to corporate criminal liability in its promulgation of Bill C-45.

3.3.4 Corporate Killing Model

The corporate killing model is an example of a specific criminal offence that focuses on a specific type of prohibited activity, workplace injury and death.

---

[21] Canada, Department of Justice, *Government Response to the Fifteenth Report of the Standing Committee on Justice and Human Rights* (Ottawa: Department of Justice, 2002) at 9, online: <http://canada.justice.gc.ca/eng/dept-min/pub/jhr-jdp/hear-aud.html>. See also the Australian *Criminal Code Act 1995* (Cth.) s. 12.1(2).

[22] *Ibid.*

[23] *Ibid.*, at 11.

This model requires an adverse consequence, serious injury or death, before corporate conduct would be considered criminal. Arguably, this is an appropriate description of Recommendation 73 of the Westray Inquiry. This model only addresses corporate criminal liability in the workplace health and safety field. Consequently, it was considered to be too narrow in Canada to sustain a general theory of corporate criminal liability, as it would not respond to corporate crimes against the environment and other corporate harms.

The Committee heard witnesses in support of and against specific corporate killing legislation. On the one hand, it would remove the corporate veil that protects individuals; however, on the other hand, it forms the possibility of "creating anecdotal legislation that does not cover the entire terrain".[24] One witness is cited in the Government Response as being in favour of the specific corporate killing legislation because in writing such a law "rather than rewriting the law of corporate criminal liability ... [it] probably invites less legal and constitutional peril".[25]

The federal government chose to use Bill C-45 to rewrite the law of corporate criminal liability generally, and not take the narrow approach of establishing a corporate killing offence in Canada. This meant that Bill C-45 applies to all corporate criminal liability, not just those related to workplace related injuries under section 217.1 of the Code. Even though this model was rejected by Canadian law makers, an initiative in this direction went ahead in the United Kingdom. The *Corporate Manslaughter and Corporate Homicide Act 2007*[26] received royal assent on July 26, 2007 and came into force on April 6, 2008. The Act creates a new indictable offence to replace the common law offence of gross negligence manslaughter, for the purpose of the prosecution of corporations:

1.   The offence

(1)   An organisation to which this section applies is guilty of an offence if the way in which its activities are managed or organised—

(a)   causes a person's death, and

(b)   amounts to a gross breach of a relevant duty of care owed by the organisation to the deceased.

(2)   The organisations to which this section applies are—

(a)   a corporation;

(b)   a department or other body listed in Schedule 1;

(c)   a police force;

(d)   a partnership, or a trade union or employers' association, that is an employer.

---

[24]   *Ibid.*, at 9.

[25]   *Ibid.*

[26]   (U.K.), 2007 c. 19.

(3) An organisation is guilty of an offence under this section only if the way in which its activities are managed or organised by its senior management is a substantial element in the breach referred to in subsection (1).

Although not yet tested in the courts, the United Kingdom's approach of using the so-called corporate killing model, is clearly a more direct and aggressive example of how to hold corporations criminally liable. As indicated by well respected English commentators, the essence of the new crime is succinctly put as follows:

... a company will be guilty of the offence if the way in which its activities are managed or organized, by its senior management, amount to a gross breach of the duty of care it owes to its employees, the public or other individuals and those failings caused the person's death. Companies and government bodies face prosecution if they are found to have caused a person's death due to their corporate health and safety failings.[27]

3.4 THE FAULT ELEMENT FOR CORPORATE LIABILITY

Criminal law requires proof of fault or criminal intent; this has often been described by the use of the Latin phrase *mens rea*. Defining fault relates to the purpose of which corporate fault finding is intended. It is trite to say that modern Canadian law regulates organizations, including corporations, in a number of different ways. Corporations are regulated for purposes of registration, taxation, unfair business competition, price fixing, workers compensation, environmental compliance, product liability, public health concerns and occupational health and safety.

Corporate criminal liability requires proof beyond a reasonable doubt of a prohibited or unlawful act and a fault element or *mens rea*. The fault element may be implied by the general requirements and criminal law jurisprudence or it may be more specifically found in the language of the Code. The crime of criminal negligence uses the fault element of wanton and reckless disregard.

Canadian courts have generally resisted holding corporations vicariously liable for the criminal offences of their employees. Rather, Canadian jurisprudence developed the identification theory of organizational criminal liability. To establish the fault element required by criminal law for an organization, a senior official or directing mind must be proven to have the fault element of the criminal offence and it will be thereby attributed to the organization because of the position of authority that individual had in its affairs. The corporation, however, will generally not be held liable if the senior official or directing mind was acting against the interests of the corporation. In that situation, the corporation itself would be a victim of the crime and not a

---

[27] Gerard Forlin & Louise Smail, eds., *Corporate Liability: Work Related Deaths and Criminal Prosecutions*, 2d ed. (London: Bloomsbury Professional, 2010) at p. 2, para. 1.3.

criminal perpetrator. Over time, Canadian jurisprudence has broadened the scope of the identification theory. However, the identification theory is not the only theory of corporate criminal liability. The identification theory and other models of corporate criminal liability are discussed earlier in this chapter.

The fault element is a particularly important issue from the perspective of a corporation. The general law relating to criminal negligence involving an individual is less concerned with this issue since the individual is without question responsible for their own actions. However, it is much different when a criminal negligence charge involves a corporation. Criminal negligence is an offence of lesser *mens rea* than murder, manslaughter, theft, fraud or assault. Corporations are practically vulnerable to allegations of criminal negligence when a member of the public is injured or killed. The question then becomes *who* in a corporation must have the fault element so that the corporation itself can be said to have committed criminal negligence. This question is not difficult when the corporation is small and the owner is also the manager. In that case, the mind of the individual owner is also the mind of the corporation. However, modern corporations may have organizational charts and structures that bear only a passing resemblance to the simpler models considered by the courts in developing the common law.

The Court of Appeal for Ontario considered this issue in *R. v. Canadian Allis-Chalmers Ltd.*[28] The defendant corporation was a foundry of large dimensions employing about 175 workers. The foundry had three bays in each of which was a travelling overhead crane, which was used to lift heavy loads and move them from one part of the bay to another. A large overhead crane was used to move a large bucket which moved sand from the sandpit in the foundry to the moulder. On one occasion, a worker was standing underneath the bucket, which was lifted by the crane, when the bucket dumped its load even though no one pulled the lever that would normally activate the dumping of the load. The worker suffered severe injuries, he then contracted pneumonia and eventually died.

The court delivered three concurring judgments all dismissing the appeal from the acquittal at trial. Of particular interest is Justice Masten's conclusion that:

> In order that there may be a conviction there must, in my opinion, be no reasonable doubt that the company itself failed to take proper precautions against and use reasonable care to avoid the danger in question, and I think that the failure of the men operating the machine to report the apparent defect was not negligence of the company itself but personal negligence of these men. In negligently omitting to do so the workmen were acting in that respect contrary to the instructions of the company; and in omitting to report they were not acting for or on behalf of the company. Their negligence was not for the company's benefit, but in opposition to its instructions. The true position is that, through their own personal negligence and for their own

---

[28]   [1923] O.J. No. 8, 54 O.L.R. 38 (Ont. C.A.).

convenience, they omitted to do what they ought to have done and what the company had ordered them to do.[29]

In Justice Orde's concurring judgment he suggested that a line be drawn between those in authority and those who are not in authority. Although he did not go on to make this determination in the present case, Justice Orde left this determination to the circumstances of each case:

> I am not prepared to hold that the negligence of a minor servant of the company, even though he may be invested with some authority, such as that of a foreman over a gang of men, is to be regarded as the criminal negligence of the company. I can see no reason for placing a corporate body in any lower position in this regard than an individual.[30]

Although this case was decided in 1923, the principles set out on organizational criminal liability were consistently adopted in Canadian courts up to the passage of Bill C-45 into law. Bill C-45, however has dramatically changed how criminal negligence is attributed to organizations, including corporations.

Another important case of alleged corporate criminal negligence was the prosecution of *R. v. Syncrude Canada Ltd.*[31] In *Syncrude*, two men, working for a contractor repairing a large tank, were asphyxiated due to exposure to nitrogen gas after going into a reactor in order to retrieve a fallen tool. The defendant, Syncrude Canada had hired an independent contractor, Western Stress Relieving Servicing Inc. to work in confined spaces. The contractor was hired to carry out repairs to the Syncrude plant near Mildred Lake, Alberta, during a plant shutdown. While servicing a reactor, in a confined space, a worker dropped a wrench. The worker descended into the reactor to retrieve the wrench and was rendered unconscious by exposure to nitrogen gas in the confined space of the reactor. A co-worker, observing the fate of the first worker who was trying to retrieve the wrench, descended into the same reactor to help and was similarly overcome by the gas. The medical evidence at the trial indicated that both men were likely overcome and rendered unconscious in seconds by nitrogen gas in the reactor.

Syncrude was subsequently charged with criminal negligence causing death. Justice Agrios, the trial judge, after a thorough examination of the development of corporate criminal negligence, acquitted the accused corporation. The basis of the trial judge's decision is informative and illustrates the pre-Bill C-45 criminal law with respect to the fault element for corporate criminal liability.

Justice Agrios concluded that it was necessary to look to the alter ego or directing mind of the corporation and that a "clear distinction is made between the acts of inferior agents or servants of the corporation, as opposed

---

[29] *Ibid.*, at para. 31.
[30] *Ibid.*, at para. 41.
[31] [1983] A.J. No. 845, 28 Alta. L.R. (2d) 233 (Alta. Q.B.).

to the acts of more responsible officers of the company";[32] the latter would attribute to the corporation criminal liability. In *Syncrude*, the employees who were responsible for the prohibited act were processing technicians who issued safe work permits. Justice Agrios, in dismissing the charges of criminal negligence, stated that:

> I cannot find that in a company with 4,000 employees, permit issuers, albeit they have the authority to implement safety procedures, can be considered the directing mind and will of the corporation, the alter ego of the corporation ... Their rank and position is not such of a nature as to justify the finding that their acts might be ascribed to the company itself so as to fix the corporation with liability for their acts or omissions.[33]

The fault element of criminal negligence derives from the individual who in fact committed the act or omission within the organization. Depending on whether or not the corporate representative falls within the directing mind test described above, their position and status determines the implied fault element of the offence against the corporation.

The fault element of corporate criminal liability was further demonstrated in the prosecution of *R. v. Canadian Liquid Air Limited*,[34] relating to a worker's death. The corporate accused made efforts to make the work area where the incident occurred free of any toxic gases. The corporation was aware that employees of a contractor would be using a cutting torch attached to an acetylene holding tank and that toxic gases must not be in the area when the torch was used. Unfortunately, the accused corporation did not succeed in making the area completely free of toxic gases, resulting in the death of a contract worker. Although the evidence established a clear breach of a duty, the Crown failed to prove beyond a reasonable doubt the fault element necessary to prove criminal negligence. Justice McKay described the requisite fault element as follows:

> ... it seems clear to me that a corporation can be in breach of either or both of the duties, and can breach the duty in a manner that shows a wanton or reckless disregard for the lives or safety of other persons ... a corporation can be reckless or wanton in its conduct or in a failure to act if its responsible officers for the action or omission in question have been reckless or wanton.[35]

The procedure for purging the toxic gases from the area in which the contract workers were working was to introduce nitrogen gas into the area. An industrial hygienist who testified at the trial said that purging with nitrogen would be a suitable procedure to adopt to ensure that there was a safe work environment. However, it was clear from the end results and the death of the worker that the purging with nitrogen did not make the area gas-free. There appears to be some suggestion in this case that the worker

---

[32]   *Ibid.*, at para. 40.
[33]   *Ibid.*, at para. 48.
[34]   [1972] B.C.J. No. 774, 20 C.R. (N.S.) 208 (B.C.S.C.).
[35]   *Ibid.*, at paras. 7-8.

who conducted the purging activity was negligent in carrying it out. However, the employer did not conduct any tests after the purging to determine if the purging had been successful. The court held that the Crown had not offered any evidence in the trial of inadequate purging techniques and no evidence of inadequate purging equipment. There was also no evidence of incompetence on the part of personnel involved in the purging and a lack of evidence on how the approved purging procedure failed. As a result, the court acquitted the corporate accused.

3.5 CATEGORIES OF OFFENCES

We have previously discussed the differences between crimes and strict liability offences in Chapter 1. The courts have had an important role in defining the categories of offences with which corporations may be prosecuted. Canadian law is made up of statutes, regulations and codes that establish offences for those who contravene them. The goal, generally speaking, is to ensure that corporations are socially responsible. Canadian statute law establishes the rules that corporations must follow. However, statutes passed by legislators have not always clearly identified the categories of offences. The most prevalent type of prosecution of corporations is for strict liability offences. Enforcement by Administrative Monetary Penalties and alternative methods to punishment is reviewed in Chapter 10. However, the predominant enforcement mechanism is the prosecution for legal contraventions of corporations by charging them with offences and prosecuting them in court.

The Supreme Court in *R. v. Sault Ste. Marie (City)*,[36] held that there are three categories of offences. This case revolutionized corporate criminal accountability in Canada. Provincial legislatures and the federal parliament both have the power to establish either true crimes or *mens rea* offences, strict liability or absolute liability offences. Although the criminal law power is constitutionally assigned to the federal government, a provincial offence may be classified as a true crime or *mens rea* offence, if it has a primary constitutional purpose that is within provincial jurisdiction. These three types of offences have been introduced early in this chapter. However, a more complete explanation is needed to understand the types of offences and the legal defence of due diligence.

(i) True Crimes or *Mens rea* offences: in *mens rea* offences, the prosecution must prove beyond a reasonable doubt the prohibited act and, either as an inference from the nature of the act committed or by additional evidence, the positive state of mind on the part of the accused, such as intent, knowledge or recklessness. In a criminal offence or "true crime", the prosecution has the onus of proof throughout the trial. The onus of proof never shifts to the accused.

---

[36] [1978] S.C.J. No. 59, 85 D.L.R. (3d) 161 (S.C.C.).

Most offences passed by the federal government are true crimes, such as those under the Code.

(ii)   Strict liability offences: in strict liability offences, the prosecution need only prove beyond a reasonable doubt that the defendant committed the prohibited act; the prosecution need not prove a fault element; and thereafter, the accused has the defence that it reasonably believed in a mistaken set of facts that, if true, would render the act or omission innocent, or that it has taken reasonable precautions to achieve compliance; these are the two branches of the due diligence defence. Most provincial offences are strict liability offences.

(iii) Absolute liability offences: in absolute liability offences, the prosecution need only prove beyond a reasonable doubt that the accused committed the prohibited act, constituting the *actus reus* of the offence. There is no relevant mental element and it is no due diligence defence that the accused was entirely without fault. Mere proof of the prohibited act will lead to a conviction. There can be no punishment by imprisonment, only a fine, for an absolute liability offence.

All offences in Canadian law fit into one of these three categories. The primary focus of this text are the first two categories, true crimes and strict liability offences. Absolute liability offences are of less concern for corporations since they involve minor offences with small fines that have little impact on their operations.

3.6   DETERMINING THE OFFENCE CATEGORY

Since statutes rarely determine the nature of the offence, regard must be made to the authorization for the law and the precise language to establish the offence. Since the decision of the Supreme Court in *Sault Ste. Marie*, one of the challenges often becomes how to determine which category an offence falls within. The Supreme Court in that decision gave some early guidance in that regard. It said:

> Offences which are criminal in the true sense fall in the first category. Public welfare offences would *prima facie* be in the second category. They are not subject to the presumption of full *mens rea*. An offence of this type would fall in the first category only if such words as "wilfully" "with intent" "knowingly" or "intentionally" are contained in the statutory provision creating the offence. On the other hand, the principle that punishment should in general not be inflicted on those without fault applies. Offences of absolute liability would be those in respect of which the Legislature had made it clear that guilt would follow proof merely of the prescribed act. The overall regulatory pattern adopted by the Legislature, the subject matter of the legislation, the importance of the penalty and the precision of the language used

will be primary considerations in determining whether the defence falls into the third category.[37]

There has been surprisingly little consideration and application of the comments of the Supreme Court in *Sault Ste. Marie* in respect of the determination of the category of offence of Canadian law. Typically the debate is between a full *mens rea* or strict liability offence. The offence may result in an individual being imprisoned, then at minimum the offence must be a strict liability offence. However, both true crimes and strict liability offences may result in individuals being imprisoned if they are convicted.

The presumption of an offence established by a provincial legislature is often that it is a strict liability rather than a true crime. The criminal law authority, under the *Constitution Act, 1867*,[38] rests with the federal government. However, it does lie with the province to establish a defence that is a true crime, in a provincial statute, if the primary purpose of the statute is not to pass criminal law but to address a separate subject matter other than criminal law, that is within the exclusive sphere of constitutional authority of the province. One such area is workers' compensation legislation.

Workers' compensation legislation has been established in Canada since 1914, to provide a no-fault system for the compensation of workers when they are injured in the course of their employment. The integrity of the workers' compensation system, and its financial viability, depends on full and complete reporting of accidents and material change in circumstances to the Boards that administer workers' compensation legislation in each Canadian province. Subject of the category of offences established in the Ontario *Workplace Safety and Insurance Act, 1997*[39] establishes several offences for contravening that statute. One provision in particular, section 149(1) states: "A person who knowingly makes a false or misleading statement or representation to the Board in connection with any person's claim for benefits under the insurance plan is guilty of an offence."

In a prosecution, the Ontario Court of Justice held that this provision was a *mens rea* and that the proof of such cannot be "gleaned", from post offence behaviour.[40] Therefore, establishing that a contravention of this provision of the *Workplace Safety and Insurance Act, 1997* amounted to a *mens rea* offence or true crime. In other words, an individual or a corporation could not be convicted unless the Crown prosecutor could prove, beyond a reasonable doubt, that the accused had the requisite mental intent to commit the offence.

---

[37]   *Ibid.*, at 182 (D.L.R.).

[38]   (U.K.), 30 & 31 Vict., c. 3.

[39]   S.O. 1997, c. 16, Sched. A.

[40]   *Ontario (Workplace Safety Insurance Board) v. Latcon Ltd.*, [2005] O.J. No. 3969 at para. 18, 2005 ONCJ 398 (Ont. C.J.).

Chapter 4

BILL C-45 – A GAME CHANGER

4.1 THE PURPOSES OF BILL C-45

Corporate criminal liability has been dramatically changed under Bill C-45.[1] Bill C-45 is a game changer in the real meaning of the phrase. The net of potential criminal liability was expanded beyond corporations to the much broader term organizations. Whether or not the organization is incorporated, whether it is a multi-national corporation or a corner store, whether it is a religious organization or registered charity, whether it is a local hospital or local volunteer association, Bill C-45 applies. Bill C-45 is also a game changer in the sense that corporate criminal liability is now expanded beyond the acts and omissions of the senior officers and boards of directors of an organization. Organizations now have liability for all representatives, and even contractors, who are not direct employees of the organization.

The Bill also overrules the approximately 145 years of common law jurisprudence in Canada dealing with the establishment of the *actus reus* and *mens rea* of corporate criminal liability. Bill C-45 established a new formula of processing organizational guilt in the courts. Bill C-45 also dramatically extends the powers of courts to impose broad new sentences on organizations and new, creative terms of probation on organizations. In short, Bill C-45, at a theoretical and practical level, is a radical change to the established law in Canada with respect to the criminal liability of organizations, including corporations.

On a practical level, however, there has been little increase in the investigation and prosecution of organizations, including corporations, by police and crown attorneys. Whether there has been an initial educational and adjustment delay in understanding and applying Bill C-45 to corporate Canada or not, remains to be seen. Although one prosecutor said, in a seminar that I chaired at the Law Society of Upper Canada during the month of June 2004, shortly after Bill C-45 had been introduced, "This legislation is very prosecutor friendly". Prosecutors have been slow in using Bill C-45 to increase the prosecution of corporations.

Corporate criminal liability and accountability was dramatically affected by the March 31, 2004 amendments to the *Criminal Code*[2] under Bill

---

[1] Bill C-45, *An Act to Amend the Criminal Code (Criminal Liability of Organizations)*, 2003, c. 21.

[2] R.S.C. 1985, c. C-46 [hereinafter the "Code"].

C-45. These changes will impact all organizations in terms of risk management and the avoidance of criminal charges. In order to assess the impact and effect of Bill C-45, it is important to first identify the purposes of the legislation. There are several means by which the purposes of new legislation can be determined: first, from the statements of intention accompanying the Bill C-45 introduction; second, the statements by, in this case, the former Minister of Justice and Attorney General for Canada, Martin Cauchon and others in the legislature, related speeches and other analysis; third, the Government's own publication: "A Plain Language Guide to Bill C-45"; and fourth, by a careful and detailed legal analysis of the legislation itself. Finally, to the limited extent that courts have considered these provisions, the jurisprudence interpreting the provisions of Bill C-45 in the courts. These approaches to determine the purpose of the legislation are briefly reviewed below.

Although the history of the legislative development of Bill C-45 is dealt with elsewhere,[3] a very brief summary of the legislative history, following the Westray disaster and recommendations of the Justice Richards public inquiry is instructive.

> A year after Westray, in 1993, a Parliamentary Sub-committee of the Standing Committee on Justice and Human Rights recommended legal changes modelled on the 1987 Law Reform Commission recommendations. In November a White Paper proposed that corporations be made liable for any "collective failure" to exercise reasonable care by any or all corporate "representatives". In 1999, the leader of Canada's democratic socialist party, the New Democratic Party ("NDP") sponsored a Private Members Bill, which died on the Order Paper following the dissolution of parliament. On 9 February, 2000, the 15th Report of the House of Commons Standing Committee on Justice and Human Rights on workplace safety and corporate liability was tabled. A year and a half later, upset by the Liberal government's continuing inaction, the NDP tabled what eventually came known as Bill C-284. This legislation was the forerunner to Bill C-45.[4]

First, the first reading of Bill C-45 provided four purposes as part of its introduction to the proposed legislation. The Government gave four purposes of Bill C-45 that were set out in the government summary that introduces the legislation. The bill amended the Code to (a) establish rules for attributing to organizations, including corporations, criminal liability for the acts of their representatives, (b) establish a legal duty for all persons directing work to take reasonable steps to ensure the safety of workers and the public, (c) set out factors for courts to consider when sentencing an organization, and (d) provide optional conditions of probation that a court may impose on an organization.

---

[3] See Chapter 2: "Background to Bill C-45" in Norman Keith, *Workplace Health and Safety Crimes*, 2d ed. (Markham, ON: LexisNexis Canada, 2009).

[4] Steven Bittle & Laureen Snider, "From Manslaughter to Preventable Accident: Shaping Corporate Criminal Liability" (October 2006) 28:4 Law & Pol'y 470 at 476.

Bill C-45 was ostensibly a reaction to the Westray disaster of May 9, 1992 when 26 workers died in a coal mine in Pictou County, Nova Scotia. Not only did Bill C-45 introduce a new, positive duty with respect to workplace health and safety in section 217.1 of the Code, it also significantly reformed how organizations, including corporations, were to be held liable under the Code. There was a significant attempt by the federal government to reform the criminal liability of organizations, including corporations in these amendments. Bill C-45 also expanded the power of courts when sentencing a corporation as well as placing it on probation.

Bill C-45 replaced the word "corporation", in the Code, with the word "organization". Therefore, it is not only large multi-national corporations who may now be held criminally liable, but organizations that may not in fact be incorporated pursuant to corporation statutes. This includes sole proprietorships, partnerships, non-profit associations and trade unions. The term "organization" has been defined now in the Code to mean "(a) a public body, corporate body, society, company, firm, partnership, trade union or municipality, or (b) an association of persons that (i) is created for a common purpose, (ii) has an operational structure and (iii) holds itself out to the public as an association of persons."[5] An organization is very broadly defined.

One of the concerns of the author, throughout this text, is that the treatment of organizations, including the corporation, in Canadian law, is a "one size fits all". This unfortunate attitude of parliamentarians that treats a multi-national corporation the same as a sole proprietorship or, a voluntary, charitable organization is patently absurd. The thought that a Boy Scout troop or a Big Sister's organization, could be subject to the same criminal law enforcement standards as a multi-national corporation that has engaged in nefarious workplace safety contraventions or environmental discharge is incomprehensible. This approach to Bill C-45, with great respect to the drafters, is not in the public interests. This concern was expressed by academics who generally favour an aggressive approach to corporate criminal liability.

> The government has decided that, regardless of the form chosen to undertake illegal activity (including public bodies and partnerships, among others) prosecution of the "organization" should be allowed. The question remains, though, whether the rationales that justify corporate criminal responsibility apply equally to all organizations ... the argument is essentially this: If you create a corporation, you accept the notion of separate legal personality with all of the benefits; however, by taking the benefits of separate legal personality, the incorporator must also accept that this other person (the corporation) can do bad things. If it does bad things, society reserves the right to punish the corporation through the criminal law.[6]

---

5   *Criminal Code*, R.S.C. 1985, c. C-46, s. 2 "Organization".

6   Darcy McPherson, "Extending Corporate Criminal Liability?: Thoughts on Bill C-45" (2004) 30 Man. L.J. 253 at 256.

What Professor McPherson seems to ignore, is that the definition of "organization" in Bill C-45 goes well beyond the traditional idea of a corporation established to make a profit in the marketplace. Trade unions, voluntary groups, and any organization whether or not it is incorporated, now fit within the definition of "organization". Hence, the concern that the Bill C-45 amendments to the Code cast too broad a net of potential criminal liability over those who have no intention to make a profit, who wish to serve society and its individual members who may be in need, but are now exposed to a draconian and serious risk of criminal liability.

Bill C-45 also, somewhat dramatically, establishes a statutory basis for organizational liability that, at least at first blush, obviates the need for the courts to rely upon or develop a theory or model of organizational liability. Unlike the discussion of the law in Chapter 2, Bill C-45 now provides statutory directions on the elements of a criminal offence committed by a corporation. Section 22.1 sets out a new test or formula for organizational guilt under the Code for offences with respect to negligence. Section 22.2 sets out a new test or model for liability for organizations, charged with offences other than negligence. This new approach is a statutory formula for establishing corporate criminal liability.

Early academic commentary and literature has analyzed and criticized this legislative change. For example, Paul Dusome has identified as many as 14 constituent elements that the prosecution must prove, in an offence of criminal negligence by an organization, including a corporation, to establish a conviction.[7] Dusome argues that Bill C-45 may actually make it harder, rather than easier, to convict a corporation of an offence under the Code.

Dusome goes on to provide some *"Charter* reflections" where he pronounces in rather strong language against the lack of availability of *Charter of Rights and Freedoms*[8] challenges by corporations to Bill C-45.

> Had corporations been granted *Charter* rights equal to those of individuals, and standing to challenge laws applicable only to corporations, government would have been faced with great difficulty in changing corporate liability standards from the common law identification theory to any other standard that might permit easier conviction of groups than under the identification theory. Under current jurisprudence, *such changes appear to be safe from Charter challenges.*[9]

The interesting aspect of Dusome's thesis is that the Charter may in fact have challenged the legislative changes under Bill C-45 if corporations had significant Charter rights. This, in the writer's view, is problematic. It appears to presume that Charter rights exercised by corporations, have an anti-

---

[7]   Paul Dusome, "Criminal Liability under Bill C-45: Paradigms, Prosecutors, Predicaments" (2007) 53:1 Crim. L.Q. 98 at 132-33.

[8]   Part I of the *Constitution Act, 1982*, being Schedule B to the *Canada Act, 1982* (U.K.), 1982, c. 11 [hereinafter the "Charter"].

[9]   Paul Dusome, "Criminal Liability under Bill C-45: Paradigms, Prosecutors, Predicaments" (2007) 53:1 Crim. L.Q. 98 at 147 [emphasis added].

democratic and anti-social purpose. This fallacy, it is respectfully suggested, flows from a negative presupposition on the existence and purpose of corporations in modern liberal democracies. This value laden assessment of the role of a corporation, has clearly influenced Dusome and others,[10] who appear to fear Charter challenges, in their views on Bill C-45. This theory is challenged by the analysis of the application of the Charter to corporations in Chapter 7 of this book.

Bill C-45 was also clearly intended to reform and make easier the establishment of criminal liability to organizations, including corporations. It is subject to constitutional restrictions on all legislation and state action under the Charter. While the literature criticizes Bill C-45 for not going far enough in establishing a simple and more compelling basis for criminal liability of organizations, including corporations, it is hard to understand how those who promote Charter rights and values for individuals, are not equally open to the Charter's application to corporations to ensure that Bill C-45 or any other state action be subject to Charter values. The presence of an anti-organization/corporation *animus* in considering the application of the Charter is unfortunate and promotes a dichotomy in Charter values.

Finally, there has been very little use of Bill C-45 in the prosecution of organizations, including corporations, since the introduction of the Code amendments. This is because corporations are prosecuted more frequently under regulatory, strict liability offences than under the Code. It remains to be seen whether there will be Charter challenges to Bill C-45, and whether or not there will be a rash of prosecutions against organizations, including corporations, arising from these amendments. However, whatever the effect of Bill C-45, it has not necessarily simplified the issue of corporate legal liability in Canada and it is, indeed, a game changer.

4.2   POLITICAL STATEMENTS ON BILL C-45 PURPOSES

Prior to reviewing some of the public statements and legislative debates with respect to Bill C-45, it is important to understand their legal significance. As courts may consider and interpret the Bill C-45 amendments to the Code, the question may arise as to whether or not the courts may use political statements and legislative debates as an aid to interpret this new legislation. Canadian courts have been traditionally reluctant in admitting and relying upon political statements and parliamentary debate in interpreting statutes in the course of their legal enforcement. For example, in the case of *Canada (AG) v. Reader's Digest Assoc. Can. Ltd.*,[11] the Supreme Court refused to admit statements made by two Ministers in the House of Commons regarding the interpretation of and purpose behind the statutes. In a later case, Justice Dickson of the Supreme Court stated, "generally speaking, speeches made in

---

[10]   Darcy McPherson, "Extending Corporate Criminal Liability?: Thoughts on Bill C-45" (2004) 30 Man. L.J. 253 at 256.

[11]   [1961] S.C.J. No. 56, [1961] S.C.R. 775 (S.C.C.).

the legislature at the time of enactment of the measure are inadmissible as having little evidential weight."[12] More than 10 years later, the Supreme Court, in a constitutional challenge, somewhat relaxed its approach for the purpose of constitutional litigation. In *R. v. Morgentaler*,[13] Sopinka J. said, speaking for the Court: "Provided that the court remains mindful of the limited reliability and weight of Hansard evidence, it should be admitted as relevant to both the background and the purpose of legislation."[14]

If there was a constitutional challenge to Bill C-45, the legislative history, including political statements and legislative debates, may be introduced into evidence and considered. In ordinary statutory interpretation, political statements and legislative debates may only be used to determine the specific purpose or mischief that parliament sought to address and correct by passing the legislation in question. Generally speaking, political statements and legislative debates may not be used to determine or interpret the specific meaning of a particular provision. Therefore, Bill C-45 may be better understood by the political speeches and legislative debates that surrounded its passage into law. Those passionate pleas and profound pronouncements about the Westray disaster will not likely affect the interpretation of the specific statutory provisions of Bill C-45. The law with respect to legislative committee and ministerial debates is reviewed later in the context of the application of the Charter to corporations in Chapter 7.

In a press release issued on June 12, 2003, the day Bill C-45 was introduced in Parliament, for first reading, the Honourable Martin Cauchon, then Minister of Justice and Attorney General of Canada, said:

> Employers must fully recognize their responsibility in providing a safe work environment. Failure to do so in a manner that endangers employee and public safety must be appropriately dealt with through our criminal laws. I am pleased to introduce measures today that will effectively modernize the law on corporate liability.[15]

At Bill C-45 second reading debate on September 15, 2003 in the House of Commons, Mr. Paul Harold Macklin, Parliamentary Secretary to the Minister of Justice and Attorney General of Canada, said:

> Fundamentally the bill has its origins in the tragic deaths of 26 miners in the Westray mine explosion in May 1992. I will not review in detail the lengthy and ultimately fruitless criminal proceedings that followed the investigation of the explosion. All members are aware that the company that operated the mine, and two of its executives, were charged with manslaughter. The trial judge ordered a stay of the charges because of problems with disclosure of

---

[12]   *Reference re: Residential Tenancies Act 1979 (Ontario)*, [1981] S.C.J. No. 57, [1981] 1 S.C.R. 714 (S.C.C.).

[13]   [1993] S.C.J. No. 95, [1993] 3 S.C.R. 463 (S.C.C.).

[14]   *Ibid.*

[15]   Department of Justice Canada, News Release, "Justice Minister Introduces Measures to Protect Workplace Safety and Modernize Corporate Liability" (12 June 2003), online: <http://canada.justice.gc.ca/en/news/nr/2003/doc_30922.html>.

evidence by the Crown. Although the appeal courts overturned that decision, the prosecution decided it could not go forward.[16]

Mr. Macklin described the results of the Public Inquiry into the Westray disaster and the growing consensus in respect of the need to reform the criminal law relating to the legal liability of corporations. He then addressed the role of the Standing Committee on Justice and Human Rights in the consensus building process that resulted in Bill C-45. He said:

> A discussion paper setting out the issues and reviewing the evidence of other countries, which had been prepared by the justice department, was provided to the committee. The committee heard from officials of the justice department and other experts. It heard moving testimony from victims and relatives of victims of industrial accidents. The 15th report of the committee recommended "that the government table in the House legislation to deal with the criminal liability of corporations, directors and officers". Clearly all parties in the House felt that it was time for fundamental reform in this area. The government in its response to the report reviewed the evidence that had been heard by the committee and agreed on the need for reform. The government also concluded that there was no perfect system in other countries that Canada could simply copy. The report therefore set out the principles that would guide the drafting of a made in Canada approach to the problem of corporate crime.[17]

He went on to describe what was characterized as an innovative step of introducing a new Occupational Health and Safety ("OHS") duty in the Code. Although Mr. Macklin reminded the House of Commons that the federal government had recently amended the *Canada Labour Code*,[18] Part II, to increase employer responsibilities, employee rights and the fines associated with the contravention of federal OHS legislation, he indicated that new Code amendments were also required. He went on to say:

> Bill C-45 builds on those changes by proposing to include in the *Criminal Code* a new section, section 217.1, which provides that everyone who undertakes, or has the authority, to direct how another person does work or performs a task is under a legal duty to take reasonable steps to prevent bodily harm to that person or any other person arising from that work or task. The importance of having such a duty in the *Criminal Code* is that if there is a breach of that duty, wanton and reckless disregard for the life or safety of people, and injury or death results from that breach, a person can be convicted of criminal negligence causing death which is punishable by up to life imprisonment, or criminal negligence causing bodily harm which is punishable by up to 10 years imprisonment.[19]

---

[16]   *House of Commons Debates*, No. 119 (15 September 2003) (P.H. Macklin), online: <http://www.parl.gc.ca/37/2/parlbus/chambus/house/debates/119_2003-09-15/HAN119-E.HTM> at 1340.

[17]   *Ibid.*, at 1335.

[18]   R.S.C. 1985, c. L-2.

[19]   *Ibid.*, at 1340.

Although the parliamentarians quoted above, and others who spoke in favour of Bill C-45, were impassioned about their concern about workplace health and safety, they generally neglected to comment on the very broad application of the new corporate criminal liability provisions of Bill C-45. A few parliamentarians commented on the very broad definition of "organization". No parliamentarian, that I have been able to identify, gave any consideration to the application of corporate criminal liability to an organization, when a "contractor" who is not an employee, could commit an offence and be a "representative" of the organization. No principle of contract law or insurance law would permit an organization to contract out of or obtain insurance for such exposure. However, parliamentarians, in their enthusiasm to embrace the tragedy of the Westray mine disaster, likely for their own political purposes, ignored in the parliamentary debate, some of the most problematic and draconian aspects of Bill C-45. It is therefore, regrettably, left to the courts to interpret and apply these provisions in the absence of any meaningful government position on the issue, at the time of passage of Bill C-45, and any meaningful debate from a legal, technical or even policy basis for these extreme broad aspects of Bill C-45.

4.3   PLAIN LANGUAGE GUIDE TO BILL C-45

The purposes of Bill C-45 can be better determined, therefore, by information provided by the government at the time of and after the presentation of legislative amendments for parliamentary review, debate and passage. In that respect, the government of Canada prepared a Plain Language Guide to Bill C-45 that is reviewed below. Further, the parliamentary research branch prepared a legislative summary and analysis of Bill C-45. These sources are instructive with respect to the purposes of Bill C-45.

The Department of Justice of the Government of Canada also prepared and provided a Plain Language Guide to Bill C-45.[20] The government's Plain Language Guide gave further background on the purposes of Bill C-45. It said:

> The government tabled Bill C-45 ... to modernize the law with respect to the criminal liability of corporations and the sentencing of corporations ... [b]ecause the *Criminal Code* covers a wide range of crimes by all kinds of persons, the legislation employs more complex and specific language ...[21]

The Plain Language Guide went on to say, "the provisions of Bill C-45 are a compilation of the existing rules with new reforms, which will modernize the law to reflect the increasing complexity of corporate structures."[22]

---

[20]   Canada, Department of Justice, *A Plain Language Guide – Bill C-45 – Amendments to the Criminal Code Affecting the Criminal Liability of Organizations*, online: <http://www.justice. gc.ca/eng/dept-min/pub/c45.pdf>.

[21]   *Ibid.*, at 2.

[22]   *Ibid.*

The emphasis in the Plain Language Guide is regarding the change that Bill C-45 makes to the criminal liability of organizations. What is striking by its absence is that there is no specific reference to the new legal OHS duty in the Plain Language Guide. However, it does provide an interesting example of how an organization may be held liable for OHS criminal negligence in the post-Bill C-45 era of the Code. The Plain Language Guide offers the following example of how an organization will be held accountable:

> For example, in a factory, an employee who turned off three separate safety systems would probably be prosecuted for causing death by criminal negligence if employees were killed as a result of an accident that the safety systems would have prevented. The employee acted negligently. On the other hand, if three employees each turned off one of the safety systems each thinking that it was not a problem because the other two systems would still be in place, they would probably not be subject to criminal prosecution because each one alone might not have shown reckless disregard for the lives of other employees. However, the fact that the individual employees might escape prosecution should not mean that their employer necessarily would not be prosecuted. After all, the organization, through its three employees, turned off the three systems ... Similarly, in the example of three employees engaging in the negligent conduct, the court would have to decide whether the organization should have had a system to prevent them from acting independently in a dangerous way and whether the lack of such a system was a marked departure from the standard of care expected in the circumstances. The court would consider, under this example, the practices put in place by the person in charge of safety at the factory and the practices of other similar organizations.[23]

The Library of Parliament, through its parliamentary research branch, prepared a legislative summary of Bill C-45.[24] Although this legislative summary was prepared in the summer of 2003, after the first reading of Bill C-45, and not after the final version of Bill C-45 was passed into law, it may still be helpful and relevant since there were very few changes to Bill C-45 in the legislative review and debate process. In providing background to Bill C-45 the subject of the identification theory of corporate criminal liability was reviewed.[25] The legislative summary stated, in that regard:

> The "identification theory" of corporate criminal liability has been criticized as inadequate over the years, both in Canada and elsewhere. Critics of this approach have pointed out that it does not reflect the reality of the internal dynamics of corporations, particularly in the case of larger corporations. Rarely do high-level corporate officials personally engage in the specific conduct or make the specific decisions that result in occupational health and safety violations or in serious workplace injury or death. However, they can

---

[23] *Ibid.*

[24] Parliamentary Research Branch of the Library of Parliament, *Bill C-45: An Act to Amend the Criminal Code (Criminal Liability of Organizations)* (Legislative Summary) David Goetz (Ottawa: Law and Government Division, 2003).

[25] For more information on the "identification theory" of corporate criminal liability see Chapter 3.

often, through actual policy decisions or otherwise, create or contribute to a corporate environment where subordinate managers, supervisors and employees feel encouraged or even compelled to cut corners on employee health and safety matters, even in the face of legal prohibitions or official corporate policy.[26]

The Parliamentary Research Branch legislative summary of Bill C-45 made a passing reference to the Westray mine disaster. Surprisingly, even though the lobbying efforts from the United Steel Workers of America union, and relatives of the Westray mine victims spearheaded the push for what became Bill C-45, the Westray disaster is not significantly recognized in the legislative summary. Further, there is no mention of the Westray disaster whatsoever in the Plain Language Guide, prepared by the federal government. Clearly, Bill C-45 was more importantly reforming the law of corporate criminal liability than just creating a new crime. The legislative summary's brief reference to the Westray disaster is as follows:

> In its submissions to the public inquiry into the Westray mine disaster of May 1992, the United Steel Workers of America called for the facilitation of corporate criminal liability and also advocated enhanced criminal accountability of corporate directors and officers ... the union recommended creating a new criminal offence aimed specifically at "directors and responsible corporate agents" who negligently fail to protect the health and safety of employees. The union conceded that the offence would likely have to be confined to situations of *criminal* negligence (*i.e.*, conduct amounting to a "marked departure" from the standard of reasonable person). However, it was thought that legislating a specific legal duty on the part of key corporate officials to take reasonable care to protect employees would facilitate their prosecution by obviating the need to establish a causal connection between the conduct of a corporate official and the death or injury of an employee.[27]

The legislative summary goes on to provide a brief overview of various provisions of Bill C-45, without further elaborating on the purpose of the bill. Interestingly, in the 14-page legislative summary, only one relatively short paragraph deals with the new OHS legal duty established by Bill C-45. That excerpt states, in the writer's view rather inaccurately, the following description of new section 217.1 of the Code:

> Clause 3 of the bill amends the *Criminal Code* by adding a new section 217.1 which will provide that those who are responsible for directing the work of others are under a legal duty to take reasonable steps to prevent bodily harm to any person arising from such work. This provision does not create a new criminal offence. However, by clarifying the existence of such a legal duty, the provision facilitates the application of the offence of criminal negligence, which is predicated, in part, on the existence of a legal duty.

---

[26]   Parliamentary Research Branch of the Library of Parliament, *Bill C-45: An Act to Amend the Criminal Code* (*Criminal Liability of Organizations*) (Legislative Summary) David Goetz (Ottawa: Law and Government Division, 2003) at 5.

[27]   *Ibid.*, at 6.

This description of the new OHS legal duty in the Code is arguably misleading in its use of the phrase "by clarifying the existence of such a legal duty", when such a duty never previously existed. This description appears to diminish the importance of the workplace health and safety aspect of Bill C-45. Bill C-45 not only establishes a new OHS legal duty, that clearly did not exist before, but it also effectively established a new health and safety crime. Further, it would appear that the legislative summary and the Plain Language Guide to Bill C-45 are primarily focused on the change to criminal liability of organizations. Both government documents were deficient in their review, analysis and implications of the new OHS legal duty in section 217.1 of the Code. The fact that Bill C-45 creates a new offence of OHS criminal negligence, for breach of the new OHS legal duty in the Code, is clearly one of the central purposes and results of Bill C-45.

Finally, the Plain Language Guide to Bill C-45 adds some further comment with respect to the role of senior officers and their acts or omissions on how they may establish criminal guilt on behalf of the organization.

> For example, if the CEO fudges financial reports and records, leading others to provide funds to the organization, both the organization and the CEO will be guilty of fraud. ... for example, a senior officer may be benefiting the organization by instructing employees to deal in goods that are stolen. A senior officer may instruct employees to buy from the supplier offering the lowest price, knowing that the person who offers to sell the goods at the lowest price can only make such an offer because the goods are stolen. The employees themselves have no criminal intent but the senior officer and the organization could be found guilty.[28]

4.4   STATUTORY FORMULA FOR PROVING ORGANIZATIONAL GUILT

One of the most significant changes to corporate criminal liability in Bill C-45 was the new approach to establishing organizational guilt. The elements that a Crown prosecutor must prove, when prosecuting an organization, including a corporation, have moved from the judge made rules of the common law to sections 22.1 and 22.2 of the Code. Further, I have reproduced below the two sections, and provided some commentary and an update on the most recent jurisprudence with respect to their interpretation. Section 22.1 deals with offences under the Code or other federal statutes that require proof of negligence by the organization, and section 22.2 relates to charges under the Code or other criminal statutes where there is no requirement of proof of negligence to secure a conviction. Therefore, this new statutory formula for improving organizational, including corporate, guilt, is essential

---

[28] Canada, Department of Justice, *A Plain Language Guide – Bill C-45 – Amendments to the Criminal Code Affecting the Criminal Liability of Organizations*, online: <http://www.justice.gc.ca/eng/dept-min/pub/c45/c45.pdf>.

for every advisor to corporations to be aware of and to be in compliance with.

> 22.1 In respect of an offence that requires the prosecution to prove negligence, an organization is a party to the offence if
>
> (a)   acting within the scope of their authority
>
> > (i)   one of its representatives is a party to the offence, or
> >
> > (ii)   two or more of its representatives engage in conduct, whether by act or omission, such that, if it had been the conduct of only one representative, that representative would have been a party to the offence; and
>
> (b)   the senior officer who is responsible for the aspect of the organization's activities that is relevant to the offence departs – or the senior officers, collectively, depart – markedly from the standard of care that, in the circumstances, could reasonably be expected to prevent a representative of the organization from being a party to the offence.[29]

Section 2 of Bill C-45 introduces two new requirements or formulas by which organizations may be held criminally liable. These two formulas are a departure from the identification theory of corporate liability. The first, section 22.1 of the Code, is in respect of offences that required proof of negligence. This section applies to the new OHS legal duty in section 217.1, that will be reviewed later in this chapter, as well as other forms of criminal negligence. This provision also recognizes that not all criminal offences have the same fault element. The second, section 22.2 deals with the new formula for establishing organizational guilt where the fault element is not negligence. In a very real sense, section 22.1 established a statutory fault element that is now the measure of negligence to establish the new offence of OHS criminal negligence, or any other criminal negligence charge. There is no requirement to rely on theories of liability developed by the courts. However, courts will still interpret and apply this statutory fault provision. In other words, new section 22.1 provides a formula for proving organization guilt for an offence with a fault element of negligence, even if it is unrelated to the new OHS legal duty in section 217.1 of the Code.

Section 22.1 sets out when an organization may be held liable for criminal negligence for the acts of its representatives and senior officers. Under the law prior to Bill C-45, a corporation could be found liable for a *Code* offence, but it was left to the common law to determine the nature and breadth of this liability. In the past, individuals within corporations have been found criminally liable by a directing mind, such as an officer or a director, committing the criminal offence. Under the identification theory the guilt or innocence of a few senior corporate executives and directors is what determined the guilt or innocence of the corporation. However, the new definitions of "representative" and "senior officer" list the individuals in this

---

[29]   Bill C-45, *An Act to Amend the Criminal Code (Criminal Liability of Organizations)*, 2003, c. 21, s. 2.

role and how they may contribute to the finding of criminal liability by the organization.

There has been some limited academic treatment of the new provisions of the Code. In "Extending Corporate Criminal Liability?: Some Thoughts On Bill C-45",[30] Darcy MacPherson analyzed his conception of the likely impact of the amendments to the Code. He described section 22.1(b) as creating "joint-liability language". He goes on to say:

> Even if the senior officer in charge of the area of corporate affairs where the offence occurred did not "depart markedly" from the standard of care that could have prevented the offence, if the other senior officers (judged collectively) "depart markedly" from that standard, this is sufficient to fulfill paragraph 22.1(b).
>
> Section 22.1 thus treats both multiple representatives committing the offence, and multiple senior officers failing to stop it, each as one for the purposes of negligence-based offences. I believe that this focus on collective action is designed to prevent what I will refer to as "avoidance of accountability by fragmentation".[31]

In this way, MacPherson says, Parliament has expressly limited the ability of an organization to avoid liability, by recognizing and accounting for the diffuse authority which characterizes most modern-day corporations. It remains to be seen if the courts will treat section 22.1 in the way MacPherson has described it.

In summary, section 22.1 is a significant change to the establishment of liability under the Code for organizations charged with offences relating to negligence. What did not change with Bill C-45, were sections 219, 220 and 221 of the Code. Section 219 is a fault element that requires evidence of "wanton or reckless disregard for the lives or safety of other persons". Section 220 deals with criminal negligence causing death to another person and section 221 deals with criminal negligence causing bodily harm to another person. Section 22.1 of the Bill C-45 amendments to the Code will primarily be used in prosecuting corporations where workplace incidents have resulted in a fatality or bodily harm to a worker or member of the public affected by the work.

Under the new Code amendments, an organization will be considered a party to the offence if one or more representatives, acting within the scope of their authority, is a party to the offence; and, if a senior officer responsible for the activity departs markedly from the standard of care expected to prevent that representative from being a party to the offence. This standard of criminal liability is extended to all organizations, not just to corporations.

The second part of section 22.2 of Bill C-45 deals with the formula for criminal liability where the fault element is a more traditional *mens rea* element associated with crimes. The fault element may be implied by the lan-

---

[30]   Darcy MacPherson, "Extending Corporate Criminal Liability?: Thoughts on Bill C-45" (2004) 30 Man. L.J. 253 at 256.

[31]   *Ibid.*

guage of the criminal offence, as interpreted by jurisprudence, or, alternatively, set out quite clearly in the language of the offence. The difficulty in establishing criminal liability of corporations in a more traditional criminal charge was intended to be addressed by the addition of section 22.2 to the Code. This new provision expressly requires that the organization intended to benefit, at least in part, from the commission of the offence, to prove the criminal offence. Further, the new definition of senior officer in section 1 of Bill C-45 is critical in this new fault element to the Code as well as section 22.1.

> 22.2 In respect of an offence that requires the prosecution to prove fault – other than negligence – an organization is a party to the offence if, with the intent at least in part to benefit the organization, one of its senior officers
>
> (a) acting within the scope of their authority, is a party to the offence;
>
> (b) having the mental state required to be a party to the offence and acting within the scope of their authority, directs the work of other representatives of the organization so that they do the act or make the omission specified in the offence; or
>
> (c) knowing that a representative of the organization is or is about to be a party to the offence, does not take all reasonable measures to stop them from being a party to the offence.[32]

This section sets out a new formula to establish when an organization may be held liable for criminal offences other than those with a fault element of negligence. An organization will be considered a party to an offence if a senior officer, with the intent, at least in part to benefit the organization and acting within the scope of his or her duty, either is (a) a party to the offence; (b) directs work to other representatives so that they commit the offence; or (c) knowing that a representative is or is about to be a party to the offence, fails to take all reasonable measures to stop them. The fault element is disjunctive, establishing three different means by which the organization may be found guilty of a criminal offence. If any one of these three alternative scenarios occurs, organizational criminal liability will be established.

In "Thoughts on Bill C-45", MacPherson examined the subsections of section 22.2. He concluded that section 22.2(a) was a codification of the common law identification theory. Furthermore, MacPherson claimed that section 22.2(b) is redundant because it replicates the meaning of the language of section 21(1) of the Code:

> ... assume that the other representative (who was directed by the senior officer) committed the offence, meaning that the other representative committed the *actus reus* with the necessary fault element. In such a case, the senior officer (by directing the other representative) would be abetting the representative in committing the offence. The senior officer would be a party to the offence pursuant to paragraph 21(1)(c) of the Code ...

---

[32] Bill C-45, *An Act to Amend the Criminal Code (Criminal Liability of Organizations)*, 2003, c. 21, s. 2.

But what if the representative who commits the *actus reus* does not have the requisite fault element to commit the offence? Clearly, paragraph 22.2(b) pertains to the fault element of the senior officer, as opposed to that of the other representative. Therefore, the statute unites the *actus reus* (of the other representative) with the fault element (of the senior officer) to hold the corporation liable.

At first blush, this might appear to be a change; however, the common law has already covered this. It has established that if one person (the senior officer) gets a second person (the other representative) to commit the *actus reus* of an offence without the knowledge of that other person, that other person is known as the "innocent agent" of the person with the guilty mind. The person with the guilty mind is then considered to be the person who "commits the offence". [33]

MacPherson claimed that section 22.2(c) made a "substantial change in the law". He claimed that this section expanded corporate criminal liability in at least four ways:

First, the section requires no active participation in the offence by anyone acting in any sort of managerial capacity or control position. An administrative assistant or member of the janitorial staff could conceivably render the corporation liable, as long as a senior officer is aware of the wrongdoing.

Second, the section does not require the senior officer who becomes aware of the misconduct to have any power in the area of the corporation's business and affairs where the crime is being or will be committed. Bill C-45 not only changes the concept of "directing mind" to the defined term of "senior officer", it also alleviates the activity-specific nature of the designation. Once a person is a senior officer, paragraph 22.2(c) can be invoked without the senior officer having the control necessary to prevent the crime.

Third, it appears that legislative drafters have decided that the Crown should be able to prosecute the corporation, even though the senior officer cannot be convicted of the underlying offence. Under *Canadian Dredge and Dock Co.*, the directing mind would generally be liable for the offence for which the corporation is convicted. The introduction of paragraph 22.2(c) changes this. Knowledge of the criminal activity of another is generally not sufficient to convict someone of being a party to a crime. Therefore, a senior officer cannot be convicted simply because he fails to stop another representative from committing an offence. But the corporation is in a different situation: a person's position as a senior officer, combined with knowledge of a crime being committed by someone connected to the corporation, is sufficient to convict the corporation of the underlying offence.

Fourth, the paragraph also means that all senior officers are expected, at a minimum, to communicate with another in order to protect the interests of the corporation ... [p]aragraph 22.2(c) seems to demand co-ordination and

[33]   Darcy MacPherson, "Extending Corporate Criminal Liability?: Thoughts on Bill C-45" (2004) 30 Man. L.J. 253 at 261.

> communication between all members of the management team, whether at
> the upper or middle levels of the corporation.[34]

The implications arising from this analysis may be troubling for some senior officers. MacPherson uses the example of the internal auditor, whose job may specifically require the identification of problematic or even illegal activity. If MacPherson's analysis of the provisions of section 22.2 are correct, then members of the organization such as an internal auditor may find their duties in direct competition. There has been no judicial consideration of these important issues as of yet.

In summary, section 22.1 provides a complex, formula for organizational guilt that did not exist in the Code prior to the Bill C-45 amendments. Courts will no longer be left exclusively to theories of corporate criminal liability, but rather must follow the provisions of section 22.2 when offences under the Code or other federal criminal statutes, allege criminal acts by corporations, other than charges for offences where the fault element is negligence.

4.5   BILL C-45 JURISPRUDENCE

There has been little prosecution, trial decisions and reasons for judgments either at trial or at appellate level, to develop jurisprudence with respect to the aspects of Bill C-45. One area of some discussion and consideration is in the sentencing and probationary term amendments to the Code under Bill C-45. Those subjects are dealt with in Chapter 9 which deals with sentencing in terms of probation for corporations. What follows is a brief description of the consideration of Bill C-45 and its significant changes in the law, to the very few cases that have yet been advanced against corporations, to which corporations have not pleaded guilty and gone to trial, and reasons for judgment have been made public. This aspect of this text, in due course, will likely need to be updated as the jurisprudence develops.

The Supreme Court in *R. v. Creighton*[35] set the standard with respect to determining criminal liability of corporations. In that case, Madam Justice McLachlin stated that the test for whether the accused's conduct constituted a marked departure from the standard of care of a reasonable prudent person in the same circumstances should not be extended to incorporate a standard of care which varies with the background and predisposition of the accused. That objective legal test has largely been adopted in Bill C-45 by the inclusion of section 22.1 into the Code.

In *R. v. Ontario Power Generation*,[36] failure to ensure public safety at an electricity generating station led to two fatalities. The Crown sought to attribute criminal responsibility to the corporation through the actions of a group manager. The Court referred to the new section 22.1 in its decision as

---

[34]   *Ibid.*, at 262-63.
[35]   [1993] S.C.J. No. 91, [1993] 3 S.C.R. 3 (S.C.C).
[36]   [2006] O.J. No. 4659 (Ont. C.J.).

linking the corporation "to the aggregated results of the actions of its key officials and their delegates".[37] However, the Court also held that the new provision was substantive in nature, and therefore could not have retrospective application. The Court then disposed of the issue with reference to the common law identification theory. An important point was made by the Court in response to the Crown contention that a person "who has supervisory or oversight authority over policy implementation within his sphere of the business *simpliciter* is a 'person in authority'".[38] The Court responded that:

> If the Crown is right, in as large and complex an organization as Ontario Power Generation, it might be said that virtually any supervisor at any level in the structure who has managerial responsibilities is a person in authority. I am tempted to agree with defence counsel's submission that such an interpretation would make redundant the enactment of Bill C-45 as well as the statement by Archibald, Jull and Roach that C-45 abolishes "the dichotomy between the setting of policy and only managing the corporation" developed by the common law concept of a directing mind.[39]

In *R. v. Tri-Tex Sales & Services Ltd.*,[40] a small electronics supply company and one of its operators were charged with making deceptive and misleading statements on several HST tax returns. The Crown attempted to attribute liability to the corporation through the actions of the operator, who was one-half of a husband and wife ownership. As in Ontario Power, the events of this case occurred before the new provisions were given Royal Assent. The Court held that the new provisions were "a fundamental change, if not a revolution, in corporate criminal liability".[41] However, as section 22.1 was a substantive amendment, it could not be applied to the instant case. The Court then applied the traditional common law identification theory analysis.

In *R. v. Great White Holdings Ltd.*,[42] a corporation which outfitted hunters, was charged and convicted for illegal possession of wildlife. Several guides from the corporation had killed two deer and brought them back to the Great White's camp. The corporation appealed its conviction on the grounds that the word "knowingly" converted the regulatory offence into a full *mens rea* offence. In making its determination, the unanimous Court avoided interpreting section 22.2 on the ground that it was not argued:

> I leave for another day the question of whether s. 22.2 of the *Code* informs the prosecution of a body corporate for a regulatory or public welfare offence that requires proof of fault. In the instant case, the Crown did not

37   *Ibid.*, at para. 6.
38   *Ibid.*, at para. 14.
39   *Ibid.*, at para. 17.
40   [2006] N.J. No. 230 (N.L. Prov. Ct.).
41   *Ibid.*, at para. 42.
42   [2006] A.J. No. 134, 384 A.R. 114 (Alta. C.A.).

proceed on the basis that one of the senior officers of the Appellant acting within the scope of his authority was a party to the offence. Nor did the Crown allege that a senior officer directed the work of other representatives of Great White Holdings Ltd. or knew that a representative of the company was or was about to be a party to the offence.[43]

In *R. v. ACS Public Sector Solutions Inc.*,[44] the Crown sought to commit a corporation for trial as a party to a breach of trust by a police officer, in relation to a contract for speeding photo enforcement. In finding that the corporation could not be committed for trial, the Court briefly addressed the submission that the actions of the corporation's operating mind could ascribe liability to the corporation. The Court held that section 22.2 "could, if applicable, provide the Crown with means of proving that ACS is a party to the offences when a senior officer such as Mr. MacPherson is a party to such offence".[45] However, the Court went on to state that since the circumstances in this case occurred before section 22.2 had been given Royal Assent, the Crown could not rely on the new provision to attribute liability to the corporation.

In *Tri-Tex Sales & Services Ltd.*, although it declined to apply the new provision, the Court held that section 22.2 would "make corporations liable for the actions of their representatives and senior officers in a manner which would not have applied prior to the enactment of these provisions".[46]

4.6   THE FUTURE OF BILL C-45

It has been said that only fools attempt to predict the future, so this brief section of the chapter will not attempt to predict the ultimate future of Bill C-45 as it amended the Code, but rather comment on the areas of concern both from a policy and a case law interpretive level. As indicated in Chapter 2, the evolution of corporate criminal liability has often been driven by moral panic. The lengthy time that it took to bring Bill C-45 to the Parliament of Canada for a vote, as ostensibly as a response to the Westray mine disaster, militates against change to any parts of Bill C-45. The legislation took from May, 1992, the date of the Westray disaster, to March 31, 2004, almost 12 years, to respond to a serious and compelling social problem. Bill C-45 does much more than simply introduce section 217.1, establishing a duty on all persons, including organizations, to take "reasonable steps" to prevent bodily harm to workers and members of the public arising from activities in Canadian workplaces. It radically changed the means by which organizations, including corporations, can be prosecuted, convicted, sentenced and given terms of probation under the Code. However, the absence of any meaningful review or debate, clause by clause, was inexcusable.

---

43   *Ibid.*, at para. 13.
44   [2007] A.J. No. 1310 (Alta. Prov. Ct.).
45   *Ibid.*, at para. 147.
46   *R. v. Tri-Tex Sales & Services Ltd.*, [2006] N.J. No. 230 at para. 43 (N.L. Prov. Ct.).

What we are left with, in my respectful view, are three important questions about the future of Bill C-45. They are as follows:

1.   Will Bill C-45 be revoked or amended?

2.   Will Bill C-45 be struck down as unconstitutional and contrary to the Charter?

3.   Will the courts interpret the problematic provisions of Bill C-45 in a liberal or conservative manner?

Will Bill C-45 be revoked or amended? In the author's opinion, it is very unlikely that Bill C-45 will be revoked or amended. Every political party in the federal parliament voted in favour, unanimously, of the Bill C-45 amendments to the Code. Notwithstanding the absence of any significant parliamentary review or clause by clause review of the Bill under the justice committee, as is the normal practice, politicians fell over themselves in commending the legislation as being an appropriate and measured response to the Westray mine disaster. Sadly, the Westray mine disaster, and the victim's families, the union that advocated on behalf of the victim's families, and the NDP, all were led to believe that Bill C-45 would reduce the likelihood of the repeat of the Westray mine disaster in Canada. The unfortunate truth is that the legislation is so complex, clumsy, problematic and unlikely to be aggressively enforced by prosecutors or the courts, that the effectiveness of the Bill in promoting workplace health and safety has been greatly diminished. The likelihood of any meaningful amendments, for the above mentioned reasons, are extremely low.

Will Bill C-45 be struck down as unconstitutional and contrary to the Charter? This is an interesting question of the application of the Charter to the rights of corporations. In Chapter 7, I review in detail the application of the Charter to corporations, since 1982 when the Charter was introduced and passed by the Parliament of Canada. Pierre Elliott Trudeau, the Prime Minister at the time, was a long-standing proponent of an individual of Charter of Rights and Freedoms for individual Canadians.

A comprehensive review and analysis of Bill C-45, and its constitutionality, is beyond the scope of this text. However, it is not unreasonable to foresee a corporation, being prosecuted under a section of the Bill C-45 amendments to the Code, raising a serious constitutional challenge, given the potential for an unlimited fine if the corporation is convicted of an offence under the Code. Whether this would relate to the crime of insider trading, fraud, or occupational health and safety criminal negligence causing death, does not matter. The thought that a corporation may pay millions of dollars in fines if convicted for an offence under the Code since there is no maximum fine schedule set out in the Code is daunting. Therefore, corporate decision makers, reasonably and responsibly considering the interests of the shareholders, may very well instruct legal counsel to raise all manner of constitutional argument, including challenges to the constitutionality of Bill C-45 itself, given the risks faced by the corporation. Such concerns, for the use of the blunt instrument of criminal prosecution against corporations, to have achieved social objectives, raises further policy issues. The constitutionality of Bill C-45 is reviewed elsewhere.

Will the courts interpret the problematic provisions of Bill C-45 in a liberal or conservative manner? The jury, quite literally, is still out on how the courts will interpret Bill C-45, and in particular, sections 22.1 and 22.2 of the Code. The movement from a judicial theory of criminal liability of corporations, discussed earlier in this chapter, towards a statutory formula of organizational guilt is novel in Canadian criminal law. Generally, penal law is interpreted conservatively, with a view to protecting the rights of the accused. However, with the tendency of moral panic, the easy target that corporations have in the criminal justice system, the often egregious facts that surround the prosecution of a corporation, it is not entirely clear that courts will maintain this tradition post Bill C-45. It is suggested, by this author, that the strict and narrow interpretation of Bill C-45, and charges against corporations, should continue as they do for charges against individuals. If the state decides that prosecution of criminal or strict liability offences against corporations is a policy model that they wish to pursue, and there is every reason to argue that the rights of a corporate accused should be no less diminished than those of an individual accused. This view was commented on by a leading Ontario prosecutor when he said:

> By 1990, the Charter had fully landed and prosecuting corporate crime became more anemic. We saw legal barriers to using the fruits of regulatory work in criminal matters. This created a legal minefield for criminal investigators and caused a divide in the informal co-operation and information sharing that had existed between regulators and the police.[47]

Therefore, the future of Bill C-45 remains very much in the hands of the court. The failure of the federal parliament to carefully review, clause by clause, the complex, interrelated changes that Bill C-45 brought to the Code unfortunately left the courts in the position of being the final judge of its meaning. As with all new statutes, Bill C-45 will be subject to interpretation, trial decisions, appeals and potential constitutional challenges.

---

[47] Murray D. Segal, "Responding to Misconduct in the Corporate World" (2007) 26:1 Advocates' Soc. J. 12 at para. 20.

Chapter 5

CATALOGUING OF CORPORATE CRIMES AND OFFENCES

5.1 INTRODUCTION

The cataloguing and organizing of offences that a corporation may be charged in Canada is a daunting task. There are literally hundreds of offences under the *Criminal Code*,[1] other federal criminal statutes, federal and provincial statutes offences that apply to Canadian corporations. There are also thousands of regulatory standards set out in regulations that also apply to a corporation and, if contravened, may result in criminal strict liability offences. In this chapter, a conceptual model for normatively cataloguing corporate offences is provided. This chapter addresses the challenging policy question of when to establish corporate crimes and offences in a rational and appropriate manner.

Cataloguing corporate crimes and offences can be done in a number of ways. Corporate offences may be catalogued by the type of offence, namely is it a true crime or strict liability offence. Cataloguing may also be organized on the basis of the subject matter that the offence deals with; such as financial market offences, public safety offences and environmental offences. Further, the cataloguing may simply list all of the offences for which corporations may be charged with, in a particular statute, such as the Code. Finally, offences may be catalogued by normally recommending the type of corporate accountability mechanism, such as administrative monetary penalties, strict liability offences and criminal offences. To provide the most meaningful and practical catalogue of offences, the author has chosen to take a blended, hybrid approach to cataloguing corporate crimes and offences which includes all of the above.

Given the current political and policy trend towards legislating more offences against corporations, it is simply amazing that there has been no government initiative to develop a comprehensive catalogue list of corporate crimes and offences in Canada. This chapter will set out a broad list, both by general category as well as by type of offences, which corporations may be charged. However, since this book's cataloguing is not intended to list every offence that corporations may face, organizations should seek advice from counsel with specialized knowledge of a particular area of the law to obtain

---

[1] R.S.C. 1985, c. C-46 [hereinafter the "Code"].

a list of legal responsibilities, offences and penalties. Specific advice should also be sought from counsel on how to avoid committing them, and also how to prevent and manage the risk associated with the subject matter of the offences.

One innovative manner in which corporate crimes and offences may be conceptualized is by the nature of the potential harm or consequence of the actions of corporations to victims and stakeholders. The extent to which there are stakeholders or innocent members of the public that may be adversely affected by corporations is a central theme in why corporations are prosecuted in the legislature. The following section is a modest attempt to conceptualize the types of crimes and offences to which corporations may be held accountable.

5.2 CONCEPTUAL MODEL FOR CORPORATE OFFENCES

5.2.1 Introducing the Victim Vulnerability-Harm Matrix

The conceptual basis for the following normative assessment of when crimes and offences are rational and appropriate is a risk model primarily for the consequences not the causes of corporate activity. Although this conceptual model recognizes that corporations have a legitimate role in society, it also acknowledges that corporate activity may cause harm to various categories of victims. The need for proof of intent to cause harm is not relevant to this assessment. When there is a risk of harm, some means of accountability of the corporation is rational and appropriate for the public interest. This model considers the degree of harm or damage potentially caused by the corporation. The model also considers the nature of the victim of the corporate action and their relative vulnerability. Both are then logically connected with various types of crimes or offences which apply to corporations.

This is a normative model of how standards and regulations ought to be enforced against corporations. At the lowest level of harm, with the least vulnerable victim, prosecution is clearly not the best model to achieve corporate accountability. This model seeks to provide various examples to illustrate the cataloguing of corporate crimes and offences, based on the nature of the victim and the severity of the consequence or harm of the conduct. This model is not an ultimate policy, political or value statement on the victims of corporate crimes. The harm suffered by them is both objective and subjective. At the highest level of harm, with the most vulnerable victim, prosecution by criminal charges is the most appropriate to achieve corporate accountability.

The measures or degrees of harm — minor, moderate and maximum — are intended to be objective. This may be measured in dollar value of loss or degree of human suffering and other loss. However, victims are often affected by corporate misconduct in very personal, non-economic ways that are unavoidably subjective. With respect to the categories of victims — internal stakeholder, external stakeholder and public — the thesis is based on who may be affected by misconduct of the corporation. Internal stakeholders, such as employees, have more influence or control over the actions of a corporation and therefore are less "vulnerable" than external stakeholders. Similarly, the external stakeholder, such as a supplier, customer, shareholders or pensioners have less influence than an "internal stakeholder" but more influence than a non-stakeholder, such as the public.

This model also postulates that the more control or influence over the conduct of the corporation, the more shared responsibility the stakeholder has for the conduct of the corporation. The more influence, hence lower vulnerability of the victim, the less support there is to use the traditional prosecution model to achieve corporate accountability. Similarly, the less control or influence the victim has with the corporation's decisions, the more appropriate traditional prosecution model would apply. The thesis behind this chart, ultimately, is that the public is the class of victim that needs the most protection by the state from corporate misconduct and most supports a traditional prosecution model of corporate accountability.

5.2.2 Conceptualizing the Victim Vulnerability-Harm Matrix

If a picture is worth a thousand words, then the following picture or matrix of the victim vulnerability-harm matrix ("VVH") may be helpful in explaining cataloguing corporate offences. On the horizontal access the categories of degree of harm have been identified to be minor, moderate and maximum. This methodology of characterization is inspired, but not entirely similar to the OHSAS 8800 British risk matrix, the Z-10 American risk matrix, and the Z-1000 Canada risk matrix for the health and safety risk for workers. The horizontal access in the VVH matrix offers a range of escalating harm that may be caused by corporate conduct, or more accurately, misconduct. An example of a minor degree of harm would be one that does not put the life or health of an individual, be it an employee, customer or member of the public, at risk. Conversely, the category of maximum degree of harm may in fact put the life of similarly situated individuals at risk.

In the VVH matrix, the degree of vulnerability is predicated on the concept that the more removed an individual or organization is from the corporation's control and decision making, the more vulnerable they are to the conduct, or misconduct, of the corporation. The role of corporate control and decision making in corporate liability was reviewed in Chapter 3. Although this approach may not be universally accepted, especially by anti-corporate worldview, in the author's view it is a reasonable policy approach to catalogue offences. It may assist in developing public policy by considering the degree of vulnerability of various individuals and organizations to the conduct, and misconduct, of corporations.

Internal stakeholders, be they employees, contractors, unions and senior management, have more knowledge of the activities of corporations, and therefore are more informed and less likely to be exposed to risk of harm by corporate misconduct. Similarly, external stakeholders, such as investors, suppliers, customers, shareholders and pensioners of a corporation, are not usually directly involved in the operations and management decisions of a corporation, but are nonetheless more interested and involved than members of the public. External stakeholders have influence and effect corporate decisions without having the same influence or control as internal stakeholders. Ultimately, the public who has no direct influence or control over the decisions of corporations, is the most vulnerable category of person who may be affected by acts and omissions of the corporation. The public relies exclusively on the state's legal authority to hold corporations accountable. Therefore, there is a sound public policy argument that the public should be the most important category of potential victim, since it is the most vulnerable to corporate misconduct that needs to be protected by laws, statutes and regulations.

What follows then is a chart or matrix that provides one approach to a catalogue of corporate offences that relates to criminal and strict liability offences.

VICTIM VULNERABILITY-HARM MATRIX OF CORPORATE RESPONSIBILITY

	Victim Category	Minor	Moderate	Maximum
DEGREE OF VULNERABILITY ↑	Public	4	7	9
	External Stakeholder	2	5	8
	Internal Stakeholder	1	3	6

DEGREE OF HARM ⟶

The above VVH Matrix of corporate responsibility is a conceptual framework for the identification and use of various policy models to achieve corporate accountability. The thesis is that the more vulnerable the victim is and the more serious the degree of harm is, the greater the policy argument in favour of the most severe sanctions against a corporation. The most severe policy sanction is use of the criminal-prosecutorial model. Conversely, the lower the degree of harm and the less vulnerable the victim category, the weaker the argument in favour for using a traditional criminal-prosecutorial model for corporate accountability.

This is certainly not the only approach to catalogue various corporate crimes and offences. However, the VVH Matrix recognizes that the more severe the harm to a victim, and the more vulnerable the victim, the higher the moral and legal justification for prosecution, by way of a criminal offence. Similarly, logic suggests that when there is a minor degree of harm, with an engaged or internal stakeholder, this is not the type of matter that should result in the use of the draconian powers of prosecution. Therefore, the above noted chart gives policy makers, corporations and the public some degree of confidence that there is a rational, objective process to determining appropriate means for corporate accountability measures. In the last chapter of the book, Chapter 10, we deal at length with corporate accountability in the form of alternative dispute resolution, alternative resolution agreements and corporate social responsibility. Argument in favour of using a non-prosecutorial model of corporate accountability is enhanced when there is not a maximum degree of harm to the public involved.

What follows, is a list of examples of the VVH Matrix of corporate responsibility.

1.   Internal Stakeholder Suffering a Minor Degree of Harm:

An allegation that employees have not been paid overtime pursuant to the legal requirements of Labour Standards legislation, be it provincial or federal. This harm, just economic harm, to an internal stakeholder, who presumably has either an individual contract or employment or collective agreement, is one where the internal stakeholders have a measure of ongoing knowledge and participation of the practices of the corporation; even if the corporation knowingly fails to meet minimum standards requirements for overtime payment, this is clearly not the type of vulnerability-harm where prosecution model of corporate accountability is advisable. Notwithstanding this analysis, it is still possible for a corporation to be prosecuted with a strict liability offence for failure to pay prescribed overtime rates under Labour Standards legislation.

2.   External Stakeholder with a Minor Degree of Harm:

An allegation of fraud under a workers' compensation system under provincial legislation; as noted below, the Ontario *Workplace Safety Insurance Act, 1997* [2] has one provision of the workers' compensation statute identified as a true crime or *mens rea* offence. However, generally, other offences under that statute and other provincial workers' compensation statutes are strict liability in nature. The workers' compensation system, is a no-fault system of providing income to workers who have been injured from work and are no longer receiving income from their employer. Like any insurance scheme, there is an accident fund from which workers are paid that is funded from stakeholders in the same industry. Employers in the same rate group, are external stakeholders. They fit within this category. The integrity and financial viability of the workers' compensation system, since workers' compensation systems in Canada are exclusively funded by employers is

---

[2]   S.O. 1997, c. 16, Sched. A.

compromised if there is fraud. Failing to acknowledge that the worker who was injured and therefore denying benefits, or not registering and therefore underfunding the system, affects other corporate employers as external stakeholders. However, there is a minor degree of harm because one particular corporate employer committing workers' compensation fraud will not substantially damage or undermine the general viability of the system, given the number of employers who are external stakeholders. Therefore, the category or degree of harm caused by workers' compensation fraud is, generally speaking, minor.

3.   Internal Stakeholder with a Moderate Degree of Harm:

Pension legislation has been established to ensure that employees, workers and their beneficiaries are treated properly and fairly under a corporate pension plan. If a corporate employer underfunds, otherwise misconducts itself with, or even defrauds the employee of pension benefits, then those internal stakeholders are affected. The harm to an employee who has their pension damaged by corporate misconduct, directly or indirectly, can be devastating for an employee's future retirement, financial security and well-being. A recent example of this took place with the Nortel bankruptcy and pension problems. Therefore, in the author's view, a moderate degree of harm rather than a minor degree of harm is caused to the victims since the vulnerability for financial security, especially at the end of one's working life, can be very significant.

4.   Public, Non-Stakeholder with a Minor Degree of Harm:

Various offences may fit within this public protection mandate of the state, where there is only a minor degree of harm to the public; one example used, under federal legislation is the proper use of pest control products in the marketplace. Although generally these products do not have potential health consequences for people, they nonetheless may pose a potential public health hazard if inappropriately used. Since they are sold by third party retail outlets, there is no internal or external stakeholder group that is uniquely exposed to this type of risk. The public has no input on any of the production or management of the production of pest control products, therefore they are more dependent on the state, and the role of the regulator to ensure that pest control products are not harmful to the public.

5.   External Stakeholder with a Moderate Degree of Harm:

External Stakeholders with some vulnerability to moderate harm is the next category. Federal legislation dealing with competition and commercial offences, primarily under the *Competition Act*,[3] is a useful example of this category. The *Competition Act* intended to ensure a level playing field not only for the benefit of the public, but primarily for competitors in the same industry. Rules against false and misleading advertising and rules against pyramid schemes are intended to generally protect those in the marketplace

---

[3]   R.S.C. 1985, c. C-34.

as much or more than the public; a moderate degree of harm to a business interest, or an individual who is a victim of a pyramid scheme by buying product that they cannot resell, places these types of offences into the external stakeholder category; because they may have significant financial effect on individuals and corporations in a particular industry, they are also considered to have a moderate degree of harm associated with those offences.

6.   Internal Stakeholder with a Maximum Degree of Harm:

Legislation that is intended to protect workers from exposure to inappropriate biological, chemical or radioactive hazards, as well as general workplace health and safety fits within this category. Employees, workers and subcontractors are internal stakeholders with the corporate defendant. Although they may participate in the prevention of health and safety risks by way of joint health and safety committees, and have the right to refuse to do unsafe work and access to information through programs such as the workplace hazardous material information system, they are still exposed to a potential maximum degree of harm. The concept behind most Canadian occupational health and safety statutes is one of an internal responsibility system, recognizing the role that internal stakeholders have in workplace health and safety, therefore the offences relating to health and safety violations by the corporate accused is arguably less serious than exposure to health, safety and life threatening hazards to the public.

7.   Public, Non-Stakeholder with a Moderate Degree of Harm:

The public is at risk from corporations polluting the air, water and land that sustains the eco-system and affects all members of society. The public (and the broader physical and natural environment), is directly or indirectly affected by pollution. Examples like Walkerton, resulted in the death of members of the public. The public has a moderate degree of potential harm from merely being exposed to pollution over which it has no control. Therefore, the author has classified environmental hazards and risk to the public as a moderate degree of harm in this VVH matrix.

8.   External Stakeholder with a Maximum Degree of Harm:

The vast majority of Canadians with any type of investments is exposed to financial market risk. Bad investments may result in financial harm and personal ruin if corporate defendants engaged in securities misconduct, insider trading and fraud. Economic harm is generally viewed as less severe than personal injury or health consequences. However, external stakeholders to the corporation, primarily investors, may have severe financial risk when there are securities legislation contraventions. Most Canadians hold, through mutual funds and personal portfolios, some measure of publicly traded securities in Canada and abroad. This creates a very broad category of external stakeholders; the state has a reasonable interest in protecting from corporate financial offences.

9. Public, Non-Stakeholder with a Maximum Degree of Harm:

Members of the public, who have no control or influence over the activities of corporations, need to be protected from the maximum harm that may be caused to them by a corporation. If corporations put the lives of the public at risk, there needs to be strong public accountability. The legislation that most specifically deals with intentional or criminal acts of corporations, that may affect the public, are represented by the Bill C-45 amendments to the Code. Apart from its application to workers, if a member of the public is affected by way of personal injury, severe health consequences or killed, by the misconduct of a corporation, through its representatives and senior officers, then Bill C-45 is a very good example of a law that will protect the non-stakeholder victim category of the public from the maximum harm that may be done by the corporation. There are likely very few examples of such corporate misconduct. Although the magnitude of the number of deaths in the Westray mine disaster would evoke, emotionally, a need to categorize the alleged offences by mine managers and the corporation in this most severe category, the victims were arguably less vulnerable because they were internal stakeholders. Employees who had some measure of control and influence, by law, over activities in the mine: this category postulates that the public, with no ability to control or influence over the potential harm caused by the corporate misconduct need to be protected, more than internal or external stakeholders. A classic example of this category would be if a nuclear reactor, operated by a corporation, was so negligently managed that it resulted in a nuclear meltdown and radiation exposure to members of the public who live in the vicinity or downwind from the nuclear incident, causing severe health consequences, injury and death.

In summary, the fundamental concept behind the VVH Matrix is that different types of misconduct by a corporation ought to result in different treatment under the law, depending on their position in the matrix. For example, there is little reason to commence a prosecution against a corporation when the degree of harm to an internal stakeholder is minor. Similarly, where the degree of harm is at its maximum to the most vulnerable, where the life of one or more members of the public is in jeopardy, this would be the most appropriate category for a corporation to be held liable under a criminal prosecution. This VVH Matrix of corporate responsibility does provide a useful framework for discussion and for policy-makers to consider in determining whether or not prosecution is the appropriate, reasonable response to any alleged corporate misconduct. Where prosecution is not advisable, other means of corporate accountability ought to be considered. These methods of achieving appropriate criminal offences accountability are discussed in Chapter 10. Apart from pure civil remedies, such as union grievances and shareholder class action lawsuits, measures such as Administrative Monetary Penalties and strict liability offences are more appropriate. The following, revised VVH Matrix illustrates the recommended policy for accountability.

VICTIM VULNERABILITY – HARM MATRIX OF CORPORATE RESPONSIBILITY

Victim Category	Minor	Moderate	Maximum
Public	4	7	9
External Stakeholder	2	5	8
Internal Stakeholder	1	3	6

DEGREE OF VULNERABILITY (vertical axis, arrow pointing up)

DEGREE OF HARM ⟶

The above review and analysis of the VVH matrix, is the basis to recommend that prosecution may not always be the best or most appropriate response. It is suggested in the VVH matrix, categories 1, 2 and 3 would not be appropriate for any type of prosecution, but other means, such as regulatory orders and administrative monetary penalties, would be much more appropriate than prosecution to achieve corporate accountability. Similarly, it is suggested that categories 4, 5 and 6 ought not to be the subject of criminal prosecution, but more appropriately be the basis of strict liability offence charges given their placement on the VVH matrix. Finally, it is arguable that criminal prosecution may be appropriate for categories 7, 8 and 9, in circumstances where the requisite mental intent of a corporate "senior officer", now prescribed by Bill C-45, has been met. In the following revised version VVH matrix referenced above, there are three separate means of achieving corporate accountability. Although this is not a complete or definitive guide for policy makers, it is a useful objective analysis that assists in understanding what is the most effective and reasonable means of achieving corporate accountability.

5.3 CRIMINAL OFFENCES AND CORPORATIONS

The Code, the primary criminal statute in Canada, was passed under the federal constitutional authority of the *Constitution Act, 1867*.[4] The federal government, in other words, has the exclusive authority to pass criminal law in Canada, precluding provinces and territories from passing laws that are in pith and substance criminal law. The Bill C-45 amendments to the Code have had a material effect on the application of the Code to corporations. As discussed in Chapter 4, Bill C-45 did a "search and replace" on the term

---

[4] (U.K.), 30 & 31 Vict., c. 3.

"corporation" and replaced it with the term "organization" throughout the Code. In addition to the Bill C-45 amendments to the Code, the definition of various terms regarding who may be charged with an offence are extremely broad. Therefore, what follows is a review of the types of offences with which a corporation may be charged, and a brief review of the terms and their definitions that permit a corporation to be charged under the Code.

The Code establishes offences and defines the circumstances in which a corporation may be charged with those criminal offences. In the Code, the term "everyone" means "persons" and "owner", and similar expressions, including "Her Majesty" and an "organization", it is an important phrase for identifying who may be charged with an offence under the Code.[5] The term "organization" is similarly broad and includes a public body, body corporate, society, company, firm, partnership, trade union or municipality, or an association of persons that holds itself out to the public as an association of persons.[6] The combined effect of the two definitions of "everyone" and "organization" in the Code is that all crime offences against corporations are based on these terms. The terms "everyone" and "organizations" apply to all corporations. Therefore, it may be argued that virtually any provision of the Code that establishes a crime with these two terms could apply to a corporation. For example, a corporation could conceivably be charged with murder if a "senior officer", who was responsible for managing an important aspect of an organization's activities, committed the act with intent in part to benefit the organization.[7]

To summarize, the term "everyone" applies to an "organization" and an "organization" includes a corporation. The term "everyone" applies to every corporation in Canada. Therefore, every offence under the Code that may be committed by an "organization" or by "everyone", is an offence with which a corporation may be charged.

The following is a list of the offences that may be committed by a corporation since they use the term "organization" or "everyone", in the applicable provisions of the Code. All numerical references are to sections of the Code.

"ORGANIZATION"

- 82- Possession without lawful excuse — criminal organizations
- 83.01-Terrorism — an entity includes an organization and can participate in terrorist activity
- 83.02- Providing or collecting property for certain terrorist activities
- 328- Theft by or from person having special property interest
- 362(1)(b)- False Pretense or false statement
- 418(1)- Selling defective stores to Her Majesty

---

[5] R.S.C. 1985, c. C-46, s. 2.

[6] *Ibid.* Broad term "organization" was part of the Bill C-45 amendments to the *Criminal Code.*

[7] Todd Archibald, Kenneth Jull & Kent Roach, *Regulatory and Corporate Liability: from due diligence to risk management* (Toronto: Canada Law book, 2010) at para. 5:40:40.

- 422(1)- Criminal Breach of Contract (wilfully breaks a contract knowing the consequence will be to endanger life, cause injury to persons or property …)

The following Code offences may be committed by "everyone". Since the term organization, including corporation, is included in the definition "everyone" at least in theory a corporation may be charged with the following criminal offences.

"EVERYONE"

- 26- Excessive force
- 46- High Treason
- 49- Acts intended to alarm Her Majesty or break public peace
- 50- Assisting alien enemy to leave Canada, or omitting to prevent treason
- 51- Intimidating Parliament or legislature
- 52- Sabotage
- 53- Inciting to mutiny
- 54- Assisting deserter
- 56- Offences in relation to members of R.C.M.P.
- 57- Forging or uttering forged passport
- 58- Fraudulent use of certificate of citizenship
- 61- Seditious offences
- 62- Offences in relation to military forces
- 65- Punishment for rioter
- 66- Punishment for unlawful assembly
- 68- Offences related to proclamation
- 70- Orders by Governor in Council
- 71- Duelling
- 74- Piracy by law of nations
- 75- Piratical Acts
- 76- Hijacking
- 77- Endangering safety of aircraft or airport
- 78- Offensive weapons and explosive substances
- 78.1- Seizing Control of ship or fixed platform

Dangerous substances

- 79- Duty of care re explosive
- 80- Breach of duty
- 81- Using explosives

Prize Fights

- 83- Engaging in prize fight

Terrorism

- 83.02- Providing or collecting property for certain activities

- 83.03- Providing, making available, *etc.*, property or services for terrorist purposes
- 83.04- Using or possessing property for terrorist purposes

Freezing of Property

- 83.12- Offences — freezing of property, disclosure or audit

Participating, Facilitating, Instructing and Harbouring

- 83.18- Participation in activity of terrorist group
- 83.19- Facilitating terrorist activity
- 83.2- Commission of offence for terrorist group
- 83.23- Harbouring or concealing
- 83.231- Hoax — terrorist activity

Corruption and Disobedience

- 119- Bribery of judicial officers, *etc.*
- 120- Bribery of officers
- 121- Frauds on the Government
- 123- Municipal corruption
- 124- Selling or purchasing office
- 125- Influencing or negotiating appointments or dealing in offices
- 126- Disobeying a statute
- 127- Disobeying order of court
- 129- Offences relating to public or peace officer

Misleading Justice

- 131- Perjury
- 136- Witness giving contradictory evidence
- 137- Fabricating Evidence
- 138- Offences relating to affidavits
- 139- Obstructing Justice
- 140- Public Mischief
- 141- Compounding indictable offence
- 142- Corruptly taking reward for recovery of goods
- 143- Advertising reward and immunity

Escapes and Rescues

- 144- Prison Breach
- 145- Escape and being at large without excuse
- 146- Permitting or assisting escape
- 147- Rescue or permitting escape
- 148- Assisting prisoner of war to escape

Sexual Offences

- 155- Incest
- 162- Voyeurism

Offences Tending to Corrupt Morals

- 163- Corrupting morals
- 165- Tied sale
- 167- Immoral theatrical performance
- 168- Mailing obscene matter
- 172- Corrupting children

Disorderly Conduct

- 173- Indecent Acts
- 174- Nudity
- 175- Causing disturbance, indecent exhibition, loitering, *etc.*,
- 176- Obstructing or violence to or arrest of officiating clergyman
- 177- Trespassing at night
- 178- Offensive volatile substance
- 179- Vagrancy

Nuisances

- 180- Common nuisance
- 181- Spreading false news
- 182- Dead body

Interception of Communications

- 184- Interception

Keeping gaming or betting house

- 201- Keeping gaming or betting house
- 202- Betting, pool-selling, book-making
- 203- Placing bets on behalf of others
- 206- Offence in relation to lotteries and games of chance

Bawdy-houses

- 210- Keeping common bawdy house
- 211-Transporting person to bawdy house
- 212- Procuring

Duties Tending to Preservation of Life

- 215- Duty of persons to provide necessaries
- 216- Duty of persons undertaking acts dangerous to life
- 217- Duty of persons undertaking acts
- 217.1- Duty of persons directing work
- 218- Abandoning child

Criminal Negligence

- 219- Criminal Negligence
- 221- Causing bodily harm by criminal negligence
- 238- Killing unborn child in act of birth
- 240- Accessory after fact to murder

Suicide

- 241- Counselling or aiding suicide

Neglect in Child Birth and Concealing dead Body

- 243- Concealing body of child

Bodily Harm and Acts and Omissions Causing Danger to the Person

- 245- Administering noxious thing
- 246- Overcoming resistance to commission of offence
- 247- Traps likely to cause bodily harm
- 248- Interfering with transportation facilities

Motor Vehicles, Vessels and Aircraft

- 249- Dangerous operation of motor vehicles, vessels and aircraft
- 249.1- Flight
- 250- Failure to keep watch on person towed
- 251- Unseaworthy vessel and unsafe aircraft
- 262- Impeding attempt to save life
- 263- Duty to safeguard opening in ice

Assaults

- 264.1- Uttering threats
- 269- Unlawfully causing bodily harm
- 270- Assaulting a peace officer
- 270.1- Disarming a peace officer
- 271- Sexual assault
- 273- Aggravated sexual assault

Kidnapping, Trafficking in Persons, Hostage Taking and Abduction

- 279- Kidnapping — forcible confinement
- 280- Abduction of person under 16
- 281- Abduction of person under 14
- 282- Abduction in contravention of custody order
- 283- Abduction

Abortion

- 287- Procuring miscarriage
- 288- Supplying noxious things

Unlawful Solemnization of Marriage

- 294- Pretending to solemnize marriage
- 295- Marriage contrary to law

Blasphemous Libel

- 296- Offence of Blasphemous Libel

Defamatory Libel

- 300- Publication of libel known to be false
- 301- Defamatory Libel
- 302- Extortion by libel

Hate Propaganda

- 318- Advocating Genocide
- 319- Public incitement of hatred

Theft

- 322- Theft
- 324- Theft by bailee of things under seizure
- 326- Theft of telecommunication service
- 327- Possession of device to obtain telecommunication facility or service
- 330-Theft by person required to account
- 331- Theft by person holding power of attorney
- 332- Misappropriation of money held under direction

Offences Resembling Theft

- 335- Taking motor vehicle or vessel or found therein without consent
- 336- Criminal Breach of Trust
- 337- Public Servant refusing to deliver property
- 338- Fraudulently taking cattle or defacing brand
- 339- Taking possession, *etc.*, of drift timber
- 339(2)- Dealer in second-hand goods
- 340- Destroying documents of title
- 341- Fraudulent concealment
- 342.1- Unauthorized use of computer

Robbery and Extortion

- 343- Robbery
- 345- Stopping mail with intent
- 346- Extortion

Criminal Interest Rate

- 347- Criminal Interest rate

Breaking and Entering

- 348- Breaking and entering with intent, committing offence or breaking out
- 351- Possession of break-in instrument
- 352- Possession of instruments for breaking into coin operated or currency exchange devices
- 353- Selling, *etc.*, automobile master key

Having in Possession

- 354- Possession of property obtained by crime
- 355- Punishment
- 357- Bringing into Canada property obtained by crime

False Pretences

- 361- False Pretence or false statement
- 363 - Obtaining execution of valuable security by fraud
- 364- Fraudulently obtaining food, beverage or accommodation
- 365- Pretending to practise witchcraft, *etc.*

Forgery and Offences Resembling Forgery

- 366- Forgery
- 370- Counterfeit proclamation, *etc.*
- 371- Telegram, *etc.*, in false name
- 372- False Messages and Indecent telephone calls
- 374- Drawing document without Authority
- 375- Obtaining, *etc.*, by instrument based on forged document
- 376- Counterfeiting stamp, *etc.*
- 377- Damaging documents
- 378- Offences in relation to registers

Fraud

- 380- Fraud
- 381- Using mails to defraud
- 382- Fraudulent manipulation of stock exchange transactions
- 383- Gaming in stocks or merchandise
- 384- Broker reducing stock by selling for his own account
- 385- Fraudulent concealment of title documents
- 386- Fraudulent registration of title
- 387- Fraudulent sale of real property
- 388- Misleading receipt
- 389- Fraudulent disposal of goods on which money advanced
- 390- Fraudulent receipts under *Bank Act*
- 392- Disposal of property to defraud creditors
- 393- Fraud in relation to fares, *etc.*
- 396- Offences in relation to mines

Falsification of Books and Documents

- 397- Books and documents
- 398- Falsifying employment record
- 399- False return by public officer
- 400- False prospectus, *etc.*
- 401- Obtaining carriage by false billing
- 402- Trader failing to keep accounts

Identity Theft and Identity Fraud

- 404- Personification at examination
- 405- Acknowledging instrument in false name

Forgery of Trade-marks and Trade Descriptions

- 406- Forging trade-mark
- 408- Passing off
- 409- Instruments for forging trade-mark
- 410- Other offences in relation to trade-marks
- 411- Used goods sold without disclosure
- 413- Falsely claiming royal warrant

Wreck

- 415- Offences in relation to wreck

Public Stores

- 417- Applying or removing marks without authority
- 418- Selling defective stores to Her Majesty
- 419- Unlawful use of military uniforms or certificates
- 420- Military stores

Breach of Contract, Intimidation and Discrimination Against Trade Unionists

- 422- Criminal breach of contract
- 423- Intimidation
- 424- Threat against internationally protected person
- 424.1- Threat against United Nations or associated personnel
- 425- Offences by employers
- 425.1- Threats and retaliation against employees (not mentioning "every one" but employer)

Secret Commissions

- 426- Secret commissions

Trading Stamps

- 427- Issuing trading stamps

WILFUL AND FORBIDDEN ACTS IN RESPECT OF CERTAIN PROPERTY

- 429- Wilfully causing event to occur

Mischief

- 430- Mischief (data, cultural property)
- 431- Attack on premises, residence or transport of internationally protected person

- 431.1- Attack on premises, accommodation or transport of United Nations or associated personnel

Other Interference with Property

- 437- False alarm of fire
- 438- Interfering with saving of wrecked vessel
- 439- Interfering with marine signal, *etc.*
- 440- Removing natural bar without permission
- 441- Occupant injuring building
- 442- Interfering with boundary lines
- 443- Interfering with international boundary marks, *etc.*

Cattle and Other Animals

- 444- Injuring or endangering cattle
- 445- Injuring or endangering other animals

Cruelty to Animals

- 445.1- Causing unnecessary suffering
- 446- Causing damage or injury
- 447- Keeping cockpit

OFFENCES RELATING TO CURRENCY

- 449- Making Counterfeit Money
- 450- Possession, *etc.*, of counterfeit money
- 451- Having clippings, *etc.*

Uttering

- 452- Uttering, *etc.*, counterfeit money
- 453- Uttering coin
- 454- Slugs and tokens

Defacing or Impairing

- 455- Clipping and uttering clipped coin
- 456- Defacing current coins

Instruments or Materials

- 458- Making, having or dealing in instruments for counterfeiting
- 459- Conveying instruments for coining out of mint

Advertising and Trafficking in Counterfeit Money or Counterfeit Tokens

- 460- Advertising and dealing in counterfeit money, *etc.*

INSTRUMENTS AND LITERATURE FOR ILLICIT DRUG USE

- 462.2- Offence (knowingly imports into Canada, exports from Canada, manufactures, promotes or sells instruments or literature for illicit drug use …)

PART XII.2 — PROCEEDS OF CRIME

- 462.31- Laundering proceeds of crime

ATTEMPTS — CONSPIRACIES — ACCESSORIES

- 463- Attempts, accessories

Other Procedural Issues

- 517- Order directing matters not to be published for specified period
- 605- Release of exhibits for testing
- 648- Restriction on publication

5.4 OTHER FEDERAL CRIMES AND OFFENCES

The Code is the primary criminal statute passed by the federal government under its criminal law power. The authority of the federal government over criminal law authorizes the passage of the Code and other federal criminal statutes. Section 96 of the *Constitution Act, 1867*,[8] describes other areas of constitutional authority that result in corporate crimes and strict liability offences being passed by the federal parliament. The scope of authority of the federal government, pursuant to section 91 of the *Constitution Act, 1867* are as follows:

> 91. It shall be lawful for the Queen, by and with the Advice and Consent of the Senate and House of Commons, to make Laws for the Peace, Order, and good Government of Canada, in relation to all Matters not coming within the Classes of Subjects by this Act assigned exclusively to the Legislatures of the Provinces; and for greater Certainty, but not so as to restrict the Generality of the foregoing Terms of this Section, it is hereby declared that (notwithstanding anything in this Act) the exclusive Legislative Authority of the Parliament of Canada extends to all Matters coming within the Classes of Subjects next hereinafter enumerated; that is to say,
>
> 1.   Repealed.
>
> 1A.   The Public Debt and Property.
>
> 2.   The Regulation of Trade and Commerce.
>
> 2A.   Unemployment insurance.
>
> 3.   The raising of Money by any Mode or System of Taxation.
>
> 4.   The borrowing of Money on the Public Credit.
>
> 5.   Postal Service.
>
> 6.   The Census and Statistics.
>
> 7.   Militia, Military and Naval Service, and Defence.
>
> 8.   The fixing of and providing for the Salaries and Allowances of Civil and other Officers of the Government of Canada.
>
> 9.   Beacons, Buoys, Lighthouses, and Sable Island.

---

[8]   (U.K.), 30 & 31 Vict., c. 3.

10. Navigation and Shipping.

11. Quarantine and the Establishment and Maintenance of Marine Hospitals.

12. Sea Coast and Inland Fisheries.

13. Ferries between a Province and any British or Foreign Country or between Two Provinces.

14. Currency and Coinage.

15. Banking, Incorporation of Banks, and the Issue of Paper Money.

16. Savings Banks.

17. Weights and Measures.

18. Bills of Exchange and Promissory Notes.

19. Interest.

20. Legal Tender.

21. Bankruptcy and Insolvency.

22. Patents of Invention and Discovery.

23. Copyrights.

24. Indians, and Lands reserved for the Indians.

25. Naturalization and Aliens.

26. Marriage and Divorce.

27. The Criminal Law, except the Constitution of Courts of Criminal Jurisdiction, but including the Procedure in Criminal Matters.

28. The Establishment, Maintenance, and Management of Penitentiaries.

29. Such Classes of Subjects as are expressly excepted in the Enumeration of the Classes of Subjects by this Act assigned exclusively to the Legislatures of the Provinces.

And any Matter coming within any of the Classes of Subjects enumerated in this Section shall not be deemed to come within the Class of Matters of a local or private Nature comprised in the Enumeration of the Classes of Subjects by this Act assigned exclusively to the Legislatures of the Provinces.

5.4.1 Competition and Commercial Offences

The federal government has passed legislation, in particular the *Competition Act*,[9] that deals with competition in the marketplace and establishes commercial offences by corporations in Canada. The *Competition Act* deals with the topics of false and misleading advertising, price-fixing and cartels, review of mergers and acquisitions, and abuse of market position and power through various pricing and other commercial strategies. This legislation is intended to facilitate fair competition and business practices in the marketplace.

---

[9] R.S.C. 1985, c. C-34.

It is beyond the scope of this text to thoroughly review the visions of the *Competition Act*. However, a brief review of the *Competition Act* may be helpful to demonstrate the nature of the offences that are established by that statute. The stated purpose of the *Competition Act*, set out at the beginning of the statute, is as follows:

> The purpose of this Act is to maintain and encourage competition in Canada in order to promote the efficiency and adaptability of the Canadian economy, in order to expand opportunities for Canadian participation in world markets while at the same time recognizing the role of foreign competition in Canada, in order to ensure that small and medium-sized enterprises have an equitable opportunity to participate in the Canadian economy and in order to provide consumers with competitive prices and product choices.[10]

The *Competition Act* is only one of 702 federal statutes that regulate Canadian corporations. That is quite apart from the provincial statutes that regulate corporations in provincial areas of constitutional authority. However, it is a critical statute that provides for competition and commercial standards and various offences related to breach of those standards by corporate activity in the marketplace. Several of the offences established by the *Competition Act* are as follows:

False or Misleading Representations

52. (1) No person shall, for the purpose of promoting, directly or indirectly, the supply or use of a product or for the purpose of promoting, directly or indirectly, any business interest, by any means whatever, *knowingly or recklessly* make a representation to the public that is false or misleading in a material respect. [Emphasis added]

Pyramid Schemes

55.1 (1) For the purposes of this section, "scheme of pyramid selling" means a multi-level marketing plan whereby

(a) a participant in the plan gives consideration for the right to receive compensation by reason of the recruitment into the plan of another participant in the plan who gives consideration for the same right;

(b) a participant in the plan gives consideration, as a condition of participating in the plan, for a specified amount of the product, other than a specified amount of the product that is bought at the seller's cost price for the purpose only of facilitating sales;

(c) a person knowingly supplies the product to a participant in the plan in an amount that is commercially unreasonable; or

(d) a participant in the plan who is supplied with the product

(i) does not have a buy-back guarantee that is exercisable on reasonable commercial terms or a right to return the product in saleable condition on reasonable commercial terms, or

(ii) is not informed of the existence of the guarantee or right and the manner in which it can be exercised.

---

[10] *Ibid.*, s. 1.1.

5.4.2 Corruption of Foreign Public Officials

Following the lead of the United States, with its *Foreign Corrupt Practices Act*,[11] Canada has also addressed the issue of bribery and the corruption of foreign public officials. Origin of both the United States and Canadian legislation in this area resulted from the December 17, 1998 ratification of the Organization for Economic Cooperation and Development Convention addressing the subject of the corruption of foreign officials, in particular for the purpose of gaining economic advantage in developing countries. The federal statute, *The Corruption of Foreign Public Officials Act*,[12] provides a detailed definition of foreign public officials, and prohibits any "person" as defined in section 2 of the Code from providing any bribe, advantage, or benefit to any kind of foreign public official. The offence provisions under this legislation establish a *mens rea* offence relating to anyone who possesses property or proceeds obtained or derived from the bribery of foreign public officials.[13] The legislation also provides a far-reaching remedy of seizing the proceeds of bribery, as defined under the legislation, incorporated by reference various seizure of the proceeds of crime, under the Code.[14]

To date there have been very few prosecutions under this legislation. Perhaps one of the reasons is the rather restrictive position taken by the Supreme Court, in the *R. v. Libman*[15] case, which interpreted the extraterritorial application of federal criminal law restrictively. The Supreme Court has held that there must be a real and substantial link between the alleged offence and Canada before any criminal liability will be imposed in Canada. The Supreme Court also held that it must take into account all relevant facts that take place in Canada that may legitimately give Canada an interest in prosecuting the offence, and the court must then consider whether there is anything in the facts that offends international comity with respect to jurisdiction. Otherwise Canada will not have authority to prosecute corporate offenders under the Act.

Interestingly, this statute provides for jail terms for individuals of up to five years and, maximum fines up to $50,000, if the matter is prosecuted by way of summary conviction and, alternatively, there is an unlimited fine for corporations charged and convicted, if the prosecution proceeds by way of indictment. The distinction between these two types of proceedings is addressed in the next chapter.

---

[11] Pub. i. 95-213, 91 Stat. 1494 (1997).
[12] S.C. 1998, c. 34.
[13] *Ibid.*, s. 3(1).
[14] *Ibid.*, s. 3(4).
[15] [1985] S.C.J. No. 56, [1985] 2 S.C.R. 178 (S.C.C.).

5.4.3 Environmental Offences

The federal government does not have exclusive jurisdiction over every type of environmental pollution, standard, spill or related activity. Federal jurisdiction over the environment normally applies when pollution is interprovincial or international. The *Canadian Environmental Protection Act*[16] has the authority to set standards and regulate the conduct of corporations which applies in federal jurisdiction. Although the mandate set out in section 2 of that legislation includes a section of the environment and human health, the enforcement measures taken by the federal government under the *Canadian Environmental Protection Act* is largely through compliance orders and prosecution. Offences under that Act are as follows:

Contravention of the Act, the regulations or agreements

272. (1) Every person commits an offence who contravenes

(a)   a provision of this Act or the regulations;

(b)   an obligation or a prohibition arising from this Act or the regulations;

(c)   an order or a direction made under this Act;

(d)   an order, direction or decision of a court made under this Act; or

(e)   an agreement respecting environmental protection alternative measures within the meaning of section 295.

Penalties

(2) Every person who commits an offence under subsection (1) is liable

(a)   on conviction on indictment, to a fine of not more than $1,000,000 or to imprisonment for a term of not more than three years, or to both; and

(b)   on summary conviction, to a fine of not more than $300,000 or to imprisonment for a term of not more than six months, or to both.

False or misleading information, etc.

273.(1) Every person commits an offence who, with respect to any matter related to this Act or the regulations,

(a)   provides any person with any false or misleading information, results or samples; or

(b)   files a document that contains false or misleading information.

Penalties

(2) Every person who commits an offence under subsection (1) is liable

(a)   on conviction on indictment, to a fine of not more than $1,000,000 or to imprisonment for a term of not more than three years, or to both, if the offence is committed knowingly;

---

[16] S.C. 1999, c. 33.

> (b) on summary conviction, to a fine of not more than $300,000 or to imprisonment for a term of not more than six months, or to both, if the offence is committed knowingly;
>
> (c) on conviction on indictment, to a fine of not more than $500,000 or to imprisonment for a term of not more than three years, or to both, if the offence is committed negligently; and
>
> (d) on summary conviction, to a fine of not more than $200,000 or to imprisonment for a term of not more than six months, or to both, if the offence is committed negligently.

Damage to environment and risk of death or harm to persons

274. (1) Every person is guilty of an offence and liable on conviction on indictment to a fine or to imprisonment for a term of not more than five years, or to both, who, in committing an offence under subsection 272(1) or 273(1),

> (a) intentionally or recklessly causes a disaster that results in a loss of the use of the environment; or
>
> (b) shows wanton or reckless disregard for the lives or safety of other persons and thereby causes a risk of death or harm to another person.

5.4.4 Labour Standards

Labour standards legislation protects employees and workers, who are all internal stakeholders. The *Canada Labour Code*[17] deals with various aspects of labour standards for federally regulated employees. Part I of the statute deals with industrial relations, including collective bargaining, strikes and lock-outs, and the role of the Canadian Industrial Relations Board. Part II deals with workplace health and safety, including the duties of employers and employees, the right to refuse to do unsafe work, the prosecution of workplace stakeholders, primarily employers, who do not follow the statute or regulations dealing with workplace safety. Part III of the statute deals with traditional labour standards issues such as hours of work, minimum wage, vacation and holidays.

This statute, in particular Part II, deals with workplace health and safety, and establishes serious strict liability offences for corporations who do not follow health and safety standards. Those provisions are as follows:

General offence

148. (1) Subject to this section, every person who contravenes a provision of this Part is guilty of an offence and liable

> (a) on conviction on indictment, to a fine of not more than $1,000,000 or to imprisonment for a term of not more than two years, or to both; or
>
> (b) on summary conviction, to a fine of not more than $100,000.

---

[17] R.S.C. 1985, c. L-2.

If death or injury

(2) Every person who contravenes a provision of this Part the direct result of which is the death of, serious illness of or serious injury to an employee is guilty of an offence and liable

    (a)   on conviction on indictment, to a fine of not more than $1,000,000 or to imprisonment for a term of not more than two years, or to both; or

    (b)   on summary conviction, to a fine of not more than $1,000,000.

Risk of death or injury

(3) Every person who wilfully contravenes a provision of this Part knowing that the contravention is likely to cause the death of, serious illness of or serious injury to an employee is guilty of an offence and liable

    (a)   on conviction on indictment, to a fine of not more than $1,000,000 or to imprisonment for a term of not more than two years, or to both; or

    (b)   on summary conviction, to a fine of not more than $1,000,000.

Defence

(4) On a prosecution of a person for a contravention of any provision of this Part, except paragraphs 125(1)(c), (z.10) and (z.11), it is a defence for the person to prove that the person exercised due care and diligence to avoid the contravention. However, no person is liable to imprisonment on conviction for an offence under any of paragraphs 125(1)(c), (z.10) and (z.11).

Officers and senior officials, etc.

149. (2) If a corporation or a department in, or other portion of, the federal public administration to which this Part applies commits an offence under this Part, any of the following persons who directed, authorized, assented to, acquiesced in or participated in the commission of the offence is a party to and guilty of the offence and liable on conviction to the punishment provided for the offence, whether or not the corporation or department in, or portion of, the federal public administration has been prosecuted or convicted:

    (a)   any officer, director, agent or mandatory of the corporation;

    (b)   any senior official in the department in, or portion of, the federal public administration; or

    (c)   any other person exercising managerial or supervisory functions in the corporation or department in, or portion of, the federal public administration.

5.4.5 Money Laundering and Terrorist Financing Legislation

The federal government has promoted legislation to deal with the growing problem of international money laundering and terrorist financing. The statute, the *Proceeds of Crime (Money Laundering) and Terrorist Financing*

Act,[18] has the object to detect and deter money laundering and financing of terrorist activities. The statute also authorizes and facilitates the investigation and prosecution of money laundering offences and terrorist activities in Canada. This statute is less directed at regulatory and social standards than it is at traditional criminal activity. Further, similar to regulatory, health and safety, and environmental statutes, it establishes offences for persons, including corporations, who contravene the provisions of the statute. The offence provisions read as follows:

General offences

74. Every person or entity that knowingly contravenes any of sections 6, 6.1 or 9.1 to 9.3, subsection 9.4(2), sections 9.5 to 9.7 or 11.1, subsection 12(1) or (4) or 36(1), section 37, subsection 55(1) or (2), section 57 or subsection 62(2), 63.1(2) or 64(3) or the regulations is guilty of an offence and liable

    (a)   on summary conviction, to a fine of not more than $50,000 or to imprisonment for a term of not more than six months, or to both; or

    (b)   on conviction on indictment, to a fine of not more than $500,000 or to imprisonment for a term of not more than five years, or to both.

Reporting — sections 7 and 7.1

75.   (1) Every person or entity that knowingly contravenes section 7 or 7.1 is guilty of an offence and liable

    (a) on summary conviction,

        (i) for a first offence, to a fine of not more than $500,000 or to imprisonment for a term of not more than six months, or to both, and

        (ii) for a subsequent offence, to a fine of not more than $1,000,000 or to imprisonment for a term of not more than one year, or to both; or

    (b) on conviction on indictment, to a fine of not more than $2,000,000 or to imprisonment for a term of not more than five years, or to both.

Defence for employees

(2) No employee of a person or an entity shall be convicted of an offence under subsection (1) in respect of a transaction or proposed transaction that they reported to their superior or in respect of property whose existence they reported to their superior.

Disclosure

76. Every person or entity that contravenes section 8

    (a) is guilty of an offence punishable on summary conviction; or

---

[18] S.C. 2000, c. 17.

(b) is guilty of an indictable offence and liable to imprisonment for a term of not more than two years.

Reporting — section 9

77. (1) Every person or entity that contravenes subsection 9(1) or (3) is guilty of an offence and liable on summary conviction to a fine of not more than $500,000 for a first offence and of not more than $1,000,000 for each subsequent offence.

Due diligence defence

(2) No person or entity shall be convicted of an offence under subsection (1) if they exercised due diligence to prevent its commission.

Registry

77.1 Every person or entity that provides information to the Centre under section 11.12, 11.13, 11.14 or 11.3 and that knowingly makes any false or misleading statement or knowingly provides false or misleading information to a person responsible for carrying out functions under this Act is guilty of an offence and liable

(a) on summary conviction, to a fine of not more than $50,000 or to imprisonment for a term of not more than six months, or to both; or

(b) on conviction on indictment, to a fine of not more than $500,000 or to imprisonment for a term of not more than five years, or to both.

Liability of Officers and Directors

78. If a person or an entity commits an offence under this Act, any officer, director or agent of the person or entity who directed, authorized, assented to, acquiesced in or participated in its commission is a party to and guilty of the offence and liable on conviction to the punishment provided for the offence, whether or not the person or entity has been prosecuted or convicted.

Offence by employee, agent or mandatory

79. In a prosecution for an offence under section 75, 77 or 77.1,

(a) it is sufficient proof of the offence to establish that it was committed by an employee, agent or mandatory of the accused, whether or not the employee, agent or mandatory is identified or has been prosecuted for the offence; and

(b) no person shall be found guilty of the offence if they establish that they exercised due diligence to prevent its commission.

5.4.6 Pest Control Products Public Protection

Federal legislation has been established to prevent unacceptable risk to the public and the environment from the use of pest control products. The potential victim is not a stakeholder, but rather the public. The applicable federal statute, *Pest Control Products Act*,[19] is primarily a public health and environmental statute that establishes various prohibitions against manufacturing, possessing, handling, storing, transporting, importing or distributing any pest control product that is not registered under the legislation. Like many federal and provincial statutes, its primary means of enforcing the statutory provisions and objectives is by establishing offences. This traditional legislative scheme, of creating strict liability offences to achieve regulatory objectives, may not always be the most effective and efficient way of ensuring regulatory compliance. A policy analysis under the VVH Matrix would suggest prosecution to enforce this statute is questionable. In any event, the relevant offence provisions under the statute are extensive and as follows:

Contravention causing risk or harm

68. (1) Every person is guilty of an offence if, in contravening this Act or the regulations, they cause

    (a) a risk of imminent death or serious bodily harm to another person;

    (b) a risk of substantial harm to the environment; or

    (c) harm to the environment.

Punishment

(2) Every person who commits an offence under subsection (1) is liable

    (a) on summary conviction, to a fine of not more than $200,000 or to imprisonment for a term of not more than six months, or to both; and

    (b) on conviction on indictment, to a fine of not more than $500,000 or to imprisonment for a term of not more than three years, or to both.

Offence committed wilfully or recklessly

(3) Every person is guilty of an offence if, while contravening this Act or the regulations, they wilfully or recklessly cause

    (a) a risk of imminent death or serious bodily harm to another person;

    (b) a risk of substantial harm to the environment; or

    (c) harm to the environment.

Punishment

(4) Every person who commits an offence under subsection (3) is liable

    (a) on summary conviction, to a fine of not more than $300,000 or to imprisonment for a term of not more than six months, or to both; and

    (b) on conviction on indictment, to a fine of not more than $1,000,000 or to imprisonment for a term of not more than three years, or to both.

---

[19] S.C. 2002, c. 28.

Contravention of regulations

69. Every person who contravenes a provision of the regulations is guilty of an offence and liable

    (a) on summary conviction, to a fine of not more than $200,000 or to imprisonment for a term of not more than six months, or to both; and

    (b) on conviction on indictment, to a fine of not more than $500,000 or to imprisonment for a term of not more than three years, or to both.

Officers, etc., of corporations

70. (1) If a corporation commits an offence under this Act, any officer, director or agent of the corporation who directed, authorized, assented to, acquiesced in or participated in the commission of the offence is a party to and guilty of the offence and liable on conviction to the punishment provided for the offence, whether or not the corporation has been prosecuted or convicted.

Duty to ensure compliance

(2) Every director and officer of a corporation shall take all reasonable care to ensure that the corporation complies with this Act and the regulations.

Offence and punishment

(3) Every person who contravenes subsection (2) is guilty of an offence and liable

    (a) on summary conviction, to a fine of not more than $200,000 or to imprisonment for a term of not more than six months, or to both; or

    (b) on conviction on indictment, to a fine of not more than $500,000 or to imprisonment for a term of not more than three years, or to both.

Offence by employee or agent

71. In a prosecution for an offence under this Act, it is sufficient proof of the offence to establish that it was committed by an employee or agent of the accused, whether or not the employee or agent is identified or has been prosecuted for the offence, unless the accused establishes that

    (a) the offence was committed without the knowledge or consent of the accused; and

    (b) the accused exercised all due diligence to prevent its commission.

5.5 PROVINCIAL OFFENCES

Canada is a confederation of the provinces, territories and the federal government. A large number of legislative subjects fall within the exclusive authority of provinces. Provinces have authority to pass statutes and regulations that set standards for corporate conduct. Provincial constitutional authority to establish offences that hold corporations accountable is circumscribed by section 92 of the *Constitution Act, 1867*.[20] Section 92 states:

Subjects of exclusive Provincial Legislation

92. In each Province the Legislature may exclusively make Laws in relation to Matters coming within the Classes of Subjects next hereinafter enumerated; that is to say,

1. Repealed.

2. Direct Taxation within the Province in order to the raising of a Revenue for Provincial Purposes.

3. The borrowing of Money on the sole Credit of the Province.

4. The Establishment and Tenure of Provincial Offices and the Appointment and Payment of Provincial Officers.

5. The Management and Sale of the Public Lands belonging to the Province and of the Timber and Wood thereon.

6. The Establishment, Maintenance, and Management of Public and Reformatory Prisons in and for the Province.

7. The Establishment, Maintenance, and Management of Hospitals, Asylums, Charities, and Eleemosynary Institutions in and for the Province, other than Marine Hospitals.

8. Municipal Institutions in the Province.

9. Shop, Saloon, Tavern, Auctioneer, and other Licences in order to the raising of a Revenue for Provincial, Local, or Municipal Purposes.

10. Local Works and Undertakings other than such as are of the following Classes:

    (a) Lines of Steam or other Ships, Railways, Canals, Telegraphs, and other Works and Undertakings connecting the Province with any other or others of the Provinces, or extending beyond the Limits of the Province;

    (b) Lines of Steam Ships between the Province and any British or Foreign Country;

    (c) Such Works as, although wholly situate within the Province, are before or after their Execution declared by the Parliament of Canada to be for the general Advantage of Canada or for the Advantage of Two or more of the Provinces.

11. The Incorporation of Companies with Provincial Objects.

12. The Solemnization of Marriage in the Province.

13. Property and Civil Rights in the Province.

14. The Administration of Justice in the Province, including the Constitution, Maintenance, and Organization of Provincial Courts, both of Civil and of Criminal Jurisdiction, and including Procedure in Civil Matters in those Courts.

---

[20] (U.K.), 30 & 31 Vict., c. 3.

15. The Imposition of Punishment by Fine, Penalty, or Imprisonment for enforcing any Law of the Province made in relation to any Matter coming within any of the Classes of Subjects enumerated in this Section.

16. Generally all Matters of a merely local or private Nature in the Province.

5.5.1 Provincial *Mens Rea* Offences

The provinces do not have constitutional authority to pass legislation that is classified as pure or primarily criminal law. However, some provincial legislation, that falls within the authority of section 92 of the *Constitution Act, 1867*, may establish offences that have been classified as true crimes. These classifications of offences, as discussed in Chapter 3, require proof of intent or same degree of wilfulness or recklessness.

One example of a *mens rea* offence in a provincial statute is in the *Workplace Safety and Insurance Act, 1997*.[21] That legislation provides for no-fault workers compensation benefits for workers who are injured arising out of or in the course of their employment. The scheme sets up an accident fund that is financed by employers and pays out compensation to injured employees. This legislation creates an number of offences, one of which at least is a provincial *mens rea* offence. The legislation states, "a person who knowingly makes a false or misleading statement or representation to the Board in connection with any person's claim for benefits under the insurance plan is guilty of an offence."[22]

This provision has been interpreted by the courts to be a *mens rea* offence or true crime, requiring proof of intent beyond a reasonable doubt.[23] In that case, it is held that the onus is on the Crown to prove that the employees representing the company that were involved in filing information with the Workplace Safety Insurance Board knew that the information being provided was false at the time that it was submitted to the Board. The court also held that *mens rea* cannot be "gleaned" from subsequent behaviour of representatives of the corporate defendant. The charges were dismissed at trial and this decision was upheld on appeal.[24]

In another prosecution under the *Workplace Safety and Insurance Act, 1997* dealing with the same provision, section 149, the court explicitly identified the offence as being one of "full *mens rea* offence".[25] The court also acknowledged that very few regulatory offences require the Crown to prove *mens rea* or wrongful intention or knowledge, but that section 149 of the *Workplace Safety and Insurance Act, 1997* was one of them.

---

[21] S.O. 1997, c. 16, Sched. A.

[22] *Ibid.*, s. 149(1).

[23] *Ontario (Workplace Safety and Insurance Board) v. Latcon Ltd.*, [2005] O.J. No. 3969, 2005 ONCJ 398 (Ont. C.J.).

[24] *Ibid.*, para. 18.

[25] *R. v. Virk*, [2002] O.J. No. 4102 at para. 10, 55 W.C.B. (2d) 464 (Ont. C.J.).

5.5.2 Provincial Strict Liability Offences

The vast majority of provincial standards for corporations found in statutes and regulations promulgated by provinces are strict liability offences. For reasons discussed above, the federal government has exclusive authority over criminal law and the provinces have only limited rights to pass true crimes, in the context of other subjects of provincial authority under the constitution. What follows is a brief summary of provincial, strict liability offences that apply to corporations.

The majority of labour or employment standards set by legislatures in Canada are at the provincial level. For example, in Ontario, labour standards are dealt with by a specific piece of legislation that deals with minimum wage, maximum hours of work, overtime provisions and related labour standards. These provincial labour standards may result in the prosecution of employers for breach of the standards. The offence under these statutes is strict liability in nature. The following are the offences established by Ontario's labour standards legislation, the *Employment Standards Act, 2000*[26] or such contraventions by corporations.

Offence to keep false records

131. (1) No person shall make, keep or produce false records or other documents that are required to be kept under this Act or participate or acquiesce in the making, keeping or production of false records or other documents that are required to be kept under this Act. 2000, c. 41, s. 131 (1).

False or misleading information

(2) No person shall provide false or misleading information under this Act. 2000, c. 41, s. 131 (2).

General offence

132. A person who contravenes this Act or the regulations or fails to comply with an order, direction or other requirement under this Act or the regulations is guilty of an offence and on conviction is liable,

    (a) if the person is an individual, to a fine of not more than $50,000 or to imprisonment for a term of not more than 12 months or to both;

    (b) subject to clause (c), if the person is a corporation, to a fine of not more than $100,000; and

    (c) if the person is a corporation that has previously been convicted of an offence under this Act or a predecessor to it,

        (i) if the person has one previous conviction, to a fine of not more than $250,000, and

        (ii) if the person has more than one previous conviction, to a fine of not more than $500,000. 2000, c. 41, s. 132.

---

[26] S.O. 2000, c. 41.

Additional orders

133. (1) If an employer is convicted under section 132 of contravening section 74 or paragraph 4, 6, 7 or 10 of subsection 74.8 (1) or if a client, within the meaning of Part XVIII.1 is convicted under section 132 of contravening section 74.12, the court shall, in addition to any fine or term of imprisonment that is imposed, order that the employer or client, as the case may be, take specific action or refrain from taking specific action to remedy the contravention. 2009, c. 9, s. 25.

As with federally-regulated workplaces, provincially-regulated workplaces also have workplace health and safety legislation passed by the provinces. Provinces across Canada play a very important role in establishing standards and enforcing them for workers across Canada. The vast majority of workers, approximately 90 per cent, or more, are provincially regulated rather than federally regulated. Therefore, when provinces set health and safety standards, they have also deemed it appropriate to establish various offences to enforce those standards, primarily against corporate employers. What follows are the offences, of a strict liability nature, established by Ontario's workplace health and safety legislation, that corporations are subject to if they contravene workplace health and safety standards.

Occupational Health and Safety Act[27]

66. (1) Every person who contravenes or fails to comply with,

    (a) a provision of this Act or the regulations;

    (b) an order or requirement of an inspector or a Director; or

    (c) an order of the Minister,

is guilty of an offence and on conviction is liable to a fine of not more than $25,000 or to imprisonment for a term of not more than twelve months, or to both.

Idem

(2) If a corporation is convicted of an offence under subsection (1), the maximum fine that may be imposed upon the corporation is $500,000 and not as provided therein.

Part of the challenge of government in the increasingly digital and complex information age is the protection of personal, private health information. Information of an individual, if misused, could be used to deny a person proper access to government services, employment, contracts, and also provide sensitive information to media outlets. Ontario, like many jurisdictions in Canada, at the provincial level, has created legislation to protect personal health information. What follows are the offence provisions that may be the subject of the prosecution of individuals and corporations, who do not respect those legal protections.

---

[27] R.S.O. 1990, c. O.1.

Personal Health Information Protection Act, 2004[28]

Offences

72. (1) A person is guilty of an offence if the person,

(a) *wilfully* collects, uses or discloses personal health information in contravention of this Act or its regulations;

(b) makes a request under this Act, under false pretences, for access to or correction of a record of personal health information;

(c) in connection with the collection, use or disclosure of personal health information or access to a record of personal health information, makes an assertion, *knowing* that it is untrue, to the effect that the person,

(i) is a person who is entitled to consent to the collection, use or disclosure of personal health information about another individual,

(ii) meets the requirement of clauses 26(2)(b) and (c),

(iii) holds the beliefs described in subsection 26 (5), or

(iv) is a person entitled to access to a record of personal health information under section 52;

(d) disposes of a record of personal health information in the custody or under the control of the custodian with an *intent* to evade a request for access to the record that the custodian has received under subsection 53 (1);

(e) *wilfully* disposes of a record of personal health information in contravention of section 13;

(f) contravenes subsection 34 (2), (3) or (4) or clause 47 (15) (a), (e) or (f);

(g) *wilfully* obstructs the Commissioner or a person known to be acting under the authority of the Commissioner in the performance of his or her functions under this Act;

(h) *wilfully* makes a false statement to mislead or attempt to mislead the Commissioner or a person known to be acting under the authority of the Commissioner in the performance of his or her functions under this Act;

(i) *wilfully* fails to comply with an order made by the Commissioner or a person known to be acting under the authority of the Commissioner under this Act; or

(j) contravenes section 70. 2004, c. 3, Sched. A, s. 72 (1) [emphasis added].

Penalty

(2) A person who is guilty of an offence under subsection (1) is liable, on conviction,

---

[28] S.O. 2004, c. 3, Sched. A.

(a) if the person is a natural person, to a fine of not more than $50,000; and

(b) if the person is not a natural person, to a fine of not more than $250,000. 2004, c. 3, Sched. A, s. 72 (2).

Millions of Canadians rely upon their pension in their retirement years to sustain a modest or adequate standard of living. Many public and private sector employees have pensions plans, of various designs, that have been an important part of their anticipated compensation, in their retirement, throughout their working years. Legislation such as Ontario's *Pension Benefits Act*,[29] is designed to set standards for the management, maintenance, investment and protection of pension benefits of retirees. In setting these standards, if the corporate employer was to breach trust and legal requirements, they may be subject to prosecution. The following strict liability offences are ones that corporations who contravene these standards are subject to.

Pension Benefits Act

109. (1) Every person who contravenes this Act or the regulations is guilty of an offence.

Idem

(2) Every person who contravenes an order made under this Act is guilty of an offence. R.S.O. 1990, c. P.8, s. 109.

Penalty

110. (1) Every person who is guilty of an offence under this Act is liable on conviction to a fine of not more than $100,000 for the first conviction and not more than $200,000 for each subsequent conviction. 1997, c. 28, s. 220 (1).

Persons re corporation

(2) Every director, officer, official or agent of a corporation and every person acting in a similar capacity or performing similar functions in an unincorporated association is guilty of an offence if the person,

(a) causes, authorizes, permits, acquiesces or participates in the commission of an offence referred to in section 109 by the corporation or unincorporated association; or

(b) fails to take all reasonable care in the circumstances to prevent the corporation or unincorporated association from committing an offence referred to in section 109. 1997, c. 28, s. 220 (1).

Penalty

(3) A person who is guilty of an offence described in subsection (2) is liable on a first conviction to a fine of not more than $100,000, and on each subsequent conviction to a fine of not more than $200,000, whether or not the corporation or unincorporated association has been prosecuted for or con-

---

[29] R.S.O. 1990, c. P.8.

victed of an offence arising from the same facts or circumstances. 1997, c. 28, s. 220 (1).

The capital markets provide for the issuance of shares and public trading of the shares, of corporations in Canada. Securities legislation is deemed to be within provincial constitutional jurisdiction. Therefore, Canada does not have a national stock exchange or a national securities regulator. In setting standards for process of "going public" maintenance of these standards and trust within the system is critical. Preventing misuse or abuse of the stock exchange system, and the issuing of shares in public companies, is a very important mandate of securities legislation and the Commissions that are established thereunder to achieve that end.

In Ontario, the *Securities Act*[30] regulates the process of "going public", and related issues. In both setting and enforcing standards, part of the process of corporate accountability is the establishment of various offences. What follows is an excerpt of the strict liability offences that a corporation may be exposed to to ensure corporate accountability in this important subject matter of provincial regulation.

Securities Act

122. (1) Every person or company that,

> (a) makes a statement in any material, evidence or information submitted to the Commission, a Director, any person acting under the authority of the Commission or the Executive Director or any person appointed to make an investigation or examination under this Act that, in a material respect and at the time and in the light of the circumstances under which it is made, is misleading or untrue or does not state a fact that is required to be stated or that is necessary to make the statement not misleading;

> (b) makes a statement in any application, release, report, preliminary prospectus, prospectus, return, financial statement, information circular, take-over bid circular, issuer bid circular or other document required to be filed or furnished under Ontario securities law that, in a material respect and at the time and in the light of the circumstances under which it is made, is misleading or untrue or does not state a fact that is required to be stated or that is necessary to make the statement not misleading; or

> (c) contravenes Ontario securities law,

is guilty of an offence and on conviction is liable to a fine of not more than $5 million or to imprisonment for a term of not more than five years less a day, or to both. 1994, c. 11, s. 373; 2002, c. 22, s. 181 (1).

5.6 FINAL THOUGHTS

The cataloguing of corporate crimes and offences in Canada is a challenging task. Depending on a corporation's business, regulatory standards pervade

---

[30] R.S.O. 1990, c. S.5.

everyday operation with risk of crimes and offences if those standards are breached by the organization. The definitions of "organization" and "everyone" in the Code expose a corporation to many charges that may never realistically occur. However, it is daunting in managing legal risk for corporations to realize the breadth of the definitions and potential exposure to criminal prosecution of corporations under the Code.

Many areas of standards for corporations, and legal enforcement of standards through strict liability offences, fall within provincial jurisdiction. Although provinces may pass crimes or *mens rea* offences, the vast majority of provincial offences are strict liability in nature. This gives rise to the defence of due diligence. This defence is explored more fully in Chapter 8 dealing with defences to corporate crimes and offences.

The conceptual model for cataloguing corporate crimes and offences was introduced and reviewed in this chapter. The thesis is that the more vulnerable the potential victim of corporate misconduct, and the more serious the harm caused by the corporate misconduct, the greater the reasonable and appropriate response is a traditional prosecution model. However, the more involved the stakeholder is in the control and influence over corporate decisions, legally and practically, and the smaller the degree of harm by the potential corporate misconduct, the less rational and appropriate it is to use the traditional prosecution model. This policy approach is not a "one size fits all" approach to political decision making on new crimes and offences for corporations. However, it is a sensible approach that will be instructive in analyzing political and policy decisions in the future. Much of the potential policy alternatives to prosecutions are discussed in Chapter 10, the future of corporate accountability.

Chapter 6

CORPORATIONS AND THE
CRIMINAL JUSTICE SYSTEM

6.1 INTRODUCTION TO THE CRIMINAL JUDICIAL SYSTEM

The prosecution of corporations necessarily draws the corporation into the criminal justice system. The prosecution of corporations with a criminal or regulatory offence is a blunt instrument, and an expensive one at that, to achieve accountability. Corporations have some unique issues that arise in the prosecution of criminal and regulatory offences. The amendments to the *Criminal Code*[1] under Bill C-45 increased the scope and application of the criminal liability of organizations in Canada. Accordingly, a greater number of persons may be exposed to criminal investigations and charges that have had no previous experience with the criminal justice system. Faced with this prospect, it is important to have a basic understanding of the criminal justice process as well as the fundamental rights the Canadian Constitution, in particular the *Charter of Rights and Freedoms*,[2] affords to each suspect and accused. The latter subject as it relates to corporations is addressed in detail in the next chapter. This chapter gives a brief description of the various procedural issues, stages of the process and legal rights that an accused has during the criminal justice process, from the time of investigation to the time an accused is either convicted or acquitted and remanded for sentencing at trial. The process for prosecution of corporations under strict liability offences is governed by provincial procedural statutes, such as the *Provincial Offences Act*.[3]

Under the Canadian Constitution, only the federal parliament has jurisdiction to enact laws that exclusively or primarily concern criminal law and procedure.[4] Most criminal law in Canada is contained in the Code and

---

[1]   R.S.C. 1985, c. C-46 [hereinafter the "Code"].

[2]   Part I of the *Constitution Act, 1982*, being Schedule B to the *Canada Act, 1982* (U.K.), 1982, c. 11 [hereinafter the "Charter"].

[3]   R.S.O. 1990, c. P.33. Note that the following discussion is intended to help persons criminally charged under the provisions of the *Criminal Code*, R.S.C. 1985, c. C-46, that will be amended or added through the enactment of Bill C-45. Also, the areas of procedure described below do not necessarily form part of every case. They provide a general overview of common stages. Every criminal proceeding has a life and history of its own and will be influenced by the particular facts of each case and the procedural decisions and options available.

[4]   *Constitution Act, 1867*, (U.K.), 30 & 31 Vict., c. 3, s. 91(27).

under the *Controlled Drugs and Substances Act*.[5] Not all offences enacted by the federal government, however, are enacted pursuant to its criminal law power. For example, the *Canada Labour Code*,[6] Part II, regulating occupational health and safety in federally regulated workplaces, is passed pursuant to the federal government's authority to regulate federal works and undertakings, and is not considered criminal law.

Canadian provinces, unlike countries such as Australia and the United States, are not permitted to make laws that are constitutionally classified criminal law. Criminal offences are established when the federal government passes a law that has moral blameworthiness and a fault element as part of the offence. It need not be passed as part of the Code to be a criminal law. For example, if a provincial statute or municipal by-law has as its primary purpose the punishment of behaviour that requires proof of intent, then those offences may be considered a *mens rea* or true crimes.

The attorney general of each province is responsible for prosecutions under the Code offences. The federal attorney general prosecutes drug offences. The same division of powers distinction is made with respect to policing. Provinces have authority to establish police forces to enforce the Code. The federal and provincial governments have authority to establish a police force to investigate drug offences and other federal offences. However, most provinces contract for the services of the national police force, the Royal Canadian Mounted Police. Only Ontario and Quebec have provincial police forces. The Code gives special powers to peace officers, which is a unique Canadian term for police officers in Canada, to enforce criminal law. The Charter is part of the constitution and the fundamental law of Canada. Attorneys general, local prosecutors and peace officers are bound to respect and comply with the Charter when enforcing the Code or strict liability offences. Regulatory strict liability offences are also resolved in these courts.

The majority of criminal cases are resolved in provincial criminal courts. Provincial court judges are appointed by the provinces and they do not sit with a jury. Provincial court judges may hear serious indictable offences, if the accused chooses to be tried in a provincial court without a jury. In such circumstances, there is no preliminary inquiry. Federal parliament has exclusive authority to appoint superior court judges, who can sit with a jury. Murder charges must be tried by a superior court judge, usually with a jury. Superior court judges may also try most other indictable offences, provided that the accused elects or chooses to be tried in this higher level of trial court. The accused may elect to be tried in the superior court, with a preliminary inquiry, and with or without a jury when the offence is an indictable offence.

---

[5]   S.C. 1996, c. 19.

[6]   R.S.C. 1985, c. L-6.

The Code applies across Canada and sets the standard of what constitutes criminal behaviour in every part of the country.[7] The Code is consistent
in setting standards of criminal conduct and behaviour throughout Canada.
No person may be convicted or discharged of a Code offence committed
outside of Canada.[8] The Code provides for some exceptions for offences on
an aircraft, ship, fixed platforms and spacecraft that are outside of Canada
but that have a designated connection with Canada.[9]

6.2 TYPOLOGY OF CRIMINAL OFFENCES

Corporations charged with offences under the Code are subject to the same
typology of offences as are individuals. The Code defines an act or omission
to be a criminal offence and how the offence is classified. All crimes in the
Code are classified as either indictable offences or offences punishable upon
summary conviction, or hybrid offences. The former represent the more serious offences with more severe penalties. Additionally, some crimes have a
hybrid type of offence being both indictable and summary conviction offences, dependent on the election of the prosecutor. This means that in most
cases the Crown has the right to select how the offence will be classified and
prosecuted.[10] Neither the court nor the defence has the right to direct the
Crown on how it must proceed. However, if the Crown fails to elect how it
will proceed, the offence is deemed to be an indictable offence for the purposes of any interim procedures such as bail hearings, preliminary inquiry or
other motions.[11]

6.2.1 Summary Conviction Offences

Summary conviction offences are criminal offences that are less serious on
the spectrum of offences under the Code.[12] Most sections of the Code enacting offences punishable on summary conviction often contain no specific
penalty provisions. If this is the case, except where otherwise provided by
law, every one who is convicted of an offence punishable on summary
conviction is liable to a fine of not more than $100,000 or to imprisonment
for six months or both.[13] This penalty provision was specifically amended
by Bill C-45 by increasing that monetary penalty from $25,000 to
$100,000 for a summary conviction offence. Nevertheless, if provided for

---

[7]   Although the *Criminal Code* is the pre-eminent source for determining offences in Canada,
there are also a number of other federal offences declared in other federal statutes and regulations, as well as provincial offences such as driving and liquor offences declared in provincial
statutes and regulations.

[8]   *Criminal Code*, s. 6(2).

[9]   *Ibid.*, s. 7.

[10]   "Crown" is used interchangeably with "prosecution" throughout this text.

[11]   *Interpretation Act*, R.S.C. 1985, c. I-21, s. 34(1)(a).

[12]   Proceedings for summary conviction offences are governed by Part XXVII of the *Criminal
Code*.

[13]   *Ibid.*, s. 787(1).

in the applicable section of the Code, some offences prosecuted by way of summary conviction will have a maximum penalty of imprisonment of 18 months.[14]

6.2.2 Indictable Offences

Indictable offences are the most serious criminal offences and accordingly, their penalties are the more severe than summary conviction offences. They are punishable by a maximum penalty of imprisonment for two, five, 10, 14 years or life imprisonment depending on the offence. For example, an accused who is charged and convicted of the new offence of Occupational Healthy and Safety ("OHS") criminal negligence causing death under Bill C-45 may receive a maximum penalty of life imprisonment. The Code provides for three categories of indictable offences:

(i)   *Absolute Jurisdiction or section 553 Offences*: This class of indictable offences fall within the absolute jurisdiction of a provincial court judge. The accused must be tried in the provincial court of the province or territory.[15]

(ii) *Section 469 Offences*: This class of indictable offences fall within the exclusive jurisdiction of the superior court of the province or territory.[16]

(iii) *Section 554 Offences*: All other indictable offences which do not fall within section 469 or section 553 allow an accused an election as to the mode of trial (discussed below); these include fraud over $5,000, criminal negligence causing death, manslaughter, *etc*.

Whether a criminal prosecution proceeds by way of summary conviction or indictment, the criminal investigation process is usually the same. The criminal process usually commences before an arrest is made as a proper and lawful investigation must be conducted by the police. Police usually do their investigation, conduct their search and seizure, surveillance and conduct witness interviews. Correspondingly, potential accused persons or organizations have various pre-charge and post-charge rights during the criminal investigation process. Some of these rights of suspects accused under the Charter are reviewed below.

6.3   THE RIGHT TO BE FREE FROM UNREASONABLE SEARCH AND SEIZURE

It is the fundamental right of every Canadian, both individual and organization, to be secure against unreasonable and arbitrary searches by the police

---

[14]   *Ibid.*, s. 264.1(a) (uttering a threat to cause death or bodily harm).

[15]   These are less serious offences; for example, theft under $5,000.

[16]   These offences are serious; for example, murder.

and to not have their property seized for use as evidence as a result of such searches. The law generally obliges no person to engage in self incrimination. This right, firmly rooted in our common law tradition, is now codified as a constitution right in section 8 of the Charter.

The Supreme Court has interpreted the purpose of section 8 of the Charter to be the protection of people's reasonable expectations of privacy.[17] This includes warrantless searches in one's home or place of business, body searches for possible production of DNA evidence,[18] the acquisition of someone's or a business' hydro information or bank records. The right to be free from unreasonable search and seizure, under section 8 of the Charter, in taking forensic DNA evidence, is protected by section 487.05 of the Code. That provision permits a provincial court judge to issue a DNA warrant for taking bodily samples for forensic DNA analysis. A provincial court judge may issue a DNA warrant where there are reasonable grounds to believe that a designated offence has been committed and that a bodily substance has been found or obtained at the scene, on or in the victim, or on anything worn or carried by the victim, or on or within the body of any person or anything or at any place associated with the commission of the designated offence. The provincial court judge, in considering a request for a DNA warrant, must consider the nature of the designated offence and the circumstances of its commission and where there is a peace officer or other person with the necessary training who is able to take the bodily sample from the suspect.

Every invasion of private property, however slight, may be considered to be a form of trespass. Generally speaking, no person has the right to enter private property except by the owner's or occupier's consent, or strictly in accordance with particular lawful authorization. Unless the police are in possession of a valid search warrant or are acting in accordance with some other specific legal authority, they have no right to enter private premises and remain there against the owner's or occupier's wishes.[19] When the police obtain a search warrant, it must meet certain substantive requirements. The search warrant must identify an alleged offence with sufficient precision to apprise anyone concerned with the nature of the offence for which evidence is being sought. The search warrant must also describe the items to be seized with enough specificity to permit the officers responsible to execute the search warrant to identify such objects and to link them to the offence described in the information and the search warrant; it must describe the loca-

---

[17]   See *Hunter v. Southam Inc.*, [1984] S.C.J. No 36, [1984] 2 S.C.R. 145 (S.C.C.).

[18]   See *R. v. Stillman*, [1997] S.C.J. No. 34, [1997] 1 S.C.R. 607 (S.C.C.).

[19]   In *R. v. Collins*, [1987] S.C.J. No. 15, 33 C.C.C. (3d) 1 (S.C.C.), the Court established a five-step process to determine the legality of a search and seizure: 1) Can the police (or State actor) conduct be characterized as a search and seizure? 2) Did the actions of the police (or State actor) intrude upon the accused's reasonable expectation of privacy? 3)Were the actions of the police authorized by law, either statutory or the common law? 4) Was the law that the police were relying on to pursue the search and seizure reasonable? 5) Was the search or seizure carried out in a reasonable fashion? The accused has the burden of persuading the court that his or her Charter rights against unreasonable searches has been infringed or denied.

tion with sufficient accuracy to enable one from the mere reading of it to know of what premises it authorizes the search.[20]

Evidence acquired as a result of an illegal search and seizure may be subject to an application for exclusion from being used as evidence at trial if it may affect the fairness of the trial.[21] However, if the prosecution can show that illegally obtained evidence was inevitably to be found, the evidence may be admissible. The court may be called upon to determine, under sub-section 24(2) of the Charter, whether the admission of the illegally obtained evidence brings the administration of justice into disrepute. Subsection 24(2) requires that evidence shall be excluded if, having regard to all of the cir-cumstances, the admission of the evidence would bring the administration of justice into disrepute. In addition to remedies under subsection 24(2) of the Charter, evidence may also be excluded under subsection 24(1) of the Char-ter. For example, if the admission of evidence undermines an accused's right to a fair trial, pursuant to subsection 11(d) of the Charter, then an order ex-cluding the evidence may be obtained by the trial judge. Evidence may be rendered unfair at trial, the way it was taken may render it unreliable or its potential for misleading the trier of fact may outweigh any such minimal probative value it may possess. Further, if the police have acted in such an abusive fashion that the court concludes that the admission of the evidence would irremediably taint the fairness of the trial itself, it may also be ex-cluded under the authority of subsection 11(d) of the Charter.[22]

6.4   THE RIGHT TO BE FREE FROM ARBITRARY DETENTION

Organizations, including corporations, cannot be physically detained. None-theless, if any of its managers or representatives are put in such a situation, they will be allowed, on behalf of the organization, to retain and instruct counsel. This will be of increasing importance with potential risk of criminal prosecution of corporations. Bill C-45 charges have, in some cases, resulted in both corporations and their president being investigated and charged with criminal offences.

A detention occurs when a person has been taken into police custody or believes that he or she does not have the option to leave when being de-tained or questioned.[23] Many people do not know exactly what the authority of the police is and will tend to err on the side of co-operation rather than caution when dealing with them. When confronted by police, even if feeling uncomfortable and pressured, individuals will often decide not to leave or defer questioning. The law clearly states that any person has the right not to

---

[20]   *Rex v. Gibson*, [1919] A.J. No. 83, 30 C.C.C. 308 (Alta. S.C.).

[21]   *Canadian Charter of Rights and Freedoms*, Part 1 of the *Constitution Act, 1982*, being Schedule B to the *Canada Act, 1982* (U.K.), 1982, c. 11, s. 24(1).

[22]   *R. v. Harrer*, [1995] S.C.J. No. 81, 101 C.C.C. (3d) 193 (S.C.C.).

[23]   See the Charter, s. 9.

be arbitrarily detained by the police. If a person was unlawfully detained by the police, without legal representation, it is possible that any evidence gathered was obtained contrary to section 10(b) of the Charter. The corresponding right of a detained person to retain and instruct a lawyer without delay and to be informed of that right is an important pre-charge right of every individual under the Charter.

6.5   INITIATION OF CRIMINAL PROCEEDINGS

When authorities make a decision to prosecute a corporation, they must follow proper procedures. Criminal proceedings, following an investigation, are usually commenced when an accused person or organization is formally charged. This may be done by the prosecution in one of two ways: 1) on the swearing of an information or 2) the issuance of an indictment. The police usually decide on the charge in consultation with the Crown prosecutor, but ultimately it is the Crown prosecutor who will decide if there is sufficient evidence to secure a conviction. If criminal charges proceed, the accused should immediately retain a lawyer or, if a lawyer cannot be afforded, apply for legal aid to have a lawyer appointed by the provincial legal aid system. There is nothing in the Code to prevent an accused representing themselves, which may become a problem since many accused who choose to act in their own capacity can clog the courts because of their unfamiliarity with criminal procedure.

An information is generally prepared for summary conviction offences or offences of a less serious nature that are to be tried in the provincial court. The information records the offence and is used to record the progress of the case. It contains information such as whether the accused was released on bail, what sort of release the accused was given, how the accused pleaded, the disposition of the case if it was tried in the provincial court, the outcome of the preliminary inquiry if the accused elected trial in the superior court, and the time and date of every appearance in court.

An indictment is a written accusation generally signed by the prosecutor in the name of the Queen alleging that an accused has committed an indictable offence. It is the formal legal document, like the information, containing the records and progress of the case, and used throughout the criminal proceedings which will be heard in the superior court of criminal jurisdiction.

6.6   ARRESTING AN ACCUSED

It is trite to say that organizations, including corporations, cannot be physically detained or arrested. Rather, the normal practice is that they are served with a Summons or Notice that they have been charged with a criminal offence under the Code or any other Act.[24] If no other method of service is

---

[24]   *Criminal Code*, s. 703.2.

provided, service on an organization may be effected by delivery to the manager, secretary or other executive officer of the organization or to any one of its branches.[25] Often a senior officer is charged together with the corporation for the same or similar criminal or strict liability offences.

Individuals are usually arrested when they are charged with a criminal offence.[26] Provincial offence statutes do not provide for the power of arrest. Section 494 of the Code sets out the arrest powers that anyone has without a judicial warrant and section 495 sets out the wider arrest powers of a police officer without a warrant. The general rule, as provided for in section 495(2), is that a peace officer shall not arrest a person without warrant for less serious offences under the Code where, in establishing the identity and securing the attendance of the person in court, securing evidence of the offence and preventing the repetition of the offence or the commission of another offence, the public interest that justice will be achieved can be satisfied by issuing an appearance notice.[27]

A judicial warrant for an arrest may be obtained under section 507(4) of the Code. In such instance, if a justice of the peace[28] considers that a case has been made out on oath for compelling an accused to answer the charge of the offence, then he or she will issue a summons unless the evidence presented discloses reasonable grounds to believe that it is necessary in the public interest to issue an arrest warrant.

The exercise of arrest powers triggers a number of ancillary powers for police officers. The Supreme Court has held that in the exercise of their arrest powers for indictable offences, police officers may enter premises without consent if there are reasonable and probable grounds to believe that the person sought is within the premises and if, before entry, they have provided proper announcement for their presence and purpose.[29] This common law power has been restricted under the Charter. Also, when exercising arrest powers, police officers may make warrantless searches incidental to the arrest.[30]

The Supreme Court in the decision of *R. v. Feeney*[31] held that the common law right to make a warrantless arrest on private premises must now be adjusted to comply with Charter rights and values. In general, an individual's privacy interest in the dwelling-house outweighs the interest of

---

[25]   *Ibid.*

[26]   For further information, see M.L. Friedland & K. Roach, *Criminal Law and Procedure: Cases and Materials*, 7th ed. (Toronto: Emond Montgomery Publications, 1994).

[27]   This is essentially a promise to appear by the accused. Should the accused not appear, he may be arrested and this will affect his or her chances of receiving bail in the future.

[28]   A Justice of the Peace is the person who presides over the case, much like a judge but with a much narrower scope of authority.

[29]   *Eccles v. Bourque*, [1974] S.C.J. No. 123, 19 C.C.C. (2d) 129 (S.C.C.); *R. v. Landry*, [1986] S.C.J. No. 10, 25 C.C.C. (3d) 1 (S.C.C.).

[30]   M.L. Friedland & K. Roach, *Criminal Law and Procedure: Cases and Materials*, 7th ed. (Toronto: Emond Montgomery Publications, 1994) at 114.

[31]   [1997] S.C.J. No. 49, 115 C.C.C. (3d) 129 (S.C.C.).

the police, and warrantless arrests in dwelling-houses are prohibited under the Charter. Under section 529.1 of the Code a justice or judge is allowed to issue a warrant to authorize a peace officer to enter a dwelling-house for the purpose of effecting the arrest or apprehension of a suspect. This judicial authorization is dependent upon the justice or judge being satisfied by information on oath in writing that there are reasonable grounds to believe that the person is or will be present and that an arrest warrant is in force anywhere in Canada or that grounds for a warrantless search exist. This provision, as well as the companion provisions in sections 529.2 through to 529.5 inclusive, were enacted in response to the Supreme Court decision in *R. v. Feeney.*

If a person is arrested, summoned or given an appearance notice for an indictable offence, he or she may be compelled to attend at a specified place and time for photographing and fingerprinting under the *Identification of Criminals Act.*[32] An accused ought to obtain legal advice before attending a police station to provide this information.

In general, after an arrest is made, a peace officer is under an obligation to release the arrestee from custody as soon as practicable and issue a summons or appearance notice[33] unless the peace officer believes on reasonable grounds that it is necessary in the public interest to detain the accused in custody having regard to the need to establish the identity of the arrestee, secure or preserve evidence relating to the offence, prevent the continuation of an offence, or to stop the arrestee from failing to appear in court.

6.7 RIGHT TO COUNSEL

The right to a lawyer, or counsel, is just as important for a corporation as it is for an individual accused. However, a corporation cannot be arrested or detained. The criminal investigative activities of the police are restricted by various rights under the common law and under the Charter, including the right of an individual to counsel under section 10(b). Section 10 states that:

> every one has the right on arrest or detention:
>
> (a)   to be informed promptly of the reasons therefore;
>
> (b)   to retain and instruct counsel without delay and to be informed of that right.

The right to legal counsel is a fundamental right of every suspect or accused. The right to legal counsel has been explained by the Supreme Court as follows:

> [W]hen an individual is detained by state authorities, he or she is put in a position of disadvantage relative to the state. Not only has this person suffered a deprivation of liberty, but also this person may be at risk of incriminating him- or herself. Accordingly, a person who is "detained" within the

---

[32]   R.S.C. 1985, c. I-1.

[33]   *Criminal Code*, s. 497.

meaning of s. 10 of the *Charter* is in immediate need of legal advice in order
to protect his or her right against self-incrimination and to assist him or her
in regaining his or her liberty.[34]

Once an individual has expressed his or her request to retain a lawyer,
the police cannot question him or her until he or she has had a meaningful
opportunity to speak with a lawyer. The same right is afforded to organizations charged with a crime. As a result of Bill C-45, every senior officer
should be aware of this right. Also, corporations should have a policy regarding when to seek the advice of a lawyer. Through its directors or officers, the organization may consult with a lawyer to ascertain its rights.
Nonetheless, once an accused has received advice from his or her lawyer,
the police can resume their questioning. Therefore, an accused should re-
member that at all times he or she is under no obligation to say anything to
the police and that by not saying anything, he or she will not be adversely
prejudiced later.[35]

It has been held by courts to be a Charter violation if the police tells an
individual accused that he or she has a right to a lawyer but then proceeds to
tell the accused that he or she does not really need a lawyer.[36] By doing so, a
police officer has been held by the courts to be depriving the accused of the
right to make a meaningful decision because the police officer is providing
advice. Further, if an accused expresses concern about his or her ability to
afford a lawyer, the police must inform him or her of the availability of legal
aid and/or duty counsel.[37]

6.8   JUDICIAL INTERIM RELEASE — A.K.A. "BAIL"

A corporate accused cannot be arrested and therefore do not need to apply
for bail. However, individuals are often charged together with corporations
and therefore this subject will be briefly reviewed. The hearing for judicial
interim release, also known as bail, is a very important part of the criminal
process. Under the reforms of the late 1960s, bail is more easily obtained
from either the police or the courts. The Code permits the police to initially
determine an accused's pre-trial release status. There are certain instances
where it is necessary for an accused to be held in custody, either because the
police have decided not to release the accused pursuant to sections 495 to
499 of the Code or because the police are unable to release the accused, as in
a case of murder. In such cases, the accused must be brought before the
courts.

---

[34]   *R. v. Bartle*, [1994] S.C.J. No. 74 at para. 16, [1994] 3 S.C.R. 173 (S.C.C.).

[35]   Charter, s. 7.

[36]   *R. v. Burlingham*, [1995] S.C.J. No. 39, 124 D.L.R. (4th) 7 (S.C.C.).

[37]   Duty Counsel is a government lawyer who is available before court to advise accused persons.
It is provided to ensure that an accused person will have the benefit of legal advice and assistance when appearing before the court unrepresented. All accused persons are entitled to assistance by Duty Counsel regardless of their financial means. The financial eligibility guidelines
governing the issuance of Legal Aid certificates does not apply to the Duty Counsel program.

Generally, there are two types of individual accused for the purposes of the judicial interim release provisions: those charged with an offence listed in section 469 of the Code, most frequently murder, and those charged with any other criminal offence. For those charged with offences not listed in section 469, an automatic right to a bail hearing results and they must be brought before a court[38] without unreasonable delay and in any event within 24 hours if a justice of the peace is available.[39] At a bail hearing, the justice of the peace is obliged to order the accused released on an undertaking without conditions with respect to the offence unless the prosecutor, having been given a reasonable opportunity to do so, shows cause why the detention of the accused in custody is justified or why a more onerous form of release ought to be ordered.[40] The criteria for release or detention are dictated by subsection 515(10) of the Code. They include: 1) where the detention is necessary to ensure his or her attendance in court, commonly referred to as the primary ground; 2) where the detention is necessary for the protection or safety of the public, commonly referred to as the secondary ground; or 3) where the detention is necessary in order to maintain confidence in the administration of justice, commonly referred to as the tertiary ground.

Accused persons charged with section 469 offences are not entitled to an automatic release hearing before a justice. On the contrary, unlike others, they must make an application for release to a judge of the superior court and bear the onus of showing cause as to why they ought to be released.[41] If they are successful in doing so, the justice must order their release and include in the record a statement of reasons for making the order.[42] The justice may also include any reasonable conditions available on the release.[43]

It is possible that an accused be denied bail and remain in pre-trial detention, no matter what offence he or she is charged with, until the end of his

---

[38] Note that the type of offence will determine which judicial stream the accused will enter for the purposes of bail (appearance before a provincial court or superior court).

[39] *Criminal Code*, s. 503.

[40] *Ibid.*, s. 515(1), (2).

[41] This reverse onus situation is also true for accused persons charged with: offences under *Criminal Code*, s. 467.11, 467.12 or 467.13, or an offence alleged to have been committed for the benefit or in association with a criminal organization; an offence under any of ss. 83.02 to 83.04 and ss. 83.18 to 83.23 or otherwise is alleged to be a terrorism offence; an offence under subss. 16(1) or (2), 17(1), 19(1), 20(1) or 22(1) of the *Security of Information Act*, R.S.C. 1985, c. O-5; an indictable offence not listed in s. 469 where the accused is not ordinarily resident in Canada (as per s. 515(6)(b)); an offence under subss. 145(2) to (5) alleged to have been committed while the accused was at large after being released in respect to another offence; having committed an offence punishable by s. 5(3), 5(4) or 6(3) of the *Controlled Drugs and Substances Act*, S.C. 1996, c.19 (as per subs. 515(6)(d) of the *Criminal Code*).

[42] *Criminal Code*, s. 515(6).

[43] These include: the supervision of the accused by a surety or sureties or, if the prosecution consents, the deposit of cash bail in lieu of finding a surety or sureties (s. 515(2)); the reporting to a designated person, such as a police officer (s. 515(4)(a)); remaining within a specified territorial jurisdiction (s. 515(4)(b)); notifying the Court of any change of address or employment (s. 515(4)(c)); abstaining from communication with named persons such as victims, co-accused, witnesses; depositing one's passport (s. 515(4)(e)); or any other condition that the Court sees fit to impose (s. 515(4)(e.1)).

or her trial. However, pre-trial custody will be given consideration and credit in plea bargain arrangements and sentencing. Although time in custody is usually given full credit in sentencing, pre-trial incarceration still amounts to a loss of personal liberty.

6.9   CROWN DISCLOSURE

Understanding the case that you have to meet is an important right of both an individual and corporate accused. Crown disclosure is the process of making the prosecution's evidentiary file available to the accused and his or her lawyer. This is a critical right to ensure a fair and transparent prosecution process. Sections 7 and 11(d) of the Charter provide an accused with a right to make full answer and defence in response to criminal charges. Crown disclosure is one of the most important rights in the criminal justice system process and as such, the Crown has an obligation to disclose to the accused all relevant information in its possession, whether it be inculpatory or exculpatory.[44] The Supreme Court has stated, "the fruits of the investigation ... are not the property of the Crown for use in securing a conviction but the property of the public to be used to ensure that justice is done."[45] In fact, the Crown has a special obligation to treat an accused fairly and provide crown disclosure. Consequently, crown disclosure must be made early in the prosecution process and ongoing disclosure of new evidence and material is a continuing duty of the Crown. Failure by the Crown to fulfil its disclosure obligation may result in Orders for disclosure or even a stay of proceedings or other redress, including costs, and will be treated as a very serious breach of professional ethics.[46]

An accused is entitled to disclosure and production of evidence where he or she can show that there is a "reasonable possibility that the information is logically probative".[47] Accordingly, the Crown must disclose all information and evidence that is in its custody, including statements that witnesses have made and any physical evidence seized. Furthermore, it must also produce information and evidence that is in its power, possession or control, such as evidence still in the hands of the police or other agents of the state that are custodians of information.[48] Correspondingly, the Crown has a duty to obtain from the investigators all relevant information and then preserve it.[49] If evidence that should have been disclosed is lost, the prosecution must explain what happened to it and if the reason provided is deemed unsatisfac-

---

[44]   See *R. v. Stinchcombe*, [1991] S.C.J. No. 83, [1991] 3 S.C.R. 326 (S.C.C.); see also *R. v. Carosella*, [1997] S.C.J. No. 12, [1997] 1 S.C.R. 80 (S.C.C.).

[45]   *R. v. Stinchcombe, ibid.*

[46]   *R. v. Chaplin*, [1994] S.C.J. No. 89 at para. 21, [1995] 1 S.C.R. 727 (S.C.C.).

[47]   *R. v. O'Connor*, [1995] S.C.J. No. 98, [1995] 4 S.C.R. 411 (S.C.C.).

[48]   For example, another government agency assisting in the prosecution.

[49]   *R. v. O'Grady*, [1995] B.C.J. No. 2041, 64 B.C.A.C. 111 (B.C.C.A.).

tory, an abuse of process or other breach of section 7 of the Charter may have occurred.[50]

If the evidence or documentation is not in the Crown's immediate possession or control, but rather in the possession and control of a third party, the accused can apply to the trial court for an order requiring the third party to disclose the relevant materials needed.[51] In a request for third party disclosure the defence counsel must demonstrate two separate requirements. First, that the material requested is relevant to an issue at trial or the competency of a person to testify at trial. Second, the documents, records or evidence are produced to the trial court for examination and the trial court then weighs the positive and negative effects of ordering a production of documents, evidence or records by third parties.

Despite this positive duty of disclosure, the Crown may choose to delay or deny production of evidence for legitimate reasons such as relevancy,[52] the protection of informers or witnesses, or the completion of an investigation.[53] Also, disclosure may be denied where justified by the law of privilege. Nonetheless, where such evidence or material is not disclosed to the defence, there remains an obligation on the prosecution to disclose the existence of that material. This permits a review at the request of the defence of the non-disclosure of the evidence in question. Finally, full crown disclosure permits the accused and defence counsel the right to full answer and defence. This promotes open access to the prosecution's case and hopefully facilitates early resolution of the charges.

6.10 THE ACCUSED'S ELECTION IN CRIMINAL CHARGES

If a corporation is charged with an indictable offence under the Code then it will have some important decisions regarding elections in the process. The Code sets out the election process for the forum of the criminal trial. After the Crown has elected how it wishes to proceed with a charge, either by indictment or by summary conviction, the accused generally has a choice as to how he or she prefers the trial to proceed. Unless the offence is one listed under either of section 553 or 469 of the Code, the accused may elect to proceed with a judge alone trial in the provincial court, or have a preliminary inquiry in the provincial court followed by a judge alone trial in the superior court of criminal jurisdiction, or a judge and jury trial in the superior court of criminal jurisdiction. If the accused is charged with an offence listed under

---

[50] *R. v. La*, [1997] S.C.J. No. 30, [1997] 2 S.C.R. 680 (S.C.C.).

[51] See *R. v. O'Connor*, [1995] S.C.J. No. 98, [1995] 4 S.C.R. 411 (S.C.C.); see also *Criminal Code*, s. 278.2.

[52] Information that is totally irrelevant need not be disclosed, but the Crown must err on the side of inclusion, disclosing all information that might be useful to the defence in making a full Inquiry.

[53] Note that this decision not to disclose evidence, though rarely exercised, can be reviewed by a judge.

section 553, they will have no choice but to face a trial by judge alone in the provincial court. Conversely, if the accused is charged with an offence listed under section 469, the superior court of criminal jurisdiction has exclusive jurisdiction over the trial and it is to be preceded by a preliminary inquiry in the provincial court. In such circumstance, the accused will nonetheless be able to select whether he or she wishes to be tried by a judge alone or by a judge and jury,[54] unless the offence is punishable by imprisonment for more than five years, in which case the attorney general may require a trial to proceed by judge and jury.[55]

If a provincial court judge declines to record an accused's election, as is his right under section 567,[56] the accused is deemed to have elected to be tried by a court composed of a judge and jury. A similar result occurs if an accused did not elect when his election was put to him under section 536, or if the accused was ordered to stand trial by a provincial court judge who continued proceedings before him as a preliminary inquiry, pursuant to subsection 555(1) of the Code.

Where an accused elects to be tried by a provincial court judge without having a preliminary inquiry, the provincial court judge shall call upon the accused to plead to the charge, and if the accused does not plead guilty, the provincial court judge shall proceed with the trial or fix a time for the trial. If the election to be tried by a provincial court judge is made before a justice who is not a provincial court judge, the justice must remand the accused to appear and plead to the charge before a provincial court judge.

Where an accused elects to have a preliminary inquiry and be tried by a judge without a jury, or a court composed of a judge and jury, or where the accused is deemed to have elected to be tried by a court composed of a judge and jury, the provincial court judge before whom the election is made will conduct a preliminary inquiry.

Sometimes, an accused may wish to change his or her election. If the original election was to be a trial in provincial court, the accused may, as of right, re-elect in writing to have a preliminary inquiry and be tried by a judge with or without a jury if the accused does so not later than 14 days before the first day of trial.[57] If the accused wishes to do so less than 14 days before the first day of trial, such re-election requires the consent of the prosecutor.[58]

If the accused had originally elected to be tried in the superior court, with or without a jury, the accused may re-elect to be tried in provincial court at any time before or after the completion of the preliminary inquiry,

---

[54] Note that s. 11(f) of the Charter confers upon any person charged with an offence the right, save for offences under military law, to be tried before a judge sitting with a jury where the maximum punishment for the offence is imprisonment for five years or a more severe punishment.

[55] *Criminal Code*, s. 568.

[56] A judge would do so to ease the procedure, if he or she wanted to prevent multiple accused persons from electing different modes of trial.

[57] *Criminal Code*, s. 561(1).

[58] *Ibid.*, s. 561(2).

provided the prosecutor gives written consent.[59] On receipt of such written re-election, the judge presiding at the preliminary inquiry shall proceed with the trial or fix a date for the trial.[60]

6.11 THE PRELIMINARY INQUIRY

One of the significant safeguards against a wrongful conviction in the Canadian criminal justice system is the preliminary inquiry. In the case of indictable proceedings, the criminal prosecution process may include the holding of a preliminary inquiry. The purpose of a preliminary inquiry is to determine whether there is sufficient evidence to require that an accused person be placed on trial for the offence they are charged with, or any other indictable offence in respect of the same set of events.[61] A corporate accused has this right just like an individual accused. Sometimes a preliminary inquiry is held pursuant to an election of the accused, as in the case of an offence where neither a provincial court judge nor a superior court of criminal jurisdiction has absolute jurisdiction.[62] A preliminary inquiry is mandatory in the case of any offences listed under section 469 of the Code. However, even in such cases, an accused may dispense with a preliminary inquiry, with the Crown's consent, by consenting to an order to stand trial pursuant to subsection 549(1).

When a preliminary inquiry is held, it is required to proceed in accordance with Part XVIII of the Code. The Crown, to obtain a committal for trial, must show sufficient evidence upon which a reasonable jury properly instructed could convict the accused. If the evidence is insufficient to result in a reasonably minded trier of fact to make a finding of guilt, the accused must be discharged. An accused is entitled to present evidence but is under no obligation to do so on a preliminary inquiry. Usually an accused will use the preliminary inquiry to examine the nature and quality of evidence in support of the Crown's case against the accused.

The role of the preliminary inquiry in safeguarding against wrongful convictions cannot be overstated. The Court of Appeal for Ontario stated the preliminary inquiry "protects an accused from trial where the Crown is unable to produce sufficient evidence to warrant the accused's committal for trial."[63] A preliminary inquiry affords an accused the opportunity to learn about and discover the case against him or her,[64] to commit a witness to details of his testimony that will later be used in cross-examination at trial should the witness' testimony differ, to challenge the strength of the evi-

---

[59]   *Ibid.*, s. 561(1).

[60]   *Ibid.*, s. 562(2).

[61]   *Ibid.*, s. 548, the test of which is set out in *United States of America v. Shephard*, [1976] S.C.J. No. 106, [1977] 2 S.C.R. 1067 (S.C.C.).

[62]   *Criminal Code*, ss. 553 and 469.

[63]   *R. v. Girimonte*, [1997] O.J. No. 4961 at para. 29, 121 C.C.C. (3d) 33 (Ont. C.A.).

[64]   *R. v. Skogman*, [1984] S.C.J. No. 32, 13 C.C.C. (3d) 161 at 171 (S.C.C.).

dence adduced by the Crown, to probe for details and facts which may allow the defence to unearth facts or witnesses who might otherwise not be available. An accused may also obtain information to prepare for Charter motions or other motions at trial at the preliminary inquiry. Conversely, the Crown may be afforded the opportunity to discover the theory of the defence, to test the strength of its evidence, and to record the sworn testimony of potentially reluctant witnesses and commit them to details prior to trial.

A preliminary inquiry will be held for an individual or an organization, or both together, as required by law. By virtue of sections 538 and 556 of the Code, an organization will appear in court by counsel or agent. The justice may, however, proceed with a preliminary inquiry in the absence of a corporate accused if it does not appear pursuant to a summons. Corporate accused should obtain legal advice before they attend the preliminary inquiry.

6.12 PRE-TRIAL CONFERENCES

There are two types of pre-trial conferences in the Canadian criminal justice system: judicial and counsel pre-trial conferences. A judicial pre-trial conference is a meeting between prosecution and defence counsel and a judge who will not preside at trial. Before a trial commences, it is sometimes advisable and necessary that a pre-hearing conference with a judge, usually referred to as a pre-trial, be held. The Code provides that a judicial pre-trial conference is mandatory in every case to be tried by a jury[65] and may be ordered in non-jury cases.[66] An accused person can also meet with the Crown for a resolution meeting to discuss possible pleas and obtain the Crown's position on a resolution without a trial prior to or even during the trial.

The judicial pre-trial conference is a rather informal proceeding generally used to identify and narrow the outstanding issues and to ensure the efficient use of court time. For such a conference to be productive, an accused should have discussed the case with his lawyer to address issues such as the anticipated length of trial, the completeness of crown disclosure, the making of admissions, arguments concerning the admissibility of evidence and applications for Charter remedies. Furthermore, many judges conducting judicial pre-trial conferences will express their views on legal issues, the appropriate penalty or the possibility of guilty plea of the accused to a lesser charge. A judicial pre-trial conference may have the benefit of exploring a possible resolution of the criminal charges without a trial.

A counsel pre-trial conference is similar to a judicial pre-trial conference. Counsel representing the Crown and the accused meet, without a judge, to discuss the case. Issues can be narrowed, facts may be agreed without the need of evidence, and possible resolution can be explored. The success of a counsel pre-trial conference is perhaps more dependent on the maturity and good faith of both counsel than a judicial pre-trial conference.

---

[65]   *Criminal Code*, s. 625.1(2).

[66]   *Ibid.*, s. 625.1(1).

Like a judicial pre-trial conference, the counsel pre-trial conference does not require charges to be resolved without a trial and the charges may proceed to trial.

6.13 TRIAL

A corporate accused may be prosecuted and taken to trial just like an individual defendant. A trial is the process in the criminal justice system by which the accused is brought to a hearing to determine if they are guilty of the charge with which they are charged. Once the procedural steps described above have been completed and the accused has made its intention to plead not guilty clear, a trial is ready to commence. A criminal trial is based on the adversarial system in the administration of justice in Canadian courts. An accused should, however, be cognizant of the right to a trial within a reasonable time, under subsection 11(b) of the Charter. Should this right be violated, a stay of proceedings pursuant to subsection 24(1) of the Charter may be warranted.

The right to be tried within a reasonable period of time is one of the most important rights of an accused. Individuals may suffer exquisite agony waiting for a determination of their criminal charges at trial. If judicial resources are not available for a speedy trial, then this prejudices the right of an accused to be fairly treated in the administration of criminal justice. Corporations have a right under subsection 11(b) of the Charter to be tried within a reasonable period of time, as well as an individual accused. However, the Supreme Court has held that in addition to an unreasonable delay in proceeding to trial, over and above that of an individual accused, "… a corporate accused must ... be able to establish that its fair trial interest has been irremediably prejudiced."[67]

Assuming that the subsection 11(b) right to a trial within a reasonable period of time under the Charter has not been violated, the start of a trial usually begins with the accused being arraigned. This consists of the accused standing before the court, there is a formal reading of the charge or charges to the accused, and a clerk asks the court how the accused wishes to plead, guilty or not guilty. The accused must then plead either guilty, or not guilty. An accused may also plead not guilty as charged but guilty to a lesser and included offence or other criminal offence on consent.

In the case of an individual, the answer to the arraignment should be done personally by the accused so that there can be no misunderstanding how he or she intends to plead. In the case of an organization, the plea, as the whole trial appearance, may be conducted by a senior officer or representative or the retained lawyer, as is permitted by the Code.[68] In the case of a corporation, a designated representative may enter the plea of not guilty at the arraignment.

---

[67]   *R. v. CIP Inc.*, [1992] S.C.J. No. 34 at para. 50, [1992] 1 S.C.R. 843 (S.C.C.).
[68]   *Criminal Code.*, ss. 556(1) and 620.

If the accused pleads guilty, as is done in the majority of criminal cases, he or she is admitting all the elements of the offence with which he or she is charged. Given the serious consequences arising from a criminal conviction, the accused must appreciate what they are pleading guilty to, with no misunderstanding. A plea of guilt must be voluntary, informed and unequivocal. If the court has some doubt whether the plea is clearly understood or unqualified, it must refuse to accept it or make inquiries to satisfy itself that the qualification or condition does not take away from the accused's intention to enter an unequivocal plea of guilty. If, on the other hand, the accused pleads not guilty, the court will proceed with a trial.[69]

If it is a trial by Judge alone, it is not incumbent on the Crown to give an opening statement. At the beginning of the trial, after the jury has been selected, the trial judge will give some opening remarks to the jury informing them of the procedure that will be followed. It is then incumbent on the prosecution to give an opening statement and call witnesses to prove every fact and circumstance constituting the offence, beyond any reasonable doubt, and tender other evidence and respond to any defence that reasonably arises on the evidence. The Crown's opening statement will outline the case it intends to present, the purpose of which is to allow the trier of fact[70] to follow the evidence that will be adduced.[71] This opening address should not be used by the Crown to argue the case. The prosecution should not refer to any evidence whose admissibility must be determined.[72] Traditionally, the accused usually had no right to make an opening statement immediately after the Crown. Nevertheless, in recent years, defence counsel have been permitted to address the trier of fact in a limited fashion, if only to say a little about their case. Most defence lawyers prefer to wait until the end of the Crown's case to address the trier of fact.

After the opening statement, the prosecutor begins to present evidence through the calling of witnesses. When Crown counsel completes an examination-in-chief of the witness following which the defence has the right to cross-examine the witness. This defence right of cross-examination is not solely limited to issues raised during examination-in-chief, but may relate to any question which is directly in issue or which relates to the credibility of the witness. Following cross-examination, the Crown has a limited right of re-examination. It is limited because the Crown cannot raise any new areas of evidence with the witness. Rather, he or she can only ask questions relating to matters arising directly out of the cross-examination.

---

[69]   *Ibid.*, ss. 622 and 623.

[70]   This refers to the judge or the jury, whomever is responsible to make findings of fact, pursuant to the accused's elected mode of trial.

[71]   Crown counsel will usually only give an opening statement during a jury trial. Nevertheless, he or she may request an opportunity to do so during a judge alone trial. Other times, the judge may request an opening summary to assist him or her in following the evidence.

[72]   This will be done during a *voir dire*, or trial within a trial, whereby the Judge, in the absence of the jury, will hear arguments to determine the admissibility of evidence.

Once the Crown concludes its case, the accused counsel may, if he or she desires, deliver an opening statement[73] and present evidence of its own to the trier of fact. This is done through legal counsel for the defence. Like the Crown did previously, the defence will call witnesses that will be examined-in-chief. The prosecution is then entitled to cross-examine the witness. Subject to stringent exceptions, the prosecution cannot usually cross-examine the accused on other acts of misconduct or discreditable conduct for the purpose of showing that by reason of the accused's bad character, he or she ought not to be believed or that he or she is likely to have committed the offence in question.[74] Defence counsel may then re-examine the witness, subject to the same restrictions the Crown was subject to during its right of re-examination.

Following the defence's case, the prosecution may be given the right to adduce reply or rebuttal evidence. Generally speaking, such evidence is only admissible if new matters that could not have been anticipated were raised by the accused. More commonly, though, the judge will invite counsel to give closing statements.[75] Where an accused counsel has elected to call evidence in defence, he or she must address the trier of fact first before the Crown. It is only if the accused elects not to call a defence that the prosecutor is required to address the trier of fact first.

After the closing statements are completed, a judge will instruct the jury, if there is one, on its role and decision. This will include instructions concerning the onus of proof, burden of proof, the presumption of innocence of the accused, the requirement that there be a unanimous verdict, the law as it relates to the specific offence or offences in question, including the elements of the crime as well as its defences. Once this charge to the jury is complete, the jury is sequestered until they reach a unanimous verdict or are unable to agree, in which case a mistrial[76] must be declared.

If the trier of fact, either a jury or a judge, finds the accused guilty, or if the accused has at any time pleaded guilty, a conviction will be registered and the matter will proceed to sentencing. If the trier of fact finds the accused not guilty, the accused is acquitted and, subject to Crown appeal, the criminal prosecution is over.

---

[73] *Criminal Code*, s. 651(2). The accused may also make an application for a directed verdict of acquittal on the basis that the Crown has failed to establish a sufficient case on which the trier of fact could convict him or her. The test to be applied is whether there is enough admissible evidence which could, if believed, result in a conviction. If there is, the trial judge is not justified in directing a verdict of acquittal and the defence will, if it so desires, adduce evidence of its own.

[74] *R. v. McNamara (No. 1)*, [1981] O.J. No. 3254, 56 C.C.C. (2d) 193 (Ont. C.A.).

[75] *Criminal Code*, s. 651.

[76] *Ibid.*, s. 653.

6.14 SENTENCING AND PROBATION

A corporation that is convicted of the offence with which it has been charged will then be remanded for sentencing and possibly terms of probation. Sentencing occurs after an accused is found guilty and convicted of a criminal offence. Canadian sentencing jurisprudence has traditionally focused on the aims of denunciation, deterrence, separation and rehabilitation.[77] There is also a goal of restorative justice that is concerned with the restoration of the parties affected by the commission of an offence. This is accomplished through rehabilitation of the offender, reparations to the victim(s) and to the community, the promotion of a sense of responsibility of the offender, and acknowledgement of the harm done. These trends have been recognized and enhanced with the Bill C-45 amendments to the sentencing provisions for organizations in the Code that are reviewed in detail in Chapter 9.

Offences find their associated punishment prescribed in the Code. An offender will thus be subject to the prescribed penalty. This includes imprisonment, fines and probation orders. Nonetheless, he or she may, if it is shown to be in his or her best interests and not contrary to the public interest, instead of being convicted, be discharged absolutely or on other conditions attached to a probation order.[78]

Organizations, including corporations, obviously cannot be incarcerated. Directors and officers may not be jailed for the offence of the corporation if they have not been charged and convicted personally. The new Bill C-45 sentencing powers for organizations are quite extensive and establish new powers for the sentencing judge. A court must take into consideration the following factors when imposing a sentence on an organization: (a) any advantage realized by the organization as a result of the offence; (b) the degree of planning involved in carrying out the offence and the duration and complexity of the offence; (c) whether the organization has attempted to conceal its assets, or convert them, in order to show that it is not able to pay a fine or make restitution; (d) the impact that the sentence would have on the economic viability of the organization and the continued employment of its employees; (e) the cost to public authorities of the investigation and prosecution of the offence; (f) any regulatory penalty that has been imposed on the organization in respect of the offence; (g) whether the organization has been convicted of a similar offence in the past; (h) any penalty that has been imposed by the organization on one of its representatives for their role in the commission of the offence; (i) any restitution that the organization is ordered

---

[77]   Law Society of Upper Canada, "Sentencing" in Law Society of Upper Canada, Ontario Bar Admission Course Reference Materials, *Criminal Law* (Toronto: Law Society of Upper Canada, 2003) at 11-1.

[78]   *Criminal Code*, s. 732(1), (2).

to make; (j) any measures that the organization has taken to reduce the likelihood of it committing a subsequent offence.[79]

The court will be able to impose a fine on an organization,[80] make an order compelling the organization to make restitution to the victims, compel the organization to establish OHS policies, standards and procedures to reduce the likelihood of the organization committing a subsequent offence and force the organization to disclose to the public information regarding the offence of which it has been convicted, the sentence it has received and any measures it is taking to prevent a recurrence of the offence.[81]

6.15 SOME FINAL THOUGHTS

The use of prosecution as a model for corporate accountability is problematic. The process for the administration of the criminal justice system is long-standing and well established. The use of criminal prosecution to enforce standards and accountability of corporations in Canadian society is a relatively new development in Canadian law. The impact of being charged with a criminal offence is somewhat balanced with the right given to suspects and accused under the Charter. The greater the risk of serious penalties, the more rights the judicial system tends to give to suspects and accused. Therefore, individuals and corporations who may be investigated for contravention of the new offences will have their legal rights under the Charter recognized and upheld by the courts. Criminal prosecutions, rights under the Charter, the presumption of innocence, sentencing and probationary terms will all be the new language of corporate decision makers and their legal advisors.

Finally, it is the author's view that the changes to the Code under Bill C-45 may have the effect of bringing greater attention to the value of prosecution to achieve corporate accountability. The public interest is enhanced by corporate governance across Canada. However, prosecution is not necessarily the best way to achieve that goal. The Bill C-45 amendments to the Code should give pause to all organizational decision makers, who can positively impact business decisions. Legal risk of prosecution is higher than ever. The development of effective management systems, which is a hallmark of the due diligence defence for strict liability offences, may be applied to all manner of business risk.

---

[79] Bill C-45, *An Act to Amend the Criminal Code (Criminal Liability of Organizations)*, 2003, c. 21, s. 14.

[80] *Criminal Code*, s. 735(1). The amount of the fine is in the discretion of the court when the offence is an indictable offence. When the offence is a summary conviction offence, the imposed fine is not to exceed $100,000 (as proposed by Bill C-45).

[81] Bill C-45, *An Act to Amend the Criminal Code (Criminal Liability of Organizations)*, 2003, c. 21, s. 18.

Chapter 7

RIGHTS OF CORPORATIONS UNDER THE CHARTER

7.1 INTRODUCTION TO CORPORATIONS AND THE CHARTER

The role of a constitution in a democracy is to reflect the values, beliefs and governance structures of the people. The Charter *of Rights and Freedoms*[1] is part of the supreme law and Constitution of Canada. Corporations have had an inconsistent experience with access to and application of the Charter. The Charter sets out the rights and freedoms of all Canadians and is intended to protect essential values in a free and democratic society. Since corporations are the primary legal means by which private and public organizations are established and operated in Canadian society, the subject of this chapter is the rights of corporations under the Charter.

There was little guidance regarding the application of the Charter to corporations from its political origins. Therefore, the courts have had a central role in interpreting the Charter and determining its application to corporations. This has been manifest in the issue of standing and limits on Charter application to corporations. The courts, however, are limited to determining the rights of corporations under the Charter one case, one right and one principle at a time. The jurisprudence has left, in the author's view, a patchwork of decisions that have resulted in a dysfunctional relationship between corporations and the Charter.

The need for corporate accountability in a modern, liberal democracy is self-evident. The tragedies of Westray, Walkerton and BP (both the world's largest oil spill at Texas City and Deep Horizons in the Gulf) evoke images of coal mine fatalities, all human suffering and death from E. coli, and a massive oil spill killing thousands of fish and animals at the hand of corporations. Corporate accountability in an age of multi-national corporations is a critical challenge for the exercise of public policy and protection. However, corporations are established by state authorized incorporation laws and play a vital role in society. In the policy of prosecution of corporations, the Charter is a necessary issue. The application of the Charter to an important legal, economic and social structure is an important subject to have

---

[1] Part I of the *Constitution Act, 1982*, being Schedule B to the *Canada Act, 1982* (U.K.), 1982, c. 11 [hereinafter the "Charter"].

functioning clearly and consistently. Corporate accountability through prosecution, in view of the recent Bill C-45 amendments to the *Criminal Code*,[2] makes the application of the Charter to corporations an area of legal and practical importance.

7.2   PARLIAMENTARY STATEMENTS REGARDING THE CHARTER AND CORPORATIONS

7.2.1   Overview

There were few references in the Charter debates to rights as they were intended to apply to corporations. Given the extensive jurisprudence interpreting the American Bill of Rights to corporations when the Canadian Charter was being drafted, this is both a surprise and disappointment. The limited references in the Parliamentary Committee proceedings were primarily concerned with the effect that the wording used in sections 2, 7 and 15 would have on the applicability of those rights to corporations. It was clear from these proceedings that only section 15, the individual equality provision of the Charter, was drafted explicitly to exclude corporations. The statements from the Ministry of Justice and other government representatives indicate that the wording in sections 2 and 7 was assumed to extend those rights only to natural persons. However, no clear statement of intent, and no clear language like in section 15, was used in drafting those provisions. The government indicated that the choice between "everyone" and "every person" was viewed as inconsequential, and the scope of those rights would be determined by their context.

Generally, the proceedings of Parliament, including debates, statements and early drafts of legislation, are relevant and admissible for interpretation by courts. However, the legislative history of a statute, while admissible, is generally accorded little weight in interpretation by the Court. As a result, the "living tree" or purposive approach to interpretation predominants adds little weight to Parliamentary or Committee statements regarding Charter rights. These types of statements, however, have become relevant in a section 1 analysis, when the courts must consider the legislative purpose of a provision that impugns the Charter.

The primary source for considering the legislative intent regarding the Charter's application to corporations was the "Special Joint Committee of the Senate and House of Commons"[3] that sat from November 6, 1980 until February 13, 1981. Other sources included the Commons Debates and Senate Debates spanning the years 1980 to 1983, as well as statements in the House and Senate with respect to the "Proposed Resolution for a Joint Address to Her Majesty the Queen respecting the Constitution of Canada". Secondary sources, including constitutional texts by Hogg, Sharpe, Taylor

---

[2]   R.S.C. 1985, c. C-46 [hereinafter the "Code"].
[3]   1st Sess., 32nd Parl., 1980.

and Bayefsky,[4] set out a comprehensive list of the documents used in the proceedings leading to the passage and patriation of the *Constitution Act, 1982.*[5]

Although there were limited references to the rights of corporations under the Charter in the Parliamentary proceedings, some general principles arose. First, it was clear that there was a general understanding that the term "person" was inclusive of corporations. The statements discussed below included discussions, in the context of women's rights, that a corporation as an "artificial person" could avail itself of a right assigned to "any person". Second, it was clear that the term "every individual", as it is used in section 15, was specifically intended to exclude corporations. Third, the Trudeau Liberal government's position with respect to the terms "everyone" and "every person" was that those two terms were effectively synonymous. The government indicated that the terms were interchangeable, and where they were used in different provisions, the content of those rights and to whom they would apply would be determined by the context. It is suggested that the application of the Charter to corporations was not carefully considered in the legislative debates and the matter was largely left to be decided by the courts.

7.2.2 Specific Sections Discussed

On January 22, 1981, the Joint Session debated a potential amendment to section 2 of the draft Charter that purported to replace the term "everyone" to "every person". This amendment was championed by Svend Robinson,[6] in response to the testimony of several women's rights groups. The reasoning for the amendment was that those groups sought to have reflected in the Charter the jurisprudence with respect to the term "person", which had historically excluded women until some landmark Canadian cases. Mr. Robinson was concerned that the terms "every person" and "every individual" had been settled, while the term "everyone" had not. Frederick Hawkes,[7] then put it to the Solicitor General/Acting Minister of Justice, Robert Kaplan (Liberal):

> You have a choice, I think, between the words "everyone", "every person" and "every individual", and if we look at the government interpretation in relation to Clause 15, they are suggesting that the words "every individual" are required to make it clear to the courts in future that we are talking about individuals, we are talking about people.
>
> I think that comes about because in law there is some possibility that the words "everyone" or the words "every person" can refer to artificially created

---

[4]   A.F. Bayefsky, *Canada's Constitution Act 1982 & Amendments: a documentary history* (Toronto: McGill-Hill Ryerson, 1989).

[5]   Being Schedule B to the *Canada Act, 1982* (U.K.), 1982, c. 11 [hereinafter the "Constitution"].

[6]   An NDP member of Parliament from British Columbia.

[7]   A PC member of Parliament.

> bodies such as corporations ... and that by using "every person", is there any possibility in law, according to the technical advice that you get, that we in fact are conferring these fundamental freedoms on corporate bodies rather than individuals?[8]

In response, Kaplan stated:

> The legal advice on which the government is operating is that there is no difference among any of those three alternatives, that the use of one or the other or the third would make no difference in the rights and freedoms that are to be provided in the constitution, and on that basis we have no objection to the change. It seems to us to be dancing on the head of a pin.[9]

In response, Hawkes noted that the section 15 deliberations led to the change from "everyone" to "every individual" to ensure that it was clear that the section 15 rights applied only to natural persons and not corporations. He then questioned Kaplan as to how that logic would apply in section 15 but not in section 2, and asked whether the government wished to leave it open that the section 2 freedoms would apply to corporations. To that, Kaplan said:

> We think it is clear with either form for the purpose of Clause 2 that human persons are intended and are covered by any of those formulations ... [W]e believe that the context makes it clear whichever of those words are used, that human persons are intended to be covered.[10]

The members then discussed the status of corporations as persons under the law. Hawkes then put to the Minister that a lawyer might be able to argue that where "every person" was used, a corporation would be able to avail itself of that right. Dufferin Roblin,[11] then put to Kaplan why there ought not to be any difference in interpreting the three expressions under section 2, but there ought to be under section 15. To that, Kaplan said:

> The rights in Clause 15 are of a nature that do not apply to nonhuman persons. Discrimination on the basis of age of a corporation is not something that Clause 15 would protect.[12]

Senator Roblin agreed, and added further that that same argument ought to apply to the fundamental freedoms in section 2. At that point, Ken Epp,[13] argued that the three expressions were not interchangeable. Epp raised the issue of abortion, and how the Code defined a "person" as a person outside the mother's womb. He claimed that changing the wording of section 2 to reflect "every person" would thrust that section into that debate. Kaplan

---

[8]   Special Joint Committee on the Senate and the House of Commons, 1st Sess., 32nd Parl., 1980, at 43:40-41.
[9]   Ibid., at 43:41.
[10] Ibid.
[11] A PC Member of the Senate.
[12] Special Joint Committee on the Senate and the House of Commons, 1st Sess., 32nd Parl., 1980, at 43:42.
[13] A PC member from Alberta.

responded by saying that "everyone" and "every person" were both neutral on that issue. In explaining that position, he said:

> Now, "individual" is somewhat more restrictive because it excludes corporations, but "everyone" and "every person" leaves open the question of how abortions are viewed in law and that is a matter that should be determined, in the view of the government, by Parliament.[14]

Then, David Crombie,[15] said to Kaplan: "Using the word "every person" brings in the connotation of a corporation. I gather there was a line of questioning dealing with economic corporations or financial corporations. I wondered if your comment in relation to those also dealt with religious corporations, religious bodies which are incorporated."[16]

Kaplan indicated that it did. In response to a question from Robert Bockstael,[17] regarding the consequences of the proposed amendment on the wording of section 7, Kaplan said:

> I think it would be logical to use one formulation or the other throughout the act wherever the same sense is intended. So my position on Clause 7 is the same as the position taken on Clause 2 ... there is no card up the government's sleeve on this, that our view is that it is truly a matter of indifference as between those two expressions ...[18]

Further, Coline Campbell[19] said:

> ... I reminded the Committee that we were on Clause 2, one of the reasons why I like "every person" in Clause 2, is that "person" has been interpreted specifically to include corporations and companies.

> I tend to feel that "person" in Clause 2 will be justified as really extending it further there.[20]

Bryce Mackasey[21] then reiterated the issue raised by Epp, and stated that "everyone" goes beyond individuals and includes corporations. He wanted to "satisfy his own mind" that an amendment to section 2 would not "... strip them unintentionally of their rights under Clause 2".[22] Ultimately, the proposed amendment in section 2 from "everyone" to "every person" was defeated.

---

[14] Special Joint Committee on the Senate and the House of Commons, 1st Sess., 32nd Parl., 1980, at 43:44.

[15] A PC member from Ontario.

[16] Special Joint Committee on the Senate and the House of Commons, 1st Sess., 32nd Parl., 1980, at 43:46.

[17] A Liberal member from Manitoba.

[18] Special Joint Committee on the Senate and the House of Commons, 1st Sess., 32nd Parl., 1980, at 43:47.

[19] A Liberal member from Nova Scotia.

[20] Special Joint Committee on the Senate and the House of Commons, 1st Sess., 32nd Parl., 1980, at 43:51.

[21] A Liberal member from Quebec.

[22] Special Joint Committee on the Senate and the House of Commons, 1st Sess., 32nd Parl., 1980, at 43:53.

In the January 23, 1981 proceedings, Robinson proposed an amendment to section 7, substituting "everyone" for "every individual". According to Robinson:

> ... the purpose of this amendment is to specify very clearly that what we are talking about in Clause 7 is precisely what we are talking about in Clause 15. That is 'natural persons' and not 'artificial persons' or 'corporations'.[23]

He referred to the government's change in section 15 from "everyone" to "every individual" as reflecting a desire to be very specific about its application to natural persons. He went on to say:

> Surely it cannot be argued that any of [s. 7] rights in any way adds to the rights of corporations ... any extension which might be made under the rubric of fundamental justice, would I submit, be covered already by protections from unreasonable search and seizure in Section 8.

> Clearly the right to life, and the right to liberty are ones which apply to natural persons, and do not apply to the corporate sector.

> So Mr. Chairman, in recognition of the fact that it is human beings we are talking about, and natural persons, very clearly in Clause 7, I suggest that the logic which compelled the government to change Clause 15 from "everyone" to "every individual" would be similarly applicable in Clause 7.[24]

In response, Perrin Beatty[25] questioned Robinson on why it would be necessary to change the wording at all if the rights under section 7 were inapplicable to corporations. He argued that the real reason for the amendment was in reaction to a proposed amendment of section 7 to include property rights, which ultimately never materialized. What followed was some discussion of the rights of small businesses and family farms with respect to the proposed property rights under section 7 if corporations were excluded. Acting Minister of Justice Kaplan then added:

> I have very little to add to what we indicated yesterday about "every person" and "every individual". We think an "individual" clearly applies to human beings only, and the other two expressions are interchangeable and that their scope is determined by the context.

> I would agree with Mr. Beatty that, if the rights provided in this clause, as amended, could extend to corporations, that they will do so if you used the word "everyone", but would not [if the amendment succeeds] ... [26]

The amendment from "everyone" to "every individual" in section 7 was rejected.

In the proceedings on January 28, 1981, Liberal MP Ron Irwin introduced an amendment to section 11 to replace "anyone" with "any person". In response, Robinson questioned why the amendment was proposed, given

---

[23]   *Ibid.*, at 44:7.

[24]   *Ibid.*, at 44:7.

[25]   A PC member from Ontario.

[26]   Special Joint Committee on the Senate and the House of Commons, 1st Sess., 32nd Parl., 1980, at 44:9.

the earlier discussions about the indifference between "everyone" and "every person". Robinson questioned whether that amendment would affect government thinking on that earlier distinction. In response, Jean Chrétien and Roger Tassé, the Minister of Justice and Deputy Minister, respectively, stated that the change was merely a grammatical change, and had no effect on the application of the rights under section 11, and should not have been considered as "opening the door" to that previous debate.[27] The amendment in section 11 from "anyone" to "any person" was passed.

In the proceedings on January 28, 1981, PC MP Hawkes questioned Jean Chrétien on the wording used in the "cruel and unusual punishment" provision in section 12. Hawkes said:

> You had the choice of "everyone", which is in the clause, but you could have put "any person", which you did in Clause 11. My previous understanding is that the word "everyone" would include artificial corporations. Is that the intent of the government to have the clause apply to artificial persons as well as human persons.[28]

In response, member Ewaschuk, a representative of the government from the Ministry of Justice, said that it was not possible to incarcerate a corporation. He further added: "[s]o it would be very unusual, you are quite right, where that would apply to anybody other than a natural person, but since the word *'everyone' is there, it would apply to corporations as well*."[29] Ewaschuk went on to say: "I do not see any problem, Mr. Hawkes, with the word 'everyone' applying to a corporation, because if in fact some judge comes up with something cruel and unusual in relation to the corporation, why should it stand?"[30]

From the Committee and related debates, some general conclusions of legislative intentions arise. First, the statements of the Solicitor General regarding sections 2, 7, and 15 illustrate an attitude that the rights were reserved for only individual human beings. In general, it appeared that the government was of the view that sections 2 and 15 were intended to apply to natural persons only. Additionally, the exchange between Bockstael and Kaplan under section 2 indicates that the government took a similar position on section 7. Due process or fundamental justices rights in section 7, however, were not conclusively considered unavailable for corporations.

Second, the governing Liberal party took a somewhat relaxed or flexible view toward the use of terms like "everyone" and "every person" as key terms that provide standing to assert rights under the Charter. This may be paradoxical, given the above discussion of the inclusion of corporations in both terms, and the government's stance on the application of the rights under the Charter. However, it is clear in some of the discussions, such as those

---

[27] *Ibid.*, at 47:31.
[28] *Ibid.*, at 47:78.
[29] *Ibid.*, [emphasis added].
[30] *Ibid.*

under sections 7, 11 and 12, that the use of terms like "everyone" and "every person" were intended or at least contemplated in respect of their application to corporations. At the very least, they left the door open for them depending on the legal or judicial context in which the issue arose.

7.2.3   Evidentiary Value of the Charter Debates

In *Constitutional Law of Canada*,[31] Hogg discusses the use of legislative history. Legislative history and debates in the interpretation of the statutes and the Charter:

> ... does not have a precise meaning. In the account that follows, I use the term to mean the documentary evidence of the events that occurred during the drafting and enactment of a statute. It may include the following elements:
>
> 1. The report of a royal commission or law reform commission or parliamentary committee recommending that a statute be enacted;
>
> 2. A government policy paper ... recommending that a statute be enacted;
>
> 3. A report or study produced outside government which existed at the time of the enactment of the statute and was relied upon by the government that introduced the legislation;
>
> 4. Earlier versions of the statute, either before or after its introduction into Parliament or the Legislature;
>
> 5. Statements by ministers or members of Parliament and testimony of expert witnesses before a parliamentary committee charged with studying the bill; and
>
> 6. Speeches in the Parliament when the bill is being debated.[32]

Professor Hogg goes on to note that there are two categories of applicable legislative history in constitutional litigation: the history of the impugned statute, and the history of the Constitution itself. Hogg notes that unlike the *Constitution Act, 1867*, there are "abundant records of the legislative history of the [Constitution]".[33] The potential sources of legislative history include:

- Seven different drafts of the Constitution, beginning on Aug 22, 1980, and ending with the enacted version March 29, 1982;

- Extensive passages from the debates of the House and Senate from the introduction to the House of the "Proposed Resolution for a Joint Address to Her Majesty the Queen respecting the Constitution of Canada", October 6, 1980 until the passage:

  - House of Commons: Dec. 2, 1981;

  - Senate: Dec. 8, 1981;

- Commons Debates, 1980–1983;

---

[31] P.W. Hogg, *Constitutional Law of Canada*, looseleaf (Toronto: Thomson Carswell, 2007).

[32] *Ibid.*, at 60-1-2.

[33] *Ibid.*, at 60-6.

- Testimony from Joint Committee of House and Senate on Constitution, Nov. 6, 1980 to Feb. 13, 1981; and
- The debates from the UK House of Commons and House of Lords leading to the passage of the *Canada Act, 1982*:
  - House of Commons: Dec. 14, 1981–Mar. 8, 1982;
  - House of Lords: Mar. 8, 1982–Mar. 25, 1982.[34]

In *R. v. Dubois*,[35] the Supreme Court of Canada confirmed that the legal status of the *Constitution Act, 1867*, is the same as that of the Constitution. Therefore, legislative history is admissible in interpretation of the latter.

There are two approaches to considering legislative history in interpreting the Charter: originalism and progressive interpretation. These two approaches each lie at the end of a spectrum of deference to the intentions of legislators. Originalism treats legislative intent as conclusive of meaning. That argument is based on the proposition that the text of the Constitution ought to be read in the sense intended by the framers, as the values of the framers are the ones which prevailed in the drafting process. This approach is said to be consistent, as the meaning of a provision would remain fixed over time. Professor Hogg states that the arguments against originalism mean that legislative history ought to be accorded "little weight in constitutional interpretation".[36] The main argument is that it is impossible to be certain of the framers' intentions, given the large number of people who contributed to the drafting of the Constitution. Even if one could identify with precision the intention of every person held to be a framer, it would still be nearly impossible to attribute the final draft of the Constitution to the particular members who voted on it.

The alternative approach is the progressive interpretation. This approach treats the Constitution as fluid, not static. The progressive approach is not necessarily inconsistent with the intention of the drafters or framers, as Hogg notes, because the drafters may have intended that the rights enshrined in the Constitution be amenable to development beyond the complicated amending formula. Patrick Monahan, in *Politics and the Constitution*,[37] argues that during the Joint Session, legislators had in mind that the courts would not be bound by their intentions in drafting the Constitution.

7.2.4 Legislative Intent Jurisprudence

Almost immediately after the Charter came into force, the Court declined to give real weight to the intentions of the drafters when interpreting it. In *Reference re Motor Vehicle Act (British Columbia) s. 94(2)*,[38] the Court heard

---

[34] *Ibid.*, at 60-6.
[35] [1985] S.C.J. No. 69, [1985] 2 S.C.R. 350 (S.C.C.).
[36] P.W. Hogg, *Constitutional Law of Canada*, looseleaf (Toronto: Thomson Carswell, 2007) at 60-8.
[37] Patrick Monahan, *Politics and the Constitution* (Toronto: Carswell, 1987).
[38] [1985] S.C.J. No. 73, [1985] 2 S.C.R. 486 (S.C.C.).

an appeal from the B.C. Court of Appeal as to the constitutionality of a provision in B.C. law that provided for a minimum period of imprisonment for
driving with a suspended licence. The provision in question was characterized as absolute liability; in other words, there was no defence available if
the offence was made out. The question before the Court was whether or not
section 7 principles of fundamental justice included only procedural rights,
or something more in the way of substantive rights. From the outset of the
majority opinion, Lamer J. made it clear that the Court was not constrained
by the intentions of legislators in interpreting the Charter:

> The overriding and legitimate concern that courts ought not to question the
> wisdom of enactments, and the presumption that the legislator could not
> have intended same, have to some extent distorted the discussion surround-
> ing the meaning of "principles of fundamental justice"...
>
> But I do not share that assumption. Since way back in time and even re-
> cently the courts have developed the common law beyond procedural safe-
> guards without interfering with the "merits or wisdom" of enactments ...[39]

With respect to the approach of the Court to Charter interpretation:

> I propose therefore to approach the interpretation of section 7 in the manner
> set forth by Dickson J. in *Hunter v. Southam Inc.* and *R. v. Big M Drug Mart
> Ltd.*
>
> In *Hunter v. Southam Inc.* this Court expressed the view that the proper ap-
> proach to the definition of the rights and freedoms guaranteed by the Charter
> was a purposive one. The meaning of a right or freedom guaranteed by the
> Charter was to be ascertained by an analysis of the purpose of such a guar-
> antee; it was to be understood, in other words, in the light of the interests it
> was meant to protect.
>
> In my view this analysis is to be undertaken, and the purpose of the right or
> freedom in question is to be sought by reference to the character and the lar-
> ger objects of the Charter itself, to the language chosen to articulate the spe-
> cific right or freedom, to the historical origins of the concepts enshrined, and
> where applicable, to the meaning and purpose of the other specific rights
> and freedoms with which it is associated within the text of the Charter. The
> interpretation should be, as the judgment in Southam emphasizes, a gener-
> ous rather than a legalistic one, aimed at fulfilling the purpose of the guaran-
> tee and securing for individuals the full benefit of the Charter's protection.[40]

Justice Lamer then considered the statements made in the Joint Session
with respect to the intended scope of protection afforded by section 7. He
referred to several statements that limited section 7 to procedural fairness,
and did not extend it to substantive due process. He then considered whether
the Joint Session remarks were admissible at all, and stated:

> In Re: Authority of Parliament in relation to the Upper House, the Court
> stated, at p. 66:

---

[39]   *Ibid.*, at paras. 18-19.

[40]   *Ibid.*, at para. 21, citing from *R. v. Big M Drug Mart Ltd.*, [1985] S.C.J. No. 17, [1985] 1 S.C.R.
295 at 344 (S.C.C.).

It is, we think, proper to consider the historical background which led to the provision which was made in the Act for the creation of the Senate as a part of the apparatus for the enactment of federal legislation. In the debates which occurred at the Quebec Conference in 1864, considerable time was occupied in discussing the provisions respecting the Senate. Its important purpose is stated in the following passages in speeches delivered in the debates on Confederation in the parliament of the province of Canada:

...

I would adopt this approach when interpreting the Charter. Consequently, the Minutes of the Proceedings and Evidence of the Special Joint Committee on the Constitution should, in my view, be considered.[41]

Justice Lamer then considered the weight that the minutes of the Joint Session ought to be given in the interpretation of section 7: "... I nonetheless believe that the logic underlying the reluctance to allow the use of materials such as speeches in Parliament carries considerable force with respect to the Minutes of the Committee as well."[42]

In *Borowski v. Canada (Attorney General)*,[43] the Saskatchewan Court of Appeal heard an appeal from a decision dismissing an action for a declaration that provisions of the *Criminal Code* exempting therapeutic abortion from prosecution were inconsistent with the Charter. In dismissing the appeal, Gerwing J., writing for the Court, considered the principles of Charter interpretation, and stated: "While legislative history in relation to the adoption of the Charter is admissible and relevant to the construction of the Charter, it is of little weight ..."[44]

Justice Gerwing did, however, note that to the extent that the minutes of the Joint Session reflected the prevailing attitude toward section 7 and the status of a foetus as "not a person", the minutes were relevant. Justice Gerwing cited from the statements of Bockstael and Kaplan, referred to above under "Section 7", for the proposition that the legislative history did not intend a radical change to the common law treatment of a foetus.[45]

A slightly different approach to weighing Parliamentary statements was taken in *Criminal Lawyers' Assn. v. Ontario (Ministry of Public Safety and Security)*.[46] There, the Ontario Court of Appeal heard an appeal from a refusal of the Privacy Commissioner to release certain OPP records following a review. The appellant argued that the provisions of the privacy legislation used to deny the request violated section 2(b) of the Charter. In a 2-1 dissent, Juriansz J. would have denied the appeal. Justice Juriansz considered the legislative history of section 2(b) and stated:

---

[41] *Reference re Motor Vehicle Act (British Columbia) s. 94(2)*, [1985] S.C.J. No. 73 at paras. 44-45, [1985] 2 S.C.R. 486 (S.C.C.).

[42] *Ibid.*, at para. 46.

[43] [1987] S.J. No. 312, 39 D.L.R. (4th) 731 (Sask. C.A.).

[44] *Ibid.*, at 752 (D.L.R.).

[45] *Ibid.*, at 754 (D.L.R.).

[46] [2007] O.J. No. 2038 (Ont. C.A.), revd [2010] S.C.J. No. 23 (S.C.C.).

Originalism is not part of the Canadian constitutional tradition. Nevertheless, the legislative history of the Charter is admissible to interpret its provisions and the question is what weight a court should give to the evidence introduced in a particular case.[47]

In *R. v. Prosper*,[48] the Court heard an appeal from a drunk driving conviction that dealt with whether or not section 10(b) of the Charter imposed a substantive obligation on the government to ensure counsel was provided to defendants upon arrest or detention. In allowing the appeal, Lamer C.J. noted that no such right could be implied from section 10(b). In declining to read a right to be provided counsel into section 10(b), he held:

> ... there is evidence which shows that the framers of the Charter consciously chose not to constitutionalize a right to state-funded counsel under section 10 of the Charter: Minutes of Proceedings and Evidence of the Special Joint Committee of the Senate and of the House of Commons on the Constitution of Canada (January 27, 1981). Specifically, a proposed amendment, which would have added the following clause to what is now section 10 of the Charter was considered and rejected:
>
> (d) if without sufficient means to pay for counsel and if the interests of justice so require, to be provided with counsel;
>
> In [*Motor Vehicles*], I stated for the majority that while these Minutes are admissible as extrinsic aids to the interpretation of Charter provisions, they should not be given "too much weight". However, it must be borne in mind that the Minutes at issue in [*Motor Vehicles*] recorded the views of civil servants on the meaning that should be given to the words "the principles of fundamental justice" found in s. 7 of the Charter, a task for which the courts are far better qualified.[49]

In *British Columbia Teachers' Federation v. British Columbia (Attorney General)*,[50] the B.C. Supreme Court heard a motion by the defendant to, among other things, strike out a demand for documents and discovery relating to the legislative intentions in passing a statute. In allowing the motion, Rice J. reviewed the applicability of extrinsic evidence in Charter cases, specifically in the context of a section 1 analysis:

> In Charter litigation, the general rule is that the legislative history of a challenged statute is admissible to determine whether the purpose of the challenged statute was to infringe a Charter right: see *R. v. Edwards Books and Art*, where parliamentary debates and a law reform commission report were admitted as evidence. Legislative history may also be used to determine whether the statute is justified as a reasonable limit under section 1 ...[51]

Justice Rice noted that legislative history had been held to be generally admissible by the Court, but went on to quote from the Court:

---

[47]   *Ibid.*, at para. 113.
[48]   [1994] S.C.J. No. 72, [1994] 3 S.C.R. 236 (S.C.C.).
[49]   *Ibid.*, at para. 30.
[50]   [2008] B.C.J. No. 2414 (B.C.S.C.).
[51]   *Ibid.*, at para. 42.

The main problem with the use of legislative history is its reliability. First, the intent of particular members of Parliament is not the same as the intent of the Parliament as a whole. Thus, it may be said that *the corporate will of the legislature is only found in the text of provisions, which are passed into law*. Second, the political nature of Parliamentary debates brings into question the reliability of the statements made. Different members of the legislature may have different purposes in putting forward their positions. That is to say the statements of a member made in the heat of debate or in committee hearings may not reflect even that member's position at the time of the final vote on the legislation.[52] [Underlining in original.]

Ultimately, Rice J. concluded that although legislative history was admissible, the scope of discovery sought by the plaintiffs was far beyond what was either admissible or useful. In general, it is acknowledged by the courts that extrinsic evidence such as legislative history is admissible for the purposes of determining the purpose of legislation pursuant to a section 1 Charter analysis.[53]

7.2.5 Initial Conclusions

Statements made by legislators with respect to the rights of corporations under the Charter were relatively infrequent and were often couched in a larger debate regarding the rights of other groups, such as women and the unborn. There was a surprising lack of meaningful, explicit statements respecting the rights of corporations or corporate defendants. What is clear from the statements is that several rights in the Charter, such as sections 2 and 15, were clearly envisioned as being applicable to natural persons only and not corporations. The debates on section 7 were a little vague, but if the government's logic was that "every person" and "everyone" were interchangeable, then an argument can be made that the legislators' awareness that corporations are generally "persons" at law implies that section 7 rights may well have been intended to apply to corporations.

Evidence of the debates surrounding the Constitution is admissible as evidence in Charter litigation. However, the traditional common law "living tree" approach toward constitutional interpretation generally leads the courts to give these statements little weight. Evidence of legislative intention, while instructive in a section 1 analysis, is seen as otherwise generally unhelpful because they do not reflect the actual substance of the language of the Charter.

Finally, this review and analysis indirectly supports the suggestion that there is a need and a means to change the relationship between the Charter and corporations. The courts have the opportunity and the responsibility to

---

[52] *Ibid.*, at para. 47, citing from *R. v. Heywood*, [1994] S.C.J. No. 101, [1994] 3 S.C.R. 761 at 788 (S.C.C.) [emphasis in original].

[53] See, for example, *R. v. Heywood*, [1994] S.C.J. No. 101, [1994] 3 S.C.R. 761 (S.C.C.); *R. v. Brown*, [2009] O.J. No. 269 at paras. 7-24 (Ont. C.J.); *R. v. Lizotte*, [2009] A.J. No. 1203 at paras. 6-9 (Alta. Prov. Ct.).

interpret the Charter in the evolving context of corporations and their accountability in law and society. The legislative history, however inadequate on the subject of the Charter's application to corporations, has not closed the door on the subject of standing, practicability and principles to the application of the Charter to corporations.

7.3   CORPORATION'S STANDING TO RAISE CHARTER ISSUES

7.3.1   Introduction to Standing

With greater penalties at stake and as a result of the trend towards more frequent prosecution of corporations, corporate defendants are becoming increasingly motivated to assert their legal rights, including those under the Charter. The right of a corporation's standing to raise Charter issues and defences has had inconsistent treatment by the courts. Although corporations are established by state action, through mandatory registration under corporation statutes, there is no consistent theory or approach in Canadian law addressing when corporations have standing to raise Charter issues in the courts. The issue of a corporation's right to raise Charter issues is one of the most important issues facing corporate defendants today. As Justice Rosenberg has said "The Charter's impact on access to justice is one of the difficult areas to assess."[54]

Some leading Charter decisions involve corporate defendants. These cases often focus on the remedial power of the court while ignoring the fundamental issue of standing. For example, in *R. v. 974649 Ontario Inc. (c.o.b. Dunedin Construction)*,[55] a justice of the peace was held to have jurisdiction to make an order for costs against the Crown for breach of its disclosure obligations, in a *quasi*-criminal prosecution against a corporation for alleged health and safety offences. The corporate defendant was granted a Charter remedy of costs against the Crown without any consideration of the issue of the corporation's standing under the Charter. The central issue in that case was the availability of a Charter remedy of costs, not who may seek the remedy.

7.3.2   Overview of Standing for Corporations

Section 52 of the *Constitution Act, 1982* provides that the Constitution is Canada's supreme law and any law inconsistent with it is of no force or effect. This provision, known as the "supremacy clause" effectively operates to invalidate any law that violates or is inconsistent with the Charter. Standing for individuals to raise Charter issues and defences exists where a liti-

---

[54] Honourable Justice Marc Rosenberg, "Introduction" in J. Cameron & J. Stribopoulos, eds., *The Charter and Criminal Justice: 25 Years Later* (Markham, ON: LexisNexis Canada, 2008).

[55] [2001] S.C.J. No. 79, 2001 S.C.C. 81 (S.C.C.) [*Dunedin Construction*].

gant is directly affected or exceptionally prejudiced by the law. The juris-prudence has also established that anyone, including a corporation, who has been charged pursuant to a law has the right to challenge that law on federal-ism, or division of powers grounds, or constitutional validity.

When a litigant does not have standing under section 52, they may ob-tain standing pursuant to their public interest. The Court has established that even where a litigant is not directly affected by legislation, he/she/it may obtain standing where: (i) there is a serious question as to validity of the leg-islation, (ii) the litigant is directly affected or has a genuine interest in the validity of the legislation, and (iii) there is no other reasonable and effective manner of bringing the matter before the Court.

Standing is also available to a corporation where it is charged crimi-nally or under a regulatory statute with an offence. The language used to express the legal rights guaranteed under sections 7 through 14 of the Char-ter, however, have important limitations in their application to corporations. The rights guaranteed in those provisions have been held to apply primarily to individuals and not to corporations. There are some exceptions including the section 8 right against unreasonable search and seizure, the section 11(b) right to be tried within a reasonable time and the section 11(d) right to a fair trial. The distinction between the corporeal nature of human beings versus the incorporeal nature of corporations has often been used to distinguish and limit the rights guaranteed by the Charter. While these arguments may have appeal on a case-by-case analysis, they often lose sight of the Charter values that are part of the constitutional foundation of Canada's free and democratic society.

7.3.3   Standing under Section 52 of the *Constitution Act*

Section 52 of the Constitution provides: "The Constitution of Canada is the supreme law of Canada, and any law that is inconsistent with the provisions of the Constitution is, to the extent of the inconsistency, of no force or ef-fect."

If a corporation objects to the application of a statute because it is ar-guably not a valid law, a constitutional issue arises pursuant to section 52. Given the supervisory nature of section 52, any court or tribunal with the power to decide questions of law may decide the constitutionality of legisla-tion. As a result, judicial review of legislation usually arises where a litigant, either an individual or a corporation, attempts to resist its application.[56]

Standing, as it applies to litigation generally, is the principle that a liti-gant needs to have sufficient interest in the outcome of the proceeding in order to properly appear before the courts. Professor Hogg, sets out six fac-tors that inform standing:

---

[56]   P.W. Hogg, *Constitutional Law of Canada*, looseleaf (Toronto: Thomson Carswell, 2007) at 59-1, 59-2.

1.   avoiding a floodgate of litigation;

2.   rationing limited resources for real, and not hypothetical, disputes;

3.   limiting the exercise of judicial power by not ruling on issues unnecessary to decide the matter;

4.   avoiding prejudice to those who might be affected but are not before the Court;

5.   avoiding the risk that a party without sufficient stake will present the case in a less than fulsome manner; and

6.   avoiding the result of a judicial decision made in a hypothetical context without a full factual record.[57]

As a result of the foregoing, a litigant's standing to raise a Charter right or defence will generally be allowed where the litigant is directly affected by the legislation in question. The traditional role of the Attorney General as the guardian of the public interest has led to the requirement that a litigant must be "exceptionally prejudiced"[58] or establish "special damage"[59] by legislation of general application in order to be entitled to declaratory relief against legislation. In *Smith v. Ontario (Attorney General)*,[60] the Court held that in order for a private litigant to challenge a law that applies to the public generally, he or she must demonstrate that the law applies differently to him or her: "[a]n individual, for example, has no status to maintain an action restraining a wrongful violation of a public right unless he is exceptionally prejudiced by the wrongful act."[61]

In essence, the Court explicitly recognized that a citizen may be proactive in challenging a law that is unconstitutional as violating the Charter and ought not be subject to prosecution in order to challenge the constitutionality of a law. This right has not been made widely available to corporations due to the personal nature of this test. However, section 52 establishes the supremacy of the Charter and the role of the courts in upholding the Charter. Therefore, this is the first legal plank in the jurisprudential platform of providing corporations with broader access to the courts to uphold the Charter, as part of the Canadian Constitution.

7.3.3.1   *Public Interest Standing*

The Court has slowly moved away from a narrow view and towards a broad view of public interest standing. This arguably establishes a second plank in the thesis of a presumption of Charter standing for corporations. In *Thorson*

---

[57]   *Ibid.*, at 59-3.
[58]   *Smith v. Ontario (Attorney General)*, [1924] S.C.J. No. 15, [1924] S.C.R. 331 (S.C.C.).
[59]   *Boyce v. Paddington Borough Council*, [1906] A.C. 1 (H.L.).
[60]   [1924] S.C.J. No. 15, [1924] S.C.R. 331 (S.C.C.).
[61]   *Ibid.*, at 333 (S.C.R.).

v. Canada (Attorney General),[62] an individual taxpayer sought to challenge provisions of a statute as part of a class action. The individual's standing was denied at both the trial and on appeal. On further appeal, the majority of the Court held that it had a discretionary power to grant standing to a litigant to challenge legislation on the basis of public interest standing. Justice Laskin, writing for the majority, held that the Court ought not to allow legislation to be "immunized" from judicial review simply because there was no party that was exceptionally prejudiced and was willing to litigate. He said:

> In my opinion, standing of a federal taxpayer seeking to challenge the constitutionality of federal legislation is a matter particularly appropriate for the exercise of judicial discretion, relating as it does to the effectiveness of process ... where all members of the public are affected alike, as in the present case, and there is a justifiable issue respecting the validity of legislation, the Court must be able to say that as between allowing a taxpayers' action and denying any standing at all when the Attorney General refuses to act, it may choose to hear the case on the merits.[63]

The Court further expanded public interest standing in *Nova Scotia (Board of Censors) v. McNeil*.[64] In that case an individual litigant was concerned with the powers exercised by the Nova Scotia Board of Censors pursuant to legislation. The individual attempted to unsuccessfully have the Attorney General challenge the legislation. He then brought an application to have the legislation and certain regulations declared unconstitutional. The lower courts granted him standing. On the appeal, Laskin J. held that although theatre owners could bring a direct challenge to the legislation, that did not mean that the private litigant could not obtain public interest standing to challenge the legislation.

In *Canada (Minister of Justice) v. Borowski*,[65] the respondent was an anti-abortion advocate who sought to invalidate provisions of the Code that exempted therapeutic abortions from the legal prohibition against abortion. Justice Martland, writing for a 7-2 majority of the Court, recognized that *McNeil* allowed standing even where there was a recognized class of persons who may have been exceptionally prejudiced by the legislation.[66] In the result, the respondent was granted public interest standing. Justice Martland then set out the test:

> I interpret these cases as deciding that to establish status as a plaintiff in a suit seeking a declaration that legislation is invalid, if there is *a serious issue as to its invalidity*, a person need only to show that he is *affected by it directly or that he has a genuine interest* as a citizen in the validity of the

---

[62] [1974] S.C.J. No. 45, [1975] 1 S.C.R. 138 (S.C.C.).
[63] *Ibid.*, at 161 (S.C.R.).
[64] [1975] S.C.J. No. 77, [1976] 2 S.C.R. 265 (S.C.C.).
[65] [1981] S.C.J. No. 103, [1981] 2 S.C.R. 575 (S.C.C.).
[66] *Ibid.*, at 595 (S.C.R.).

legislation and that there is *no other reasonable and effective manner in which the issue may be brought before the Court.*[67]

In *Finlay v. Canada (Minister of Finance)*,[68] the appellant was a person receiving social assistance who sought to challenge federal cost-sharing as unconstitutional, in an attack on the sufficiency of the provincial legislation governing social assistance. Justice Le Dain set out the issues that were of concern to the courts in granting public interest standing:

> The traditional judicial concerns about the expansion of public interest standing may be summarized as follows: the concern about the allocation of scarce judicial resources and the need to screen out the mere busybody; the concern that in the determination of issues the courts should have the benefit of the contending points of view of those most directly affected by them; and the concern about the proper role of the courts and their constitutional relationship to the other branches of government.[69]

The outcome of these four cases was a more liberal test with respect to public interest standing. The courts have discretion to grant standing where:

1. the action raises a serious legal question;

2. the plaintiff/applicant has a genuine interest in the validity of the legislation; and

3. there is no other reasonable and effective manner to bring the issue before the Court.

This public interest standing test has clear application for corporations. Often a corporation has a legitimate interest and the means to test whether a law or state action contravenes the Charter. Further, a corporation may be the only person with the means to fund the litigation. However, public interest standing, in and of itself, is too narrow a plank upon which the platform presumption of Charter standing for corporations can be built.

For example, in *Hy and Zel's Inc. v. Ontario (Attorney General)*,[70] a corporation and a number of its employees sought a declaration that a provision of holiday closing legislation requiring stores to close on Sunday violated the freedom of religion right in section 2(a) of the Charter. On the issue of standing, the majority held that since there was very little evidence led by the applicants, there was a more reasonable and effective manner of bringing the matter before the Court. After considering *Finlay*, Major J., writing for the majority, held:

> a court's ability to consider standing at the outset "depends on the nature of the issues raised and on whether the court has sufficient material before it, in the way of allegations of fact, considerations of law, and argument, for a

---

[67] *Ibid.*, at 598 (S.C.R.) [emphasis added].

[68] [1986] S.C.J. No. 73, [1986] 2 S.C.R. 607 (S.C.C.).

[69] *Ibid.*, at para. 32.

[70] [1993] S.C.J. No. 113, [1993] 3 S.C.R. 675 (S.C.C.).

proper understanding at a preliminary stage of the nature of the interest asserted."[71]

Andrew Lokan, in *Constitutional Litigation in Canada*,[72] claims that the Court has demonstrated a "clear trend toward applying [public interest standing] more restrictively."[73] He referred to *Hy & Zel's* for the proposition that the Court was unwilling to extend public interest standing to legitimate parties, such that: "… a party wishing to challenge the validity of legislation may be better off violating the law and risking criminal sanctions than bringing a freestanding challenge in good faith to determine its legal position."[74]

In *Corp. of Canadian Civil Liberties Assn. v. Canada (Attorney General)*,[75] a public advocacy, non-profit organization sought to invalidate certain provisions of Canadian national security and intelligence legislation, to the extent that the investigative powers provided for within violated the Charter. Justice Charron held that the merits of the application were relevant when deciding if there was a serious issue as to the invalidity of the legislation.[76] Justice Charron went on to state that standing ought not to be granted where, on the balance of probabilities, it can be shown that the legislation will be subject to attack by private litigants.[77] In that case, the lack of adjudicative facts led the majority to conclude that there was no serious issue, nor was it the most reasonable and effective way to bring the matter before the Court.

Finally, in *Canadian Bar Assn. v. British Columbia*,[78] the CBA sought declarations that the Government of British Columbia and Attorney General were not providing adequate legal aid services, which breached the Charter. Justice Brenner, in dismissing the application, reviewed the quartet of Supreme Court cases and held that the test for public interest standing could only be applied on a direct challenge to legislation. While the Court had expanded public interest standing in *Finlay*, it was done incrementally and with caution.[79] He concluded that:

> [t]he plaintiff correctly submits that the principles governing public interest standing must be applied in a "liberal and generous manner". In *Canadian Council of Churches*, Cory J. stated that "the post-Charter era calls for a liberal and purposive approach to standing". However, he also emphasized that the approach must remain balanced (at 250). In my view, the balanced ap-

---

[71]   *Ibid.*, at para. 17, citing from *Finlay v. Canada (Minister of Finance)*, [1986] S.C.J. No. 73 at para. 16, [1986] 2 S.C.R. 607 (S.C.C.).

[72]   A.K. Lokan & C.M. Dassios, *Constitutional Litigation in Canada*, looseleaf (Toronto: Thomson Carswell, 2006).

[73]   *Ibid.*, at 3-8.

[74]   *Ibid.*, at 3-9.

[75]   [1998] O.J. No. 2856, 40 O.R. (3d) 489 (Ont. C.A.).

[76]   *Ibid.*, at 503 (O.R.).

[77]   *Ibid.*, at 519 (O.R.).

[78]   [2006] B.C.J. No. 2015 (B.C.S.C.).

[79]   *Ibid.*, at para. 37.

proach will not be served by removing the requirement that the "serious issue" must relate to invalidity of legislation, or to a public act undertaken
without or in excess of statutory authority.[80]

In conclusion, although there has been a liberalization of the test for
public interest standing, it is not clear that corporations have a consistent
access to public interest standing under the Charter. Courts have been more
sympathetic to individuals than organizations, including corporations, in the
area of public interest standing, even though corporations employ individuals, are managed by individuals and have individual investors. There has yet
to be a clear decision by the Court on the full extent of public interest standing available to corporations under the Charter. This is the second legal
plank to support a broader platform for Charter standing for corporations
under Canadian law.

7.3.4 Standing as a Defendant

The third plank to support a broader legal platform for Charter standing for
corporations arises when a defendant is charged with an offence. In *R. v. Big
M Drug Mart Ltd.*,[81] the corporation was charged with the offence of selling
goods on Sunday in violation of the *Lord's Day Act.*[82] Chief Justice Dickson,
writing the majority opinion in a unanimous decision, considered section 52:

> Section 52 sets out the fundamental principle of constitutional law that the
> Constitution is supreme. The undoubted corollary to be drawn from this
> principle is that no one can be convicted of an offence under an unconstitu-
> tional law. The respondent did not come to court voluntarily as an interested
> citizen asking for a prerogative declaration that a statute is unconstitutional.
> If it had been engaged in such "public interest litigation" *it would have had
> to fulfill the status requirements laid down by this Court in the trilogy of
> "standing" cases* ...[83]

The purpose of the *Lord's Day Act* to compel observance of the Christian Sabbath, Sunday, was held to be a violation of section 2(a) of the Charter. The fact that a corporation may not enjoy the right to freedom of
conscience and religion, a decidedly individual and spiritual freedom, was
held by Dickson C.J. to be irrelevant. The constitutionality of the legislation
was held to not depend on the specific rights enjoyed by the appellant corporation. The Court held that a corporation could challenge the constitutionality of the law if the purpose and/or effect of the legislation, that was the
basis of the prosecution, violated the Charter.

---

[80]   *Ibid.*, at para. 46.

[81]   [1985] S.C.J. No. 17, [1985] 1 S.C.R. 295 (S.C.C.).

[82]   R.S.C. 1970, c. L-13.

[83]   *R. v. Big M Drug Mart Ltd.*, [1985] S.C.J. No. 17 at para. 38, [1985] 1 S.C.R. 295 (S.C.C.)
[emphasis added].

In *Irwin Toy Ltd. v. Québec (Attorney General)*,[84] the issue of a corporation's standing arose when it sought a declaration that certain provisions of Quebec consumer protection legislation banning advertising directed at children younger than 13 years of age, violated the Charter. In a 3-2 majority decision, it was held that the provisions of the legislation that called for imprisonment for violation could not be challenged by a corporation, since a corporation could not be jailed. Since only the corporation was charged, and no individual was at risk of imprisonment, there was no recourse to section 7.[85] The majority distinguished *Big M* as follows:

> A plain, common sense reading of the phrase "Everyone has the right to life, liberty and security of the person" serves to underline the human element involved; only human beings can enjoy these rights. "Everyone" then, must be read in light of the rest of the section and defined to exclude corporations and other artificial entities incapable of enjoying life, liberty or security of the person, and include only human beings. In this regard, the case of R. v. Big M Drug Mart Ltd., supra, is of no application. *There are no penal proceedings pending in the case at hand, so the principle articulated in Big M Drug Mart is not involved.*[86]

This decision does not consider the legislative debates and is the low watermark for corporations to get standing to raise Charter defences in criminal or regulatory prosecutions.

The Court then returned to the *Big M* approach when it granted standing to *Wholesale Travel Group Inc.*[87] In that case, the corporation was charged with misleading advertising pursuant to federal competition legislation. On the issue of standing to raise sections 7 and 11(d) of the Charter to challenge the legislative provisions, Lamer C.J. distinguished *Irwin Toy* on the basis that there were no individual penal consequences involved in the former.[88] Chief Justice Lamer rejected the argument that a finding of invalidity with respect to human beings ought to lead only to invalidating the provision that applied to individuals and not corporations. However, he also added the following proviso:

> ... these provisions apply to both individual and corporate accused. However, if the provisions in question applied only to corporations, the Charter analysis would, in my view, be very different. For example, provisions which applied exclusively to corporations could not be challenged on the basis that they combined absolute liability with imprisonment, for the simple reason that a corporation cannot be imprisoned.[89]

---

[84]   [1989] S.C.J. No. 36, [1989] 1 S.C.R. 927 (S.C.C.).
[85]   *Ibid.*, at para. 93.
[86]   *Ibid.*, at para. 96 [emphasis added].
[87]   [1991] S.C.J. No. 79, [1991] 3 S.C.R. 154 (S.C.C.).
[88]   *Ibid.*, at para. 22.
[89]   *Ibid.*, at para. 27.

An extension of the corporation's standing to raise Charter defences occurred in a civil case, *Canadian Egg Marketing Agency v. Richardson.*[90] The respondent corporation was the subject of civil action by the Canadian Egg Marketing Agency pursuant to regulatory legislation prohibiting inter-provincial marketing of eggs in the Northwest Territories. The corporation raised sections 2(d) and 6 of the Charter in its defence, alleging that the legislation violated its freedom of association and mobility rights. At trial, the corporation was granted public interest standing. When the case was appealed to the Court, Justices Iacobucci and Bastarache, writing for the 7-2 majority, held that the corporation did not need to obtain public interest standing, but could rely on the *Big M* principle. The majority recognized that:

> [p]rior to this decision, the respondents could not obtain standing to invoke the Charter using the exception created by this Court in [*Big M*], because they were not facing penal proceedings. In our opinion, it is now time to expand the exception to allow corporations to invoke the Charter when they are defendants in civil proceedings instigated by the state or a state organ pursuant to a regulatory scheme.[91]

The majority went on to explain its reasoning for expanding Charter standing in a civil matter:

> Our expanding the *Big M Drug Mart* exception to civil proceedings in these limited circumstances is not intended to provide corporations with a new weapon for litigation. *The purpose of the expansion is to permit a corporation to attack what it regards as an unconstitutional law when it is involuntarily brought before the courts pursuant to a regulatory regime set up under an impugned law.* Surely, just as no one should be convicted of an offence under an unconstitutional law, no one should be the subject of coercive proceedings and sanctions authorized by an unconstitutional law.[92]

The combined effect of *Big M, Wholesale Travel* and *Canadian Egg Marketing*, is to broaden the right of corporations to raise Charter issues. Those cases are very similar to the principles of public interest standing and recognize the important interests that corporations have in Charter litigation.

7.4   CORPORATIONS AND SPECIFIC CHARTER RIGHTS

The third plank in the argument or "platform" for broader access by corporations to the Charter includes the specific due process rights under the Charter. Sections 7 to 14 of the Charter guarantee various legal rights to those persons charged with offences. The Charter debates inferred that these rights

---

[90]   [1998] S.C.J. No. 78, [1998] 3 S.C.R. 157 (S.C.C.).

[91]   *Ibid.*, at para. 34. Note that the majority also stated, at para. 35: "Generally speaking, a party seeking to invoke the Charter may be granted standing under four broad heads: as of right, the *Big M Drug Mart* exception, public interest standing, and under residuary discretion. As already noted, these respondents could have been granted standing in this Court under the residuary discretion."

[92]   *Ibid.*, at para 44 [emphasis added].

were available to all legal persons, including corporations. However, the courts have not always taken this approach.

7.4.1 Section 7

Section 7 of the Charter provides that "Everyone has the right to life, liberty and security of the person and the right not to be deprived thereof except in accordance with the principles of fundamental justice."

In *Irwin Toy*, discussed above, the Court held that a corporation did not have standing to rely upon section 7:

> In our opinion, a corporation cannot avail itself of the protection offered by s. 7 of the Charter. First, we would have to conceive of a manner in which a corporation could be deprived of its "life, liberty or security of the person". We have already noted that it is nonsensical to speak of a corporation being put in jail. To say that bankruptcy and winding up proceedings engage s. 7 would stretch the meaning of the right to life beyond recognition. The only remaining argument is that corporations are protected against deprivations of some sort of "economic liberty".[93]

However, a number of years later, in *Wholesale Travel* the Court took a more liberal approach to corporations seeking standing under section 7. In that case, Lamer C.J. held that section 7 was available as a defence for a corporation charged with a regulatory offence, where the legislation in question also could affect individuals. As a result, it appears that *Wholesale Travel* did not necessarily expand the Charter rights of corporations so much as it reaffirmed the *Big M* principle that no person can be convicted of an unconstitutional law.

Cases that followed *Wholesale Travel* appear to apply that same approach to denying a corporation standing under section 7.[94] However, an interesting exception arose in *Agat Laboratories Ltd.*[95] In that Alberta case, the corporate defendant was charged with a number of regulatory offences, for which Crown disclosure was ordered by the Court. As a result of the Crown's failure to comply, the corporation sought costs under section 24(1) for a violation of its section 7 rights. The Court tied the corporations' right to Crown disclosure to section 7 and the ability to make a full answer and defence. The Crown argued that costs were not available to a corporation under section 24(1). The Court held:

> [a]s previously indicated, the Crown relies on R. v. Irwin Toy Inc., supra, and R. v. Wholesale Travel Group Inc., supra, as support for that proposition. However, those cases do not address the question of remedies for a

---

[93] *Irwin Toy v. Québec (Attorney General)*, [1989] S.C.J. No. 36 at para. 94, [1989] 1 S.C.R. 927 (S.C.C.).

[94] See, for example, *R. v. Church of Scientology of Toronto*, [1997] O.J. No. 1548 (Ont. C.A.); *Main Rehabilitation Co. v. Canada*, [2004] F.C.J. No. 2030 at paras. 4-5 (F.C.A.); *R. v. 1260448 Ontario Inc. (c.o.b. William Cameron Trucking)*, [2003] O.J. No. 4306 at paras. 14-16 (Ont. C.A.).

[95] [1998] A.J. No. 304 (Alta. Prov. Ct.).

Charter breach. Any discussion in those cases about economic interests centres on whether those interests are covered by section 7 of the Charter, not whether economic remedies are available to corporations under section 24(1) if a Charter breach is found. ... In my view, there is nothing in the Charter itself nor in the case law which would prohibit a corporate accused from receiving an economic remedy under section 24(1) of the Charter if it is found that one of its Charter rights has been violated.[96]

7.4.2 Section 8

Section 8 of the Charter provides that "everyone has the right to be secure against unreasonable search or seizure." It is now well established that corporations have standing with respect to unreasonable search and seizure. In *Canada (Combines Investigation Acts, Director of Investigation and Research) v. Southam Inc.*,[97] the Court did not question the trial judge's holding that section 8 applied to corporations. In that case a regulatory investigative agency entered the corporate respondent's premises to examine documents. The lack of prior authorization of the search in the legislation was held to be inconsistent with section 8, and the legislation was invalidated.

7.4.3 Section 9

Section 9 of the Charter provides that "everyone has the right not to be arbitrarily detained or imprisoned." Given the general interpretation of section 7 as inapplicable to corporations as a guaranteed right, and that section 9 rights are limited to detention and imprisonment, it seems obvious that section 9 would be inapplicable to corporations as well. It is trite to say that a corporation, *per se*, may not be detained or imprisoned. In *R. v. 741290 Ontario Inc.*,[98] the Court stated: "The unavailability of some provisions of the Charter is obvious from a mere reading of the section: for example, a corporation cannot be arrested, detained or imprisoned, and thus the rights in ss. 9 and 10 have no application to it."[99]

7.4.4 Section 10

Section 10 of the Charter provides that "everyone has the right on arrest or detention (a) to be informed promptly of the reasons therefore; (b) to retain and instruct counsel without delay and to be informed of that right; and (c) to have the validity of the detention determined by way of *habeas corpus* and to be released if the detention is not lawful." Again, there is no jurisprudence establishing standing for corporations under section 10. However, on the same analysis as sections 7 and 9, it seems highly likely that the right is

---

[96]   *Ibid.*, at paras. 27 and 29.
[97]   [1984] S.C.J. No. 36, [1984] 2 S.C.R. 145 (S.C.C.) [*Hunter*].
[98]   [1991] O.J. No. 215 (Ont. Prov. Div.).
[99]   *Ibid.*, at para. 13.

not available to corporations. Corporations have no physical body to arrest or detain.

7.4.5 Section 11

Section 11 of the Charter provides a number of substantive rights when a person is charged with an offence.[100] In *R. v. Wigglesworth*,[101] the Court set a reasonably low threshold for what constitutes an offence. It described the rights under the general language of section 11 "charged with an offence" broadly: "The rights guaranteed by s. 11 of the Charter are available to persons prosecuted by the State for public offences involving punitive sanctions, *i.e.*, criminal, *quasi*-criminal and regulatory offences, either federally or provincially enacted."[102]

There is no available jurisprudence that directly addressed the right under section 11(a) of the Charter for corporations. However, corporations arguably share this right with individuals.

In *R. v. CIP Inc.*,[103] a corporation charged in relation to a fatal industrial accident argued that its section 11(b) right to be tried in a reasonable time had been infringed. The language used by the Charter applies to the right to trial within a reasonable period of time for all defendants, including corporations. After considering *Big M* and *Hunter*, among other authorities, the Court held that the corporation had standing to raise s. 11(b) concerns and said: "[t]he right to a fair trial is fundamental to our adversarial system. Parliament has seen fit to accord that right constitutional protection. I can

---

[100] Section 11 of the Charter: Any person charged with an offence has the right

    (a)   to be informed without unreasonable delay of the specific offence;

    (b)   to be tried within a reasonable time;

    (c)   not to be compelled to be a witness in proceedings against that person in respect of the offence;

    (d)   to be presumed innocent until proven guilty according to law in a fair and public hearing by an independent and impartial tribunal;

    (e)   not to be denied reasonable bail without just cause;

    (f)   except in the case of an offence under military law tried before a military tribunal, to the benefit of trial by jury where the maximum punishment for the offence is imprisonment for five years or a more severe punishment;

    (g)   not to be found guilty on account of any act or omission unless, at the time of the act or omission, it constituted an offence under Canadian or international law or was criminal according to the general principles of law recognized by the community of nations;

    (h)   if finally acquitted of the offence, not to be tried for it again and, if finally found guilty and punished for the offence, not to be tried or punished for it again; and

    (i)   if found guilty of the offence and if the punishment for the offence has been varied between the time of commission and the time of sentencing, to the benefit of the lesser punishment.

[101] [1987] S.C.J. No. 71, [1987] 2 S.C.R. 541 (S.C.C.).

[102] *Ibid.*, at para. 16.

[103] [1992] S.C.J. No. 34, [1992] 1 S.C.R. 843 (S.C.C.).

find no principled reason for not extending that protection to all accused."[104]
And further:

> Any accused, corporate or human, can be denied full answer and defence by
> reason of delay. A corporation is just as vulnerable to the deterioration of
> recollection which can prejudice any person on trial for an offence. Its wit-
> nesses, like those of any accused, can die, move away, or disappear. If, as
> seems clear, the right of an accused to make full answer and defence is a
> fundamental principle of the Canadian system of justice, and if that system
> regards corporations as being susceptible to the same criminal process as
> humans, it would seem to follow that protection of the fairness of a corpora-
> tion's trial is a concern which is well within ... section 11(b).[105]

Therefore, corporations are guaranteed the Charter right to be tried in a reasonable time under section 11(b).[106] The reasoning in *CIP* is perhaps the Court's
broadest statement of a corporation's Charter rights and supports a broader approach to standing to assert Charter rights by corporations generally.

Regarding section 11(c), *R. v. Amway Corp.*,[107] held that it was anach-
ronistic to suggest that both the corporate officer and the corporation itself
were both witnesses when it was only the officer being examined. He held:

> In my view, it would strain the interpretation of s. 11(c) if an artificial entity
> were held to be a witness. Such a metamorphosis could not be justified on
> the basis that the rules of evidence on an examination for discovery do not
> restrict the person testifying to personal knowledge.
>
> Applying a purposive interpretation to s. 11(c), I am of the opinion that it
> was intended to protect the individual against the affront to dignity and pri-
> vacy inherent in a practice which enables the prosecution to force the person
> charged to supply the evidence out of his or her own mouth. Although dis-
> agreement exists as to the basis of the principle against self-incrimination, in
> my view, this factor plays a dominant role.[108]

Therefore, corporations have not been permitted standing to assert the right
against being compelled to be a witness against oneself under section 11(c).

In *R. v. Auto Clearing (1982) Ltd.*,[109] several corporate defendants were
charged under the *Highway Traffic Act* as the registered owners of cars
driven through red lights monitored by police cameras. Since the driver
could not be identified but the owner could, the corporations were charged.
They challenged the provision of the legislation as violating section 11(d), as
the onus was upon the owner to prove that he/she/it was not driving the car
at the time, and that the driver was not authorized to do so. Although Singer
J. ultimately rejected the application to strike down the provision, he stated:

---

[104] *Ibid.*, at para. 33.

[105] *Ibid.*, citing from *R. v. 741290 Ontario Inc.* (1991), 2 O.R. (3d) 336 at 351-352.

[106] See also *R. v. Deslauriers*, [1992] M.J. No. 502, 83 Man. R. (2d) 7 (Man. C.A.), where an interesting argument distinguishing between s. 11(b) rights as they apply to private as opposed to
public corporations was rejected.

[107] [1989] S.C.J. No. 3, [1989] 1 S.C.R. 21 (S.C.C.).

[108] *Ibid.*, at paras. 34-35.

[109] [2007] S.J. No. 360 (Sask. Prov. Ct.).

Section 11 deals, exclusively, with a person charged with an offence. It has long been settled that corporations (who are never in danger of going to jail) may invoke section 11(d) and that quasi-criminal charges under traffic safety legislation fall within the definition of an offence for the purposes of section 11(d). There is no requirement that a person be subject to imprisonment for section 11 rights to apply.[110]

Cases dealing with a corporation's rights to have standing under section 11(e), (f), (g), (h) or (i) do not exist. Given that (e) and (f) deal with bail and imprisonment, it seems unlikely that they will apply to corporations. Although there is no jurisprudence to support this contention, it is logical that section 11(g), (h) and (i) would likely apply to corporations. The rights against conviction under *ex post facto* laws, against double jeopardy, and the benefit of the lower sentencing do not disclose any identifiable distinction between conviction of a human being versus a corporation. The broad policy statement in *CIP* with respect to fair trials is the high watermark of corporate rights under the Charter.

7.4.6 Section 12

Section 12 of the Charter provides that "everyone has the right not to be subjected to any cruel and unusual treatment or punishment". There are no reported cases dealing with a corporation's standing to raise the Charter prohibition against cruel and unusual punishment. However, the legislative debates appear to support an intention of the framers of the Charter to permit corporations to assert this right. It is unclear whether the incorporeal nature of a corporation would preclude this right applying to a corporate defendant. In *R. v. Smith*,[111] Lamer J., as he then was, set out the test for cruel and unusual punishment:

> The criterion which must be applied in order to determine whether a punishment is cruel and unusual within the meaning of s. 12 of the Charter is, to use the words of Laskin C.J. in Miller and Cockriell, supra, at p. 688, "whether the punishment prescribed is so excessive as to outrage standards of decency". In other words, though the state may impose punishment, the effect of that punishment must not be grossly disproportionate to what would have been appropriate.[112]

Other cases have dealt with section 12 in terms of minimum sentences[113] and driving suspensions.[114] Therefore, it is possible that section 12 rights may be extended to a corporation, although the issue has not yet been addressed.

---

[110] *Ibid.*, at para. 36. See also, for example, *R. v. Unity Auto Body Ltd.*, [1988] S.J. No. 275 at 401 (Sask. Q.B.): "On the other hand, I cannot believe that those who drafted the Charter had in mind that s. 11(d) would not apply to corporations."

[111] [1987] S.C.J. No. 36, [1987] 1 S.C.R. 1045 (S.C.C.).

[112] *Ibid.*, at para. 53.

[113] *R. v. Kumar*, [1993] B.C.J. No. 2266, 85 C.C.C. (3d) 417 (B.C.C.A.).

[114] *R. v. Ross*, [1985] B.C.J. No. 1073, 32 M.V.R. 261 (B.C.S.C.).

7.4.7 Section 13

Section 13 of the Charter provides that "a witness who testifies in any proceedings has the right not to have any incriminating evidence so given used
to incriminate that witness in any other proceedings, except in a prosecution
for perjury or for the giving of contradictory evidence". In *Thomson Newspapers Ltd. v. Canada (Director of Investigation and Research, Restrictive
Trade Practices Commission)*,[115] the Court held that a corporation was incapable of self-incrimination. However, the representative of the corporation
acting as witness could, of course, avail him or herself of section 13. This
decision is similar to the narrow approach taken in *Amway Corp*. Therefore,
a corporation cannot avail itself of the right against self-incrimination.

7.4.8 Section 14

Section 14 of the Charter provides that "[a] party or witness in any proceedings who does not understand or speak the language in which the proceedings are conducted or who is deaf has the right to the assistance of an
interpreter." There are no cases dealing with a corporation's right to an interpreter. Given the use of "witness" in that right, and the analysis above
under sections 11(c) and 13, it seems unlikely that this right would apply to a
corporation. Other specific Charter rights cases, such as *Amway Corp.*, have
established that it is the corporate representative who is the witness, and
therefore it is that individual, and not a corporation, who can avail him or
herself of section 14.

7.4.9 Summary on Standing of Corporations

The investigation and prosecution of corporations is part of the growing
trend of law enforcement initiatives demanded by the Canadian polity. Corporations are often an easy target for blame for a variety of external effects
of their internal decisions and actions. Standing for corporations is a critical
issue for access to justice regarding Charter rights and defences. Consistent
with the presumption of innocence and right to a fair trial under section
11(d) of the Charter, it is suggested that corporate defendants have a legitimate interest in pursuing Charter rights and defences. However, to date, corporations have been given limited standing to raise Charter issues and
defences.[116] The jurisprudence pursuant to section 52 of the *Constitution Act,
1982* and public interest standing, are not sufficiently broad to protect the
legitimate and lawful interests of organizations, including corporations. Further, the application of Charter rights to corporate defendants has been inconsistently applied.

---

[115] [1990] S.C.J. No. 23, [1990] 1 S.C.R. 425 (S.C.C.).

[116] Andrew Bernstein, "The Yoke of Canadian Egg: Corporate Standing Under the Charter" (2000)
33:2 Can. Bus. L.J. at 247.

In the author's view, there is a need for a more broad-based, principled approach to Charter standing for corporations. A new approach ought to start with the proposition that corporations, which are legal persons established by state mandated public statutes, ought to have a presumption of standing to raise Charter issues very broadly. If the current trend towards criminalizing more activities that corporations may engage in continues, it is respectfully submitted that a new approach to recognizing Charter rights of corporations is necessary to balance state power, uphold constitutional values, and preserve the rule of law. I have argued that the three separate legal planks support a new principle: they are based on the Charter as part of the fundamental law of Canada, the broadening of the test for public interest constitutional litigation and the Charter jurisprudence providing legal rights to corporate defendants. These three planks, or legal arguments, when viewed together, can adequately establish a broad legal basis or platform to support a "presumption of Charter standing" for corporations.

The Charter is intended by its origins, purpose and principles, to protect the fundamental rights of an accused from state actions, regardless of their legal identity or status. Therefore, all defendants, including corporations, should have a presumption of Charter standing to raise Charter issues and defences as part of this great legal tradition of the presumption of innocence. Further, where it is clear from the text of a specific Charter right that has no application to the corporation, public interest standing supports a presumption of Charter standing for corporations to uphold the liberty of their officers, directors or employees that may be at risk. This is a reasonable extension of *Wholesale Travel* case supported by a liberal approach to the test for public interest standing on Charter issues. A presumption of Charter standing for corporations is a more principled approach to access to justice and would provide corporations with a greater access to raise and protect constitutional rights and values.

7.5 A PURPOSIVE APPROACH TO CHARTER JURISPRUDENCE RELATING TO CORPORATIONS

7.5.1 Principles Without Common Sense

The first major decision of the Court in assessing the Charter's application to corporations involved a very individual right, freedom of religion. Who would have thought that a corporation could assert freedom of religion regarding days of religious observance? Common sense indicates that a corporation has no "soul to save" and therefore ought not to be afforded rights based on freedom of religion. Was the Charter meant to provide economic rights to corporations under the guise of freedom of religion? Yet the Court based this decision on a principled approach that "… no one can be convicted of an offence under an unconstitutional law."[117] As a result, both indi-

---

[117] *R. v. Big M Drug Mart Ltd.*, [1985] S.C.J. No. 17 at para. 38, [1985] 1 S.C.R. 295 (S.C.C.).

viduals and corporations may *prima facie* argue that a law they are charged with violating is invalid as it is inconsistent with the Constitution. In allowing a corporation to challenge a law based on the allegation that it violated the right to freedom of religion guaranteed by section 2(a) of the Charter, the Court held:

> Any accused, whether corporate or individual, may defend a criminal charge by arguing that the law under which the charge is brought is constitutionally invalid. The argument that the respondent, by reason of being a corporation, is incapable of holding religious belief and therefore incapable of claiming rights under s. 2(a) of the Charter, confuses the nature of this appeal. ... It is the nature of the law, not the status of the accused, that is in issue.[118]

The Court later held that where there were penal proceedings, if a law was found to be unconstitutional because it violated individual rights, the corporation could also benefit from this finding since they could not then be prosecuted under an unconstitutional law.[119]

The value of a principled approach was demonstrated outside of the penal prosecution area. Corporations may now allege that a law is constitutionally invalid based on violations of rights held only by individuals, when the corporation is a defendant in a civil proceeding. The Court held:

> Prior to this decision, the respondents could not obtain standing to invoke the Charter using the exception created by this Court in R. v. Big M Drug Mart Ltd., [1985] 1 S.C.R. 295, because they were not facing penal proceedings. In our opinion, it is now time to expand the exception to allow corporations to invoke the Charter when they are defendants in civil proceedings instigated by the state or a state organ pursuant to a regulatory scheme. ... a party seeking to invoke the Charter may be granted standing under four broad heads: as of right, the Big M Drug Mart exception, public interest standing, and under residuary discretion.[120]

In summary, although there are now several routes by which corporations may claim Charter protection, they do not necessarily resonate with a "common sense", man-on-the-street understanding of the Charter. The Court's reliance on a principled approach to the Charter's application to corporations fails to be consistent with the purpose of the Charter.

7.5.2 Common Sense without Principles

The broadly worded due process provision of the Charter has been given a different interpretation by the Court. The Court held in a first, clumsy attempt by a corporation to assert section 7 rights, that a corporation "cannot avail itself of the protection offered by section 7", as a corporation cannot be

---

[118] *Ibid.*, at paras. 39 and 41.

[119] *Ibid.*

[120] *Canadian Egg Marketing Agency v. Richardson*, [1998] S.C.J. No. 78 at paras. 34-35, [1998] 3 S.C.R. 157 (S.C.C.).

deprived of life, liberty, or security of the person.[121] Although *Big M* clearly had the effect of protecting the economic security of a business corporation, the Court resiled from that position in *Irwin Toy*. With respect to life and liberty the Court said:

> We have already noted that it is nonsensical to speak of a corporation being put in jail. To say that bankruptcy and winding up proceedings engage s. 7 would stretch the meaning of the right to life beyond recognition.[122]

The Court went on to hold that a corporation could not be deprived of security of the person, as this phrase did not encompass economic rights in the form of property rights.[123] The Court, purporting to rely on a so-called "common sense" application of the Charter, held that the term "everyone" was held only to apply to human individuals:

> That is, read as a whole, it appears to us that this section was intended to confer protection on a singularly human level. A plain, *common sense* reading of the phrase "Everyone has the right to life, liberty and security of the person" serves to underline the human element involved; only human beings can enjoy these rights. "Everyone" then, must be read in light of the rest of the section and defined to exclude corporations and other artificial entities incapable of enjoying life, liberty or security of the person, and include only human beings.[124]

The Court also held that the corollary of this proposition is that individuals representing corporations cannot invoke section 7 so as to grant the corporation rights which it does not possess.[125] This reasoning clearly ignores the practical realities and legal theories relating to how corporate decisions are made by individuals within the corporation.

This "common sense" approach to constitutional interpretation has been repeatedly invoked to prevent corporations from alleging violations of section 7 in situations where there were no penal proceedings. This has resulted in decisions that:

a)   sections 17(1-2) of the *Federal Courts Act* do not violate section 7 by preventing the addition of the crown as a co-defendant in the provincial courts,[126]

b)   corporations cannot avail themselves of the protection against self incrimination offered by this section,[127] and

---

[121] *Irwin Toy Ltd. v. Québec*, [1989] S.C.J. No. 36 at para. 94, [1989] 1 S.C.R. 927 (S.C.C.).

[122] *Ibid.*

[123] *Ibid.*, at paras. 94-95.

[124] *Ibid.*, at para. 96 [emphasis added].

[125] *Ibid.*

[126] *Dywidag Systems International, Canada Ltd. v. Zutphen Brothers Construction Ltd.*, [1990] S.C.J. No. 27 at para. 7, [1990] 1 S.C.R. 705 (S.C.C.).

[127] *British Columbia Securities Commission v. Branch*, [1995] S.C.J. No. 32 at paras. 36-37, [1995] 2 S.C.R. 3 (S.C.C.). See also, *Thomson Newspapers Ltd. v. Canada*, [1990] S.C.J. No. 23, [1990] 1 S.C.R. 425 (S.C.C.).

    c)   the release of a document under the *Access to Information Act* would not deprive individuals associated with the corporation of their rights to "life liberty and security of the person".[128]

In short, the so-called "common sense" interpretive approach was used by the Court to restrict the application of the Charter to corporations. This approach was very results-oriented and lacked a more intellectual approach to the application of the Charter. In the author's view, this approach failed to weigh the principles of Charter interpretation and the broad purpose of section 7 in the administration of justice.

7.5.3 A Purposive Approach

The need for a purposive approach to the application of the Charter is illustrated by the following questions. Should courts deny corporations constitutional rights because it is just "common sense", or should a "principled approach" that recognizes the value that is protected by the Charter right prevail over "common sense"; or is there a better approach? Moreover, is there any consistency in either approach as it applies to corporations? The Court certainly moved beyond *Irwin Toy* towards a purposive approach in the *Wholesale Travel* case. The Court allowed corporations to challenge legislation on the basis that it violated sections 7 and 11(d).[129] However, in doing so it did not explicitly state that this section applied to a corporate defendant; rather, to a penal provision that applied both to corporations and to individuals. The corporate defendant had standing to allege that the law violated both sections 7 and 11(d) of the Charter. The Court also ominously opined that the constitutional analysis might be "very different" if the statutory provision had applied to corporations alone.[130] Therefore, *Wholesale Travel* left section 7 and related due process rights of corporations in a state of uncertainty.

    There clearly is a need for a more consistent, credible approach to defining constitutional rights of corporations. This may be defined as a purposive approach; one that does consider the broad purposes of the Charter on the one hand, but does not, in the result, defy a common sense application of the text.

    The closest the Court has come to recognizing a purposive interpretation of the Charter to corporations is found in the *CIP* decision. *CIP* would suggest that whether a corporation may claim the protection of this right will depend on: "…whether it can establish that it has an interest falling within the scope of the guarantee, and one which accords with the purpose of that provision".[131]

---

[128] *Tridel Corp. v. Canada Mortgage and Housing Corp.*, [1996] F.C.J. No. 644, at paras. 85-87 (F.C.T.D.).

[129] *R. v. Wholesale Travel Inc.*, [1991] S.C.J. No. 79, [1991] 3 S.C.R. 154 (S.C.C.).

[130] *Ibid.*, at paras. 27-29.

[131] *R. v. CIP Inc.*, [1992] S.C.J. No. 34 at para. 22, [1992] 1 S.C.R. 843 (S.C.C.).

CIP is an interesting case for the Court to redefine and expand the rights of corporations under the Charter. First, it deals with a workplace injury to a worker that resulted in charges under Ontario's *Occupational Health and Safety Act.*[132] There was no individual defendant, simply a corporation, charged with a strict liability, regulatory offence of failing to provide a safe workplace which resulted in a workplace injury. The right asserted by the corporate defendant was a right to a trial within a reasonable period of time pursuant to section 11(b) of the Charter. In the seminal decision of the Court in *R. v. Askov,*[133] Justice Cory's primary concern was the "exquisite agony"[134] that an individual suffered in waiting to stand trial if there was unreasonable delay. In other words, section 11(b) was significantly an individual right or concern about access to justice in a timely fashion, more so than a right that would naturally or obviously apply to corporations. However, Justice Cory also identified other societal concerns of expeditious trials, availability of witnesses, proper provision of state resources to the administration of justice, in his section 11(b) analysis.

Although the section 11(b) jurisprudence has progressed beyond the *Askov* test, it is profound that the Court attempted to reconcile and indeed broaden the rights of corporations under the Charter under this *CIP* section 11(b) case. As Tollefson observes:

> at one level, *CIP* can be read as an attempt by the Court to survey and rationalize its corporate Charter rights jurisprudence. If indeed this was the intention, the exercise must be considered as an abject failure. ... the Court ultimately, and not without equivocation, seems to endorse a natural entity theory of the corporation, leaving its jurisprudence more confused and troubling than before.[135]

Notwithstanding the observations of Professor Tollefson, *CIP* is an effort by the Court to focus more on the purpose of the Charter right and Charter values generally, than the previous section 7 due process jurisprudence of the Court.

The Court goes on, in *CIP*, to recognize that by providing access to justice for corporations to argue Charter rights, a related access to justice is provided for individuals who make up the corporation, either as directors, officers, employees or investors, as well as individuals who, in future cases, may seem to rely upon the Charter jurisprudence relating to corporation rights to pursue their own rights. Therefore, *CIP* not only focuses on the purpose of Charter values but also the access of all persons, including individuals and corporations, to argue Charter values in particular circumstances, especially prosecutions with penal sanctions.

---

[132] R.S.O. 1990 c. O.1, as amended.

[133] [1990] S.C.J. No. 106, [1990] 2 S.C.R. 1199 (S.C.C.).

[134] *Ibid.*, at para. 43.

[135] Chris Tollefson, "Corporate Constitutional Rights and the Supreme Court of Canada" (1993 – 1994) 19 Queen's L.J. 309 at 343.

In *CIP* the Court established a test that requires a corporate defendant to prove through real evidence before the trial court, that it has suffered "irremediable prejudice"[136] in order to establish a contravention of the section 11(b) right to a trial within a reasonable period of time. In other words, the Court, while recognizing the purpose and value behind a trial within a reasonable period of time, also contextually interprets how the right ought to be applied to a corporation in a manner that is consistent with the variation and identity of an individual and a corporation. In other words, while respecting the purpose of section 11(b) of the Charter the Court also applied a certain amount of contextual common sense to the application of the constitutional right to a corporation.

Although *CIP* is not a panacea to reconciling the diverse and inconsistent jurisprudence of Charter rights of corporations, it is an important step in a direction for its consistency. *CIP* supports a broader application of Charter rights to corporations in a manner which decides the importance of access to justice, on a case-by-case basis, when corporations are before the courts as litigants, and in particular, defendants. It is an approach that considers, in a principled manner, both the purpose of the Charter generally, the Charter value in particular that is being considered in the case, as well as applies a measure of common sense or practical application of the Charter right in the context of providing access to justice. This approach, it is suggested, is a more useful, progressive and consistent approach in the application of the Charter to corporations.

7.6 CHARTER REMEDIES FOR CORPORATIONS

Charter remedies are important if the Charter rights are to be taken seriously. Expansion of corporate liability to all corporate "representatives" who commit offences, and "senior officers" who fail to prevent such crimes is now enshrined in law under Bill C-45. This not only highlights the personal exposure of individual to legal risk but also risks for the corporation. The broader approach to corporate accountability and liability under Bill C-45 ought to result in expanding and clarifying the role of Charter rights and remedies for corporations.

The Charter debates, regarding the application of constitutional rights to corporations, has provided little guidance on the Charter's application to corporations. This is not only regrettable, but also consistent with the Canadian judicial approach of minimizing the intention of the legislature as positive evidence of the interpretation of various legislative initiatives, including the Charter. Section 24 of the Charter provides for two types of remedies. Section 24(1), provides very general, remedial provisions on the following language: "Anyone whose rights or freedoms, as guaranteed by this Charter have been infringed or denied may apply to a court of competent jurisdiction

---

[136] *R. v. CIP Inc.*, [1992] S.C.J. No. 34 at para. 50, [1992] 1 S.C.R. 843 (S.C.C.).

to obtain such remedy as the court considers appropriate and just in the circumstances."

Depending on the type of Charter violation, courts have interpreted this provision broadly. Remedies for Charter violations have included orders by a court as follows:

1. Refusal to permit a witness to be called by the prosecution when the prosecutor has contravened the corporation and individual rights to not testify against themselves;[137]

2. The remedy of a stay of proceedings for a contravention of Crown obligations to investigate and prosecute fairly, and with due regard for full disclosure, and an absence of conflict of interest on the part of a Ministry of Labour engineer in the prosecution of a corporation;[138]

3. And the remedy requiring the prosecution to pay the legal costs of the corporate defendant for failure to provide full, complete and timely disclosure.[139]

A more specific remedial provision is provided in section 24(2) of the Charter. That provision states: "Where, in proceedings under subsection (1) a court concludes that evidence was obtained in a manner that infringed or denied any rights or freedoms guaranteed by this Charter, the evidence shall be excluded if it is established that, having regard to all the circumstances, the admission of it in the proceedings would bring the administration of justice into disrepute."

This sub-remedial provision of the Charter provides for the exclusion of evidence that has been illegally obtained. This will be the primary remedy for a court to consider when there has been a breach of the right to be free from unreasonable search and seizure under section 8 of the Charter. A review of the section 8 Charter discussion above, will indicate both when and how a corporation may argue, in a prosecution of a criminal or strict liability offence, that section 8 has been contravened. Once a contravention of section 8 has been determined, then there will be a further determination by the court if the administration of justice has been brought into disrepute by the manner in which the illegally obtained evidence was obtained. The corporation, just like an individual, is entitled to bring an application to have evidence excluded prior to or during a criminal or strict liability prosecution.

The Supreme Court has set down four overriding principles for the interpretation and application of the Charter and for fashioning Charter remedies. Those four principles, as set out by McLachlin C.J.C. of the Supreme Court, are as follows:

---

[137] Unreported decision of Ontario Provincial Court, Judge Harris dated December 20, 1989.

[138] Unreported decision of Justice of the Peace, B. Booth, confirmed on appeal, in *R. v. VTC Industrial Coating Ltd.*, [1996] O.J. No. 5478, 32 W.C.B. (2d) 7 (Ont. Prov. Div.), affirmed on appeal and digested as 38 W.C.B. (2d) 437.

[139] *R. v. 974649 Ontario Inc.*, [2001] S.C.J. No. 79, 206 D.L.R. (4th) 444 (S.C.C.).

First, s. 24(1), like all Charter provisions, commands a broad and purposive interpretation ... moreover, it is remedial, and hence benefits from the general rule of statutory interpretation that accords remedial statutes a "large and liberal" interpretation ... the language of this provision appears to confer the widest possible discretion on a court to craft remedies for violations of Charter rights.[140]

The second proposition flows from the first: s. 24 must be interpreted in a way that achieves its purpose of upholding Charter rights by providing effective remedies for their breach ... through the provision of an enforcement mechanism, s. 24(1) "Above all else ensures that the Charter will be a vibrant and vigorous instrument for the perception of the rights and freedoms of Canadians."[141]

The Third proposition guiding the interpretation of section 24 is that subs. (1) and (2) must be read together to create a harmonious interpretation. The conjunction of the two subsections, one dealing with remedies in general and the other dealing with exclusion of evidence that would bring the administration of justice into disrepute, suggests that both are concerned with providing remedies for Charter breaches ... Thus this phrase must be interpreted in a way that produces just and workable results for both the grant of general remedies and the exclusion of evidence in particular.[142]

The final proposition is that s. 24 should not be read so broadly that it endows courts and tribunals with powers that they were never intended to exercise. The jurisdictions of Canada's various courts and tribunals are fixed by Parliament and the legislatures, not by judges ... Legislative intention is the guiding light in identifying courts of competent jurisdiction.[143]

With the Chief Justice of Canada's words in mind, since corporations play an important and integral part of Canadian society, there is a sound basis for corporations to seek and obtain Charter remedies, together with individuals. To achieve a Charter remedy, one must first identify a Charter right that has been contravened or violated. This chapter has carefully reviewed the development of Charter rights by corporations, in court decisions, as a result of the absence of the framers of the Charter addressing the issue in the Charter debates. However, as mentioned above, Bill C-45 has changed and enhanced the risk of criminal liability of organizations, including corporations. Therefore, organizations and corporations, as well as individuals, should be free to look to the Charter for fair and equitable treatment in Canadian law. Where various Charter rights have been contravened by state regulators, against organizations, including corporations, then there is no sound reason or logic that would deny corporations equal access to Charter remedies.

---

[140] *Ibid.*, para. 18.
[141] *Ibid.*, para. 19.
[142] *Ibid.*, para. 21.
[143] *Ibid.*, para. 22.

Chapter 8

DEFENCES TO CRIMINAL AND STRICT LIABILITY OFFENCES

8.1 INTRODUCTION TO DEFENCES

A corporate accused has the right to defend the allegations with which it has been charged. It may defend the charges that it has committed an offence just like an individual accused. The prosecution process provides that the corporate accused has the right to make answer and defence. A defence to a charge of a criminal or strict liability offence is any legal principle or rule that provides a justification or excuse for the commission of the offence. A corporation that is charged with an offence may raise any defence known in law to answer the charges that it is facing in court. Once the prosecution has called its evidence, filed exhibits and put in its case, it remains open to defence counsel for a corporation to call evidence and make argument to raise any and all defences available to the corporate defendant. This chapter deals with defences to criminal and strict liability charges available to corporations.

The availability and nature of a defence largely relates to the nature of the charge. For example, some strict liability offences under environmental and occupational health and safety legislation explicitly provide for the defence of due diligence. Similarly, some provisions of the *Criminal Code*[1] that apply to corporations also have various limiting factors, and therefore explicit or implicit defences in the actual wording of the offence. It is always open for a corporate defendant to argue that the prosecution has not proven the offence beyond a reasonable doubt. Although, strictly speaking, this is not considered a defence in law, it will be a complete answer to the charge that the Crown has not proven the case beyond a reasonable doubt and the charge will be dismissed. In the prosecution of corporations and individuals, a distinction has developed in the jurisprudence between a defence that is a *justification* and a defence that is an *excuse*.

Generally speaking, a *justification* will challenge the wrongfulness of the action that technically may constitute the offence. A justification in law, which is a complete defence to charges, is supported by the theory that the accused should not be punished in the circumstances because the *justification* negates the charge. As the Supreme Court has said, "... the values of

---

[1]   R.S.C. 1985, c. C-46 [hereinafter the "Code"].

society, indeed of the criminal law itself, are being better promoted by disobeying a given statute than by observing it."[2] On the other hand, an *excuse* is a defence to a criminal or strict liability offence that relies upon, "a realistic assessment of human weakness, recognizing that a liberal and humane criminal law cannot hold people to the strict obedience of laws in emergency situations where normal human instincts, whether of self-preservation or altruism, overwhelmingly impel disobedience".[3] Whether a justification or an excuse, both will answer and defend against the charge.

The majority of the jurisprudence regarding the law of defences under the Code deals with individuals, and not corporations, charged with offences. However, in strict liability offences, many of the charges are against corporations and there is broader jurisprudence regarding defences for corporations. In the pre-Bill C-45 era, a corporation charged with any offence could raise issues with respect to the alleged illegal conduct being the action of an employee who is not a directing mind of the corporation. Further, a corporate defendant could argue that the employee committing the offence, if a directing mind, was acting outside of their assigned field of responsibility or operation. In any event, since Bill C-45[4] has now codified the elements of the criminal offence committed by a corporation, much of the jurisprudence with respect to defences available to corporations under the Code are now of more historical than legal significance.

This chapter is divided into headings dealing with defences to criminal charges and defences to strict liability charges. Although criminal and strict liability offences are similar, there are different defences available. Since there is no requirement to prove a requisite mental intent for strict liability offences, the Supreme Court in *R. v. Sault Ste. Marie*[5] established the defence of due diligence. This is a major distinction in the law of defences for corporations. There may in fact be more defences available to corporations charged with strict liability offences than criminal offences. Therefore, a separate review of defences for strict liability offences from charges under the Code is appropriate and necessary.

8.2 DEFENCES TO CRIMINAL OFFENCES

8.2.1 Procedural Defences

Procedural defences provide a complete defence to criminal charges, and in many cases, strict liability charges as well. They are identified as procedural defences because the defence involves a concern or complaint by the defence about how the investigatory, prosecutorial or trial process has affected

---

2   *R. v. Perka*, [1984] S.C.J. No. 40, 14 C.C.C. (3d) 385 at 396-397 (S.C.C.).
3   *Ibid.*, at 398 (C.C.C.).
4   Bill C-45, *An Act to Amend the Criminal Code (Criminal Liability of Organizations)*, 2003, c. 21.
5   [1978] S.C.J. No. 59, 40 C.C.C. (2d) 353 (S.C.C.).

the defendant. The result of a successful procedural defence is that there is a stay, or legal stoppage of the prosecution, rather than a dismissal of the charges. The effect of a stay, for all practical purposes, is the same as a finding of "not guilty" and a dismissal of the charges. However, if a procedural defence has been resolved in favour of the corporate defendant, it will not have the satisfaction of knowing that its charges have been fully dealt with on the merits and the charges dismissed.

The first type of procedural defence is a request for a judicial stay based on the contravention or violation of the *Charter of Rights and Freedoms*.[6] The rights of corporations to pursue Charter remedies are discussed in Chapter 7 of this text. The corporation must establish that it has standing to raise a Charter issue, since not all Charter rights are clearly available to corporate defendants, as they are to individual defendants. Charter remedies are available under section 24 of the Charter, which have at times resulted in a stay of criminal, or even strict liability offences, when Charter rights of the corporation have been infringed.

Other procedural defences that are available to corporations include but are not necessarily limited to time limitations, entrapment, the rule against multiple convictions, *res judicata* and issue *estoppel* and abuse of process. These procedural defences, except the defences of abuse of process, are addressed in this section. Abuse of process is covered in the following section.

The procedural defence of a limitation period is only available for a criminal charge prosecuted on summary conviction. In such a case, the prosecution must be commenced against the corporation not more than six months after the point in time where the subject matter of the alleged defence arose.[7] The Code does not provide for a limitation period for an indictable offence or when the Crown chooses, in the case of a hybrid offence, to proceed by way of indictment. Therefore, for example, a prosecution for criminal negligence causing injury or death, an indictable offence, has no limitation period.

The procedural defence of entrapment is based on the idea that when the design, planning and commission of an offence is undertaken by a law enforcement official, then an accused may not be successfully prosecuted. Early development of the entrapment procedural defence is recognized by the U.S. Supreme Court.[8] A thorough discussion of the entrapment defence was provided by the Supreme Court in *R. v. Amato*[9] in 1982. *Amato* was charged with trafficking in drugs and was charged when an undercover police officer and an informer had repeatedly and persistently requested drugs from the individual appellant. A strong dissenting decision by Estey J., high-

---

[6]   Part I of the *Constitution Act, 1982*, being Schedule B to the *Canada Act, 1982* (U.K.), 1982, c. 11 [hereinafter the "Charter"].

[7]   *Criminal Code*, s. 721(2).

[8]   *Sorrells v. United States*, 287 U.S. 435 (S.C. 1932).

[9]   [1982] S.C.J. No. 72, [1982] 2 S.C.R. 418 (S.C.C.).

lighted the origins of the doctrine from common law recognition, and now enshrined in section 7(3) of the Code, that criminal courts are permitted to adopt common-law defences. Justice Estey went on to set out three principles that characterize entrapment: first, that the police instigate an offence through their conduct to ensnare the accused; second, that the police scheme for the purpose to obtain evidence for the prosecution of the accused for the instigation of a crime; and third, that the crime was induced through deceit, fraud, trickery, reward or other means.[10]

The procedural defence found in the *R. v. Kienapple*[11] case, stands for the proposition that a defendant cannot be convicted twice for the same offence, or substantially the same offence. This procedural defence is normally applied at the end of a trial, and after a conviction of a corporate defendant on one count, which is either identical to or substantially the same as a second or third count, resulting in the other count or counts being stayed. This defence is normally described as the rule against multiple convictions.

The procedural defence of *res judicata* is based on the general fairness principle that if the legal issue has already been clearly decided by a judicial proceeding, that the same issue or matter cannot be re-litigated, or be the basis for a further prosecution. The principle of *res judicata* has a number of applications, including the more narrow procedural defence of issue *estoppel*. Issue *estoppel* may be raised as a procedural defence, for example, where the same point of law had been determined at a previous criminal trial, and therefore the prosecutor was not permitted to make allegations in a second trial, that were inconsistent with that previous determination.[12] The American use of the phrase "double jeopardy" is part of the Canadian legal principle of *res judicata*. The elements of this defence include the previous legal determination was final, that the previous judicial proceeding had appropriate jurisdiction to deal with the issue, that the same legal decision or issue is in question in the present case as was the live issue in the previous case, and the parties in the previous case are the same as the parties in the current case.[13]

8.2.2 Abuse of Process

The procedural defence of abuse of process is best understood as the authority that courts have to govern their own process and prevent prosecutions to abuse judicial process. A prosecution may be stayed if the judicial decision-maker is persuaded that there has been a breach of acceptable standards by the prosecuting authorities. The accused will benefit from successfully arguing that there has been an abuse of process since it will result in the charges being stayed. In that respect, it may be a viable strategy of a corporate ac-

---

[10]   *Ibid.*

[11]   [1974] S.C.J. No. 76, [1975] 1 S.C.R. 729 (S.C.C.).

[12]   *R. v. Wright*, [1965] O.J. No. 985, 45 C.R. 38 (Ont. C.A.).

[13]   *R. v. Duhamel*, [1984] S.C.J. No. 58, [1984] 2 S.C.R. 555 (S.C.C.).

cused to raise an abuse of process argument before or during a prosecution. Abuse of process is the right to be free from unlawful, inappropriate conduct of government officials and prosecutors in the course of an investigation or prosecution.

The legal test to make out an allegation of abuse of process as a procedural defence to charges was first clearly set out by the Supreme Court in *R. v. Jewitt*.[14] Chief Justice Dickson wrote a unanimous decision that a trial judge, in the trial of an offence, had residual power or authority and discretion to end proceedings in a case of abuse of process. Chief Justice Dickson specifically adopted the conclusions of Dubin J.A. of the Court of Appeal for Ontario in *R. v. Young*.[15]

The legal test for abuse of process can be found in the Supreme Court decision of *R. v. Amato*.[16] Justice Estey said a prosecution should be prevented on the basis of abuse of process "where the executive action leading to the charge and its prosecution is offensive to the principles on which the administration of justice is conducted by the courts."[17] In *R. v. Young*, Dubin J.A. said that there is an evolving nature to the legal test of abuse of process where:

> ... compelling an accused to stand trial would violate those fundamental principles of justice which underlie the community's sense of fair play and decency and to prevent the abuse of a court's process through oppressive or vexatious proceedings.
>
> It is a power, however, of special application which can only be exercised in the clearest of cases.[18]

In *R. v. Conway*,[19] L'Heureux-Dubé J. confirmed "that courts must have the respect and support of the community in order that the administration of criminal justice may properly fulfil its function."[20]

Chief Justice McLachlin further defined the test for abuse of process in *R. v. Scott*,[21] when she said:

> In summary, abuse of process may be established where: (1) the proceedings are oppressive or vexatious; and, (2) violate the fundamental principles of justice underlying the community's sense of fair play and decency. The concepts of oppressiveness and vexatiousness underlie the interest of the accused in a fair trial. But the doctrine evokes as well the public interest in a fair and just trial process and the proper administration of justice.[22]

---

[14]   [1985] S.C.J. No. 53, 20 D.L.R. (4th) 651 (S.C.C.).

[15]   [1984] O.J. No. 3229, 46 O.R. (2d) 520 (Ont. C.A.).

[16]   [1982] S.C.J. No. 72, 140 D.L.R. (3d) 405 (S.C.C.).

[17]   *Ibid.*, at 442 (D.L.R.).

[18]   [1984] O.J. No. 3229 at para. 88, 46 O.R. (2d) 520 (Ont. C.A.).

[19]   [1989] S.C.J. No. 70, [1989] 1 S.C.R. 1659 (S.C.C.).

[20]   *Ibid.*, at para. 8.

[21]   [1990] S.C.J. No. 132, [1990] 3 S.C.R. 979 (S.C.C.).

[22]   *Ibid.*, at para. 70.

Therefore, in an argument to advance the defence of abuse of process, one is best advised to satisfy both aspects of the test set out by McLachlin C.J.C. above. How this legal test will be established on the evidence is largely to be determined on the facts of each case. The examples of abuse of process, delineated later in this chapter, will review the scope of the meaning and application of the legal test.

8.2.2.1 *Forum and Proof of Abuse of Process*

The proper forum to raise an abuse of process defence was once considered to be within the exclusive jurisdiction of a superior court. In *R. v. Jewitt*,[23] however, Dickson C.J.C. referred to the power of all trial courts to effectively deal with matters relating to abuse of process. The exception to this trend is where the trial is not within reach or it is the trial process or decision-maker that is the subject of the concern.[24] Therefore, the proper forum for the application for an appropriate remedy for an abuse of process is now generally considered to be the trial court; either in a pre-trial motion[25] or at trial.[26]

The onus of proof in an application for abuse of process is on the accused. It is generally agreed that the onus of establishing that there has been an abuse of process, of whatever kind, lies with the person or party that makes the assertion. This was accepted by Estey J. in *R. v. Amato*.[27]

The burden of proof in an application for abuse of process is on a balance of probabilities, a civil standard. It has been suggested that this burden of proof should be modified by the requirement that a court only make a finding of an abuse of process in the clearest of cases. Courts will require the assertion of a violation of the Charter to be proven on a balance of probabilities. A compromise between the burden of proof for abuse of process and Charter case law was attempted to be struck by Barry J. in *R. v. Kenny*.[28] In that decision, the justice said:

> I believe that the reference to the "clearest of cases" applies to determining the proper remedy as opposed to determining whether or not there has been a violation of the Charter. I accept the submission of defence counsel that, whether the argument is based on common law abuse of process or abuse under the Charter, to establish the abuse, the accused should merely have to establish, on a balance of probabilities, that to compel him to stand trial in the circumstances of the case would violate those fundamental principles of justice which underlie the community sense of fair play and decency or would be otherwise oppressive.[29]

---

23   [1985] S.C.J. No. 53, 20 D.L.R. (4th) 651 (S.C.C.).

24   See *R. v. Rahey*, [1987] S.C.J. No. 23, 39 D.L.R. (4th) 481 (S.C.C.).

25   *R. v. VTC Industrial Coatings Ltd.*, [1995] O.J. No. 4978 (Ont. Prov. Div.).

26   *R. v. Mardave Construction (1990) Ltd.*, (1993), 13 L.W. 1329-009 (Ont. Prov. Div.).

27   [1982] S.C.J. No. 72, 140 D.L.R. (3d) 405 (S.C.C.).

28   [1991] N.J. No. 253, 68 C.C.C. (3d) 36 (Nfld. T.D.).

29   *Ibid.*, at 45 (C.C.C.).

8.2.2.2   Abuse of Process and the Charter

The Charter, as part of the *Constitution Act, 1982*,[30] is part of the fundamental law of Canada. The law of abuse of process is part of the common law regarding the due administration of justice in our legal system. One of the many instances in which the common law and the Charter overlap is the law of abuse of process.

In *R. v. Young*,[31] the Court of Appeal for Ontario appears to have treated the common law doctrine of abuse of process as having been entirely in section 7 of the Charter. The Saskatchewan Court of Appeal has specifically held that the doctrine of abuse of process is subsumed in section 7 in the sense that a finding of an abuse of process would necessarily mean that an accused's rights under section 7 would have been infringed without any justification under section 1 of the Charter.[32] The issue of whether or not the doctrine of abuse of process is subsumed in section 7 of the Charter, unfortunately, was not decided. However, the Court did make the following comment regarding that issue:

> The parties to this appeal were agreed that the common law doctrine of abuse of process was now subsumed in s. 7. The trial judge accepted this proposition as did all the members of the Court of Appeal although in neither of the courts below was there much analysis of the relationship between the two.[33]

This is a problem for a corporate accused who generally is regarded as having no section 7 rights. The Charter is integral to the administration of justice, just as the common law doctrine of abuse of process. Therefore, it is reasonable to expect that the doctrine of abuse of process would be subsumed into the broader constitutional rights of the Charter. Initial support for this view is found in the decision of the Supreme Court in *Reference re Motor Vehicle Act (British Columbia) s. 94(2)*.[34] In that decision, Lamer C.J.C. stated:

> Sections 8 to 14 [of the Charter] address specific deprivations of the "right" to life, liberty and security of the person in breach of the principles of fundamental justice, and as such, violations of s. 7. They are therefore illustrative of the meaning, in criminal or penal law, of "principles of fundamental justice"; they represent principles which have been recognized by the common law, the international conventions and by the very fact of entrenchment in the Charter, as essential elements of a system for the administration of justice which is founded upon a belief in the dignity and worth of the human person and the rule of law.[35]

---

[30]   Being Schedule B to the *Canada Act, 1982*, (U.K.), 1982, c. 11.

[31]   [1984] O.J. No. 3229, 46 O.R. (2d) 520 (Ont. C.A.).

[32]   *R. v. Keyowski*, [1986] S.J. No. 137, 49 Sask. R. 64 (Sask. C.A.), affd [1998] S.C.J. No. 28, [1988] 1 S.C.R. 657 (S.C.C.).

[33]   *Ibid.*, at para. 5.

[34]   [1985] S.C.J. No. 73, [1985] 2 S.C.R. 486 (S.C.C.).

[35]   *Ibid.*, at para. 61.

It remained to be seen how far the courts would relate the two areas of law until the Supreme Court decision of *R. v. O'Connor.*[36] In *O'Connor*, the accused was charged with a number of sexual offences alleged to have occurred when he was a priest at a native residential school. The offences allegedly occurred approximately 25 years prior to the trial and involved former students of the school. Approximately one month before the trial was to begin, it was adjourned at the request of the accused because of a delay in disclosure of certain material by the Crown. Then there was an application for the records of the therapists, psychologists and psychiatrists by the defence, but they were not given notice of the application. The application was granted and an order of disclosure was made. After the commencement of the trial, it became clear that not all of the material had been disclosed that had been ordered disclosed. The Supreme Court described the conduct of the Crown as shoddy and inappropriate, but not in violation of the accused's right to make full answer and defence. However, in respect of the issue of abuse of process and the Charter, it clarified the relationship between the doctrine of abuse of process and the Charter.

Justice L'Heureux-Dubé reviewed this important issue and wrote:

> I recognize that this court has consistently, albeit implicitly, considered abuse of process separately from the Charter ...

> I also recognize that, despite these strong parallels, the common law and Charter analyses have often been kept separate because of the differing onus of proof upon the accused under the two regimes ... It is important to remember, however, that even if a violation of s. 7 is proved on a balance of probabilities, the court must still determine what remedy is just and appropriate under s. 24(1). The power granted in s. 24(1) is in terms discretionary, and it is by no means automatic that a stay of proceedings should be granted for a violation of s. 7. On the contrary, I would think that the remedy of a judicial stay of proceedings would be appropriate under s. 24(1) only in the clearest of cases. In this way, the threshold for obtaining a stay of proceedings remains, under the Charter as under the common law doctrine of abuse of process, the "clearest of cases".

> As a general rule, however, there is no utility in maintaining two distinct approaches to abusive conduct ...

> The principles of fundamental justice both reflect and accommodate the nature of the common law doctrine of abuse of process. Although I am willing to concede that the focus of the common law doctrine of abuse of process has traditionally been more on the protection of the integrity of the judicial system whereas the focus of the Charter has traditionally been more on the protection of individual rights, I believe that the overlap between the two has now become so significant that there is no real utility in maintaining two distinct analytical regimes. We should not invite schizophrenia into the law.[37]

---

[36] [1995] S.C.J. No. 98, [1995] 4 S.C.R. 411 (S.C.C.).

[37] *Ibid.*, at paras. 67-68, 70-71.

Justice L'Heureux-Dubé then provided a summary of the relationship between the common law doctrine of abuse of process and section 7 of the Charter:

> Where life, liberty or security of the person is engaged in a judicial proceeding, and it is proved on a balance of probabilities that the Crown's failure to make proper disclosure to the defence has impaired the accused's ability to make full answer and defence, a violation of s. 7 will have been made out. In such circumstances, the court must fashion a just and appropriate remedy, pursuant to s. 24(1). Although the remedy for such a violation will typically be a disclosure order and adjournment, there may be some extreme cases where the prejudice to the accused's ability to make full answer and defence or to the integrity of the justice system is irremediable. In those "clearest of cases", a stay of proceedings will be appropriate.[38]

8.2.2.3   Entrapment

The combined effect of the decisions in *Jewitt*[39] and *Amato*[40] has been to recognize a lawful excuse for the commission of an offence when there is conduct by law enforcement authorities that is fundamentally incompatible with the due administration of justice. The procedural defence of entrapment, discussed above, is one that prevents a person from being convicted when his or her offence has been directed, caused or instigated by the conduct of law enforcement officials. In *Amato*, Estey J. considered the two positions that support the concept of entrapment. First, there is the position that entrapment should be viewed as a positive substantive law defence. Second, there is the position that entrapment should be viewed as part of the doctrine of abuse of process. Justice Estey concluded that entrapment must be seen as part of the second position: such conduct constitutes abuse of process. The government's instigation of an offence, or entrapment, operates as a bar to proceedings not because the elements of the offence have not been made out, but because a court should refuse to condone such activity and conduct on the part of government law enforcement officials.

8.2.2.4   Promise Not to Prosecute

Corporate accused may raise the procedural defence of a breach of an undertaking not to prosecute. It appears to be a well-settled principle that if the Crown gives an express undertaking or promise not to prosecute and subsequently breaches that undertaking or promise, then there is a basis to prevent the prosecution on the grounds of abuse of process. The rationale in support of this was espoused by Krever J. in *R. v. Crneck*,[41] when he said:

---

[38]   *Ibid.*, at paras. 83.
[39]   [1985] S.C.J. No. 53, 20 D.L.R. (4th) 651 (S.C.C.).
[40]   [1982] S.C.J. No. 72, 140 D.L.R. (3d) 405 (S.C.C.).
[41]   [1980] O.J. No. 3724, 116 D.L.R. (3d) 675 (Ont. H.C.J.).

... agreements made by a representative of the Attorney-General after consideration and consultation with experienced police officers should — because the representative symbolically and in reality is the embodiment of our society's idea of fairness in the administration of justice — should, I say, be carried out.[42]

Another case of a breach by the Crown of an undertaking not to prosecute was the decision of the Court of Appeal for Ontario against a corporation, in *R. v. Abitibi Paper Co.*[43] In that case, the accused corporation operated a paper mill and began discussions with a senior official of the Ontario Ministry of the Environment respecting a program for the improvement of its secondary effluent system. The objective was to eliminate or at least reduce the pollution of a local river. In dialogue with government officials, satisfaction was expressed with the progress of the program. The company was led to believe that it would not be prosecuted. One month later, the company was charged with 22 counts of violating the *Environmental Protection Act*. The trial judge stayed the charges for abuse of process. The case was appealed to the Court of Appeal. The Court of Appeal upheld the trial judge's decision and affirmed the validity of abuse of process for the breach of a Crown undertaking not to prosecute the corporation.

In a case similar to the decision in *Abitibi Paper Co.* a court found that there was an abuse of process when an implied undertaking not to prosecute was held out by government officials.[44] When Northwood Pulp Timber Ltd. expanded its mill, it was advised by the Ministry of the Environment that it did not require a permit to discharge sludge into the nearby river. In an annual review, the ministry singled out the company for the sludge release problem. After some demands by and negotiations with the ministry, the company was formally advised that it had a year to cease discharges into the river. During that year, the company ran a pilot project to explore the possibility of processing the sludge through the primary clarifier. The company worked diligently towards a solution even though the technology was very limited in this area. When it became apparent that the pilot project had not worked out and the year had expired, the company was charged. The court held that the charges amounted to an abuse of process, on a balance of probabilities, and the charges were stayed.

A further example of an undertaking not to prosecute arose in *R. v. Todglen Construction Ltd.*[45] The court stayed the charges when an inspector was found to have entered into an undertaking not to prosecute the accused and the inspector subsequently unilaterally revoked the undertaking and commenced prosecution. The Ministry of Labour inspector had, in the course of an investigation under the applicable health and safety legislation,

---

[42]   *Ibid.*, at para. 22.

[43]   [1979] O.J. No. 4246, 99 D.L.R. (3d) 333 (Ont. C.A.).

[44]   *R. v. Northwood Pulp Timber Ltd.*, [1992] B.C.J. No. 2690, 9 C.E.L.R. (N.S.) 289 (B.C. Prov. Ct.).

[45]   (1994), 13 L.W. 1343-003 (Ont. Prov. Div.).

asked a project superintendent for a statement. The superintendent expressed some concern about the potential liability of his employer and himself. The inspector gave an assurance that neither the superintendent nor his employer would be charged if the superintendent co-operated and provided a written statement. The superintendent provided the statement. Several months later, in breach of his undertaking, the inspector swore out an Information against the employer/contractor of the superintendent. The court held that there had been a breach of the undertaking that had been given by the inspector and that this amounted to oppressive conduct which would offend the community's sense of decency and fair play. The court then went on to say:

> The only question left is whether a stay of proceedings is the remedy. In *Ke-yawski v. Her Majesty the Queen*, the Supreme Court of Canada said that a stay of proceedings to remedy an abuse of process is available where compelling an accused to stand trial would violate those fundamental principles of justice which underline the community's sense of fair play and decency, or where the proceedings are oppressive or vexatious.
>
> In my opinion this is a case of abuse of process and the remedy is a stay of proceedings.[46]

The charges were stayed with an order of $51,000 in legal costs assessed against the Ministry of Labour. The authority of a trial justice to make an award of costs was resolved in *R. v. 974649 Ontario Inc.*[47]

8.2.2.5   *Inappropriate Advantage in Civil Claim*

It is an abuse of process to use criminal or *quasi*-criminal prosecution to collect or gain advantage in a civil claim or debt. The commencement of charges against a person will normally be held to be an abuse of process if the dominant purpose of the prosecution is to collect payment or gain advantage in a civil debt.[48] This applies to an individual or a corporation. In *R. v. Waugh*,[49] where the court said:

> In order to stay criminal proceedings on the ground that they were commenced to effect collection of a civil debt or to enforce some other civil remedy it must clearly be shown that such was the sole and only purpose for their commencement.[50]

There are additional reasons to suggest that a threat to commence a criminal or *quasi*-criminal prosecution to collect a civil claim may amount to an abuse of process. For example, if there is an outstanding civil claim arising from a construction project, there is good reason to conclude that it would be an abuse of process for one contractor to threaten to call in the

---

[46]   *Ibid.*, at 4, 5.

[47]   [1995] O.J. No. 2330, 101 C.C.C. (3d) 48 (Ont. Gen. Div.), revd [1998] O.J. No. 4735 (Ont. C.A.), affd [2001] S.C.J. No. 79 (S.C.C.).

[48]   *R. v. Sparks*, [1981] O.J. No. 3308, (1982), 65 C.C.C. (2d) 476 (Ont. Co. Ct.).

[49]   [1985] N.S.J. No. 315, 68 N.S.R. (2d) 247 (N.C.S.C.).

[50]   *Ibid.*, at para. 42.

Ministry of Labour and have charges laid under the applicable health and safety legislation as a means to compel payment or to collect the debt.

In *R. v. Leroux*,[51] the accused was charged with using false pretences for obtaining the complainant's signature on a promissory note. The complainant made some effort to negotiate repayment. When the efforts to settle the matter failed, the complainant went to the police and swore out an Information leading to the accused's arrest. The complainant testified at trial that he did not want to take the criminal proceedings against the accused. He had only done so because the accused had not offered a reasonable settlement. The accused was convicted at trial, but appealed. On appeal the accused was acquitted on the grounds that he had been charged under the wrong section of the Code, but the court went on to say:

> It was abundantly clear from the evidence of the complainant that he was endeavouring to obtain repayment of the amount which he had been compelled to pay to the bank upon his promissory note. He admitted quite frankly that he tried to get the matter settled in some way by the accused, either by partial payment or by security or otherwise, and that he told the accused that if he did not get it settled he would swear out a warrant for his arrest. In effect, the complainant, by threatening prosecution, endeavoured to obtain payment of a debt. What was done in this case amounted to an abuse of process of the Court and should not be tolerated ... The criminal law was not enacted for the assistance of persons seeking to collect civil debts.[52]

In a more recent case,[53] originating from the Northwest Territories, the accused found itself charged with fraud for keeping a false log in an attempt to reduce payments owing to the complainant. The police laid charges and advised the complainant not to contact the accused. Contrary to the direction of the police, the complainant made contact and offered to try to have the charges dropped if the accused would pay the amount owing. The accused did not accept the so-called offer to settle. The complainant did not disclose the settlement offer to the police or to the prosecutor. The complainant testified at the trial of the accused that the sole interest in the charges was to obtain the money that it believed was due. The court stayed the charges and held that the case amounted to an attempt to collect a civil debt. The court went on to say that the Crown was under responsibility to enter a stay of proceedings upon learning all the facts even if the police were unaware of the underlying motives for the prosecution.

In *R. v. Bristow*,[54] the accused was charged with theft over $1,000. The accused had received money from an investor but used it for his personal purposes and therefore had committed the *prima facie* offence of theft. The accused had been threatened by the complainants prior to their contacting

---

51   [1928] O.J. No. 45, [1928] 3 D.L.R. 688 (Ont. C.A.).

52   *Ibid.*, at para. 23.

53   *R. v. Inuvik Coastal Airways Ltd.*, [1983] N.W.T.J. No. 40, 51 A.R. 115 (N.W.T.S.C.).

54   [1990] B.C.J. No. 2218, 11 W.C.B. (2d) 127 (B.C.S.C.).

the police and had been told that he would go to jail if he refused to sign documents designed to exclude him from a company. The accused did sign the documents, but the complainants went to the police anyway in order to pre-empt a civil claim by the accused. The court ultimately decided, upon a review of all the evidence, that the prosecution was in essence a private prosecution whose dominant purpose was to obtain a civil benefit.

Finally, this area of abuse of process impacts on the situation where a private prosecution is initiated and advanced by a private citizen rather than by a Crown Attorney. For example, if a private prosecution is commenced and if the dominant purpose for the prosecution is the collection of an outstanding civil debt, the prosecution may be stayed as an abuse of process. The nature of the private prosecution, especially where the complainant also becomes the prosecuting party, would increase the likelihood of an improper motive being easily established against the complainant. Private prosecutions may not be properly initiated under the applicable health and safety legislation for the dominant purpose of collecting or avoiding a civil debt.

8.2.2.6   Unfair Selective Prosecution

A corporation that is unfairly and selectively prosecuted by manifestly unfair means or for oppressive reasons, may be able to argue that there is an abuse of process. This concept was considered in the case of *R. v. Miles of Music Ltd.*[55] In that case, the accused was a disc jockey who was being prosecuted for copyright infringement in an apparent effort to establish a test case under federal copyright legislation. The relevant authorities had misled the accused into believing that no licence was available to carry out his activities. This occurred when there was a pending investigation. Subsequently, the authorities commenced a prosecution of the accused for carrying out his business activities without such a licence. A police raid was carried out on the accused, and all of his tapes were seized, effectively putting him out of business.

The trial court held that the search and seizure was an abuse of process and that the accused had been unfairly singled out for prosecution. At the Court of Appeal, the majority disagreed with the trial judge's decision. In a strong dissent, however, Blair J. roundly criticized the prosecution and described it as oppressive. The majority of the court concluded that this was not the "clearest of cases" in which the doctrine of abuse of process should be applied.

In *R. v. Northwood Pulp Timber Ltd.*,[56] the accused company operated a large pulp mill with two pulping process lines near a major city. Water for the process was taken from the river but was treated to remove sediments before it was used. The sludge from this treatment was discharged back into

---

[55]   [1989] O.J. No. 391, 74 O.R. (2d) 518 (Ont. C.A.).

[56]   [1992] B.C.J. No. 2690, 9 C.E.L.R. (N.S.) 289 (B.C. Prov. Ct.), affd [1995] B.C.J. No. 2380 (B.C.S.C.).

the river. In 1988, the Ministry of the Environment required the company to find an alternative to discharging the sludge into the river. While two lines were shut down, the treatment system malfunctioned and effluent exceeding the toxicity limits of the accused's permit entered the river. The Ministry of the Environment investigated and charged the company with three counts of violating the environmental legislation. The facts at trial revealed that the accused company was the only pulp mill in the province required to deal with the problem, that there was no known technology to deal with the problem, that the standard for the particular effluent was set lower than the influent, and that the accused had performed its own investigation without finding a solution. The court said:

> The accused argues that it has been singled out by a regulatory agency, has been assigned the task of developing a solution to a complex problem in a limited time, has made diligent efforts in good faith to find and implement a solution, and has proceeded with a proposal solution on the basis of a pilot project with the full knowledge of a regulatory agency ... In my opinion, the conduct of the ministry can be characterized as unfair and oppressive.[57]

The court also commented that the defence of due diligence can exist at the same time as an abuse of process for an oppressively selective prosecution. On the basis of the finding of the abuse of process and the second branch of the defence of due diligence, the court stayed the charge in question.

In a similar case, charges were laid for violation of an environmental statute.[58] A company had engaged in the construction of a culvert crossing a stream. As a result, deleterious substances were released into the stream. The company had a permit for the purpose of constructing the culvert. However, it was not legally possible to construct the culvert without violation of another statute, the one for which the company was charged. At trial there was a conviction. On appeal, the appellant raised for the first time the defence of abuse of process. The court, in staying the charges on appeal, stated:

> In circumstances such as this, it is in my view not fair and just that the appellant should be required to face a charge of having committed an offence by doing the very act which it was permitted to do by the same administering authority.[59]

8.2.2.7   Crown Misconduct

Crown prosecutor misconduct towards an accused in a prosecution should be sufficient to support a finding of abuse of process. Prosecutors have special authority and responsibility to uphold principles of fair play and decency in the administration of justice. An accused, whether represented by a lawyer or not, should be reasonably free from fear of intimidation by the prosecutor.

---

[57]   *Ibid.*, at 303 (C.E.L.R. (N.S.)).

[58]   *R. v. Boise Cascade Canada Ltd.*, [1994] O.J. No. 1309, 14 C.E.L.R. (N.S.) 93 (Ont. Gen. Div.), revd [1995] O.J. No. 1977, 24 O.R. (3d) 483 (Ont. C.A.).

[59]   *R. v. Boise Cascade Canada Ltd.*, [1995] O.J. No. 1977 at para. 10 (Ont. C.A.).

This flows from the traditional and continuing view of the prosecutor as more than a mere advocate and partisan player in a legal tug-of-war to obtain a conviction.

This duty not to intimidate an accused was set out over 56 years ago by the Supreme Court when Rand J. said:

> It cannot be over-emphasized that the purpose of a criminal prosecution is not to obtain a Conviction, it is to lay before a jury [*ie.*, trier or fact] what the Crown considers to be credible evidence relevant to which is alleged to be a crime ... The role of prosecutor excludes any notion of winning or losing; his function is a matter of public duty than which in civil life there can be none charged with greater personal responsibility. It is to be efficiently performed with an ingrained sense of dignity, the seriousness and the justness of judicial proceedings.[60]

The role of the prosecutor is to both administer and uphold the integrity of the administration of justice. Any conduct on the part of the prosecutor that would result in discrediting the administration of justice would be a violation of the concept of the prosecutor's clear legal and ethical responsibilities. As one author has put it: "Perhaps as no other trial counsel the prosecutor's raison d'être is the carrying out of the public duty spoken by Mr. Justice Rand. There is no question but that his pre-eminent duty is to the state and its ideals of justice, along with its system of administering those ideals."[61]

Fundamental to the proper conduct by the prosecutor is the fair and proper treatment of the accused. If an accused is unrepresented, the prosecutor has an obligation to ensure that all reasonable evidence, arguments, submissions and rights that may benefit the accused be brought to the attention of the trial justice. If an accused does not have a lawyer, the prosecutor may not take advantage of that fact.

Crown prosecutors have responsibilities in law beyond the common law duties, set out above, towards the accused. For example, in Ontario the Law Society of Upper Canada's *Rules of Professional Conduct* deal directly with this issue. In particular, those ethical rules make it clear that: "The prosecutor should not do anything which might prevent the accused from being represented by counsel or communicating with counsel."[62] This rule was apparently breached by a prosecutor in the course of preparing for a prosecution when he contacted an individual accused the night before the trial. The accused told the prosecutor that he had a lawyer. The prosecutor told the accused that he did not care about that and he still wanted to see if the individual accused was prepared to enter into an arrangement to testify against the corporate co-accused, his employer, and received some consideration for the withdrawal of the charges against the individual accused.

---

[60]   *R. v. Boucher*, [1954] S.C.J. No. 54, [1955] S.C.R. 16 at 23-24 (S.C.C.).

[61]   B.G. Smith, *Professional Conduct for Canadian Lawyers* (Toronto: Butterworths, 1989) at 167-69, 173.

[62]   Law Society of Upper Canada, *Rules of Professional Conduct Handbook*, 1995 ed. (as amended to November 25, 1994), Rule 10(9).

When this conduct of the prosecutor was brought to the attention of the trial judge, the prosecution was prevented from withdrawing the charges against the individual accused and compelling him to testify against the corporate accused. In that ruling Harris J. referred to the conduct of the prosecutor towards the accused as "grossly improper".[63]

Another example of a prosecutor's misconduct took place in the case of *R. v. Port Colborne (City)*.[64] That case was the first prosecution of a fire department and fire chief under health and safety legislation in Canada. The prosecution had been party to an agreement of all counsel, well in advance of trial, that the trial of the corporate accused and two individuals accused should take place concurrently. Several weeks before trial both of the individuals accused were served with two subpoenas purporting to compel them to testify against each of the other two accused. A letter was also served with the subpoena on each of the individuals accused that said, among other things, "call me at [telephone number] one week prior to the trial date in order to review the questions I am likely to ask you, so that you will feel more comfortable testifying in court".[65]

Justice Girard described the conduct of the Ministry of Labour's self-admitted normal pre-trial tactic as a "terrible practice".[66] He went on to state: "It is difficult to understand how that can ever be allowed even if the prosecution feels that in a certain set of circumstances it would be appropriate."[67] His Honour did not find that the above-mentioned conduct of the prosecution was conducted with malice or evil intent and therefore declined to stay the charges on the basis of abuse of process. However, he did grant an Order quashing the subpoenas and directed that the Crown could not call either of the accused to testify against each other or their employer. This leads to the next subject of whether or not there needs to be clear or intentional misconduct of the prosecutor to establish abuse of process generally.

8.2.2.8   *Crown Misconduct Not Required*

Intentional misconduct by the Crown prosecutor clearly may amount to an abuse of process. However, Crown misconduct is not necessarily required to prove abuse of process. The case of *R. v. Keyowski*,[68] addressed the issue of whether Crown misconduct of an intentional nature was required to establish the abuse of process argument. In that case, the accused was charged with criminal negligence causing death. After two juries had been unable to agree on a verdict, the Crown sought to try the accused for a third time. In that

---

[63]   *R. v. Steen Contractors Ltd.*, (20 December 1989), Harris J. (Ont. Prov. Div.).

[64]   (31 January 1992) (Ont. Prov. Div.).

[65]   *Ibid.*, at para. 3.

[66]   *Ibid.*, at para. 5.

[67]   *Ibid.*

[68]   [1988] S.C.J. No. 28, 40 C.C.C. (3d) 481 (S.C.C.).

context, the defence moved that the charges be stayed on the grounds of abuse of process. Justice Wilson, for a unanimous Court, said:

> To define "oppressive" as requiring misconduct or an improper motive would, in my view, unduly restrict the operation of the doctrine. In this case, for example, where there is no suggestion of misconduct, such a definition would prevent any limit being placed on the number of trials that could take place. Prosecutorial conduct and improper motivation are but two of many factors to be taken into account when a court is called upon to consider whether or not in a particular case the Crown's exercise of its discretion to re-lay the indictment amounts to an abuse of process.[69]

Therefore, it is clear that there is no requirement that there be proof of any misconduct on the part of the Crown in order to establish an abuse of process. The misconduct of a prosecutor or government inspector clearly would establish a *prima facie* case of abuse of process. It may also be more difficult to establish an abuse of process without evidence of Crown misconduct. Crown misconduct, however, is now not a necessary prerequisite to establish abuse of process.

8.2.2.9   Remedies For Abuse of Process

Corporate accused may seek several types of judicial remedies for a finding of abuse of process. The law of abuse of process has infrequently analyzed the appropriate remedy for an abuse of process. This is perhaps the result of the nature of the development of the doctrine. The early cases that recognized the doctrine of abuse of process evolved as part of the trial court's power to control its own proceedings. Specifically, courts stated that they needed to be able to prevent proceedings from continuing due to the conduct, act or omission of the Crown that amounted to abuse of process. The power of a trial judge to control proceedings was usually defined as the power to stay proceedings. A stay is the most complete remedy that could be invoked when there has been an abuse of process. A stay of proceedings is the equivalent to an acquittal after a full trial and a dismissal of the charges. Charges that are stayed may not ever be proceeded with, absent a successful appeal. Charges that are stayed may not be laid again on the grounds that there has already been a final determination on the charges. A full discussion of the nature of the remedy of a stay is found in *R. v. Amato*.[70]

The further development of the law relating to the doctrine of abuse of process may see additional remedies being added to the judicial remedial repertoire. For example, in the case of *R. v. Steen Contractors Ltd.*[71] the trial judge refused to permit the prosecutor to call an individual as a witness who had been an accused and had been approached by the prosecutor the evening before the trial to "cut a deal" and turn into a Crown witness against his em-

---

[69]   *Ibid.*, at para 3.

[70]   [1982] S.C.J. No. 72, [1982] 2 S.C.R. 418 (S.C.C.).

[71]   (20 December 1989), Harris J. (Ont. Prov. Div.).

ployer, the corporate accused. When the trial judge refused to permit the prosecutor to call the witness, the prosecutor refused to call any other witnesses and the case was dismissed. This remedy of refusing to permit the prosecution to call a witness had, in that case, a similar effect to a stay of proceedings. However, the prosecution could have proceeded with the case and called other witnesses to establish a *prima facie* case for the Crown. This case demonstrates that the court will fashion an appropriate remedy for the facts of each case in which there is an abuse of process.

The remedy for an abuse of process should be responsive to the nature of the misconduct and the effect that it has on the merits of the case and the due administration of justice. When an accused has proven on a balance of probabilities that the prosecutor or the investigators, or both, have unfairly or oppressively treated the accused by initiating or continuing with judicial proceedings, charges may be stayed for abuse of process. This authority lies in the residual power of the trial court to prevent oppressive or vexatious proceedings, to prevent prosecutorial misconduct and to preserve public confidence in the justice system: *R. v. Young*;[72] *R. v. Conway*;[73] *R. v. D. (E.)*.[74] However, the abuse of process must not only offend the community's sense of fair play and decency but it must also be the clearest of cases for a stay to be the proper remedy: *R. v. Power*.[75]

The common law doctrine of abuse of process is now subsumed or included in sections 7 and 11(h) of the Charter. The principles of fundamental justice, provided for in section 7, and a fair trial, under section 11(b) of the Charter, includes the doctrine of abuse of process. The doctrine of abuse of process now has been given constitutional authority under the Charter: *R. v. Keyowski*;[76] and *R. v. O'Connor*.[77]

The Supreme Court has held that where the right of the innocent not to be convicted is dependent on the right to make full answer and defence then the Charter must carefully protect that right. One means of protecting the right to make full answer and defence is by providing the strong remedy of a stay to deter prosecutors and investigators from violating that important right. Where the method and means of the investigation are biased and intent on misdirecting the evidence and investigation, the appearance of a fair trial cannot occur. To protect the due administration of justice, the public respect for the judicial system, and the fair trial right of the accused, the Supreme Court has stated that a stay is the appropriate remedy: *R. v. Seaboyer*,[78] and *R. v. O'Connor*.[79]

---

72   [1984] O.J. No. 3229, 46 O.R. (2d) 520 at 551 (Ont. C.A.).

73   [1989] S.C.J. No. 70, 70 C.R. (3d) 209 at 222 (S.C.C.).

74   [1990] O.J. No. 958, 57 C.C.C. (3d) 151 at 161 (Ont. C.A.).

75   [1994] S.C.J. No. 29, 89 C.C.C. (3d) 1 at 10 (S.C.C.).

76   [1988] S.C.J. No. 28, 40 C.C.C. (3d) 481 at 483 (S.C.C.).

77   [1995] S.C.J. No. 98, [1995] 4 S.C.R. 411 (S.C.C.).

78   [1991] S.C.J. No. 62, 83 D.L.R. (4th) 193 at 261-64 (S.C.C.).

79   [1995] S.C.J. No. 98, 130 D.L.R. (4th) 235 at 275-77 (S.C.C.).

8.2.3 Substantive Defences

Substantive defences available to corporations charged with criminal and strict liability offences may result in a dismissal of the charges and a finding of "not guilty". Unlike procedural defences, substantive defences are based primarily on two principles. First, that the accused is presumed in law, both under the common law and under section 11(d) of the Charter, that the corporate defendant is presumed innocent until proven guilty. Second, the burden of proof on the Crown in a penal prosecution is to establish the prohibited act beyond a reasonable doubt. Therefore, it is quite accurate to say that the failure of the Crown to prove a criminal offence, or any element thereof, beyond a reasonable doubt, will result in a dismissal of the charges. This does not necessarily mean that the corporate accused was innocent of the wrongdoing, but merely as a result of the above mentioned two principles, the Crown cannot prove the charge or charges beyond a reasonable doubt.

Bill C-45 clearly changes the method by which corporations are charged with offences. Section 22.1 deals with offences that are based on a fault standard of negligence, as defined under the Code. Section 22.2 deals with the fault elements of a corporation when charged with an offence other than an offence involving allegations of negligence under the Code. Therefore, it is available for a corporation to raise a defence that one or more elements required to be proven in the formula for establishing guilt under either section 22.1 or 22.2 of the Code, have not been proven beyond a reasonable doubt. If a reasonable doubt remains with respect to any aspect or element of the offence, or any defence offered by the defence with some evidence, then it is a complete defence and the charges will be dismissed.

This fundamental aspect of Canadian criminal law may also be considered a substantive defence. In addition to these principles, other substantive defences are known in Canadian law. Some defences to criminal charges are clearly only available to an individual and would not be available to a corporation. For example, the defences of intoxication, mental disorder and automatism, and insanity are defences only available for individuals. Further, most criminal defences have been provided either in the Code or developed in the case law, from the experience of individual defendants raising these defences. Therefore, what follows is a brief review of substantive defences to corporations charged with offences under the Code. It remains to be seen, with the advent of Bill C-45, and the statutory formula for guilt set out in sections 22.1 and 22.2 of the Code, whether new defences, interpreting those provisions, will be made available for corporate defendants.

Defences that fall within the category of substantive defences include provocation, self-defence, necessity and duress. The defence of provocation is normally available for an individual defendant. It typically is used by an individual to reduce the charge of murder to manslaughter rather than amount to a complete defence. The theory behind provocation is that it may cause an otherwise ordinary person to act in an involuntary manner. Generally speaking, provocation will not be available to a corporate defendant.

Self-defence relates to an accused's apprehension of harm and perception of the need to use force or other means to protect oneself. This defence is primarily available for individuals and not corporations. The Supreme Court has held that a person may qualify for the defence of self-defence even though the individual was not being unlawfully treated or assaulted. The Court said, "an honest but reasonable mistake as to the existence of an assault is permitted ... the existence of an assault must not be made a kind of pre-requisite for the exercise of self-defence to be assessed without regard to the perception of the accused. This would amount to, in a sense to trying the victim before the accused".[80] Since a corporate defendant may not likely have a reasonable apprehension of death or a grievous bodily harm, it is not likely that this defence will be available for a corporate accused.

The defence of necessity holds some interest and potential application for a corporate defendant. As a substantive defence, it is available only in very limited circumstances. In the prosecution of *R. v. Morgentaler*,[81] the well known abortion doctor, the Court of Appeal held that the defence of necessity should not have been left to the jury when doctors were charged with violating a Code provision that required approval of a hospital committee before an abortion was performed. The charge could also have been laid, potentially, against a corporate accused that operated an abortion clinic. The Supreme Court did not ultimately deal with this defence since it declared the Code provision relating to approval of abortions by a hospital committee in contravention of women's rights under section 7 of the Charter.

The substantive defence of necessity was also considered by the Supreme Court in *R. v. Perka*,[82] where it stressed that only when an accused faced immediate or urgent circumstances could it raise the defence. The decision in *Perka* was applied to a municipal corporation, charged with a contravention of a strict liability offence when a firefighter drowned in the course of a water rescue of civilians. Although there was little discussion of the defence in that case, it did appear to open the door for a corporate defendant, charged with a criminal or strict liability offence, to raise the defence of necessity.[83]

The substantive defence of duress, similar to that of necessity, may occur when an accused commits a crime in response to some extraordinary, external pressure. Duress is normally understood, especially with an individual accused, to be threats of harm against the accused, or a person known to or close to the accused. The classic example of the defence of duress, for an individual accused, is one who commits a crime or assists in the commission of a crime with a knife held to his or her throat. Section 17 of the Code is

---

[80]   *R. v. Pétel*, [1994] S.C.J. No. 1 at para. 21, 87 C.C.C. (3d) 97 (S.C.C.).

[81]   [1985] O.J. No. 2662, 22 C.C.C. (3d) 353 (Ont. C.A.), revd [1988] S.C.J. No. 1 (S.C.C.).

[82]   [1984] S.C.J. No. 40, [1984] 2 S.C.R. 232 (S.C.C.).

[83]   *R. v. Colborne (City)*, [1992] O.J. No. 2555 (Ont. Prov. Div.).

very restrictive in its application of the defence of duress when there are immediate threats of death or bodily harm. The common law defence of duress, arguably, is broader. Similar to the substantive defences of provocation, self-defence and necessity, courts have generally required the accused to satisfy an objective standard that a reasonable person would have acted in the manner in which the accused did, to satisfy the defence of duress. Generally, there has to be no safe way to escape when there is a potential safe avenue of escape.[84] A common law defence of duress may be applied when a third party, such as a relative or close friend, is threatened. This defence may include the well-being of a corporation if it was at risk of corporate survival. It may be limited to a personal service corporation that is the alter ego of the individual owner.

In summary, the traditional substantive defences of provocation, self-defence, and duress are not likely to be easily available to corporate defendants. The defence of necessity, however, has had some broader application for a corporate accused. However, if circumstances arise where the consideration of these defences is applicable, it should be remembered that the mere raising of an evidentiary basis of the defence, consistent with the legal test for the defence, may make the defence available. In other words, if the accused is charged with a crime, it does not have to establish these defences on a balance of probabilities. Unlike the defence of due diligence for a corporation in a strict liability offence, defences available to criminal charges apply whenever there is a reasonable doubt about their existence, based on some evidence for the court to consider. These defences require the accused to point to evidence that a reasonable person in the circumstances of the accused, would act in a similar manner.

Substantive defences to crimes are not particularly well suited to criminal charges against corporations. Criminal defences, both those found in the Code and in the case law, overwhelmingly focus on the application of criminal law to the individual in society, and not the corporation. As discussed above, this still may be an area of law that will evolve given the developments in Bill C-45.

8.3   DEFENCES TO STRICT LIABILITY OFFENCES

8.3.1   Defences Generally

Many of the defences available to a corporation charged with a criminal offence, may also be made available to corporations charged with a strict liability offence. It has been argued earlier in this text that there is a great deal of similarity between criminal and strict liability offences against corporations since, *inter alia*, a corporation cannot be imprisoned. The *Provincial Offences Act*,[85] the statute governing the prosecution of strict liability of-

---

[84]   *R. v. Hibbert*, [1995] S.C.J. No. 63, 99 C.C.C. (3d) 193 (S.C.C.).
[85]   R.S.O. 1990, c. P.33.

fences in Ontario, confirms the availability of justifications and excuses at common law, including criminal law defences: "Every rule and principle of the common law that renders any circumstance a justification or excuse for an act or a defence to a charge continues in force and applies with respect to offences, except insofar as they are altered or inconsistent with this or any other Act."[86]

This provision will not apply to a defence relating to criminal intent since there is no constituent mental element required for proof of a strict liability offence. However, where criminal defences exist in relation to the prohibited act, and in relation to other elements of the offence relevant to a strict liability offence, then this section of the Act preserves those defences. Therefore, when reviewing the potential defences of a corporation to strict liability offences, one should have regard to the defences that might be available to a corporation when charged with a criminal offence.

8.3.2 Defence of Due Diligence

Strict liability offences have been extensively reviewed and compared to criminal offences in Chapter 3 of this text. In *R. v. Sault Ste. Marie*,[87] the Supreme Court held that in a strict liability offence, the onus of proof shifts to the defendant to establish the defence of due diligence. The shifting of the onus of proof was not seen as unfair since the defendant generally had more knowledge of what was done to avoid the commission of the prohibited act than had the regulator. It is expected that the defendant would advance the defence of due diligence through evidence within its knowledge, if it was available. There are two separate branches of the due diligence defence:

   (i)   In the first branch, the defendant must prove that it reasonably believed in a mistaken set of facts which, if true, would render the prohibited act or omission innocent.

   (ii) In the second branch, the defendant must prove that it took all reasonable steps to avoid the particular prohibited event.

The primary defence in a strict liability prosecution of a regulatory offence is the defence of due diligence. Other defences known in law may also be available to a strict liability offence. The basis of the defence is that it would be legally and morally improper to convict a person of an offence when they have taken all reasonable precautions to ensure compliance with the applicable legislation. The availability of the due diligence defence in *Cancoil Thermal Corp.*,[88] confirmed that the common law defence of due diligence, as defined in *Sault Ste. Marie*, is always available in a strict liability offence. The court dealt with the issue of the specific exclusion of the statutory defence of due diligence in the case of an offence under the Ontario

---

[86]   *Ibid.*, s. 80
[87]   [1978] S.C.J. No. 59, 40 C.C.C. (2d) 353 (S.C.C.).
[88]   [1986] O.J. No. 290, 27 C.C.C. (3d) 295 (Ont. C.A.).

Occupational Health and Safety ("OHS") legislation. The law stated that certain OHS offences were offences of absolute liability, taking away the defence of due diligence. In answering this question, the court ruled as follows:

> ... if section 14(1)(a) [now section 25(1)(a)] were treated as creating an absolute liability offence, it would offend s. 7 of the Canadian *Charter of Rights and Freedoms,* the right to life, liberty and security of the person and the right not to be deprived thereof except in accordance with the principles of fundamental justice.[89]

The court went on to comment that since under section 66(1)(a), a violation of section 25(1)(a) of the applicable health and safety legislation may attract a term of imprisonment, the combination of absolute liability and the potential penalty of imprisonment was a violation of section 7 of the Charter. The court concluded that to avoid a violation of section 7 of the Charter, section 25(1)(a) of the applicable OHS legislation must, at minimum, be treated as creating a strict liability offence.

8.3.3 Mistake of Fact Branch of Due Diligence

The first branch of the due diligence defence is based on a mistake of fact not mistake of law. Proof of the first branch of the due diligence defence is facilitated by meeting the test set down by the Supreme Court in the *Sault Ste. Marie* case. However, in order to establish the first branch of the due diligence defence, also known as the mistaken fact branch, the following elements must be proven:

1.   The accused believed in a mistaken set of facts.

2.   If the mistaken set of facts were true, they would render the act or omission innocent.

3.   The belief by the accused was deemed reasonable by the court.

An important decision interpreting the first branch of the due diligence defence is the prosecution of *R. v. London Excavators & Trucking Ltd.*[90] In that case, the accused had been hired by a general contractor to perform excavating services for the extension on a new hospital. The equipment operator came into contact with a concrete structure that was not on any of the design drawings. The equipment operators stopped the backhoe, and made an enquiry of a representative of the general contractor. He was advised by the representative of the general contractor that the concrete object was part of a footing of an old nursing station and that it should be removed. However, when the backhoe operator resumed his excavating activity, and dug into the concrete structure, he severed several major power cables from a local hydro utility that were connecting the hospital to the power grid. Al-

---

[89]   *Ibid.,* at 299 (C.C.C.).

[90]   [1998] O.J. No. 6437, 40 O.R. (3d) 32 (Ont. C.A.).

though no one was seriously injured, London Excavators & Trucking Company Ltd. was prosecuted by Ontario's Ministry of Labour.

The company relied upon the first branch of the due diligence defence. However, the Court of Appeal for Ontario, to which lower court decisions were appealed, held that the defence had not been made out. The Court of Appeal held that before beginning the work, more detailed and objective inquiries should have been made by the excavating contractor. Further, when the unexpected contact was made with the concrete structure, the excavating contractor could not merely rely upon the word of a supervisor of the general contractor, but had to establish more reliably that there was no safety hazard. The court held that it was not objectively reasonable for the backhoe operator, on behalf of London Excavators & Trucking Ltd., to simply rely on the statements made by the supervisor of the general contractor once an unexpected concrete obstacle was encountered. A lower court conviction was upheld by the Court of Appeal.

8.3.4   Reasonable Precautions Branch of Due Diligence

The second branch of due diligence is more frequently relied upon by corporate accused than the first branch. The second branch of the due diligence defence is established by proving the above mentioned legal test. Practically speaking, it is facilitated by the development of an effective management system. This may include a financial, manufacturing product, consumer products, environmental or health and safety management system. Regarding health and safety legislation, this means the internal responsibility system of shared duties and responsibilities of various workplace stakeholders is manifest in an effective management system.

One example of a successful due diligence defence based on a management system was found in the prosecution of *Kenaidan Contracting Ltd.*[91] The court had held that the prosecution had proven a contravention of the applicable provisions of the OHS statute in Ontario with which the accused had been charged. However, the court went on to assess whether or not the company had made out the second branch of the due diligence defence. Based on the following factors, the court concluded that the company had established the second branch of the due diligence defence, often referred to as the reasonable precautions branch:

1. There had been a pre-construction meeting in which workplace health and safety was considered as part of the overall planning of the project.

2. A supervisor employed by the contractor was on site at all times to deal with subcontractor issues including health and safety issues.

---

[91]   Unreported decision of Justice of the Peace Kitchen, January 12, 1995.

3.   An external health and safety consultant had been retained to inspect the project, from time to time, to ensure compliance with the established health and safety programs.

4.   There were regular health and safety meetings held at a construction project with all workers.

5.   Senior representatives from the contractor attended a weekly project meeting, at which health and safety on the project was an issue.

6.   The contractor's supervisor and health and safety consultant had clear authority to stop work if any worker was put in danger.

7.   The contractor was never made aware of the concerns relating to the issue of a subcontractor that related to the full-arrest charges against the contractor.

8.   The court determined that the health and safety program and the presence of a full-time supervisor were adequate to meet the requirements of the employer under the applicable OHS statute and that the employer had done all that could reasonably be expected of it in the circumstances.

8.3.5 Reverse Onus and the Charter

A major difference between criminal and strict liability offences is in the reverse onus placed on an accused to prove the due diligence defence. The two branches of the due diligence defence, according to *Sault Ste. Marie*, clearly placed an onus of proof on the accused to prove the defence. That this was a departure from the long-standing Anglo-Canadian legal presumption of innocence was significant. The Supreme Court indicated in *Sault Ste. Marie* that the accused had the onus of proof to demonstrate that it made out one of the defences in the two branches of the due diligence defence. The standard required by the accused was a civil standard of proof that is proof on a balance of probabilities.

The validity of the reverse onus on the accused to prove the defence of due diligence has been challenged under the Charter. In *R. v. Wholesale Travel Group Inc*,[92] the Court of Appeal for Ontario said the reverse onus offended the presumption of innocence in section 11(d) of the Charter. The same issue came up in a prosecution under the Ontario *Occupational Health and Safety Act* in *Ellis-Don Ltd. v. Ontario*.[93] The Court of Appeal rendered a split decision, 2-1, in favour of the view that the reverse onus on the accused was a violation of the presumption of innocence found in section 11(d) of the Charter, and that it could not be saved or justified by section 1 of the Charter.

---

[92]   [1989] O.J. No. 1971, 63 D.L.R. (4th) 325 (Ont. C.A.), vard [1991] S.C.J. No. 79 (S.C.C.).
[93]   [1990] O.J. No. 2208, 1 O.R. (3d) 193 (Ont. C.A.), revd [1992] S.C.J. No. 33, [1992] 1 S.C.R. 840 (S.C.C.).

The Crown appealed both *Wholesale Travel Group* and the *Ellis-Don* case to the Supreme Court. The former was heard and decided first. In *Wholesale Travel Group*, the Court reversed the Court of Appeal for Ontario decision and held that the statutory and common law reverse onus on accused to prove, on a balance of probabilities, the defence of due diligence did not offend the Charter. The Court was divided on the question of whether there was a contravention of the Charter and whether, if this was the case, the infringement was saved and justified by section 1 of the Charter. However, the arguments to ultimately justify the reverse onus on the accused in a strict liability offence were generally accepted by the majority of the Court to include the nature of the offence and the policy reasons behind the prosecution of corporations for false advertising, polluting and health and safety offences. Placing a reverse onus on an accused in a regulatory, strict liability offence was held not to contravene the Charter.

With the Supreme Court in the *Wholesale Travel Group* case permitting a reverse onus, the subsequent result in *Ellis-Don* came as no surprise. In *Ellis-Don*, the Supreme Court released a very brief decision allowing the Crown's appeal. In so doing, the Court adopted its own reasoning from *Wholesale Travel Group*, and rejected the argument that an accused's right under subsection 11(d) of the Charter is paramount over the concerns of the OHS regulator in enforcing strict liability offences. Therefore, an accused in an OHS offence is required to prove both of the branches of the due diligence defence, on a balance of probabilities.

Essentially, when an individual accused or a corporate accused is charged with a strict liability offence, they are presumed innocent until such time as the Crown has proven a *prima facie* case, beyond a reasonable doubt. Once the Crown has discharged its burden to prove the prohibited act or omission beyond a reasonable doubt, then the burden of proof shifts to the accused to prove the defence of due diligence. Although the standard of proof on the accused is a civil standard, rather than a criminal standard, the Supreme Court has held that it is an acceptable requirement for a strict liability offence and does not infringe the Charter.

8.4   DEFENCE OF OFFICIALLY INDUCED ERROR

Corporations may also rely upon the substantive defence of officially induced error to strict liability offences. The defence relates to the repugnancy of convicting an accused who has taken a course of conduct or action as a result of considered and reasonable reliance on the advice or representation of an official of the applicable government agency. The notion that the law should be obeyed is critical for the enforcement of regulatory standards. However, the law is not intent upon punishing those who have tried to determine the law through a reasonable inquiry of a government official and failed. This area of the law has undergone recent developments that will be canvassed hereafter.

The Court of Appeal for Ontario addressed the defence of officially induced error when it dealt with the question of whether an accused could argue the defence of Crown estoppel or officially induced error of law in response to legislative charges under the applicable health and safety legislation. This consideration of the defence of officially induced error occurred in the case of *R. v. Cancoil Thermal Corp.*[94] In examining the defence of officially induced error, the court said:

> The defence of "officially induced error" is available as a defence to an alleged violation of a regulatory statute where an accused has reasonably relied upon the erroneous legal opinion or advice of an official who is responsible for the administration or enforcement of the particular law. In order for the accused to successfully raise this defence, he must show that he relied on the erroneous legal opinion of the official and that his reliance was reasonable. The reasonableness will depend upon several factors including the efforts he made to ascertain the proper law, the complexity or obscurity of the law, the position of the official who gave the advice, and the clarity, definitiveness and reasonableness of the advice given.
>
> I agree with the following statement made by Professor Barton in the article referred to [(1979-80), 22 C.L.Q. 314 at p. 331:
>
> "Where the advice is given by an official who has the job of administering the particular statute, and where the actor relies on this advice and commits what is in fact an offence, even if the agency cannot be estopped does it follow that the actor should not be excused? To do so is not to condone an illegality or say that the agency is estopped into a position of illegality, but to recognize that the advice was illegal but excuse the actor because he acted reasonably and does not deserve punishment."[95]

The Court of Appeal went on to comment further: "But, although it may at times overlap with the defence of due diligence, the defence of 'officially induced error of law' is separate and distinct and can be asserted, in the same way as other defences."[96]

It is clear that the defence of officially induced error will lead to an acquittal under the applicable health and safety legislation if the defendant can prove, on a balance of probabilities, that it was misled by an inspector and that reliance on the erroneous legal opinion of the official was reasonable. Ordinarily, a mistake of law will not be successfully raised as a defence to a criminal or *quasi*-criminal charge or as a regulatory defence. Officially induced error, however, may constitute a valid defence. Of course, whether the defence can be successfully established will depend on whether the opinion of the official was reasonable in the circumstances and whether it was reasonable for the defendant to follow it.

It is now certainly open to a defendant to argue that it has been misled by either the advice or conduct of an official of the occupational health and

---

[94]   [1986] O.J. No. 290, 14 O.A.C. 225 (Ont. C.A.).

[95]   *Ibid.*, at 232 (O.A.C.).

[96]   *Ibid.*, at 232-33 (O.A.C.).

safety department of the applicable health and safety legislation. The inspector has been appointed for the purpose of inspection and examination of the workplace and has wide powers to enforce compliance with the Act and its regulations.

Several other strict liability offence prosecutions have considered and followed the decision in *Cancoil Thermal Corp.* In one motor vehicle case, the accused was accused of driving while his licence was under suspension contrary to the *Motor Vehicle Administration Act*. The accused had been directed to move his vehicle by a police officer and the court concluded that the defence of officially induced error was available on the basis that the accused operated the motor vehicle on the reasonable belief that he had been directed to do so by the police officer.[97]

In another case, the accused were alleged to have fished in a particular area while using mobile gear during a closed season, contrary to the *Atlantic Fishery Regulations*. The court held that the type of operation engaged in by the accused, although illegal, had been carried on for years with the tacit approval of the Department of Fisheries. Interestingly enough, no formal or direct approval had ever been provided by a person in authority. Defence was deemed to be one of strict liability and therefore the defence of officially induced error was applicable to such a charge. In all of the circumstances, the court held that it would be an affront to natural justice to convict the accused and therefore acquitted the accused.[98]

A further example of the use of officially induced error in a provincial offence prosecution as a complete defence was found in the decision of *R. v. Mitri*,[99] where the accused was alleged to have driven when prohibited to do so by law. The accused had been in court when it was ordered that his licence be suspended for one year. His lawyer advised him that the length of the suspension was likely to be reduced pursuant to a sentence appeal and he instructed his lawyer to appeal. Approximately three months later, the accused received a facially valid driver's licence in the mail. He contacted his lawyer to confirm his qualification to drive and was told that the lawyer would get back to him if there was any problem about his licence. The court held that the issuance and delivery of the licence constituted "legal advice" that the accused could legally drive. Further, the court stated that reliance on this advice was not unreasonable, given the accused's belief that the length of the suspension would be reduced on his sentence appeal. In the circumstances, it was reasonable for him to conclude that the sentence appeal had been successful. The court, on all of the above facts, concluded that the accused had established the defence of officially induced error and entered an acquittal.

---

[97]   *R. v. Wabasca*, [1987] A.J. No. 1757 (Alta. Prov. Ct.), affd 3 W.C.B. (2d) 414 (Alta. Q.B.).

[98]   *R. v. Johnson and Wilson*, [1987] N.B.J. No. 1148, 78 N.B.R. (2d) 411 (N.B. Prov. Ct.).

[99]   [1989] O.J. No. 1873 (Ont. Prov. Ct.).

The successful application of the defence of officially induced error by a corporation occurred in the Nova Scotia case of *R. v. Provincial Foods Inc.*[100] In that case, the corporate accused was charged with violation of a City of Halifax ordinance for unlawfully occupying a building for the purpose of manufacturing, preparing and packaging vegetable products without first obtaining an occupancy permit. As a result of a discussion between the corporation's principal and a city clerk, the principal mistakenly believed that he had received suitable permission to proceed with his enterprise. The principal relied on the clerk's description of Provincial Food's business operations and the subsequent occupancy permit issued by the city as sufficient authority to carry on with his business.

In addressing the question of whether the mistakes were mistakes of law or of fact, the court said: "Thus whether the mistake created by an official is one of law or of facts, if it has been acted upon by the defendant to his detriment, it is a proper basis for the defence of 'officially induced error'."[101] The court went on to dismiss the charges on the authority that the defence of officially induced error was established by the evidence.

After the Court of Appeal decision in *Cancoil Thermal Corp.* and the decision in *Provincial Foods*, the case of *R. v. Dubeau*[102] was decided. The accused was charged with the offence of carrying on a business of firearms and ammunition sale, without a permit, when selling guns at a series of garage sales. The accused was acquitted on an application of *Cancoil Thermal Corp.* since he had asked the local firearms officer specifically about permits for garage sales and had made other efforts to understand the complexities of the law. Finally, in *R. v. Erotica Video Exchange Ltd.*,[103] two corporate accused were held to have made out a lawful excuse because of their reliance on the approval of the obscene videos they had retailed by the British Columbia Film Board.

Further, in the Supreme Court decision of *R. v. Jorgensen*,[104] Lamer C.J.C., in a supporting judgment, on different reasons, extensively reviewed the legal defence of officially induced error. The accused was charged with knowingly selling obscene material without lawful justification or excuse. The accused was convicted at trial and the conviction was upheld on appeal. The accused had raised the fact that the eight films in question had received approval from the Ontario Film Review Board. In considering the matter at the Supreme Court, Lamer C.J.C., said: "Officially induced error of law exists as an exception to the rule that ignorance of the law does not excuse ... extensive regulation is one motive for creating a limited exception to the rule

---

[100] [1991] N.S.J. No. 684, 109 N.S.R. (2d) 209 (N.S. Prov. Ct.), affd [1992] N.S.J. No. 38, 111 N.S.R. (2d) 420 (N.S. Co. Ct.).

[101] *R. v. Provincial Foods Inc.,* [1991] N.S.J. No. 684 at para. 35 (N.S. Prov. Ct.).

[102] [1993] O.J. No. 489, 80 C.C.C. (3d) 54 (Ont. Gen. Div.).

[103] [1994] A.J. No. 1008, 163 A.R. 181 (Alta. Prov. Ct.).

[104] [1995] S.C.J. No. 92, 129 D.L.R. (4th) 510 (S.C.C.).

that *ignorantia juris neminem excusat*."[105] The steps set down in the reasons for judgment may be paraphrased as follows:

1. Was the error actually one of law or of mixed law and fact?
2. Did the accused consider the legal consequences of his actions?
3. Was the advice obtained from the appropriate official?
4. Was the advice reasonable in the circumstances?
5. Was the advice given by the official erroneous?
6. Did the accused rely on the erroneous advice of the official?[106]

Chief Justice Lamer went on to state: "Ignorance of the law remains blame-worthy in and of itself. In these specific instances, however, the blame is, in a sense, shared with the state official who gave the erroneous advice."[107] In the result, the accused were acquitted by the Supreme Court. This decision, together with the decision of the Court of Appeal for Ontario in *Cancoil Thermal Corp.*, is for the proposition that there is a valid defence of offi-cially induced error for all accused who are charged with health and safety law offences.

The challenge in proving the defence of officially induced error was seen in *R. v. Timminco Ltd.*,[108] a decision of the Ontario Court of Justice. In that case, the Ministry of Labour had been inspecting a mining plant for ap-proximately eight years and had often viewed a crown press machine in op-eration. On occasion, Ministry of Labour inspectors had been directed to various parts of the crown press, although not specifically to the rear part where workers were not normally required to work. A worker was killed when, without authorization, he went behind the machine and placed his head and torso in a moving part that was not protected by a guard. The worker died as a result of his injuries. At trial, Justice Beasley held that the mere presence of Ministry of Labour inspectors at the facility and in the vi-cinity of the crown press did not amount to the defence of officially induced error. The court held that there was no evidence of specific advice being given that the crown press and, in particular, the moving part at the back of it, was in complete compliance with the applicable section of the regulation for mines and mining plants relating to the guarding of moving parts. Hence, there was no subsequent specific reliance upon such advice by the employer, which was necessary in that particular case as part of the defence of offi-cially induced error. However, the presence of Ministry of Labour inspectors in the plant and around the crown press was relevant evidence for the de-fence of due diligence. In the result, Justice Beasley dismissed the charge against the employer on the basis of, among other reasons, the defence of due diligence.

---

[105] *Ibid.*, at para. 25.

[106] *Ibid.*, at paras. 28-30, 33-35.

[107] *Ibid.*, at para. 36.

[108] [2004] O.J. No. 5324, 37 C.C.E.L. (3d) 46 (Ont. C.J.).

8.5   DEFENCES AND CORPORATE ACCOUNTABILITY

This chapter has set out the main defences available to a corporation when facing criminal or strict liability charges. The subject of legal defences is particularly challenging in the area of criminal charges against a corporation, where defences have been largely fashioned to apply to individuals rather than corporations. As discussed in Chapter 5, analysis of Bill C-45 clearly requires some interpretation by courts with respect to the various elements of a charge involving negligence, in s. 22.1 of the Code and for non-negligence charges against corporations, under s. 22.2 of the Code. However, these are still relatively early years in the interpretation of Bill C-45 and a great deal has been left uncertain by the above mentioned provisions of Bill C-45.

Defences to strict liability offences are more clearly defined and available for corporate accused. The case law has developed around the various rights and opportunities of corporations to raise defences to strict liability offences. The result is a more developed case law, with an emphasis on the two branches of the due diligence defence, in strict liability offences. The predominant branch of the due diligence defence, the second branch, focuses on establishment of a system by the corporate accused, to prevent the commission of the offence. The establishment and effective implementation of a management system to ensure compliance with the law and prevent the strict liability offence from being committed, is a complete defence to strict liability charges involving products liability, security irregularities, environmental missteps and workplace health and safety incidents.

The defences available in strict liability offences, more so than criminal offences, promote the concept of corporate accountability. Developing a management system to ensure compliance with regulatory statutes, is a positive development from the jurisprudence that followed the Supreme Court's decision in *Sault Ste. Marie.* The development of broad principles of Corporate Social Responsibility have often found their origins, in an attempt to establish management systems to deal with regulatory standards.

The mere existence of the due diligence defence, however, in the author's view, is not sufficient to deal with the broader issues of how to achieve corporate accountability. Corporations have far reaching effects on the lives of Canadians, financial markets, consumer products, environmental and workplace safety, even if their potential impact does not amount to the commission of the offence. Further, the effective use of prosecution as a means of ensuring corporate accountability is reactive not proactive. The prosecutorial method of corporate accountability requires identification of the offence, proper investigation and evidence gathering of the offence, proper and successful prosecution of the corporation for committing the offence and then dealing with potential defences, including the defence of due diligence.

It is the author's view that a broader, more holistic approach to providing corporate motivation and accountability is a more effective and proactive means of ensuring the establishment of effective corporate accountability. The prosecution process, as it has been said before, is both a blunt and expensive instrument to achieve corporate accountability. The subject of broader and more innovative methods to establish effective corporate social responsibility is addressed in Chapter 10. First, however, this text will consider the sentencing and probationary process that corporations may be held accountable by, if they have been prosecuted, taken to trial and a conviction results.

Chapter 9

SENTENCING AND PROBATION FOR CORPORATE OFFENDERS

9.1 INTRODUCTION TO SENTENCING

After the prosecution of a corporation at trial, if there is a finding of "guilty" and a conviction is registered, then there is the punishment process called sentencing. This chapter addresses the sentencing and probationary principles and process for corporate offenders. Charges against corporations, both *mens rea* or strict liability offences, are similar in the prosecution process and have similar approaches in sentencing. As with individual offences, corporate offences are punished in a manner that reflects the nature of the offence, the offender, and the effect on the victim or community. However, unlike sentencing an individual, sentencing the corporate offender may consider the impact that the corporation has on its industry, its community and society as a whole.

The current law regarding sentencing corporate offenders in *mens rea* and strict liability offences will be reviewed and compared. Then the law of sentencing for criminal and strict liability offences of corporate offenders will be reviewed. Recent changes to the *Criminal Code*[1] in Bill C-45 expanded the framework for sentencing corporate offenders.[2] That framework may also serve as a model for reform in the sentencing of corporate offenders for strict liability offences across Canada. A review of sentencing jurisprudence also supports the need for a more integrated and principled approach to sentencing corporate offenders, regardless of the type of offence for which they have been convicted. The terms of probation for corporations is another change brought about by Bill C-45.

Sentencing the corporate offender is an important and often overlooked subject in the administration of criminal justice. In a free enterprise economic system, the market, not the criminal justice system, is the means to reward good and correct bad conduct. However, when prosecutions are used to achieve corporate accountability, then sentencing becomes important, for corporate accountability. Traditional legal sentencing texts often neglect the

---

[1] R.S.C. 1985, c. C-46 [hereinafter the "Code"].

[2] Bill C-45, *An Act to amend the Criminal Code (criminal liability of organizations)*, S.C. 2003, c. 21.

subject or only briefly address sentencing the corporate offender.[3] Sentencing the corporate offender, in both *mens rea* and strict liability offences, has primarily focused on deterrence. This approach to sentencing has ignored the broader purpose and social context of the standards that corporations have failed to achieve. Although the theory of deterrence has been the subject of criticism in the literature for sentencing generally, it has not been reviewed extensively regarding corporate offenders.[4] Sentencing the corporate offender should look beyond deterrence and consider the opportunity for corporate rehabilitation for the broader public interest. Corporations have an important role in society as employers, taxpayers, producers, suppliers and consumers. Therefore, sentencing the corporate offender should consider and recognize this broader role that corporations have in society to give meaningful accountability and corrective sentences that broadly consider the public good.

Sentencing an individual or an organization that has been convicted of a criminal or strict liability offence is among the most significant and difficult decisions that the criminal justice system is called upon to make. Most criminal charges in Canada are resolved by way of a plea of "guilty" rather than a plea of "not guilty" and a trial. Therefore, sentencing in most prosecutions is often the most important process since the issue of guilt or innocence has been resolved by way of a guilty plea.

After a conviction, the judge has to follow the requirements of the Code or other applicable statutes in sentencing the accused. Sentencing, however, largely remains a matter of judicial discretion, with only a limited number of offences defining minimum penalties. Sentencing, as a discretionary process in the Canadian criminal justice system, is largely left in the hands of lawyers and judges on a case-by-case basis. Under the Code, judges are required to base sentencing on the overriding principle of proportionality. The Code states the principle of proportionality as follows: "A sentence must be proportionate to the gravity of the offence and the degree of responsibility of the offender."[5] However appropriate this may be in sentencing individuals, this provision provides very little assistance in sentencing corporations. We will review general sentencing principles and then the specific principles that have been added to the Code under Bill C-45.

9.2   GENERAL SENTENCING PRINCIPLES

Sentencing the corporate offender convicted of a criminal offence starts with an understanding of general sentencing principles in the Code. Provincial

---

[3]   For example, Clayton C. Ruby, *Sentencing*, 7th ed. (Markham, ON: LexisNexis Canada, 2008) is one of the few texts that has a chapter on the subject of sentencing the corporate offender, but it only devotes a brief 11-page chapter to the subject out of 1138 pages in the text; see pp. 478-89.

[4]   A.N. Doob & C.M. Webster, "Sentence Severity and Crime: Accepting the Null Hypothesis" (2003) 30 Crime and Justice: A Review of Research 143.

[5]   *Criminal Code*, s. 718.1.

statutes that provide for the prosecution of provincial strict liability offences, provide little guidance in sentencing corporations. The amendments to the Code in 1996[6] were a reaction to the prevailing consensus that there was a significant overuse of incarceration as a punishment for individuals con-victed of criminal offences in Canada.[7] They introduced restorative justice sentencing principles in addition to traditional sentencing principles of deter-rence and retribution. However, these principles have little direct application to the corporate offender. Further, the 1996 amendments made no specific reference to the corporate offenders.

The principles of sentencing introduced in 1996 are clearly set out in s. 718 of the Code.

> **718.** The fundamental purpose of sentencing is to contribute, along with crime prevention initiatives, to respect for the law and the maintenance of a just, peaceful and safe society by imposing just sanctions that have one or more of the following objectives:
>
> a)   to denounce unlawful conduct;
>
> b)   to deter the offender and other persons from committing offences;
>
> c)   to separate offenders from society, where necessary;
>
> d)   to assist in rehabilitating offenders;
>
> e)   to provide reparations for harm done to victims or to the community; and
>
> f)   to promote a sense of responsibility in offenders, and acknowledgment of the harm done to victims and to the community.

Although these general principles of sentencing are more easily applied to individual offenders, they also apply to corporate offenders. The difficulty of providing a specific set of criteria for sentencing any offender, are set out by one author as follows:

> Statements of general principle must, inevitably, be so generalized as to ap-pear to be an attempt to be all things to all people. If they are not, injustice will result in far too many cases. That is because, for example, it is obvious that in sentencing many offenders deterrence should be emphasized while in sentencing many others rehabilitation should be emphasized. Moreover, leg-islating that one goal or the other is to be preferred, even if only in cases where there is doubt encourages less effort at performing the judge's real task of deciding which objectives should be emphasized in the case at hand and less effort at fashioning a sentence that might serve both ends, if the

---

6   *Criminal Code*, s. 742. In 1996 Parliament enacted Bill C-41, *An Act to Amend the Criminal Code (sentencing) and other Acts in consequence thereof,* 1st Sess., 35th Parl., reforming Cana-da's sentencing regime and explicitly incorporating restorative principles into Part XXIII of the *Criminal Code*. Section 718.2(e) sets out principles of sentencing and stipulates that judges consider "all sanctions other than imprisonment that are reasonable in the circumstances, with particular attention to the circumstances of aboriginal offenders". This provision mandates that incarceration be the sanction of last resort for all offenders at sentencing.

7   The Supreme Court of Canada in *R. v. Gladue*, [1999] S.C.J. No. 19 at para. 52, [1999] 1 S.C.R. 688 (S.C.C.) acknowledged that Canada's incarceration rate of approximately 130 inmates per 100,000 of population placed it at second or third highest among industrialized democracies.

judge cannot say that one or the other goal should be emphasized. The idea is to encourage judges to fashion the best possible sentence, not to encourage those who would like to avoid the trouble of doing the job properly, by allowing them to rely upon a principle that says "if in doubt as to what should be emphasized in a given case emphasize rehabilitation" or deterrence or some other objective.[8]

Other authors have considered the 1996 amendments to the Code and provided further insight into the purpose and effect of sentencing criteria set down by law. For example, Clayton Ruby said:

> The new provisions are a step towards more standardized sentencing, ensuring the uniformity of approach. The *Code* remains silent on what ought to be done when conflicts arise between the various sentencing objectives. Similarly, judges retain the discretion to decide which of the six enunciated principles apply in each case.[9]

9.3   CONSISTENCY IN THE SENTENCING OF CORPORATIONS

The purpose of prosecuting and sentencing a corporation under the Code is very similar to a prosecution of a corporation under a strict liability offence. The focus in both types of prosecutions is on stakeholders and public safety and security in various forms. Given the large number of regulatory prosecutions relative to the small number of prosecutions of corporations under the Code, the sentencing of corporations in strict liability offences is arguably just as or even more important than under the Code. The approach to sentencing a corporate offender not only requires a consistent principled approach to sentencing, but also a consideration for the corporation's important role, both present and future, in modern society.

The subject of sentencing is really about how to punish the offender. As advocated by Marinos and Doob, "we must understand punishment in a larger social context, and not try to understand it solely in terms of its criminal justice functions".[10] A court ought to consider "… the integration of economic considerations, the traditional focus of business, with environmental and social imperatives".[11] This is why a broader set of principles that consider the nature of the corporate offender, the nature of the offence, the effect on the victim and its broader social impact, is critical for a principled approach in sentencing corporations convicted of both *mens rea* and strict liability offences. Individual cases should always result in a sentence tailored for that specific situation. The provision and consideration of specific factors

---

[8]   T.W. Ferris, *Sentencing: Practical Approaches* (Markham, ON: LexisNexis Canada, 2005) at 11-12.

[9]   Clayton C. Ruby, *Sentencing*, 7th ed. (Markham, ON: LexisNexis Canada, 2008) at 21.

[10]   A.N. Doob & V. Marinos, "Reconceptualizing Punishment: Understanding the Limitation on the Use of Intermediate Punishment" (1995) 2 U. Chicago L. Sch. Roundtable 413 at 424.

[11]   M. Kerr, R. Janda & C. Pitts, *Corporate Social Responsibility: A Legal Analysis* (Markham, ON: LexisNexis Canada, 2009) at 9.

for sentencing corporate offenders will ensure that their status and place in society will be part of the sentencing process. Monetary deterrents alone, it is submitted, cannot address these complex interrelated principles. Otherwise fines, regardless of how large, will become a cost of doing business.

As with sentencing individuals, the substantive principles of sentencing corporate offenders ought to be known and consistent for sentencing to be rational and responsive in each case. The fundamental principle of sentencing under s. 718.1 of the Code, that the sentence must be proportionate to the gravity of the offence and the degree of responsibility of the offender, applies to both corporate and individual offenders. Proportionality principles include the gravity of the offence, the blameworthiness of the accused, the harm caused to a victim arising from the commission of the offence, the potential harm that the offence indicates, and the degree of participation by the defendant in committing the offence.[12] Section 718.2(b) of the Code introduced the parity principle; that there should be similar sentences imposed on similar offenders for similar offences in similar circumstances.

This principle has been generally adopted by sentencing courts in strict liability offences, as well as under the Code, to reinforce the continued importance of deterrence. Therefore, parity is of little assistance in identifying what a correct or creative, non-monetary penalty is, in the process of sentencing the corporate offender. Since imprisonment is not available for punishing the corporate offender, apart from individual charges against corporate officers and directors, courts have demonstrated a lack of a thoughtful, creative and principled approach to sentencing corporate offenders.

The courts have relied upon the somewhat simple, obvious theory of specific and general deterrence to impose varying degrees of monetary fines and penalties. Both types of deterrence, "… attempt to prevent crime by threatening punishment".[13] The notion of deterrence has little impact on corporate offenders, and their decision makers, in a matter that has measurably prevented corporations from becoming offenders. Further, a general theory of deterrence lacks any connection with opportunities to improve the conduct of corporations in the future. However, as will be reviewed in the next sections, legislative change and jurisprudence does hold some promise for improving the sentencing of corporate offenders.

9.4   BILL C-45 AND SENTENCING

The Code underwent significant amendments in the area of sentencing in 1996, under Bill C-41, regarding sentencing generally. The non-sentencing and probationary amendments under Bill C-45 were the earlier subject of Chapter 4. In 2004, Bill C-45 also amended sentencing

---

[12]   Allan Manson, *The Law of Sentencing* (Toronto: Irwin Law, 2001) at 84-92.

[13]   J.V. Roberts & D.P. Cole, *Making Sense of Sentencing* (Toronto: University of Toronto Press, 1999) at 6.

provisions for organizations including corporations was specifically addressed. The sentence of a corporate offender must be proportionate to the gravity of the offence and the degree of responsibility of the offender.[14] Punishment of corporate offenders involves the applicability of statutory sentencing requirements and judicial discretion in a factual matrix. The punishment of a corporate offender by deterrence poses the problem that the corporate offender may simply pass the fine on to the consumer or end user of its services.[15]

To deal with this challenge for *mens rea* offences, Parliament amended the Code on March 31, 2004 and now requires the trial judge to consider mandatory considerations for sentencing for corporations. The court that imposes a sentence on a corporate offender *must* take into account eight additional aggravating and mitigating factors:

> A court that imposes a sentence on an organization shall also take into consideration the following factors:
>
> a)   any advantage realized by the organization as a result of the offence;
>
> b)   the degree of planning involved in carrying out the offence and the duration and complexity of the offence;
>
> c)   whether the organization has attempted to conceal its assets, or convert them, in order to show that it is not able to pay a fine or make restitution;
>
> d)   the impact that the sentence would have on the economic viability of the organization and the continued employment of its employees;
>
> e)   the cost to public authorities of the investigation and prosecution of the offence;
>
> f)   any regulatory penalty imposed on the organization where one of its representatives in respect of the conduct that formed the basis of the offence;
>
> g)   whether the organization was – or any of its representatives who were involved in the commission of the offence were – convicted of a similar offence were sanctioned by a regulatory body for similar conduct;
>
> h)   any penalty imposed by the organization on a representative for their role in the commission of the offence;
>
> i)   any restitution that the organization is ordered to make or any amount that the organization has paid to a victim of the offence; and,
>
> j)   any measures that the organization has taken to reduce the likelihood of it committing a subsequent offence.[16]

These Bill C-45 amendments were complemented by additional probationary authority to the courts, which is addressed below. However, unlike the new mandatory factors to be considered in sentencing an organization, the

---

[14]   *Criminal Code*, s. 718.1.

[15]   Clayton C. Ruby, *Sentencing*, 7th ed. (Markham, ON: LexisNexis Canada, 2008) at 478, § 12.2.

[16]   *Criminal Code*, s. 718.21.

probationary authority added to the Code is discretionary at the instance of the Court.[17] The value and flexibility of creative probation orders, is very consistent with rehabilitation of the corporate offender and the broader concept of corporate social responsibility. In other words, the state, through the power of the criminal justice system, and in particular, sentencing terms of probation, has an important role to play in establishing and motivating appropriate corporate conduct. Further, in achieving the goals of corporate social responsibility, through the sentencing process, "… the state remains a vital, necessary player in the regulation of corporate conduct".[18]

One of the fundamental purposes of sentencing is to contribute, along with crime prevention initiatives, to respect for the law and the maintenance of a just, peaceful and safe society.[19] Bill C-45 did not amend or change any pre-existing sentencing principle in the Code or in criminal law jurisprudence. However, it established a new list of criteria for sentencing organizations in the Code that must be considered by the sentencing judge. Like the 1996 general sentencing amendments, these amendments were intended to provide further legislative direction to the courts in sentencing. Although many of the principles under new section 718.21 of the Code have been previously considered in cases dealing with sentencing principles, they are especially important in view of the new formula for organizational criminal liability.

Section 718 of the Code deals with the general purpose of sentencing an accused after a conviction. Bill C-45 added section 718.21 to this sentencing provision in order to expand and to clarify factors that the court must consider when imposing a sentence on an organization. The use of the word "must" in section 718.21 makes consideration of these 10 new sentencing criteria for an organization mandatory. These new sentencing powers of the court are not limited to accused who are convicted of a breach of section

---

[17]   See s. 732.1 (3.1) of the *Criminal Code*:

The court may prescribe, as additional conditions of a probation order made in respect of an organization, that the offender do one or more of the following: (a) make restitution to a person for any loss or damage that they suffered as a result of the offence; (b) established policies, standards and procedures to reduce the likelihood of the organization committing a subsequent offence; (c) communicate those policies, standards and procedures to its representatives; (d) report to the court on the implementation of those policies, standards and procedures; (e) identify the senior officer who is responsible for compliance with those policies, standards and procedures; (f) provide, in the manner specified by the court, the following information to the public, namely (i) the offence of which the organization was convicted, (ii) the sentence imposed by the court, and (iii) any measures that the organization is taking – including any policies, standards and procedures established under paragraph (b) – to reduce the likelihood of it committing a subsequent offence; and (g) comply with any other reasonable conditions that the court considers desirable to prevent the organization from committing subsequent offences or to remedy the harm caused by the offences or to remedy the harm caused by the offence.

[18]   M. Kerr, R. Janda & C. Pitts, *Corporate Social Responsibility: A Legal Analysis* (Markham, ON: LexisNexis Canada, 2009) at 493-94.

[19]   *Criminal Code*, s. 718.

217.1, the new offence of Occupational Health and Safety ("OHS") criminal negligence. They apply to all criminal offences with respect to which organizations may be charged and convicted.

The Bill C-45 amendments added 10 additional factors in the Code that must be considered by courts when sentencing organizations. These sentencing factors are each reviewed below. Factor (a) is any advantage realized by the organization as a result of the offence. Presumably, this would include any money saved by failing to invest in regulatory compliance that could have prevented the offence from occurring. For example, this may also include specific decisions to forgo or delay implementation of safety devices or environmental management systems with respect to dangerous equipment, machinery or processes because of the cost involved.

Factor (b) requires the court to consider the degree of planning that went into the offence along with the duration and complexity of the offence. Here, a distinction can be made between those offences that are committed with relatively little planning, and those that require careful planning and execution on behalf of the organization. For example, the new offence of OHS criminal negligence does not require proof of planning to result in a conviction. It only requires proof of negligence as set out in section 219 of the Code. In *R. v. Miller Shipping Co.*,[20] a corporation was convicted under the *Canada Labour Code* of three offences in relation to the accidental death of an employee. In deciding the sentence, the Court stated that s. 718.21(b):

> … raises the issue of *mens rea* and is perhaps more applicable to true criminal offences not the regulatory offences that the accused has been convicted of committing. Generally speaking regulatory offences are concerned with a failure to adhere to some regulated standard and are more similar in their fault elements to civil negligence than criminal activity. Despite this a regulatory breach can result in a great deal of harm occurring and by the same token the reason or the manner in which the breach occurs can be an aggravating factor.[21]

Factor (c) allows the court to consider any attempt taken by an organization to avoid paying a fine or restitution. Converting or concealing assets will not assist an organization to receive a reduced fine; in fact, it may lead to an increased penalty. In "Thoughts on Bill C-45", MacPherson characterizes this factor as "redundant", as it appears to involve a continuation of the offence by making the organization "judgment-proof".[22] The author's view is that MacPherson's view is somewhat narrow since these sentencing provisions will apply to all convicted corporations.

The economic impact of a sentence on the organization, as well as the impact on the employment of employees, is considered under factor (d). In OHS regulatory prosecution cases, however, it has been determined that

---

[20]   [2005] N.J. No. 157 (N.L. Prov. Ct), affd [2007] N.J. No. 412 (N.L.T.D.).

[21]   *Ibid.*, at para. 17.

[22]   D. MacPherson, "Extending Corporate Criminal Liability: Some Thoughts on Bill C-45" (2004) 30:3 Man. L.J. 253 at 277.

while this is a valid sentencing factor, it will not be given as much weight as other factors.[23] This may be due to the competition between the need for deterrence and punishment, and the realization that in many organizations the true punishment is borne by those not in effective control, such as shareholders in a corporation.

Factor (e) makes the cost of prosecution and investigation of the offence a consideration in sentencing. It is not clear if this is limited to police investigation and prosecution or if it may also apply to regulatory investigations and prosecutions. MacPherson identified this as one of the most problematic factors. It would appear that an organization may be sentenced more harshly for electing to proceed with a full trial, which has troubling implications with regard to the presumption of innocence in the Charter.

Factor (f) involves any regulatory penalty imposed arising out of events or conduct that also formed the basis of strict liability charges to the health and safety criminal negligence offence or other regulatory offence. Regulatory charges will usually be dealt with after, not before, a criminal charge. Therefore, this provision may only be applicable if there is a joint criminal and regulatory prosecution that is resolved by a joint trial or a joint plea bargain.

Factor (g) looks to previous convictions or regulatory sanctions for similar conduct, either of the organization or one of its representatives, as factors to be considered in sentencing. Evidence that the organization has a history of similar convictions or behaviour will likely result in an increased penalty. This factor is much broader than just looking at a prior criminal record. It will now mandate a much broader review.

Factor (h) concerns whether the organization has imposed any penalty on a representative for his or her role in an offence. This may be a mitigating factor for the organization, when it has recognized the role of a representative in causing the offence and taking steps to prevent a recurrence. However, it may also be an aggravating factor if the organization has unfairly disciplined or discharged a representative as a scapegoat for the organization's crime. MacPherson came to a similar conclusion when stating:

> This would encourage the corporation to attempt to off-load its responsibility by "pointing the finger", as it were, at one of its representatives. While a genuine show of remorse is an accepted mitigating factor, this usually does not involve blaming and penalizing someone else. I suspect that the legislative drafter added this to give organizations an incentive to maintain internal discipline.[24]

Factor (i) requires the court to consider any restitution ordered or amount paid to the victim by the organization. In *R. v. Fiesta Party Rentals*

---

[23] *R. v. Miller Shipping*, [2005] N.J. No. 157, 245 Nfld. & P.E.I.R. 312 at para. 28 (N.L. Prov. Ct.); *R. v. Tech-Corrosion Service Ltd.*, [1986] A.J. No. 40, 43 Alta. L.R. (2d) 88 at 92 (Alta. Q.B.).

[24] D. MacPherson, "Extending Corporate Criminal Liability: Some Thoughts on Bill C-45" (2004) 30:3 Man. L.J. 253 at 281.

(1984) Ltd.,[25] the corporate defendant had made a $20,000 donation to a charity in the name of the victim of a workplace accident. The court held that although the defendant was not entitled to a dollar-for-dollar credit for such a charitable donation it was a mitigating factor to be taken into account with all of the other factors. This type of mitigating factor will now be considered in sentencing corporate offenders.

Finally, factor (j), any measures taken by the organization to reduce the likelihood of committing subsequent offences, can be considered as evidence of how seriously the organization is in preventing a recurrence. A genuine display of efforts to improve regulatory compliance by, for example, developing an effective management system to reduce the risk of further incidents, regardless of the area of regulations, will likely be a significant mitigating factor in determining an appropriate sentence. This appears to codify the common law principle of taking subsequent ameliorative behaviour and remorse into account when determining sentence for a crime.

In *R. c. Transpavé inc.*,[26] a Quebec corporation pleaded guilty to criminal negligence in relation to the death of an employee. The Court considered the new sentencing guidelines when determining an appropriate fine. In the *Transpavé* case, the new provision was reviewed by Chevalier J., of the Quebec Court in respect of the corporate accused. The Court examined each subparagraph individually in order to come to a conclusion of a fine of $100,000, which was characterized as fair given the co-operation and remorse shown by the family-owned business. His Honour said the following:

> [10] It must however be noted that nor the corporation nor any of its employees knew that the conveyor plank detection lever could get stuck and unstuck. There was an optical beam safety system to restrict access to the place where the accident took place and it is without the knowledge of the corporation nor its management that it had been neutralized at the time of the accident.

> [11] *Transpavé* is not a multinational but a family corporation. It employs up to one hundred employees during production period. It has never paid dividends to its owners-shareholders, reinvesting year after year its profits in order to modernize and remain competitive. Its owners have also been very marked by this accident. They had called the next day a psychologist to help the employees. They had personally called every employee to inform them of the place and date of the funerals of their colleague. They went to the funeral home to offer their sympathies to Mr. L'Écuyer's family and had reiterated their condolences at the hearing through their attorney. It is therefore not an insensitive corporation as we often see.

> [12] With regards to the factor analysis to take into account, it must be noted that *Transpavé* has derived no advantage from the perpetration of the offence.

---

[25]   [2000] A.J. No. 1679 (Alta. Prov. Ct.), aff'd [2001] A.J. No. 1778 (Alta. Q.B.).

[26]   [2008] J.Q. no. 1857 (Que. Ct. (Crim & Penal Div.)).

[13] There was no planning or preparation of any sort to commit the offence. There was, prior to the accident, a Health and Safety Committee at *Transpavé* as well as a Code of Conduct, regulations and standards that employees had to follow. It is therefore not in an active nor positive fashion that the corporation has committed the offence but by its inaction, in a passive way without planning.

[14] The corporation has not tried to hide assets or convert some of them in order to declare itself incapable of paying a fine. It has all to the contrary spent many hundreds of thousands of dollars to ensure that no other tragic accident could occur.

[15] The fine that the tribunal must impose must not put in danger the viability of the corporation and cause the loss of employment to the hundred employees that have good salaries.

[16] No charge of regulatory penal nature had been taken against *Transpavé* or its management concerning the facts at the origin of this file. If there had been, the maximal fine that the corporation could have been ordered to pay is $20,000.00.

[17] *Transpavé* has never been condemned, nor its management, for a similar crime or a similar behaviour constituting a regulatory penal offence.

[18] As stated above, *Transpavé* has spent in 2006 more than half a million dollars to put its two plants at the safety level of Europe, which is higher than the one in force in North America. It is more than what CSST was asking for but it is in order to ensure that such an accident never occurs again. In 2006 and 2007, the corporation has made direct expenses of close to a quarter of a million dollars in direct investments in health and safety to increase the safety level of the corporation.

[19] *Transpavé* has also complied with all the recommendations of CSST. In June 2007, the Health and Safety Manager to the Laurentides regional office insisted on "congratulating both parties, management and union for having succeeded in implementing in less than one year a structure and culture of health and safety management at a high level standard".

[20] In 2007, the net profits of the corporation amounted to close to three quarters of a million dollars.

[21] The more than three quarters of a million dollars spent in 2006 and 2007 by *Transpavé*, to correct the situation and to be at the vanguard, must be taken into account to evaluate the fine that must be imposed since this amount almost guarantees that such an accident will not reoccur.

[22] The parties suggest, jointly, that a fine of $100,000.00 would satisfy the ends of justice.

[23] The tribunal must ratify this suggestion as the Quebec Court of Appeal reminds in *Bazinet vs. R.* rendered on January 8, 2008, unless it considers that the suggested fine is unreasonable, contrary to the public interest, inadequate or capable of bringing the administration of justice in disrepute.

[24] The suggested fine takes into account the more than $750,000.00 spent by Transpavé in 2006 and 2007 in the field of occupational health and safety.

[25] This fine even though significant allows the survival of the corporation and the continuation of 100 jobs.

[26] It underlines the importance of the acknowledgement by *Transpavé* of its fault and of its sense of responsibility that it manifested afterwards.

[27] The suggested fine is not unreasonable in the circumstances, it respects the sentence determination principles and is in compliance with the factors that must be taken into account.[27]

9.5   PROVINCIAL OFFENCES ACT SENTENCING PROVISIONS

In contrast to the extensive sentencing provisions of the Code both generally and the new sentencing and probationary terms of the Bill C-45 amendments, there is virtually no direction given under the *Provincial Offences Act* ("POA")[28] for sentencing in a regulatory strict liability offence conviction in Ontario. Similar provincial legislation is also lacking in respect of sentencing a corporation in strict liability offences in other provinces. The POA does not have a stipulated purpose or sentencing criteria for strict liability offences under the POA. In short, sentencing is left to the parties to make submissions and have a sentence imposed by the trial justice.[29] A conviction under a Part III offence under the POA may result in the court directing a pre-sentence report be prepared by a probation officer.[30] The contrast between the Code and the POA with respect to sentencing provisions is stark and without support in law, logic or public policy.

The POA may provide for imposition of terms of probation. Upon conviction of an offence under Part III of the POA, the court has the discretion to impose a suspended sentence and probation,[31] probation and a fine or imprisonment[32] or probation and a sentence of less than 90 days to be served on an intermittent basis, for example, on weekends.[33] There are no probationary provisions specifically for corporate offenders.

Probationary terms under the POA, unlike the sentencing provisions, provide little guidance on the terms of probation. For example, a corporate defendant may be required to pay compensation or restitution.[34] However, these provisions are virtually never used in sentencing since there are no statements of purpose or principles of sentencing.

---

[27]   *Ibid.*

[28]   R.S.O. 1990, c. P.33.

[29]   *Ibid.*, s. 57(1).

[30]   *Ibid.*, s. 56(1).

[31]   *Ibid.*, s. 72(1)(a).

[32]   *Ibid.*, s. 72(1)(b).

[33]   *Ibid.*, s. 72(1)(c).

[34]   *Ibid.*, s. 72(3)(a).

9.6   SENTENCING JURISPRUDENCE FOR CORPORATE OFFENDERS

Deterrence has been the central basis for sentencing of the corporate offenders up to the present time. Although deterrence has been rejected by criminologists for the individual offender, leading to the "null hypothesis", it is still the primary concept used in sentencing corporations.[35] As other commentators have said about the limit of deterrence, "A fine itself may be inappropriate under certain circumstances ... because it does not serve the functions that a punishment is suppose to serve for that particular offence."[36] What remains remarkably absent from the vast majority of both criminal and strict liability sentencing decisions relating to corporate offenders, is the constructive use of effective terms of probation and alternative means of sentencing the corporation to improve their level of legal compliance and corporate social responsibility. A move in this direction, however, has been made more available by the Bill C-45 amendments to the Code. As discussed above, these provisions compel courts to consider broad sentencing principles in each case where a corporation is convicted, and gives discretionary power to courts to consider much broader terms of probation.

There has been little application of the sentencing or probationary terms due to the paucity of corporate prosecutions since the Bill C-45 amendments. In one recent example discussed above, *Transpavé*,[37] a Quebec corporation was sentenced after pleading guilty to criminal negligence causing death of an employee arising from a workplace fatality. The court considered the new sentencing provisions of the Code for corporations in determining the appropriate fine. Justice Chevalier said:

> Transpavé is not a multinational but a family corporation. It employs up to one hundred employees during production period. It has never paid dividends to its owners-shareholders, reinvesting year after year its profits in order to modernize and remain competitive. Its owners have also been very marked by this accident. They had called the next day a psychologist to help the employees. They had personally called every employee to inform them of the place and date of the funerals of their colleague. They went to the funeral home to offer their sympathy to Mr. L'Écuyer's family and had reiterated their condolences at the hearing through their attorney. It is therefore not an incentive corporation ... with regards to the factor analysis to take into account, it must be noted that Transpavé has derived no advantage from the perpetration of this offence ...[38]

Sentencing of corporate offenders for strict liability offences, prosecuted in Ontario under the POA, have almost exclusively relied on the prin-

---

[35] A.N. Doob & C.M. Webster, "Sentence Severity and Crime: Accepting the Null Hypothesis" (2003) 30 Crime and Justice: A Review of Research 143 at 191-92.

[36] A.N. Doob & V. Marinos, "Reconceptualizing Punishment: Understanding the Limitation on the Use of Intermediate Punishment" (1995) 2 U. Chicago L. Sch. Roundtable 413 at 426.

[37] *R. c. Transpavé*, [2008] J.Q. no. 1857 (Que. Ct. (Crim & Penal Div.)).

[38] *Ibid.*, at paras. 11-12.

ciple of deterrence. Deterrence theorizes that the punishment of a corporation will deter both it and other corporations aware of the corporate offender's sentence from committing the same or similar offences in the future. In a limited sense, the law itself is intended to be both a specific and general deterrence against offences being committed. This is particularly true for offences that corporations may commit. Ignorance of the law is not an excuse or a defence for a corporation, just as it is not an excuse or defence for an individual.

Deterrence, according to Daniel Nagin, does not have the desired effect of deterring or preventing crime.[39] The courts have also recognized that a normative theory of punishment, through deterrence is not always appropriate.[40] However, the use of the deterrence theory of sentencing overlooks the important role that corporations have in our modern, complex society. Further, the primary focus on deterrence in sentencing corporate offenders in strict liability offences is, in the author's respectful view, a missed opportunity for positive change for the specific corporation, the industry in question and for corporations throughout Canadian society. The opportunity to promote corporate social responsibility through sentencing, has largely been missed by the courts in sentencing corporate offenders convicted of strict liability offences.

Several strict liability sentencing cases illustrate this point. First, is the long-standing decision of *R. v. Cotton Felts Ltd.*[41] In that decision, the Court of Appeal for Ontario dealt with the appropriateness of a sentence given by a trial judge for a conviction under the regulation pursuant to the *Occupational Health and Safety Act.*[42] The case involved a worker who had his arm caught and injured and ultimately amputated in an industrial establishment in Toronto. Although the Crown had proposed a range of fine in the amount of $4,000 to $6,000, with the maximum fine available for a corporate defendant at the time being $25,000, the trial judge, imposed a fine of $20,000. Reviewing the fitness of the sentence, on the second level of appeal to the Court of Appeal for Ontario, Mr. Justice Blair, writing for the court, set out the now well known statement with respect to sentencing factors of a corporation convicted under health and safety legislation in Ontario, and across Canada:

> The amount of the fine will be determined by a complex of considerations including the size of the company involved, the scope of the economic activity in issue, the extent of actual and potential harm to the public, and the maximum penalty prescribed by statute. *Above all*, the amount of the fine will be determined by *the need to enforce regulatory standards by deterrence.*[43]

---

[39]   Allan Manson, *The Law of Sentencing* (Toronto: Irwin Law, 2001) at 84-92.

[40]   *R. v. P. (B.W.)*, [2006] S.C.J. No. 27, 209 C.C.C. (3d) 97 (S.C.C.).

[41]   [1982] O.J. No. 178 (Ont. C.A.).

[42]   S.O. 1978, c. 83.

[43]   *R. v. Cotton Felts Ltd.*, [1982] O.J. No. 178 at para. 19 (Ont. C.A.) [emphasis added].

This decision is quoted and followed in virtually every sentencing hearing under the *Occupational Health and Safety Act.* The decision predates the substantial amendments to the *Occupational Health and Safety Act* known as Bill 208, which increased the maximum fine for a corporation by 2,000 per cent from $25,000 to $500,000. The Court of Appeal for Ontario had not revisited its decision in *Cotton Felts Ltd.* since the August 15, 1990 increase in these fines for a corporation. An interesting and often overlooked part of the decision *Cotton Felts Ltd.* relies upon two criminal prosecutions of corporations to emphasize the importance and role of deterrence.

In *R. v. Hoffman-LaRoche Ltd.,*[44] a criminal prosecution under the *Combines Investigation Act*[45] for predatory pricing, the Court emphasized the need for deterrence for the corporate offender and indicated that the fine must be substantial and significant such that it not be viewed as a mere licence for illegality by other corporations.

In the prosecution of *R. v. K-Mart Canada Limited,*[46] the corporation was convicted of the criminal offence of contravening provisions of the *Labour Relations Act*[47] of Ontario. The corporate offender had hired a security service that provided undercover anti-union infiltrators into the union with the intention of interfering with and defeating a union organizing drive. In reviewing the sentence on appeal, Howland C.J.C. said, the $25,000 fine did not "adequately reflect the gravity of the offence and was an error in principle. The fine must not be tantamount to a licence fee to commit illegal activity, but must be sufficiently substantial to warn others that such illegal activity will not be tolerated. We consider that a fine of $100,000.00 would be appropriate in the circumstances".[48] Therefore, the influence of deterrence in sentencing against corporate offenders in criminal prosecutions influenced the decision in *Cotton Felts Ltd.* that established deterrence, both specific and general, as the most important consideration in sentencing a corporate offender in criminal and strict liability offence. However, there has been no recognition of the charges in the Code relating to sentencing, in Bill C-41 and C-45, in recent strict liability sentencing decisions.

The sentencing of a corporate offender charged and convicted with an environmental offence, was considered at length by the court in *R. v. United Keno Hills Mine Ltd.*[49] In that prosecution of a strict liability environmental offence, the corporate defendant pleaded guilty to depositing waste in Yukon territorial waters in excess of the waste discharge limits prescribed by a water licence, thereby contravening the *Northern Inland Waters Act.*[50]

---

[44]   [1980] O.J. No. 3782, 30 O.R. (2d) 461 (Ont. H.C.J.), affd [1981] O.J. No. 3075 (Ont. C.A.).

[45]   R.S.C. 1970, c. C-23.

[46]   [1982] O.J. No. 54 (Ont. C.A.).

[47]   R.S.O 1970, c. 232.

[48]   *Ibid.*, para. 15.

[49]   [1980] Y.J. No. 10 (Y.T. Terr. Ct.).

[50]   R.S.C. 1970, c. 28, s. 6(1).

In assessing the appropriate fine, as a deterrent, the Territorial Court Judge Stuart, said:

> To fairly determine a deterrent fine, the capacity of each corporate offender to deflect or absorb a fine should be assessed. Thereby such matters as profits, assets, current financial status, and characteristics of the relevant market must be before the court. ... Evidence establishing corporate finances and relevant marked characteristics is essential in a system of sanctions reliant almost exclusively on fines.[51]

The current legislative sentencing provisions in the Code and the POA, and comparable provincial legislation, are not consistent with one another, especially with corporate offenders. In both regimes, the judicial trend in sentencing corporate offenders relies primarily on deterrence. The theory of deterrence has been significantly criticized and credibly challenged in criminology literature for sentencing individuals under the Code.[52] Punishing corporate offenders merely results in either a fine being absorbed, passed on to the consumer, or in extreme cases contributes to failure of the corporation. However, such an approach to sentencing will not likely deter potential corporate offenders and misses an opportunity for positive change, for both the corporate offender, and the potential onlookers in the industry and society as a whole.

The Bill C-45 amendments to the sentencing and probationary provisions in the Code, for corporate offenders, are a thoughtful addition to the sentencing process. They compel prosecutors and courts, who may often feel they have neither the time nor the resources to inquire into a number of sentencing criteria, to review the specified sentencing criteria for corporations set out in the Code. This may assist in a more meaningful sentencing process that will address how the corporation will change to prevent future offences. However, the majority of corporate offenders are charged with strict liability and not *mens rea* offences. Therefore, the absence of any similar provisions in the POA for strict liability offences in Ontario, and most Canadian provinces, remains a significant problem for sentencing the corporate offender.

9.7   A PRINCIPLED APPROACH IN SENTENCING CORPORATIONS

The principled approach towards sentencing that first arose in the mid-1990s, and for corporations on March 31, 2004, were important steps towards establishing clear, rational basis for sentencing corporations. In dealing with the issue of what is a principled approach towards sentencing the corporate offender, it is suggested that at least three questions must be asked

---

[51]   *R. v. United Keno Hills Mine Ltd.*, [1980] Y.J. No. 10 at para. 30 (Y.T. Terr. Ct.).

[52]   For example, Clayton C. Ruby, *Sentencing*, 7th ed. (Markham, ON: LexisNexis Canada, 2008) is one of the few texts that has a chapter on the subject of sentencing the corporate offender, but it only devotes a brief 11-page chapter to the subject out of 1138 pages in the text; see pp. 478-89.

and answered. First, what is the nature of the offence? Is it under the Code or is it a strict liability offence. What is the nature of the offender? What is the role of the victim in sentencing the corporate offender? What is the broader purpose of sentencing a corporation in an era of corporate social responsibility?

What is the nature of the offence? An offence against a corporation, be it *mens rea* or strict liability, is intended to direct corporate behaviour in a positive manner, by holding a corporation liable, for the benefit of society. If a corporation commits an offence and is convicted, a principled approach in sentencing must, in the author's view, consider the nature of the offence. To achieve this general questions need to be asked. What was the purpose of the offence, what was the effect on individuals, the environment or society as a whole? What degree of damage, injury, breach of trust was involved? These must all be considered as part of a principled approach to sentencing. In this respect, considering the nature of the offence is similar to the provisions of the Code for individuals as well as corporations.

What is the nature of the offender? As discussed earlier, a new formula for *mens rea* for both negligence and non-negligence offences under the Code, introduced under Bill C-45, result in the corporate offender being treated very similarly to a strict liability corporate offender. It is the nature of the organization, its size, complexity of management and decision making authority, that should also be considered in a principled approach to sentencing corporate offenders.

What is the role of the victim in sentencing the corporate offender? There can be several levels of victims when a corporation commits a *mens rea* or strict liability offence. In the area of criminal fraud, for example, there may be a number of shareholders or members of the public who have suffered financially when a corporation has committed a fraud. That group of victims should be clearly definable, and their interest in sentencing, especially under probationary term of restitution, is fairly clear and discrete. On the other hand, as in the Walkerton example, citizens who died or were rendered very ill from the E. coli breakout may be less easily identified as victims of Frank and Stan Koebel's criminal activity or the municipal or provincial government's failure to meet existing clean water regulatory requirements. A further example of the problematic role of the victim in sentencing corporate offenders is found in prosecutions under health and safety legislation. Workers are barred from suing their employers or supervisors or co-workers, as a result of workers' compensation legislation creating a "no fault" system which bars lawsuits against employers and guarantees minimum compensation to workers who are injured on the job.[53] Therefore, the need for consideration of a number of factors on the effect of victims and potential victims of corporate offences is critical in the sentencing process.

---

[53]   *Workplace Safety and Insurance Act, 1997*, S.O. 1997, c. 16, Sched. A., s. 28.

In sentencing corporations on a principled basis, what is the broader purpose of sentencing a corporate offender in an era of corporate social responsibility? Corporations are established by state authorized, public statutes. As such, the sentencing process must take that into account in sentencing. Although not limited to the broad concept of corporate social responsibility, this is a helpful starting point for establishing a principled approach to sentencing corporate offenders.

Given the important and complex role that corporations play in modern society, there is a strong basis to argue that sentencing criteria and terms of probation ought to encourage the principles of corporate social responsibility. Although corporate social responsibility has not been specifically legislated in Canada, its principles are being recognized internationally to refine and redefine the role of a corporation in modern society. Further, principles of corporate social responsibility may be used by regulators, prosecutors and the judiciary in the sentencing process to enhance the traditional goals of sentencing offenders. These concepts are further developed in the next chapter of the book.

9.8   INTRODUCTION TO PROBATION

Probation is intended to rehabilitate not punish the offender. Probation has evolved to become an important part of the criminal justice system that is often considered to be part of the sentencing process. Rather than incarcerating an individual, or setting a monetary penalty or fine to punish the offender, courts have also looked to terms of probation to attempt to rehabilitate the offender. Sentencing clearly involves punishment and retribution, probation looks at the potential for rehabilitation and restoration of the offender. Probation has not been frequently used in the prosecution and sentencing of corporations.

The origins of probation largely focus on the individual offender. The origins of probation in the English legal system date back to the early 1800s when Matthew Davenport Hill began the practice of releasing young offenders into the guardianship of local citizens, on specified conditions in the city of Birmingham. The person to whom the young offender was discharged, often a member of the clergy, was to keep a close eye on the offender, assist in their education and moral instruction, and also ensure that they did not get into further difficulty.[54]

In the United States, a Boston shoemaker by the name of John Augustus, played a similar role in mitigating penalties imposed by criminal courts on young offenders and those who are dependent on alcohol. Mr. Augustus would often approach the court, before a trial, and ask that the offender be bailed to him under his care, and he would assist in rehabilitation both before

---

[54]   Allan Manson, *The Law of Sentencing* (Toronto: Irwin Law, 2001) at 219.

and after a trial and sentencing, to assist the accused dealing with their alcoholism and also lack of employment skills.[55]

The 20th century in modern western democracy saw the development of an institutionalized probation system. The state mandated probationary system was run by the government, and staffed by professional probation officers. Probation officers became employees of the civil service at the provincial level in Canada, and carried out orders and directions of the court with respect to terms of probation. The vast majority of these probationary orders were, of course, directed at individual offenders.

The issues with respect to the eligibility for probation, the specific statutory terms of probation, revoking probation, breaching probationary conditions, and related consequences are beyond the scope of this work. However, suffice it to say that until Bill C-45 amendments to the *Criminal Code* on March 31, 2004, terms of probation were rarely considered or used in the sentencing of a corporate offender. Corporate offenders, prior to Bill C-45, were largely treated as an individual that needed to be punished and they were provided with a fine, according to the nature of the offence. The broader concept of corporate social responsibility and improving the performance of corporations vis-à-vis stakeholders, as set out in Chapter 1, was beyond the consideration of both the prosecuting attorney and the courts. In short, there was very little consideration of how probation may be used as an appropriate tool in sentencing and correcting the behaviour of the corporate offender.

9.9 PROBATION AND THE CORPORATE OFFENDER

Prior to Bill C-45, there were no specific provisions in the Code dealing with terms of probation for a corporate offender. No terms of probation were set out that were mandatory or even advisory under the Code and apparently little thought or jurisprudence existed with respect to the application of probation to corporate offenders.

Some application of probationary terms for corporate offenders was considered under the POA for strict liability offences in Ontario. Section 72 of the POA provided for a probationary order to be issued against a corporate offender that is convicted of a provincial, strict liability offence rather than a criminal offence. The scope of probationary orders has been very narrowly applied under the POA as well as the Code. One noteworthy case was the well known prosecution of *R. v. Bata Industries Ltd.*[56] In that case, a corporate defendant, together with three directors of the corporate defendant, were charged with various offences under the *Environmental Protection Act*[57] of Ontario and under the *Water Resources Act.*[58]

---

[55] *Ibid.*, at 220.
[56] [1995] O.J. No. 2691 (Ont. C.A.).
[57] R.S.O. 1980, c. 141.
[58] R.S.O. 1980, c. 361.

The case centred on the improper storage of chemical waste in drums approximate to Bata's manufacturing facility in Batawa, Ontario. Over time, the storage drums had deteriorated with the result that chemical waste leaked into the ground causing a deleterious effect on the natural environment. The corporation and two directors were ultimately convicted. By simply allowing the barrels of chemicals to sit, rust and eventually degrade to the point where they leaked the chemicals into the natural environment various offences have been committed.

One of the issues in the case considered by the Court of Appeal for Ontario was with respect to the application of the trial judge's probationary order. The trial judge had ordered the corporate defendant not to indemnify the two individual defendants, who were also convicted, by payment of their fine. This order was made as a term of probation.

The judgment of the Court of Appeal, delivered by Osborne J.A. on September 18, 1995, reversed that probation order. *Bata* appealed that part of the first appeal court's decision that affirmed the non-indemnification provision of the probation order made by the trial judge. The part of the trial judge's probation order prohibiting *Bata* from indemnifying Marchant and Weston[59] for their fines had been upheld on the first level of appeal.

In his assessment of the reasons of both the trial judge and the appeal court judge, Osborne J.A. said that "the main purpose of the indemnification prohibition term of the Bata probation order was to ensure that Marchant and Weston were appropriately punished. Both the trial judge and the appeal court judge seem to have concluded that this could only be accomplished if Marchant and Weston personally bore the burden of paying the fines imposed upon them".[60]

Justice Osborne went on to say that "using the indemnification prohibition to serve this purpose was improper because section 72(3)(c) of the *Provincial Offences Act* specifies deterrence and rehabilitation of the defendant, that is Bata, as the prescribed purposes of a probation order. It does not seem to have been Cosgrove J.'s intention in imposing the prohibition to deter Bata, or other corporations, from engaging in environmentally objectionable activities. As I have said, the focus of the indemnification prohibition in the Bata probation order was on Marchant and Weston."[61]

Justice Osborne indicated that if *Bata* is to be prohibited from indemnifying Marchant and Weston, the prohibition should occur by virtue of section 136 of the Ontario *Business Corporations Act*, and not by virtue of a probation order. According to section 136(1) of the Ontario *Business Corporations Act*,[62] indemnification is permitted if the directors acted honestly, "in good faith and in the reasonable belief that their conduct was lawful. If

---

[59]   *R. v. Bata Industries Ltd.*, [1993] O.J. No. 1679 (Ont. Gen. Div.), vard [1995] O.J. No. 2691 (Ont. C.A.).

[60]   *R. v. Bata Industries Ltd.*, [1995] O.J. No. 2691 at para. 19 (Ont. C.A.).

[61]   *Ibid.*, at para. 20.

[62]   S.O. 1982, c. 4.

Marchant and Weston did act honestly, in good faith and in the reasonable belief that their conduct was lawful, the probation order contradicts the legislative scheme of the Ontario *Business Corporations Act*."[63]

In the result, the court ruled indemnification prohibition in the *Bata* probation order was not appropriate and should be struck out of the probation order. The net effect of the Court of Appeal for Ontario's decision in *Bata* was to have a chilling effect on the application of probationary orders to corporations. Prosecutors and regulators determined that it was simply easier to have a high fine imposed on a corporation rather than to impose terms of probation, that might be challenged in court. This, of course, was unless the corporation agreed on a plea bargain agreement to a specific term of probation.

In the author's view, terms of probation may be useful for requiring a corporation to make commitments to improve business practices, environmental, health and safety, financial securities, and other related regulatory compliance. However, prosecutors are often reluctant or even loathe to agree to such terms since they would rather simply get the "big fine" and the related headline and personal recognition for achieving this "big fine" rather than improving the conduct of the particular corporation through terms of probation. This has all changed, of course, with the Bill C-45 amendments relating to terms of probation.

9.10 BILL C-45 AND NEW TERMS OF PROBATION

Bill C-45 dramatically changed the law of probation for corporate offenders. First, there were procedural changes. Section 721 of the Code, as amended by Bill C-45, is the statutory authorization for the preparation of a presentence report by a probationary officer. The report prepared by a probation officer is an important aspect of the criminal justice system with respect to sentencing and follow-up on offenders. The Lieutenant Governor in Council may make regulations prescribing the types of offences for which a court may require such a report. Subsection 721(3) delineates the mandatory required contents of a report by a probation officer. Subsection 721(1), before the Bill C-45 amendments, exempted corporations from the preparation of a report by a probation officer. This exemption continues for the new term "organization". However, it is not clear, given the broad additional optional conditions of probation, whether or not there is any significance to this exemption for organizations. This section remains the same, with the exception that "corporation" is replaced with the new term "organization". An accused organization will not require a probation report, *per se*; however, reference should be made to new probationary powers set out later in this section.

Second, there were substantive changes. Section 732.1 of the Code provides both compulsory and optional terms of probation. Subsection

---

[63]   *R. v. Bata Industries Ltd.*, [1995] O.J. No. 2691 at para. 26 (Ont. C.A.).

732.1(2) sets out conditions of probation that the offender must always comply with; namely, keep the peace and be of good behaviour, appear before the court when required to do so by order of the court, and notify the court or a probation officer in advance of any change of name or address, and promptly notify the court or the probation officer of any change of employment or occupation. In addition, optional conditions of probation are listed in subsection 732.2(3). Bill C-45 adds additional optional terms of probation in subsection 732.1(3.1). The definition of "optional conditions" is extended to include the conditions set out in subsection 3.1, which is listed below.

> (3.1) The court may prescribe, as additional conditions of a probation order made in respect of an organization, that the offender do one or more of the following:
>
> (a) make restitution to a person for any loss or damage that they suffered as a result of the offence;
>
> (b) establish policies, standards and procedures to reduce the likelihood of the organization committing a subsequent offence;
>
> (c) communicate those policies, standards and procedures to its representatives;
>
> (d) report to the court on the implementation of those policies, standards and procedures;
>
> (e) identify the senior officer who is responsible for compliance with those policies, standards and procedures;
>
> (f) provide, in the manner specified by the court, the following information to the public, namely,
>
>   (i) the offence of which the organization was convicted,
>
>   (ii) the sentence imposed by the court, and
>
>   (iii) any measures that the organization is taking – including any policies, standards and procedures established under paragraph (b) – to reduce the likelihood of it committing a subsequent offence; and
>
> (g) comply with any other reasonable conditions that the court considers desirable to prevent the organization from committing subsequent offences or to remedy the harm caused by the offence.
>
> (3.2) Before making an order under paragraph (3.1)(b), a court shall consider whether it would be more appropriate for another regulatory body to supervise the development or implementation of policies, standards and procedures referred to in that paragraph.

Bill C-45 added new optional terms of probation specifically for organizations convicted of criminal offences. There was no predecessor provision in the Code dealing with orders of probation specifically for corporations or organizations. The result of this addition to the Code will likely be a higher level of post-conviction scrutiny of organizations by the courts, probation officers and other regulatory bodies. This change in the Code integrates the new offences under sections 22.1, 22.2, and 217.1, the new sentencing and probationary powers of the courts, with, for example, OHS regulators.

This section gives courts special powers with respect to terms of probation just for organizations. These provisions would not apply to an individual who has been convicted of a criminal offence. Probation orders may include restitution, establishing corporate policies, standards and procedures, communicating them to its representatives, reports on their implementation, identify the senior officer responsible for compliance and reporting to the court on the progress of improved occupational health and safety policies, standards and procedures. These are steps that are determined by the court to ensure there are no repeat offences.

Subsection 732.1(3.1)(a) of the Code allows a court to order an organization to make restitution for any loss or damage that they suffered as a result of the offence. Remoteness of such loss or damage is not addressed, which raises the question of how remote damage must be before this section will not apply. Since workers' compensation legislation provides a no fault system of benefits to compensate injured workers and their dependents in the event of a lost time workplace injury. This subsection raises questions of whether additional compensation may be part of a restitution order. For example, in a workplace injury where there has been a conviction of a corporation, the loss will be the subject of the other compensation.

Subparagraph (b) of this new probationary provision of the Code allows the court to require an organization, after a conviction, to establish policies, standards and procedures to reduce the likelihood of the organization committing a subsequent offence. This probationary power of the courts is similar to current requirements under current provincial statutes and regulations across Canada. The Bill C-45 legal duty requires "reasonable steps" to prevent bodily harm. However, if there is such a failure to take those reasonable steps and a conviction results, then the court is now authorized to impose policies, standards and procedures that ought to have been in place to reduce the likelihood of a recurrence of the accident, injury or death in the workplace. Criminal courts do not have any previous authority or experience in establishing policies, standards and procedures for corporations. The governmental regulator that does have authority and experience in regulating policies, standards and procedures is the applicable regulator to review and recommend these standards. Therefore, it is very likely that this provision, if invoked as an appropriate probationary order, will be put in the hands of the applicable regulator, rather than the police and probationary officers for ongoing scrutiny.

Subparagraph (c) gives a court the authority to order that the policies, standards and procedures that have been required be communicated to its representatives. Communication is a critical component to an effective management system of any kind. Therefore, this probationary order appears to be consistent with the requirement for an improvement in the management system of the organization that has been convicted to ensure that a recurrence of the offence is prevented.

Subparagraph (d) requires the organization to report to the court on the implementation of those policies, standards and procedures. This heightened accountability for the organization to report its improvement to the management system complements the new above-mentioned probationary orders. Further, it holds the organization accountable, to a criminal court, for the improvement to its management system by legislating and communicating new policies, standards and procedures. Further, subparagraph (e) allows the court to identify a senior officer of the organization who is responsible for compliance with those policies, standards and procedures.

Subparagraph (f) is novel and may be controversial. It allows a court to compel the organization to provide information to the public regarding the offence with which the organization was convicted, the sentence imposed by the court, and any measures that the organization is taking to reduce the likelihood of committing a subsequent offence. In practical terms, this may require an organization to take out an ad in a national newspaper identifying that it has been charged and convicted with the offence. The organization will also be required to identify the nature of the sentence imposed on the organization, and any individual employed by the organization, as the case may be. Further, the organization may also be required to tell the public, in this national advertisement, that it has been compelled by a probationary order to take certain steps to improve its policies, standards and procedures. These types of probationary orders, often known as public shaming orders, have become increasingly popular in the United States. Public shaming as a form of punishment has its historical roots in the middle ages in Europe when individuals convicted of crimes were publicly flogged, placed in public stocks, and made the subject of very public hangings. It is open to speculate whether public shaming of corporations is really a constructive probation order.

Subparagraph (g) also gives the court a broad power to compel the organization to comply with any other reasonable conditions that the court considers desirable to prevent the organization from committing the offence again or to remedy the harm caused by the offence. This would permit the court to order the organization to comply with regulatory statutes and regulations, provide training to managers, supervisors and workers, and to ensure that an effective management system was in place. These further powers of the court, under the probationary powers of the Code, are broader than the provisions of any provincial or federal statute.

Only a few cases have yet considered the new terms of probation under Bill C-45. In *R. v. Hub Oil Co.*,[64] a corporation was convicted on charges relating to the death of two workers and injury of several others. As part of the sentence, the Court considered the new provisions of section 732.1(3.1).

---

[64]   [2005] A.J. No. 1455 (Alta. Q.B.).

On the consent of both parties, the Court held that these provisions were procedural in nature, and thus could be applied retrospectively to the events of the accident which occurred before Bill C-45 came into force. It is interesting to note that the Court applied section 732.1(3.1)(g) in ordering that a $200,000 fine be used to create bursaries for education in Workplace Safety, and to pay for the education of the children of the workers who died in the accident. Although there has been no subsequent treatment of this factor, *Hub Oil* may be a forerunner to more creative probationary orders against organizations.

In *R. v. SSI Micro Ltd.*,[65] a corporation pleaded guilty to failing to properly supervise two workers who were electrocuted during the erection of a cell phone tower, pursuant to the *Canada Labour Code*. In deciding sentence, the Court considered the submission of the defence that the corporation's representative be compelled to give presentations to schools and workplaces about the accident and workplace safety in general. This submission was made with reference to the optional conditions of section 732.1(3.1). The Court ultimately rejected this submission and said:

> I do agree such presentations have an educational component. They may deter some employers but there is a risk that the pool of employers who may be deterred would be limited to those where the presentations were made and perhaps some others through word of mouth. There are five employers listed on the proposed venues submitted by the defendant. I do not find that the deterrent effect of a company having to give a half hour to an hour presentation would or could accomplish the necessary deterrent and denunciatory effect that a sentence has to attempt to achieve in this case. [66]

Subparagraph 732.1(3.2) gives a court the power to consider the most appropriate regulatory body to supervise the development and implementation of the policies, standards and procedures referred to in the previous subparagraph. In other words, a court may reasonably consider the role and authority of the applicable regulator, as established by the applicable statute, to supervise this aspect of the new probationary powers of the court. This provision clearly indicates the need for a close working relationship between the applicable regulator, the police, the crown attorney and court in the prosecution, sentencing and probationary orders relating to the offence.

In summary, terms of probation may be helpful in achieving improved corporation accountability, if they are fully engaged by the police, regulator and prosecuting attorney, as well as the corporate defendant, to achieve meaningful change in the behaviour of the corporation. Terms of probation may potentially be more helpful, especially for a broad definition of corporate stakeholders, than are fines, even large ones. However, it takes more effort, thought and creativity to look at the marketplace in which the corporate offender has been operating to correct its behaviour, than to simply ask

---

[65] [2008] N.W.T.J. No. 26 (N.W.T. Terr. Ct.).

[66] *Ibid.*, at para. 48.

for a big fine. However attractive a big fine is for, a prosecutor, their career and prestige, that motive is not relevant for the purpose behind society's interest in prosecuting and punishing corporate offenders. Corporate offenders may be more reasonably managed, controlled and deterred from committing criminal or regulatory offences, if they knew that strict conditions of probation may be imposed if they engage in unlawful activity.

Chapter 10

NEW DIRECTIONS IN CORPORATE ACCOUNTABILITY

10.1 A PRINCIPLED APPROACH TO CORPORATE ACCOUNTABILITY

Corporate accountability covers a broad range of methods, from criminal prosecutions to corporate social responsibility. Just as corporations have evolved from royal charter to statutory availability, corporation accountability is also evolving. The idea that the modern corporation should be held accountable for its actions by criminal sanctions was largely a development of the 20th Century. Other means of corporate accountability have developed that are less draconian and arguably more effective. The emergence of corporate social responsibility occurred by the 1950s.[1] By this time, corporate crime had become widespread, business schools across North America had begun a concerted effort to promote improved corporate behaviour.[2] Corporate social responsibility ("CSR") was not born out of a specific criminal scandal that rocked the consciousness of the people, but largely from moral decision making of business itself. Unlike more severe laws and punishment stemming from single incidents and moral panic, CSR is largely a concept and movement driven by corporations themselves.

The idea of corporate philanthropy and giving back to the community was one that was alive and well since before the Great Depression. In 1951, *Harvard Business Review* published a piece by Abrams, the chairman of the board of directors of Standard Oil of Jersey, where he implored fellow corporate officers and directors to "think of themselves as professionals in the manner of physicians and lawyers, imbued with responsibilities going beyond the narrow bound of their daily work".[3] Abrams went on to say that management should see itself as a good corporate citizen. "Business managers can more effectively contribute to the solution of the many complex social problems of our time. There is no higher responsibility, there is no higher duty of professional management."[4] The altruism of Abrams, how-

---

[1]   William Frederick, *Corporation, Be Good! The Story of Corporate Social Responsibility* (Indianapolis: Dog Ear Publishing, 2006).

[2]   *Ibid.*, at 6.

[3]   *Ibid.*, at 7.

[4]   *Ibid.*, at 8.

ever, was quickly challenged by Howard Bowen in 1953[5] and later by Milton Freedman, of the Chicago School of Economics.

The 1960s and 1970s saw the introduction of business morality and CSR into a more thought-out and organized corporate initiative. Frederick facilitated this by delineating five requirements of every CSR plan:[6] first, the plan should be based on the current economic climate; second, the plan should be based on the new and emerging concepts of management and administration, including using scientific methodology; third, an adequate CSR plan will understand that it must learn from the past to prevent future mistakes; fourth, a CSR strategy will recognize that the behaviour of individual businessmen is a function of the social role they play in business and in society; and fifth, a CSR plan takes a real and deliberate effort to create an effective plan.

A principled approach towards accountability of corporations requires at least four questions that must be addressed. What is the nature of the community standard or legal requirement that the corporation must meet? What is the nature of the corporation's breach of the standard or legal requirement? What is the effect on the stakeholders or victim of the corporation's breach of the standard or legal requirement? What is the broader purpose of punishing or holding the corporation accountable for its breach of the standard or legal requirement?

What is the nature of the community standard or legal requirement? An offence committed by a corporation, be it *mens rea* or strict liability, is intended to prohibit, control and direct corporate behaviour in a positive manner for the benefit of society with a specific legal requirement. If a corporation fails to meet a legal standard, it may be charged, convicted and sentenced. A principled approach must consider the nature of the offence, the stakeholder or victim, and the nature of the offender. In other words, what was the purpose of the offence, what was the effect of the breach on individuals, environment or society as a whole. In setting community standards and legal requirements for corporations, are we making isolated morality statements or establishing broad principles of socially acceptable behaviour. To use the Garland analysis, does the law set standards for corporations to promote market freedom or the democratization of social life and culture.[7] What degree of damage, injury, breach of trust was involved must all be considered as part of a principled approach. In this respect, considering the nature of the community standards that establish the legal requirements or offence that will be enforced is critical to the role of corporate accountability.

---

[5]   Frank Abrams, *The Social Responsibilities of the Businessman* (New York: Harper and Brothers, 1953).

[6]   William Frederick, *Corporation, Be Good! The Story of Corporate Social Responsibility* (Indianapolis: Dog Ear Publishing, 2006).

[7]   David Garland, *The Culture of Control* (Chicago: University of Chicago Press, 2001) at 87-99.

It is also important in a principle approach to corporate accountability to know the nature of the corporation's breach of the standard or legal requirement. As discussed earlier, the new formula for corporate guilt for both negligence and non-negligence offences under the *Criminal Code*,[8] introduced under Bill C-45, results in the corporate criminal offender being treated very similarly to a corporate strict liability offender. Since corporate criminal liability may now be more easily proven, should aggressive prosecution and higher fines be more frequently pursued? This will depend on the nature of the breach of the standard or legal requirement in question. The nature of the organization, its size, complexity of management role as an employer and the nature of the breach should also be considered in a principled approach to corporate accountability. Specific consideration must also be given to the nature of the corporation in question.

What is the effect on the stakeholder or victim in the corporation's breach of the standard or legal requirement? There can be several levels of victims when a corporation commits a *mens rea* or strict liability offence. As set out in Chapter 5, possible victims may be identified as internal and external stakeholders and the public. For example, in the area of capital markets fraud, there may be a number of shareholders who have suffered financially when a corporation commits an offence; but the public may also be indirectly affected as well. The group of stakeholders and victims should be clearly definable, and their damage or injury flowing from the breach of the standard or legal requirement clearly identified.

In the Walkerton example, citizens who died or were rendered very ill from the E. coli outbreak may be less easily satisfied by the municipal and provincial government's failure to meet existing clean water regulatory requirements. When a corporation permits a workplace death, as seen in the Westray Mine Disaster, prosecution does not directly affect the victim's family. Workers and their families are barred from suing their employers, supervisors or co-workers, as a result of workers' compensation legislation that establish a "no fault" system which provides compensation to workers who are injured on the job.[9] There is a need to consider these and other factors, regarding the effect of stakeholders and potential victims of corporate offences in the corporate accountability process.

Finally, it is important to ask, what is the broader purpose of punishing or holding accountable the corporation for its breach of standards or legal requirements? Is prosecuting and sentencing a corporate offender by fines for deterrents the best way to stop illegal activity at a corporate level and promote corporate social responsibility? The review of Administrative Monetary Penalties, Alternative Dispute Resolution and Corporate Social Responsibility in this chapter is intended to address those questions.

---

[8]   R.S.C. 1985, c. C-46 [hereinafter the "Code"].

[9]   *Workplace Safety and Insurance Act, 1997*, S.O. 1997, c. 16, Sched. A., s. 28.

10.2 ADMINISTRATIVE MONETARY PENALTIES

10.2.1 Introduction to Administrative Monetary Penalties

Administrative Monetary Penalties ("AMP") are a relatively new development in the area of corporate accountability. The theory behind AMPs is that rather than use the prosecution process, a corporation may be directly assessed with monetary penalties for a legal contravention. AMPs are more civil than criminal both in terms of legal process and stigma. One of the interesting aspects of AMPs is that since criminal or strict liability charges are not laid, there is no prosecution process, no Charter rights, no trial and there is no sentencing hearing to determine an appropriate penalty for the crime or offence committed by the corporation. AMPs get right to the penalty without a prosecution.

AMPs circumvent the rights and protections of the criminal justice system for any corporation assessed with an AMP. If criminal prosecutions are a blunt and expensive instrument for corporate accountability, then AMPs are a pointed and economic means of achieving corporate accountability. AMPs can be tailored to the specific administrative and regulatory goals, by a specialized regulatory body or administrator, rather than a generic judge or justice of the peace in a criminal or *quasi*-criminal prosecution.

A further issue with respect to AMPs is whether or not there is a right of appeal and how it establishes a reverse onus on the corporation that is otherwise unconstitutional under section 11(d) of the *Charter of Rights and Freedoms*.[10] There is also the question of whether or not AMPs should be used as a replacement of regulatory or criminal prosecution or in addition to them. Put another way, the issue is if AMPs are used will corporations be free from double jeopardy, as protected by section 11(h) of the Charter, or are corporations potentially exposed to both prosecution and the penalties associated with AMPs?

Several court challenges to very high AMPs, imposed in various regulatory regimes, have been made on the basis of their constitutionality. There may be some point where the AMPs are so high that they are really a disguised criminal or strict liability penalty. Can the legislatures and policy makers across Canada compromise or even deny the rights and protections of the prosecution process and under the Charter for the purpose of pursuing pointed and economic corporate accountability? These issues remain to be fully resolved. The authority of legislatures to pass AMPs that are more akin to criminal and regulatory prosecution than administrative properties, is an important legal and policy issue.

---

[10] Part I of the *Constitution Act, 1982*, being Schedule B to the *Canada Act, 1982* (U.K.), 1982, c. 11 [hereinafter the "Charter"].

10.2.2 Comparison with Criminal and Strict Liability Offences

Corporate offenders may face a number of state authorized methods of accountability for their corporate decisions, and their adverse effects both internally and externally from the corporation. This section will address the similarities and differences between AMPs and offences. This review will identify the advantages and disadvantages of the different models of corporate accountability. The first similarity is that they are all legal approaches prescribed by statute, to achieve the same goal, corporate accountability. Common law, or judicial decisions, cannot impose an AMP or criminal or strict liability offence on corporations without legal authority. All of these means of corporate accountability are driven by the decisions of the respective legislatures and authorized by a democratic process. Therefore, what the Canadian people want, through their democratically elected representatives, the people get, within legal and constitutional limits. This tension of what a democratic society wants, is partially embodied in section 1 of the Charter, is the so-called "saving" provisions that permits certain Charter violations in a "free and democratic society". Ostensibly, policy advisors and political decision makers are presumed to have taken into account the values of the Charter, discussed above, as well as the saving provision, section 1 of the Charter.[11] However, there remains some tension between the rights of corporations under the Charter and the decisions of policy makers to take away those rights by imposing AMPs rather than establishing criminal or strict liability offences, for the purpose of the accountability of corporations.

Second, AMPs are very different than both criminal and strict liability offences.[12] Although some differences between criminal and strict liability offences are important, both are still offences in law and recognized as such under the Charter. Both use the prosecution to process corporations in a public court process to pursue corporate accountability.[13] However, since AMPs are not offences *per se* in the ordinary meaning of the term, and as prescribed under the Charter, they do not provide the same due process or procedural protection as do offences. The debate on the constitutionality of AMPs raises concerns about very high monetary AMPs being imposed in similar, if not identical, circumstances to the possibility of a criminal or regulatory charge being laid.[14] However, AMPs are not offences *per se* and do not provide a corporation with the protections of the trial process. Therefore, the second point of comparison between AMPs and criminal strict liability offences is that the former are not offences, whereas the latter are both offences.

Third, the similarity between AMPs and criminal and *quasi*-criminal offences, is that they both flow from alleged contravention or violation of

---

[11]   See Chapter 7, Rights of Corporations under the Charter.
[12]   See Chapter 3, Models of Corporate Liability and Categories of Offences.
[13]   See Chapter 1, Introduction to Corporate Crime and Accountability.
[14]   See section 10.2.6 of this chapter.

the applicable statute or regulatory standard. For example, several corporations have recently been charged with contravening both the Bill C-45 occupational health and safety criminal negligence provisions of the Code as well as Ontario's *Occupational Health and Safety Act.*[15] Similarly, AMPs require a threshold decision by regulatory officials that the corporate entity has contravened a statutory or regulatory standard. There is usually a thorough evidentiary and technical investigation prior to the decision of a particular securities, environmental, health and safety or food safety regulator before the imposition of AMPs. The regulator must determine that there is a contravention of the statute or regulation prior to issuing an AMP. Therefore, if a corporate business enterprise is charged with an offence or assessed with an AMP, they are both predicated on an alleged contravention of a statutory or regulatory standard. The offence requires proof beyond a reasonable doubt in a court of law, whereas the AMP only requires proof gathered by the regulator to itself.

Fourth, an important distinction between AMPs and offences is the lack of due process, evidentiary protections and constitutional rights including rights under the Charter when a corporate entity is alleged to have contravened a statutory or regulatory standard. The Code and strict liability offence statutes, prescribe various steps that prosecutors must take in order to facilitate fairness in the prosecution process. These are addressed in detail in Chapter 6. Further, the courts have, for over 100 years, set down various standards, tests and procedural rights of defendants, both individual and corporations, when charged with offences.

Charter protections are afforded to a corporate defendant when charged with an offence. Rights of corporations under the Charter are extensively discussed in Chapter 7.[16] In contrast, AMPs provide little if no procedural rights and protections for their recipients. The good faith of regulators as well as the technical expertise of regulators, are often the only material protections to prevent an AMP from being issued against a corporation. There is no pre-charge scrutiny of AMPs by a Justice of the Peace, no duty on a prosecutor to be a "minister of justice" in scrutinizing a charge before it is laid,[17] and supervisory role of the court to ensure that frivolous and vexatious charges are not proceeded with at any point during a prosecution. If AMPs are assessed against a corporation, the simple obligation of the corporation is to rectify any ordered contravention and to pay the monetary penalty. Any right of appeal is after the fact of the AMP being assessed so it is not a procedural right of fairness and fundamental justice. Part of this difference between AMPs and offences is that there is no fundamental right to be

---

15   Reference to the criminal and *Occupational Health and Safety Act quasi*-criminal prosecution against *1531147 Ontario Ltd. o/a Millennium Crane Rentals Ltd.* and *Metron Construction*, both before the courts at the time of writing.

16   See Chapter 7, Rights of Corporations under the Charter.

17   See the role of a Crown Attorney as interpreted by the Supreme Court of Canada in *R. v. Boucher*, [1954] S.C.J. No. 54, [1955] S.C.R. 16 (S.C.C.).

presumed innocent and to make full answer and defence to the charges before the assessment of the contravention being accepted by a court or the sentencing and imposition of a penalty. The right to be presumed innocent has long existed in the common law and is now enshrined in the Charter.[18]

Fifth, the long recognized "golden thread of English law", the presumption of innocence, now enshrined in section 11(d) of the Charter, guides all other procedural and substantive rights during the course of an investigation and prosecution of an offence, be it criminal or strict liability offence. No such right exists for the assessment of an AMP. The presumption of innocence excuses an individual accused from having to testify in his own defence, requires the prosecution to always prove the alleged contravention of the statutory regulatory provisions, and supports various procedural protections throughout the prosecution and trial process. AMPs provide none of these protections to the corporate accused. In contrast, AMPs afford no presumption of innocence, no right to make full answer and defence and also no procedural and substantive rights prior to an assessment of contravention of the statute of regulations. Further, AMPs presumptively hold the corporation in contravention as a prerequisite to the penalty being imposed. This is arguably the most serious limitation of the rights of a corporation when assessed with an AMP.

Sixth, imposition of a penalty or sentencing is dramatically different against a corporation between the AMP process and the prosecution process. An AMP presumptively assesses a contravention of the statutory regulatory provision and issues a penalty at the same time. The quantum of the penalty may be strictly imposed by law or may be the subject of discretion of the regulator or regulatory oversight tribunal with AMPs. In either case, the regulator, and not a third party judicial decision maker, will assess a penalty against the corporation. In contrast, in a prosecution, an imposition of a penalty by way of a sentencing hearing, can only take place after a finding of guilt that a corporation has committed an offence. The finding of guilt against the corporation requires proof beyond a reasonable doubt, the criminal standard of proof, for both a criminal and strict liability offence.

The sentencing process involves a sentencing hearing, dealing with all issues relevant to sentencing and assessment of penalty. A full opportunity to call evidence, make submissions and argue case law and precedent is available to a corporate defendant charged and convicted with an offence during a sentencing hearing. The sentencing hearing, principles and process is discussed in Chapter 9.[19] The right of a convicted corporate defendant to participate fully in a sentencing hearing is another right enshrined by law that is not enjoyed by a corporation that receives an AMP. However, the penalty is not usually the subject of consultation between the regulator and the corporation receiving the penalty. Therefore, the penalty or punishment

---

[18]   See s. 11(d) of the Charter.
[19]   See Chapter 9, Sentencing and Probation for Corporate Offenders.

process is significantly different between the AMP and the prosecution regime.

Seventh, is the availability of appeals. There are some similarities and differences between the AMPs regime and prosecution of offences. In a prosecution, be it under the Code or a strict liability offence, there is always a right of appeal. An appeal is typically available on issues of both fact and law, with different tests being set out for the appeal court to consider. On questions of fact or mixed fact in law, deference is given to the trial court or tribunal.

AMPs, on the other hand, do not always provide for an appeal. AMPs may be imposed by regulators under statutory authority without providing a full right of appeal. In such circumstances, there is an administrative law right to a judicial review. However, the grounds for judicial review are largely jurisdictional, set high standards and are limited to principles of natural justice, they do not afford *per se* a full right of appeal.

The subject matter of an appeal can also be a similarity or a difference between AMPs. Some statutory regimes that provide for AMPs to be imposed against corporations also provide a full right of appeal. However, others limit the right of appeal to a "due diligence" type of answer and defence. For example, the *Financial Institutions and Deposit Insurance System Amendment Act*[20] provides for a due diligence defence under section 34 of that statute while others do not provide a right of appeal at all.

10.2.3 AMPs and Corporate Deterrents

AMPs provide a clear and specific monetary penalty for corporations who contravene published statutory and regulatory standards. However, as discussed above, corporations are not afforded a presumption of innocence or the right to make full answer and defence with AMPs. Once the regulator has determined and assessed that an AMP is appropriate, they may be issued. The policy debate is whether an AMP is a mere punishment for corporate decision makers who do not comply with the law, or do they provide a general deterrent, to other corporations in the regulated field, to comply with the law and not engage in contraventions. In other words, does an AMP deal with specific or general deterrents, or both.

Specific deterrent, the subject of a great deal of sentencing literature and jurisprudence, relates to a specific penalty imposed on a specific offender for a specific offence. In contrast, a general deterrent theory is that other members of a regulated group, or society as a whole, will take notice of a particular penalty on an offender, and as a result of general deterrents, be deterred from getting the same contravention. Deterrence in sentencing the corporate offender is addressed in Chapter 9.

---

[20]   R.S.C. 1985, c. 18 (3rd Supp.), s. 34.

The role of AMPs as general deterrents was considered by the Supreme Court in *R. v. Cartaway Resources Corp.*[21] The facts and background are succinctly summarized by the Court in the first two paragraphs:

> In the autumn of 1994, a group of securities brokers, including Robert Hartvikson and Blayne Johnson, banded together to make a quick profit. They orchestrated the purchase of Cartaway Resources Corporation ("Cartaway") and funnelled some mining claims into Cartaway through a shelf company. Without disclosing to investors the material change in Cartaway's business to a mining exploration firm, they entered into a private placement, which they split among friends and other employees of First Marathon Securities Limited ("First Marathon").

> The British Columbia Securities Commission (the "Commission") found that Hartvikson and Johnson had breached s. 61 of the Securities Act, R.S.B.C. 1996, c. 418 (the "Act") — the prospectus requirement — by splitting the private placement, and thereby relying on a prospectus exemption to which they were not entitled. The Commission further found that it was in the public interest to impose the maximum financial penalty of $100,000 under s. 162 of the Act. On this appeal, we are not concerned with Hartvikson and Johnson's other dealings.[22]

The Court then went on to consider the proper standard of review of the role of the British Columbia Securities Commission and the 5.1 million dollars in trading profits earned by Mr. Hartvikson and Mr. Johnson, in assessing the suspension from involvement in publicly traded companies and a maximum fine, under the legislation, of an Administrative Monetary Penalty in the amount of $100,000 each. Although the British Columbia Court of Appeal had reduced the quantum of the AMP, the Supreme Court reversed the appellant court decision and reinstated the maximum AMP proposed by the Commission, for, among other reasons, general deterrents. The Court said:

> In my view, nothing inherent in the Commission's public interest jurisdiction, as it was considered by this Court in *Asbestos, supra*, prevents the Commission from considering general deterrents in making an order. To the contrary, it is reasonable to view general deterrents as an appropriate, and perhaps necessary, consideration in making orders that are both protective and preventative. Ryan J.A. recognized this in her dissent: "The notion of general deterrents is neither punitive nor remedial. A penalty that is meant to generally deter is a penalty designed to discourage or hinder like behaviour in others" (para. 125).[23]

Therefore, it appears that the Supreme Court has accepted the notion that AMPs play an important role in providing general deterrents, in a securities regulatory regime, to protect the public and to discourage securities mischief by other players in the market. This logic would likely apply to other regulated spheres where AMPs are established in Canadian law.

---

[21] [2004] S.C.J. No. 22, 238 D.L.R. (4th) 193 (S.C.C.).

[22] *Ibid.*, at paras. 1-2.

[23] *Ibid.*, at para. 60.

10.2.4 AMPs and Due Diligence

AMPs and due diligence have, at first blush, very little to do with each other. They are distinct and separate concepts in law. The due diligence defence is a defence enshrined by the Supreme Court in *R. v. Sault Ste. Marie (City)*[24] and applies only to strict liability offences. This judicial decision effectively established new law in providing a reverse-onus defence in a non-*mens rea* defence. There is a comprehensive review of the due diligence defence in Chapter 8. However, there is some blurring of distinctions in the area of AMPs and due diligence in providing some measure of due diligence as an answer to AMPs on an appeal or the assessment of a penalty. In other words, the language of the due diligence defence, discussed in Chapter 8,[25] has some application to both the assessment of the contravention and quantum of monetary penalty imposed by the AMP. For example, pursuant to the *Financial Consumer Agency of Canada Act*,[26] the statutory due diligence answer is available for the imposition of an AMP on an affected corporation.

An example of the application of due diligence principles is a factor for assessing the quantum of the penalty, similar to a sentence, reference can be made to the *Agriculture and Agri-food Administrative Monetary Penalties Act*.[27] The statute actually prohibits the application of due diligence principles for the purpose of assessment of the AMP.[28] However, it allows for the quantum of the penalty to be mitigated by the degree of advertence or inadvertence associated with the contravention.[29]

Finally, it is worth noting that some statutes which impose AMPs have gone so far as to essentially prohibit due diligence principles from being applied to either the assessment of an AMP in the first place, or in the quantum of the AMP. For example, the recent amendments to the *Environmental Protection Act*[30] in Ontario expressly eliminate the application of a due diligence defence to the environmental penalty.

10.2.5 AMPs and Double Jeopardy

The concept of double jeopardy has developed from common law jurisprudence over the centuries from England to being enshrined in the Charter.[31] When a corporation is charged and either acquitted or convicted of an offence, be it criminal or strict liability, that will end the matter, subject to the right of appeal of both parties. The principle upon which a corporate or other defendant may rely to ensure that it is not charged, prosecuted or convicted

---

[24]   [1978] S.C.J. No. 59, 85 D.L.R. (3d) 161 (S.C.C.).
[25]   See Chapter 8, Defences to Criminal and Strict Liability Offences.
[26]   S.C. 2001, c. 9.
[27]   S.C. 1995, c. 40.
[28]   *Ibid.*, s. 18.
[29]   *Ibid.*, s. 4(3).
[30]   R.S.O. 1990, c. E.19, s. 182.3(10).
[31]   See the Charter, s. 11(h).

of the same offence twice, is the principle of double jeopardy. Enshrined under the Charter, this principle is extremely important to protect the rights and the due administration of justice of all defendants, including corporations, not to be tried and convicted twice for the same offence.

However, since an AMP is not based on the prosecution of an offence for which rights of a defendant are enshrined, then the question that arises is whether an AMP is equivalent to a conviction, for the purposes of avoiding further enforcement by means of prosecution. This issue remains unresolved and unanswered in Canadian law.

10.2.6 Constitutionality of AMPs

The constitutionality and potential excesses of AMP penalties could have been the first subject of this section of this chapter, however, given recent court decisions it is now generally accepted that AMPs are legitimate, constitutional remedies and the subject has been relegated to more of a policy and academic discussion than a serious legal objection to AMPs. Hence, the comments on the constitutionality of AMPs that follow in this text have been left to the end of this section on Administrative Monetary Penalties.

AMPs have had their constitutionality under the Charter. As discussed in Chapter 7, there is limited application of the rights of section 7 of the Charter to corporations. The more significant right for corporations under the Charter, that was subject of judicial challenge regarding the nature and quantum of AMPs, is section 11 of the Charter.

The courts have been asked to consider several constitutional challenges to the character, nature, process, right of appeal and quantum of penalty in determining whether or not an AMP falls within the appropriate constitutional authority and whether or not it may contravene section 11 or other provisions of the Charter.

The Supreme Court in *Martineau v. Canada (Minister of Natural Revenue)*,[32] was called upon to determine whether a Notice of Ascertained Forfeiture, under the *Customs Act* was a proceeding that was subject to the constitutional protection afforded to persons charged with an offence under the Charter. In particular, the Court was called upon to determine whether or not the powers under the *Customs Act* amounted to an offence or were more consistent with a civil proceeding or AMP. If the Supreme Court determined that the AMP was a penal offence, it would be subject to review under the Charter. The Court stated "a distinction must therefore be drawn between penal proceedings on the one hand and administrative proceedings on the other. Only penal proceedings attract the application of section 11 of the *Charter*".[33]

The Court considered three primary aspects of the *Customs Act* provisions to resolve this issue. The Court first considered the objectives of

---

[32] [2004] S.C.J. No. 58, 247 D.L.R. (4th) 577 (S.C.C.).
[33] *Ibid.*, at para. 23.

the *Customs Act* and the forfeiture provision, then the purpose of the sanction and finally the process leading to the imposition of the sanction. After careful review of these considerations, the Court came to the following conclusion:

> To characterize the appellant as a "person charged with an offence" would have a significant impact on the entire body of legislation whose purpose is taxation and economic regulation. To recognize an alleged offender in these spheres as a "person charged with an offence" even where he or she is not in fact charged, would undermine the effectiveness of the system and substantially increase the cost of administering it.
>
> In this context, an analysis of s. 124 of the *C.A.* and its related provisions shows that the process they establish is not penal in nature and that the sanction provided for does not have true penal consequences within the meaning of *Wigglesworth*.
>
> Therefore, rule 236(2) of the *F.C.R.* does not violate s. 11(c) of the *Charter* by requiring the appellant, as plaintiff in an action under s. 135 of the *C.A.* to submit to an examination for discovery.
>
> For these reasons, the court dismissed the appeal from the bench.[34]

Courts since *Martineau* have upheld the constitutionality of AMPs. Therefore, the question remains, for corporations and their legal advisors, what rights if any exist to demand fair process, fundamental justice and reasonable treatment during the investigation and imposition of AMPs. The short answer is to review the statutes and cases interpreting the appeal provisions for those particular AMPs. The more involved answer is the application of administrative law principles. Although the body of administrative law is somewhat general and less defined than the rights of defendants in criminal and strict liability offences under the Charter, they nonetheless provide some supervisory authority to the courts when regulators and administrative tribunals go to the extreme of ignoring fairness and the imposition of penalties including AMPs.

10.3 ALTERNATIVE DISPUTE RESOLUTION AND CORPORATE ACCOUNTABILITY

There is a need to rethink corporate accountability beyond prosecution and the traditional criminal justice system. The evolution of corporate accountability must recognize the important role of the corporation in society and the politics of redistribution.[35] Prosecution of corporations is a blunt and expensive instrument that is not always effective or desirable. Corporate accountability can benefit from the considerable literature and experience of Alternative Dispute Resolution ("ADR") to achieve a broader array of outcomes than can prosecutions. ADR has become well accepted in the Cana-

---

[34] *Ibid.*, at paras. 87-90.

[35] Jock Young, *The Vertigo of Late Modernity* (Los Angeles: Sage Publishing, 2007) at 38-40.

dian justice system for civil matters, with settlement rates approaching 90 per cent through the use of negotiation, mediation and arbitration to resolve civil actions.[36] The ADR emphasis on appropriate resolution has significantly reduced the number of commercial lawsuits that proceed to trial.[37] In the family law area, collaborative law, where each party has a lawyer in a negotiating setting, has assisted many parties to resolve disputes that are emotionally charged.[38] Although ADR has been a transforming trend in the administration of civil justice in Canada, it has yet to be a significant force in the public policy of corporate accountability.

The ADR literature does not deal extensively with criminal law.[39] Other than limited application in restorative justice principles, the criminal justice system remains primarily focused on retributive justice through a system of prosecution, conviction and punishment.[40] Both *mens rea* and strict liability offences against corporations lend themselves readily to the application of ADR principles. When the liberty of the subject is not an issue, when the accused is not an individual, ADR has tremendous advantages. There is some support for this approach in the recommendations of Professor Michael Code and the Honourable Patrick J. Lesage in their report on how to improve the administration of justice in large, complex criminal prosecutions.[41]

The ADR movement historically was more a reaction to the dissatisfaction with delays, costs, inefficiencies and failures of the civil justice system than a creative, proactive solution. Macfarlane states "some of the most significant innovations in developing an early and informal dispute resolution process have grown out of the dissatisfaction felt by some members of the profession with the limits of traditional litigation to bring peace and closure to their clients."[42] On the one hand, the ADR movement has largely focused on procedural change regarding how disputes may be resolved and avoided in the future. On the other hand, courts have generally been associated with substantive, constitutional change, such as race relations in *Brown*

---

[36] Julie Macfarlane, *The New Lawyer: How Settlement is Transforming the Practice of Law* (Vancouver: UBC Press, 2008).

[37] Julie Macfarlane, *Dispute Resolution: Readings and Case Studies* (Toronto: Emond Montgomery Publications, 2003) at 622-26.

[38] *Ibid.*, at 396-407, and 410.

[39] For example, in one of the course text, Julie Macfarlane, *Dispute Resolution: Readings and Case Studies* (Toronto: Emond Montgomery Publications, 2003) there were only seven pages specifically dealing with criminal matters, according to the index, pages 425-31 inclusive.

[40] Julie Macfarlane, *Dispute Resolution: Readings and Case Studies* (Toronto: Emond Montgomery Publications, 2003) at 425-27.

[41] The Honourable Patrick J. Lesage, C.M., Q.C. & Professor Michael Code, *Report of the Review of Large and Complex Criminal Case Procedures* (Ontario: Ministry of the Attorney General, November 2008) submitted to the Honourable C. Bentley, Attorney General, online: <http://www.attorneygeneral.jus.gov.on.ca/english/about/pubs/lesage_code/lesage_code_report _en.pdf>.

[42] Julie Macfarlane, *The New Lawyer: How Settlement is Transforming the Practice of Law* (Vancouver: UBC Press, 2008) at 7.

v. Board of Education[43] in the United States and abortion rights in *R. v. Morgentaler*[44] in Canada. Therefore, ADR is generally more appropriate as a model of dispute resolution than a legal process that sets precedent and addresses constitutional issues.

In civil matters, ADR involves case management, mandatory mediation, judicial pre-trial conferences and cost consequence rules tied to formal offers to settle which have changed the civil procedure process into a pro-settlement system of procedural justice.[45] The use of ADR to address corporate accountability, may be better called upon to augment rather than replace higher fines. More constructive and flexible processes that engage the opportunity of social change is critical in a society that Jock Young describes as increasingly porous.[46] ADR also provides lawyers, defendants and judicial officials creative, constructive and conciliatory processes in the resolution of disputes.[47] ADR can be, as Dana Curtis says, "an agent of change".[48]

Governments are straining under the costs of funding a public prosecution office, a public court system and lengthy trial, including the prosecution of corporations. Limits on public resources for the administration of justice are being strained. One author noted, "the realization among policy makers of an acute need for change in public justice systems has been a watershed in many North American jurisdictions and has led to the initiation of dozens of programs that encourage and facilitate early negotiations and assessment of resolution possibilities".[49] The tremendous public cost of investigating and prosecuting corporations is staggering. Ruby states that the public cost of prosecuting corporations is a major reason why so few prosecutions of corporations are brought forward in the criminal justice system.[50]

The role of ADR and the role of lawyers as agents of change is not without its challenges. Lawyers have been criticized that "... there are certainly obvious financial advantages to the profession of settling after, rather than before, the most costly steps in litigation (usually discover-

---

[43] 347 US 483 (1959).

[44] [1988] S.C.J. No. 1 (S.C.C.).

[45] For example, the Ontario *Rules of Civil Procedure*, which came into force in 1985, introduced Rule 49 offers that encouraged, by their procedural mechanism, serious offers of settlement to be made as soon as possible; putting an unreasonable litigant at significant risk of paying a punitive order for costs, even if they had a measure of success; see *Rules of Civil Procedure*, R.R.O. 1990, Reg. 194, Rule 49.

[46] Jock Young, *The Vertigo of Late Modernity* (Los Angeles: Sage Publishing, 2007) at 38-40.

[47] Julie Macfarlane, *The New Lawyer: How Settlement is Transforming the Practice of Law* (Vancouver: UBC Press, 2008) at 3.

[48] Dana Curtis, "Reconciliation and the Role of Empathy" in James J. Alfini and Eric R. Galton, eds., *ADR Personalities and Practice Tips* (Washington, D.C.: American Bar Association Section of Dispute Resolution, 1998) at 62.

[49] Julie Macfarlane, *The New Lawyer: How Settlement is Transforming the Practice of Law* (Vancouver: UBC Press, 2008) at 8.

[50] For example, Clayton C. Ruby's text, *Sentencing*, 7th ed. (Markham, ON: LexisNexis Canada, 2008), is one of the few criminal law texts that has a chapter on the subject of sentencing the corporate offender; however, the chapter only devotes a brief 11 pages out of 1138 to sentencing corporate offenders; see pp. 478-89.

ies)".[51] Although some lawyers have pioneered the field of ADR, the legal profession generally has been dragged into the ADR process by clients and policy makers.

ADR in civil litigation has been broadly recognized as a success.[52] The public and politicians remain cautious on the value of ADR in the criminal justice system, due to the perceived failure of both the retributive and the restoration of justice models.[53] The prosecution of corporations may not be as effective to achieve corporate accountability as ADR. The realities of the new social media, increased transparency and globalization present ADR as a viable approach to corporate accountability.

One recent example in the evolution of corporate accountability has developed in federal environmental prosecutions. Environmental Protection Alternative Measures ("EPAM") are an alternative to regulatory prosecution for a contravention of the *Canadian Environmental Protection Act 1999* ("CEPA").[54] An EPAM is agreement that is negotiated and mediated between the defendant and the Attorney General of Canada, prosecuting under the CEPA. EPAMs are established by CEPA and those provisions set out who is eligible for an EPAM, what are the potential terms and limits on EPAMs, and how they must be documented and enforced.[55] Some of the alternative measures are the development of pollution prevention measures, reduction of toxic substances emissions, installation of better pollution control technology systems, and measures taken to clean up environmental damage.

The advantages of an EPAM for a defendant include the ability to use ADR to negotiate a constructive solution when a legal contravention of CEPA occurs. There is also a reduction of the legal costs of a lengthy trial, avoiding a conviction and a record of offence.[56] The advantages for the federal CEPA regulator include negotiating terms that improve the environment, motivating the defendant to invest in environmental protection measures, and achieving the public purpose of CEPA rather than simply imposing a fine against the offending organization.

The EPAM becomes a public document and is available for media scrutiny. The CEPA environmental registry is made available to the public, the media and all interested parties on the Internet.[57] This environmental ADR addresses one of the primary criticisms of ADR, namely the failure to

---

[51]   Julie Macfarlane, *The New Lawyer: How Settlement is Transforming the Practice of Law* (Vancouver: UBC Press, 2008) at 85.

[52]   For a conceptual overview of ADR offered by Professor P. Emond see: Julie Macfarlane, *Dispute Resolution: Readings and Case Studies* (Toronto: Emond Montgomery Publications, 2003) at 104-106.

[53]   *Ibid.*, at 9-10.

[54]   S.C. 1999, c. 33.

[55]   *Ibid.*, ss. 295-309.

[56]   In many commercial and public contracts, a corporation may be precluded from tendering a bid if they have a criminal, health and safety, or environmental record of conviction.

[57]   See online: <http://www.ec.gc.ca/lcpe-cepa/default.asp?lang=En&n=66B8D849-1>.

uphold legal standards and make publication of the same. Fiss argues that this type of ADR promotes peace through settlements, rather than justice, based on the rules of law.[58] In short, the evolution of EPAMs gives the stakeholders the opportunity to engage in negotiation and mediation in a process that achieves the broader purpose of public welfare statutes.

In summary, the ADR process can achieve many more objectives than a large AMP or fine to a corporate offender arising from a prosecution. Corporate fines generally get passed on to customers and end users. The use of ADR to address contraventions of capital markets, environmental, occupational and public safety laws will require a strong legislative mandate. Leadership in this area is an especially ripe opportunity for policy makers who understand the critical role that corporations play not only in the economy but also in social transformation in a turbulent age.[59] Macfarlane sets out the following challenge to the legal profession and system of justice: "the role of law and legal advice in a model of conflict resolution advocacy is perhaps the most complex, contentious and challenging dimension of the practice of the new lawyer."[60] For lawyers both prosecuting and defending corporate offenders, in both *mens rea* and strict liability offences, this task may be a meaningful contribution to social justice and corporate social responsibility.

10.4 CORPORATE SOCIAL RESPONSIBLITY

10.4.1 Introduction to Corporate Social Responsibility

Corporate Social Responsibility ("CSR") is also synonymous with sustainable business practices and responsible corporate governance. CSR has been described as a "form of corporate self-regulation integrated into a business model ... business would embrace responsibility for the impact of their activities on the environment, consumers, employees, communities, stakeholders and all other members of the public sphere."[61] CSR has also been expressed as a legal concept that guides and encourages the regulation of corporate activity in a manner that requires business corporate decisions to be based on ethical principles. Deviations from these principles of corporate social responsibility, may be reflected in a breach of standards under the Code or strict liability offences, or both. This view is supported by Robert Riech who argues that, "... governments should set the agenda for social responsibility by the way of laws and regulation that will allow a business to conduct themselves responsibly".

---

[58]   Owen M. Fiss, "Against Settlement" in Julie MacFarlane, *Dispute Resolution: Readings and Case Studies* (Toronto: Emond Montgomery Publications, 2003) at 69-70.

[59]   Julie Macfarlane, *Dispute Resolution: Readings and Case Studies* (Toronto: Emond Montgomery Publications, 2003) at 198-99.

[60]   Julie Macfarlane, *The New Lawyer: How Settlement is Transforming the Practice of Law* (Vancouver: UBC Press, 2008) at 167.

[61]   Corporate Social Responsibility, defined; Wikipedia online: <http://en.wikipedia.org/wiki/Corporate_social_responsibility> at p. 1.

A move towards CSR and away from prosecutions requires support from regulators and prosecutors as well as corporations. The pursuit of higher fines against corporate offenders by crusading prosecutors is a form of "tunnel vision" that has been the well documented cause of many wrongful convictions in Canada and the United States.[62] CSR provides a broader mandate for corporate accountability and offers a broader choice of accountability tools. Some elements of criminal law now may facilitate CSR. Bill C-45 took a small step towards that direction since it may provide for ongoing regulatory scrutiny as part of a probationary order. However, Bill C-45 does not provide sufficient authority for such CSR concepts as an independent private sector inspector general.[63]

One of the first steps towards establishing legal recognition of the principles of CSR came on December 16, 2008, when the Danish parliament adopted a Bill making it mandatory for the largest companies in that country to include information on corporate social responsibility in their financial reports.[64] Seven elements of corporate social responsibility have been introduced by governments and regulatory bodies around the world.[65] Several authors have identified seven legal principles that identified with and reasonably defined the application of corporate responsibility. Those principles are a useful list for legislators and regulators to consider in establishing principles and criteria for a sentencing in terms of probation for corporate offenders. The seven principles of corporate social responsibility are as follows:

1. Integrated, sustainable decision making: This requires corporate leaders and decision makers to consider the full scope of social and environmental impact of their decisions;

2. Stakeholder engagement: This requires corporate decision makers to broadly define their stakeholders, and to engage them in the decision making regarding corporate goals and activities;

3. Transparency: This requires corporations to provide regular, periodic public reports on their social and environmental performance measured against relevant criteria;

4. Consistent best practices: Corporations commit to achieving the highest reasonable best practices, as may be required by statutes, regulations and codes, in the execution of their business activity;

---

[62] Margaret Beare, "Shouting Innocence from the Highest Rooftops" in Margaret Beare, ed., *Honouring Social Justice: Honouring Dianne Martin* (Toronto: University of Toronto Press, 2008) at 24.

[63] Kenneth E. Jull, "Corporate Criminal Liability: Outside the Penalty Box" in Margaret Beare, ed., *Honouring Social Justice: Honouring Dianne Martin* (Toronto: University of Toronto Press, 2008) at 245.

[64] M. Kerr, R. Janda & C. Pitts, *Corporate Social Responsibility - A Legal Analysis* (Markham, ON: LexisNexis Canada, 2009) at 6.

[65] *Ibid.*, at 1.

5. Precautionary principle: Corporate decision making that errs on the side of caution, when it relates to social and environmental issues, rather than requiring proof beyond a reasonable doubt of risk of harm from business activity, before it is restrained; and

6. Accountability: Corporations, and their officers and directors, must be openly accountable for the social and environmental impact and potential harm of a failure to meet proper best practices;

7. Community interest: Corporations must undertake initiatives and programs that contribute to the social, cultural, economic and environmental enrichment of the communities in which they operate.[66]

CSR can and should be addressed proactively, by statute and regulation, and also reactively by creative sentencing of corporations. Probationary terms for corporate offenders may reflect CSR principles. However, when corporations transgress the law, the failure to use appropriate sentencing and probationary tools is a gross omission from the tools necessary to achieve the movement towards CSR. As Fisse and Braithwaite observed:

> Where corporations are sanctioned for offences [*i.e.*, fines], in theory they are supposed to react by using their internal disciplinary systems to bring home individual accountability, but the law now makes little or no attempt to ensure that such a reaction occurs. The impact of enforcement can easily stop with a corporate pay-out of a fine or a monetary penalty, not because of any socially justified departure from the traditional value of individual accountability, but rather because it is the cheapest or most self-protective course for the corporate defendant to adopt.[67]

10.4.2 Corporate Social Responsibility Defined

At some level, it might be suggested that the idea of CSR is self defining; corporations are encouraged to behave in a manner which is "socially responsible". However, any such simplistic definition is illusory. While various definitions for CSR have been advanced by different governments and organizations, common themes may be seen in their overarching concern for human rights, labour rights, safety standards and occupational health and safety, and issues relating to environmental responsibility.

CSR may be viewed as the principle that corporations should respond to interests apart from, and in addition to, those of their shareholders.[68] However, the definitions of CSR advanced by governments and international organizations have tended to focus on corporate efforts to balance their economic activities with broader stakeholder interests. For example, the Gov-

---

[66]   *Ibid.*, at 91.

[67]   B. Fisse & J. Braithwaite, *Corporations, Crime and Accountability* (Cambridge: Cambridge University Press, 1993) at 1.

[68]   Canadian Democracy and Corporate Accountability Commission, Final Report, "The New Balance Sheet Corporate Profits and Responsibility in the 21st Century" (January 2002) at 5.

ernment of Canada takes the position that "CSR is generally understood to be the way a company achieves a balance or integration of economic, environmental, and social imperatives while at the same time addressing shareholder and stakeholder expectations".[69] However, it also suggests that CSR is "an evolving term that does not have a standard definition or a fully recognized set of specific criteria".[70]

A similar definition was adopted by the European Commission in 2006 as part of its most recent policy communication on CSR, which defined it as: "a concept whereby companies integrate social and environmental concerns in their business operations and in their interaction with their stakeholders on a voluntary basis".[71]

The United Kingdom defines CSR as: "how business takes account of its economic, social and environmental impacts in the way it operates — maximizing the benefits and minimizing the downsides".[72] Finally, what may be the broadest definition is offered by the United Nations: "CSR can be defined as the overall contribution of business to sustainable development".[73]

The World Business Council for Sustainable Development ("WBCSD") provides that "Corporate social responsibility is the commitment of business to contribute to sustainable economic development, working with employees, their families, the local community and society at large to improve their quality of life".[74] Amnesty International advocates for mandatory "global standards on business and human rights that will apply across borders to all companies ... (which) ... will provide governments with clear, common guidelines on how to address corporate behaviour on human rights".[75] A more specific call for action is made by the Corporate Responsibility Coalition ("CORE"), which argues that voluntary CSR efforts are insufficient and calls for "mandatory social and environmental reporting, enhanced directors' duties, and access to justice for affected communities".[76]

---

[69] *Ibid.*

[70] Industry Canada, "Corporate Social Responsibility", Overview, online: <http://www.ic.gc.ca/eic/site/csr-rse.nsf/eng/home>.

[71] The European Commission, Communication from the Commission to the European Parliament, The Council and the European Economic and Social Committee, "Implementing the Partnership for Growth and Jobs: Making Europe a Pole of Excellence on Corporate Social Responsibility" COM (2006) 136.

[72] U.K., Department of Trade and Industry, "Corporate Social Responsibility: A Government Update" (2004).

[73] United Nations, "CSR and Developing Countries - *What scope for government action?*", Sustainable Development Innovation Briefs, Issue 1 (February 2007).

[74] World Business Council for Sustainable Development, "Corporate Social Responsibility *The WBCSD's journey*" (January 2002) at 2.

[75] Amnesty International, "Address by Irene Khan, Secretary General of Amnesty International to the Opening Plenary of the Global Compact Leadership Summit 2007" (Public Statement presented to the Global Compact Leadership Summit 2007, July 5, 2007).

[76] The Corporate Responsibility Coalition and Save the Children U.K., D. Doane & A. Holder, "Why Corporate Social Responsibility is failing children" (2007).

Despite this apparent diversity of definitions, some authors have identified underlying themes which they suggest may define the concept.[77] They suggest that CSR may be viewed as an effort to integrate economic considerations with environmental and social needs, as well as corporate efforts to balance the interests of diverse stakeholders. As such, it may be viewed as a diverse set of practices which include "stakeholder engagement, company-wide commitments and strategies, measurable targets for improvement, training, CSR management practices, and public reporting".[78]

It might be noted that each of these definitions is wide ranging and provides little information regarding the policies and practices which advocates of CSR may be expected to advance. However, it has been suggested that this need not be seen as problematic, as what is "socially responsible" must be evaluated in the context of current issues and needs.[79] Thus, the broad scope of most conceptions and definitions of CSR may permit it to adapt to novel or evolving social needs. As such, CSR may emerge as a constantly evolving concept, rather than a fixed set of goals or practices.[80]

10.4.3 Objectives of Corporate Social Responsibility

Although a single definition for CSR may be elusive or even undesirable, clear themes emerge when one considers corporate efforts to behave in a socially responsible manner. These themes relate in many ways to the very origins and original purpose of corporations that were reviewed in Chapter 2. In particular, CSR activities appear to focus on four common ends: human rights, labour standards, safety standards and occupational health and safety, and issues relating to environmental responsibility.

The concern over human rights expressed by CSR advocates appears to have taken two primary forms. First, corporations are encouraged not to engage in human rights abuses in the course of their operations.[81] Additionally, while they may be compelled to comply with the national laws of the countries in which they operate, corporations are encouraged not to be complicit in encouraging or enabling human rights abuses carried out by governmental actors.[82] In cases where compliance with national law would require human rights violations, corporations have been encouraged to withdraw their operations from those nations.

CSR has been used to advocate increased labour standards in the international context. This has included support for the right to representation by

---

[77]   M. Kerr, R. Janda & C. Pitts, *Corporate Social Responsibility - A Legal Analysis* (Markham, ON: LexisNexis Canada, 2009) at 31.

[78]   *Ibid.*, at 32.

[79]   *Ibid.*, at 5.

[80]   *Ibid.* See also Industry Canada, "Corporate Social Responsibility", Overview, online: <http://www.ic.gc.ca/eic/site/csr-rse.nsf/eng/home>.

[81]   Canadian Democracy and Corporate Accountability Commission, Final Report, "The New Balance Sheet Corporate Profits and Responsibility in the 21st Century" (January 2002) at 8.

[82]   *Ibid.*

trade unions, the abolition of child labour and compulsory labour, and the abolition of discrimination based on grounds such as religion, race and gender.[83] As with the promotion of human rights, these labour standards may require corporations who practice CSR to adhere to a higher standard than that imposed by the prevailing national laws.

This concern for labour standards has also included calls for enhanced safety standards, and increased focus on Occupational Health and Safety ("OHS") as part of CSR. In particular, the exploitation of workers in the developing world has been tied to "devastating consequences on the health and safety of the workers involved".[84] Some organizations, including the WBCSD, have indicated that OHS should form a central part of any corporation's involvement in CSR initiatives.[85]

The WBCSD suggests that like labour standards, OHS forms a core part of a business operation, and as such, they may be expected to exert a high degree of control over them in practicing CSR. In contrast, however, any one business may have only a very attenuated influence over the legal regime in place at the national level. Recognizing this, support for OHS has been explicitly included in the CSR strategies of several nations, including the United Kingdom, France and Germany.[86]

Finally, CSR has also been used to encourage increased corporate consideration of environmental issues. Numerous aspects of corporate activity may be identified which have a large impact on the environment, including manufacturing, transport, resource usage, and the generation of polluting emissions or by-products.[87] In attempting to minimize these impacts, the environmental aspects of CSR have been related to the sustainable development movement, in part due to the observation that the environmental issues targeted by that movement are frequently seen as resulting from corporate action.[88] However, it has also been argued that, antagonism aside, this is a relationship of necessity, as the goal of environmental sustainability may be out of reach without the resources and innovation of the international corporate sector.[89]

---

[83]   *Ibid.*

[84]   *Ibid.*, at 10.

[85]   World Business Council for Sustainable Development, "Corporate Social Responsibility *The WBCSD's journey*" (January 2002) at 4.

[86]   European Commission, Directorate-General for Employment, Social Affairs and Equal Opportunities Unit D. 2, "Corporate Social Responsibility - National public policies in the European Union" (September 2007).

[87]   M. Kerr, R. Janda & C. Pitts, *Corporate Social Responsibility - A Legal Analysis* (Markham, ON: LexisNexis Canada, 2009) at 12.

[88]   *Ibid.*, at 18.

[89]   M. Kerr & M.C. Cordonier Segger, "Corporate Social Responsibility: International Strategies and Regimes" in M.C. Cordonier Segger & C.G. Weeramantry, eds., *Sustainable Justice: Reconciling Economic Social and Environmental Law* (Leiden: Martinus Nijhoff, 2005).

10.4.4 Drivers of Corporate Social Responsibility

CSR has a number of positive motivators or "drivers". It has been reported that the majority of companies currently publicly report their efforts on environmental and social issues, with approximately 90 per cent of European companies and 59 per cent of American companies including such information in their annual reports, or separate companion reports.[90] In Canada, such activities appear to have increased dramatically over the past decade, where the reporting rate for companies listed on the Toronto Stock Exchange was 35 per cent in 2001, but had risen to 60 per cent in 2003, and stands at 80 per cent as of 2007.[91] Meanwhile, even critics of CSR note that it has "won the battle of ideas".[92] The impetus behind this dramatic rise in participation in CSR comes from several sources, including public demand, the activities of NGOs, government encouragement or legislation, as well as voluntary action stemming from a corporation's own business interests.

Private citizens have increasingly come to question the role of corporations in society, and the manner in which they operate.[93] In part, this may be traced to the rise of transnational corporations, and the perception that such bodies may be effectively able to evade traditional forms of legal control.[94] This in turn has led to increased public pressure for corporations to behave in a manner which is socially responsible. Some corporations have responded to this social pressure by adopting CSR practices.[95]

In Canada, growing public concern over the role of corporations led to the establishment of the Canadian Democracy and Corporate Accountability Commission ("CDCAC"), a privately funded body which studied how to encourage greater CSR on the part of Canadian corporations.[96] CDCAC conducted public opinion polls, and found that "72 per cent believe that corporate executives should take social-responsibility concerns (impacts on communities, employees, the environment, and charitable activity) into account in pursuing profits."[97] In contrast, only 20 per cent believed that the only responsibility of a corporation was to enhance its competitiveness and profits.

Concern over corporate activity amongst the general public is reflected in the establishment of NGOs to advocate particular policy positions. These

---

[90]   M. Kerr, R. Janda & C. Pitts, *Corporate Social Responsibility - A Legal Analysis* (Markham, ON: LexisNexis Canada, 2009) at 33.

[91]   *Ibid.*, at 33-34.

[92]   C. Crook, "The Good Company" in "A Survey of Corporate Responsibility" *The Economist* (January 20, 2005) 374: 8410.

[93]   E. Broadbent, "The New Balance sheet: Corporate profits and Responsibility in the 21st Century" in *Responding to Globalization* (Queen's Annual Business Law Symposium 2002) at 1.

[94]   M. Kerr, R. Janda & C. Pitts, *Corporate Social Responsibility - A Legal Analysis* (Markham, ON: LexisNexis Canada, 2009) at 36.

[95]   *Ibid.*, at 35.

[96]   Canadian Democracy and Corporate Accountability Commission, Final Report, "The New Balance Sheet Corporate Profits and Responsibility in the 21st Century" (January 2002) at Preface.

[97]   *Ibid.*, at 15.

bodies have grown in number from the 1960s onwards, with some achieving considerable influence, including consultative status at the United Nations.[98] Many major international NGOs, including Greenpeace, the World Wildlife Federation and Oxfam, have specifically targeted the corporate sector to encourage action in areas as diverse as human rights, the environment, labour and other externalities, areas frequently advanced as a component of CSR.[99]

Governments have responded to the public pressure regarding the effects of corporate conduct on both the environment and the community at large with both legislation, and support for voluntary CSR initiatives.[100] These efforts may be illustrated by observing that a number of countries, including Canada,[101] the United Kingdom,[102] Germany,[103] France,[104] and the European Commission,[105] have departments which have specifically undertaken considerations of CSR.

A number of studies have supported the argument that corporate involvement in CSR activities may serve to enhance profitability. As early as 2001, the *Financial Times* noted that "Even on a sector-by-sector basis, shares of companies with a superior environmental or human rights record appear to outperform. Clean chemical companies will outperform dirty ones, clean oil companies will outperform dirty oil companies."[106] Similar observations have been made in respect of the mutual funds industry, with socially responsible investing growing at a rate markedly faster than the industry as a whole.[107] Several possible explanations for these results suggest themselves.

First, the support for corporate accountability found amongst the population at large is also reflected in the ranks of investors. In the CDCAC studies on attitudes toward corporate responsibility, it was found that 72 per cent of Canadians felt that corporations should have accountability that extends

---

[98] M. Kerr, R. Janda & C. Pitts, *Corporate Social Responsibility - A Legal Analysis* (Markham, ON: LexisNexis Canada, 2009) at 37.

[99] *Ibid.*

[100] *Ibid.*, at 51.

[101] Canadian Democracy and Corporate Accountability Commission, Final Report, "The New Balance Sheet Corporate Profits and Responsibility in the 21st Century" (January 2002) at 5.

[102] The United Kingdom, Department for Business Innovation & Skills, online: <http://webarchive.nationalarchives.gov.uk/+/http://www.berr.gov.uk//whatwedo/sectors/sustainability/corp-responsibility/page45192.html/>.

[103] Germany, Federal Ministry of Labour and Social Affairs, online: <http://www.csr-in-deutschland.de/portal/generator/4420/startseite.html>.

[104] France, France's National Sustainable Development Strategy, online: <http://www.diplomatie.gouv.fr/en/france-priorities_1/environment-sustainable-development_1097/sustainable-development_6420/france-national-sustainable-development-strategy_6422/index.html>.

[105] European Commission, Enterprise and Industry, Policies, online: <http://ec.europa.eu/enterprise/policies/sustainable-business/corporate-social-responsibility/index_en.htm>.

[106] Geoffrey Heal, "Mastering Investment: The bottom line to a social conscience" *Financial Times* (July 2, 2001).

[107] Canadian Democracy and Corporate Accountability Commission, Final Report, "The New Balance Sheet Corporate Profits and Responsibility in the 21st Century" (January 2002) at 5.

beyond their profit margins.[108] However, an even larger number of share-holders, 74 per cent, accepted the same principle.[109] In contrast, only 20 per cent of the shareholders surveyed felt that the only responsibility of the corporation was to operate competitively and generate profits.

These beliefs are reflected in the practice of Socially Responsible Investing ("SRI"), which has taken hold among some investors, and encourages the consideration of the "social and environmental consequences of investments".[110] In the United States, SRI has been observed to be growing at a faster rate than all other investment assets under professional management, with the total value of SRI assets estimated at $2.71 trillion in 2007.[111] Thus, the adoption of a corporate position on CSR may be seen in part as a response to shareholder demand.

In addition to this, it may be argued that the adoption of a CSR program has the effect of improving a corporation's image, with potential attendant business upsides. Again referring to the CDCAC studies, 75 per cent of Canadians (and a full 78 per cent of Canadian shareholders) thought that the government should not make purchases from companies with a poor history of social responsibility. As the Canadian Federal Government already ties procurement contracts to the employment-equity performance of bidder's for contracts of over $200,000, there is no reason in principle why this policy could not be extended to consider other matters falling under the rubric of CSR.[112]

Apart from responding to the desires of individual investors, or acting out of concern for their public image and profits, corporations may also be encouraged to adopt CSR by other sources of corporate capitalization, including lending bodies and insurers.[113] To encourage this, the United Nations Environment Programme ("UNEP") has created the UNEP Statement by Financial Institutions on the Environment & Sustainable Investment ("UNEP Financial Initiative"), which requires signatories to "... regard compliance with applicable environmental regulations and the use of sound environmental practices as important factors in demonstrating effective corporate management."[114] As of 2009, the UNEP Financial Initiative has been

---

[108] E. Broadbent, "The New Balance sheet: Corporate Profits and Responsibility in the 21st Century" in *Responding to Globalization* (Queen's Annual Business Law Symposium 2002) at 2.

[109] *Ibid.*

[110] M. Kerr, R. Janda & C. Pitts, *Corporate Social Responsibility - A Legal Analysis* (Markham, ON: LexisNexis Canada, 2009) at 47.

[111] The Social Investment Forum, *2007 Report on Socially Responsible Trends in the United States* (Washington D.C.: Social Investment Forum, 2007) at ii.

[112] Human Resources Development Canada, online: <http://www.servicecanada.gc.ca/cgi-bin/search/eforms/index.cgi?app=prfl&frm=lab1168&ln=eng>.

[113] M. Kerr, R. Janda & C. Pitts, *Corporate Social Responsibility - A Legal Analysis* (Markham, ON: LexisNexis Canada, 2009) at 49-51.

[114] United Nations Environment Programme (UNEP), Finance Initiative, Innovative Financing for Sustainability, "UNEP Statement by Financial Institutions on the Environment & Sustainable Development" (May 1997) at 2.3, online: <http://www.unepfi.org/fileadmin/statements/fi/fi_statement_en.pdf>.

signed by over 180 financial institutions, including some of the largest banks in the United States, such as Citigroup, JP Morgan Chase and the Bank of America.[115] Likewise, both the World Bank, and the International Financial Corporation ("IFC") make their loans conditional on compliance with environmental and social standards.[116]

UNEP has also issued a statement in respect of the insurance industry, the UNEP Statement of Environmental Commitment by the Insurance Industry ("UNEP Insurance Statement").[117] The UNEP Insurance Statement commits signatories to "reinforce the attention given to environmental risks in our core activities. These activities include risk management, loss prevention, product design, claims handling and asset management".[118] As such, signatory insurance agencies may be expected to consider a company's practices in relation to CSR in the provision of insurance policies.

10.4.5 Criticisms of Corporate Social Responsibility

While CSR has attained both widespread attention and acceptance in recent years, its principles and assumptions have not gone without criticism.[119] These criticisms have tended to fall broadly into three categories: arguments that corporate responsibility directed solely to shareholders is socially beneficial, observations that in certain situations CSR may create new problems apart from addressing existing ones, and finally, the suggestion that some CSR initiatives may amount to little more than corporate promotion efforts, while distracting public attention from more effective means of addressing social issues.

The suggestion that corporate actors need to engage in activities classed under the practice of CSR to benefit society has been criticized by those who believe that companies run solely to profit their shareholders not only provide a social good, but will naturally seek to accommodate their stakeholders.[120] The pursuit of corporate profit may serve broad social purposes. This view was recognized from the emergence of free market systems in the 18th century. This theory was memorably put by Adam Smith in *The Wealth of Nations*:

---

[115] United Nations Environment Programme (UNEP), Finance Initiative, Innovative Financing for Sustainability, "Our Members" online: <http://www.unepfi.org/signatories/index.html?&no_cache=1>.

[116] International Finance Corporation, "Environmental and Social Standards" online: <http://www.ifc.org/ifcext/sustainability.nsf/Content/EnvSocStandards>.

[117] United Nations Environment Programme (UNEP), Finance Initiative, Innovative Financing for Sustainability, "Statement of Environmental Commitment by the Insurance Industry" online: <http://www.unepfi.org/statements/ii/index.html>.

[118] *Ibid.*, at 2.1.

[119] See generally, "A Survey of Corporate Social Responsibility" *The Economist* (January 20, 2005) 374: 8410.

[120] C. Crook, "The Good Company" in "A Survey of Corporate Responsibility" *The Economist* (January 20, 2005) 374: 8410.

It is not from the benevolence of the butcher, the brewer, or the baker, that we expect our dinner, but from their regard to their own interest. We address ourselves, not to their humanity but to their self-love, and never talk to them of our own necessities but of their advantages.[121]

In the modern context, it has been suggested that profit may be viewed as a measure of the value that a corporation creates for society, if the price that people are willing to pay for goods reflects the value that people attach to them, and the costs associated with production reflects the cost incurred by society in their production.[122] Such a company run solely for profit would further benefit the public by supplying its employees with wages, its customers with a product they desire, and may in turn act as a customer to companies which supply it with the goods and materials it needs to conduct its own business.[123] Further, if the company is to persist, all of these groups must be satisfied in their transactions with it. Thus, the company's self-interest provides a powerful incentive to benefit groups with a direct interest in the corporation's actions, provided that it is properly situated in a competitive market.

Some applications of CSR principles have attracted criticism when carried to a logical extreme. For example, while the promotion of Western ideals of human rights and labour standards in developing nations may appear to be laudatory, a refusal to deal with nations which do not meet these high standards may have adverse consequences. Such a refusal may not result in an improvement in the lives of the affected people, and may cause net harm.[124]

It has been observed even in the absence of Western labour standards, the citizens of such a nation may benefit from continued wages and employment, conditions which may not be otherwise available to them. Further, direct foreign investment may serve to stimulate economic development.[125] As such, withdrawal from nations which do not meet international labour standards may result in reduced investment, with a loss of its attendant benefits, in some developing nations.

In some cases, a corporate withdrawal from developing nations may occur in response to public scrutiny of their labour practices, and an attendant backlash which harms the corporation's image.[126] In such instances, withdrawal would be motivated by the corporation's financial interests, rather than a consideration of the actual best interests of the citizens of the

---

[121] Adam Smith, "An Inquiry into the Causes of the Wealth of Nations" *The Wealth of Nations* (1776), at Book I, Chapter. II.

[122] "Profit and the Public Good" in "A Survey of Corporate Social Responsibility" *The Economist* (January 20, 2005) 374: 8410.

[123] C. Crook, "The Good Company" in "A Survey of Corporate Responsibility" *The Economist* (January 20, 2005) 374: 8410.

[124] *Ibid.*

[125] "The Union of Concerned Executives" in "A Survey of Corporate Social Responsibility" *The Economist* (January 20, 2005) 374: 8410.

[126] *Ibid.*

developing nation. Problematically, some voluntary or mandatory codes may encourage such corporate behaviour. An example of this may be viewed in the CDCAC Final Report, which suggested that where a corporation's activities in a country may result in violations of human rights standards, and protests to the government regarding this are ineffective, the company should be obliged to withdraw from that jurisdiction.[127] However, CDCAC continued to explicitly state that it was not calling for Canadian minimum-wage standards to be applied to corporations acting in the developing world, noting that such calls would "remove a legitimate competitive advantage from an economically less developed part of the world".[128]

In other instances, corporations have trumpeted their withdrawal from nations with poor labour standards.[129] Such actions may not adequately weigh the interests of stakeholders in developing nations, effectively keeping them in poverty, where they might otherwise have made an income well above the standards of their nation.[130]

While it may be difficult to find fault with the donation of funds to what may be admittedly worthy causes, it has been suggested that the equation is less clear when the money you choose to give is not your own. In the case of corporate executives, the donation of corporate funds represents an outlay of money ultimately owned by the shareholders of the corporation, rather than the executive in their personal capacity.[131] In turn, this may have the effect of simply shifting the source of money given to charity; shareholders, who might have expected to give money to charity on their own behalf, may now find the company they invest in making these decisions for them.

Questions have also been raised whether executive officers are the persons most suited to deciding which social initiatives are most deserving of funding. While a corporation's profits, or lack thereof, may be easily measured, concepts such as "social justice" or "environmental sustainability" may be less susceptible to evaluation.[132] Further, questions may arise as to which objectives are most worthy of the finite pool of resources dedicated to CSR, and whether a particular proposal may work to those ends more efficiently than another. It is uncertain that corporate executives are better placed to answer these questions than government officials, or indeed, private citizens,

---

[127] Canadian Democracy and Corporate Accountability Commission, Final Report, "The New Balance Sheet Corporate Profits and Responsibility in the 21st Century" (January 2002) at 5.

[128] Ibid., at 6.

[129] C. Crook, "The Good Company" in "A Survey of Corporate Responsibility" The Economist (January 20, 2005) 374: 8410.

[130] "The Union of Concerned Executives" in "A Survey of Corporate Social Responsibility" The Economist (January 20, 2005) 374: 8410.

[131] Ibid.

[132] "The World According to CSR" in "A Survey of Corporate Social Responsibility" The Economist (January 20, 2005) 374: 8410.

and whether numerous corporations, acting separately, can produce an optimal or even effective policy to address global problems.[133]

Concerns such as this may be exacerbated by the observation that almost all attempts to institute CSR would involve some initial costs, namely, the costs the corporation incurs to undertake their chosen initiative.[134] In cases where these initial costs are not outweighed by a net social benefit, or worse, where they create unintended social costs themselves, society would have been better off in the absence of such well meaning, but ill executed CSR endeavours. The accountability of such corporate decision makers in respect to their CSR practices has also been questioned.[135] Unlike politicians who may be expected to face public scrutiny come election time, the mechanisms of accountability for corporate charitable contributions are primarily internal.

Well meaning encouragement of CSR on the part of government or NGOs may also be perverted in instances where they act as a barrier to the entry of new firms into the marketplace.[136] In such cases established corporations may even support initiatives which will result in costs to them as they may benefit over time from reduced competition. However, such anti-competitive effects do not obviously act in the public interest.[137]

Some CSR practices have the potential to benefit both the community and increase the corporation's profitability. This may be achieved through enhanced public goodwill, or access to diversified sources of funding. While this may present opportunities in which both corporations and external stakeholders benefit from CSR practices, it may also encourage corporations to engage in token CSR to gain public goodwill without placing too much of a burden on their finances. As a result this "token CSR" may fail to create the lasting benefits that advocates of CSR would hope for, and may serve to prevent actions which would effectively regulate corporate behaviour.[138]

It has been suggested that CSR undertaken as a public relations exercise may serve to distract attention from issues relating to business ethics or practices while doing little to alleviate the underlying problems.[139] Further, by focusing attention on the corporation's relations with the environment and social stakeholders at large, some CSR may offer little to address problems with corporate management which focus their harms on corporate

---

[133] "Profit and the Public Good" in "A Survey of Corporate Social Responsibility" *The Economist* (January 20, 2005) 374: 8410.

[134] "The Union of Concerned Executives" in "A Survey of Corporate Social Responsibility" *The Economist* (January 20, 2005) 374: 8410.

[135] C. Crook, "The Good Company" in "A Survey of Corporate Responsibility" *The Economist* (January 20, 2005) 374: 8410.

[136] "Profit and the Public Good" in "A Survey of Corporate Social Responsibility" *The Economist* (January 20, 2005) 374: 8410.

[137] *Ibid.*

[138] C. Crook, "The Good Company" in "A Survey of Corporate Responsibility" *The Economist* (January 20, 2005) 374: 8410.

[139] *Ibid.*

shareholders, such as misleading financial disclosure, or excessive executive compensation.[140]

In some instances, the public impression of action created by CSR initiatives may serve as a substitution for, or an argument against, legislative or regulatory control which may have served as a more effective control of corporate behaviour.[141] This potential has led some organizations which create voluntary standards, such as UNEP to caution that "Voluntary initiatives must be seen as part of an integrated policy and regulatory framework", and should not be used as a replacement or substitutions for regulation.[142]

10.4.6 Voluntary Versus Mandatory Corporate Social Responsibility

The CSR literature has hotly debated the costs and benefits of voluntary versus mandatory imposition of CSR. CSR is driven by a number of factors, including the corporation's self interest, public pressure, NGOs, lender and insurer requirements and government regulation or legislation. It may be observed that some of these drivers, such as public pressure, or non-binding covenants, act to constrain corporate behaviour only as far as the corporation decides to regulate its own behaviour. In this sense they may be termed "voluntary" CSR. In contrast, compliance with legislation is typically mandatory, and as such may create hard requirements for corporations to engage in specified CSR practices.

Apart from the apparent bright line division between the voluntary nature of some covenants, and the binding nature of legislation, other forces may operate to mandate CSR practices without the requirement for governmental action. For example, requirements for the adoption of CSR practices may become effectively mandatory when they are adopted by large lending agencies or insurers as a condition of doing business. Likewise, socially responsible investing may exert strong pressures to engage in CSR where it is adopted by institutional investors, or perhaps by stock exchanges as a condition for listing.[143] In such cases there may be an overwhelming business argument for adopting at least some CSR practices. A similar effect may be imagined if CSR requirements were to be implemented by professional regulatory bodies, such as the Ontario College of Pharmacists, or the College of Physicians and Surgeons of Ontario. In such a scenario, compliance with the

---

[140] J. Kazanjian, "The Broadbent-Bennett Report and the Trouble with Tribbles", in *Responding to Globalization* (Queen's Annual Business Law Symposium, 2002) at 17-18.

[141] M. Kerr, R. Janda & C. Pitts, *Corporate Social Responsibility - A Legal Analysis* (Markham, ON: LexisNexis Canada, 2009) at 99.

[142] United Nations Environment Programme (UNEP), "Voluntary Initiatives: Current Status, Lessons Learnt and Next Steps", UNEP Discussion Paper, based on the UNEP Multi-Stakeholder Workshop on Voluntary Initiatives (Paris, September 20, 2000).

[143] Social Investment Forum, *2007 Report on Socially Responsible Investing Trends in the United States* (Washington D.C.: Social Investment Forum, 2007) at ii.

specified practices would become a non-legislated requirement for practicing in a given profession.

Corporations may also bind themselves to selected CSR practices through the contracts they choose to sign with suppliers, financial institutions or other corporations. Such contractual provisions may find their origin in the internal codes of conduct adopted by one party to the contract.[144] For example, some corporations such as Bombardier Inc. have included provisions in their Code of Ethics which require their suppliers and partners to also adhere to its standards, which include provisions for OHS as a component of CSR.[145]

While such CSR initiatives may have been agreed to by the corporation as a part of the contract negotiation, after the execution of the contract, they would be binding in their effect on the parties to the contract. Further, some situations may present a corporation with little choice other than to agree to bind themselves to the CSR initiatives required by a business partner. For example, small or medium sized businesses may have little negotiating power in regards to standard procurement contracts offered by major suppliers.

Finally, corporations may be bound to standards of behaviour similar to CSR through court decisions which find contrary practices to be tortious. For example, in the United States, the tort of public nuisance may be invoked where a public right is interfered with, by the defendant's unreasonable conduct, and the defendant failed to take reasonable precautions to prevent, control or minimize the harm resulting from their conduct.[146]

Such claims have frequently been brought against corporations accused of engaging in environmentally irresponsible practices.[147] While these claims have frequently been rejected on the ground that they raise non-justifiable political questions, a recent decision of the Second Circuit overturned such a dismissal, allowing a claim from eight state attorneys general to proceed against a collection of American electric power companies on the premise of their greenhouse gas emissions.[148] Should this claim, or others based on similar principles, ultimately result in a finding that the corporation was liable and result in an award of damages, the threat of similar litigation may act as a potent, preventative constraint on corporate behaviour.

The number of voluntary initiatives promoting compliance with various CSR standards has expanded in recent years so that they now number

---

[144] C. Crook, "The Good Company" in "A Survey of Corporate Responsibility" *The Economist* (January 20, 2005) 374: 8410.

[145] Bombardier, "Code of Ethics and Business Conduct", at 14 and 19, online: <http://www.bombardier.com/files/en/supporting_docs/CODE_EN_2005.pdf>.

[146] C. Crook, "The Good Company" in "A Survey of Corporate Responsibility" *The Economist* (January 20, 2005) 374: 8410.

[147] *Ibid.*

[148] *State of Connecticut, et al. v. American Electric Power Company Inc., et al.*, (2009) 582 F.3d 309.

in the thousands.[149] As they are created without the need for a legislative process, such initiatives may be implemented more quickly than a legislative response.[150] As such, they may offer a means to address sudden or rapidly developing issues.[151] Further, as such standards are privately adopted and implemented, they do not require administrative or financial support from the government in order to operate.[152]

The lack of a legislative process also provides a greater ability for voluntary initiatives to be tailored to the needs of the industries they are targeted at.[153] This stems in part from the fact that they may be drafted and implemented by the very corporations or industry groups they are ultimately intended to apply to.[154] In turn, this adaptability to corporate needs may encourage greater compliance, or more rapid adoption. The process of drafting, adopting and implementing voluntary CSR programs may also encourage cultural changes within the corporation, promoting proactive actions by the management responsible for adopting the standard.[155]

However, while voluntary initiatives thus have several advantages, they have been criticized, particularly with regard to their non-binding nature, which has led to questions regarding their effectiveness in practice.[156] In fact, a 2003 study by the Organization for Economic Cooperation and Development has suggested that few voluntary initiatives in respect of the environment have resulted in improvements significantly above the outcome which might have been expected without them.[157]

Several explanations may be offered for this lack of effectiveness. First, due to their voluntary adoption, voluntary CSR initiatives inevitably fail to capture all industry members.[158] This problem may be particularly acute where those corporations which resist the adoption of voluntary standards are also those with the worst records in the field the standards address. Further, in the absence of effective enforcement measures, even those com-

---

[149] United Nations Environment Programme (UNEP), "Voluntary Initiatives: Current Status, Lessons Learnt and Next Steps", UNEP Discussion Paper, based on the UNEP Multi-Stakeholder Workshop on Voluntary Initiatives (Paris, September 20, 2000).

[150] *Ibid.*

[151] C. Crook, "The Good Company" in "A Survey of Corporate Responsibility" *The Economist* (January 20, 2005) 374: 8410.

[152] *Ibid.*

[153] *Ibid.*

[154] *Ibid.*

[155] United Nations Environment Programme (UNEP), "Voluntary Initiatives: Current Status, Lessons Learnt and Next Steps", UNEP Discussion Paper, based on the UNEP Multi-Stakeholder Workshop on Voluntary Initiatives (Paris, September 20, 2000).

[156] *Ibid.*

[157] M. Kerr, R. Janda & C. Pitts, *Corporate Social Responsibility - A Legal Analysis* (Markham, ON: LexisNexis Canada, 2009) at 31.

[158] United Nations Environment Programme (UNEP), "Voluntary Initiatives: Current Status, Lessons Learnt and Next Steps", UNEP Discussion Paper, based on the UNEP Multi-Stakeholder Workshop on Voluntary Initiatives (Paris, September 20, 2000).

panies that do adopt a voluntary code may be able to disregard it where they are motivated to do so by other business interests.[159]

Problems may also arise where voluntary standards are drafted by industry members and fail to adequately address the social or environmental concerns they are addressed to. However, such an insufficient standard may still be used to create a show of action to garner public support, possibly all they were intended to do in the first place.[160] A particular damaging instance of this has been termed "regulatory capture", and occurs where the existence of voluntary standards are used to argue against the adoption of mandatory regulations or legislation.[161] In such cases, meaningful action may be prevented by ineffective voluntary actions.

While several organizations such the European Commission have defined CSR to encompass only voluntary initiatives, others, such as the government of Denmark, have passed legislation which mandates some minimum forms of CSR.[162] Legislative measures were contemplated in Canada, in the private members initiative, by Bill C-300 to regulate the behaviour of Canadian extraction companies in developing countries. Such mandatory initiatives, whether they arise from legislation or other sources, have a number of benefits which are missing in voluntary initiatives.

The clearest difference between mandatory initiatives and voluntary CSR initiatives is the enforceability of the former.[163] Where mandatory CSR requirements emerge from legislation, the specific mode of enforceability may be provided by that legislative document, and may include specific penalties which transgressors will be subject to, often through access to the courts.

The penalization of those who contravene mandatory CSR requirements might be expected to encourage higher levels of compliance with mandatory requirements. For example, the threat of a sufficiently substantial monetary penalty would be expected to engage the self-interest of the corporation so as to encourage it to proactively comply with the standard. This ability may be particularly important in situations where it is necessary to force corporate compliance with a CSR standard that is unlikely to be adopted voluntarily.[164] Such situations may arise where the CSR initiative

---

[159] The Corporate Responsibility Coalition and Save the Children U.K., D. Doane & A. Holder, "Why Corporate Social Responsibility is failing children" (2007) at 13.

[160] C. Crook, "The Good Company" in "A Survey of Corporate Responsibility" *The Economist* (January 20, 2005) 374: 8410.

[161] M. Kerr, R. Janda & C. Pitts, *Corporate Social Responsibility - A Legal Analysis* (Markham, ON: LexisNexis Canada, 2009) at 99.

[162] The European Commission, Communication from the Commission to the European Parliament, The Council and the European Economic and Social Committee, "Implementing the Partnership for Growth and Jobs: Making Europe a Pole of Excellence on Corporate Social Responsibility" COM (2006) 136.

[163] M. Kerr, R. Janda & C. Pitts, *Corporate Social Responsibility - A Legal Analysis* (Markham, ON: LexisNexis Canada, 2009) at 99.

[164] *Ibid.*, at 100.

will require dramatic corporate outlays to achieve, or will require the drastic alteration of normal business practices to achieve a pressing social or environmental need. Further, as this enforceability applies equally to all corporate actors who are subject to the CSR requirement, mandatory requirements avoid to some extent the problem of the refusal of some corporations to sign on to voluntary initiatives.[165]

There are several drawbacks associated with mandatory methods of imposing CSR, particularly when they emerge from legislative efforts. In contrast to the speed of adoption which may be achieved through voluntary measures, the time consuming nature of legislative undertakings may make regulatory solutions less responsive to quickly evolving situations.[166] Further, it has also been observed that legislation tends to be less tailored to industry needs, an issue which may be important where the regulation will apply to corporations in different sectors and of different sizes.[167]

Interestingly, while the potential for enforcement action and penalties have already been noted as the benefits of mandatory CSR, these same attributes also create downsides. For instance, with regard to regulation, the costs of enforcement are placed on the government, and limited enforcement resources may lead to increased evasive activity.[168] Further, some commentators have noted that monetary penalties may be insufficient to encourage compliance in all cases, and may come to be seen as merely another cost associated with the business.[169] In such instances, even mandatory regulations may be insufficient to regulate corporate behaviour.

While both voluntary and mandatory CSR have advantages and disadvantages, the debate as to whether CSR is best pursued through voluntary or mandatory means has been ongoing for some time.[170] Some governments, such as the European Commission, have defined CSR to include only corporate actions which are made on a "voluntary basis".[171] Likewise, as early as 1992 the United Nations supported the use of private voluntary initiatives to address both environmental and social issues.[172] In contrast, some govern-

---

[165] *Ibid.*

[166] United Nations Environment Programme (UNEP), "Voluntary Initiatives: Current Status, Lessons Learnt and Next Steps", UNEP Discussion Paper, based on the UNEP Multi-Stakeholder Workshop on Voluntary Initiatives (Paris, September 20, 2000) at 3.

[167] M. Kerr, R. Janda & C. Pitts, *Corporate Social Responsibility - A Legal Analysis* (Markham, ON: LexisNexis Canada, 2009) at 102.

[168] *Ibid.*, at 101.

[169] J. Bakan, *The Corporation: The Pathological Pursuit of Profit and Power* (Toronto: Viking Canada, 2004) at 79.

[170] M. Kerr, R. Janda & C. Pitts, *Corporate Social Responsibility - A Legal Analysis* (Markham, ON: LexisNexis Canada, 2009) at 93.

[171] The European Commission, Communication From The Commission To The European Parliament, The Council and the European Economic and Social Committee, "Implementing the Partnership for Growth and Jobs: Making Europe a Pole of Excellence on Corporate Social Responsibility" COM (2006) 136.

[172] The United Nations, Agenda 21, at Section IV, "Financial Resources and Mechanisms", online: <http://www.un.org/esa/dsd/agenda21/res_agenda21_33.shtml>.

ments, such as that of Denmark, have introduced mandatory CSR reporting requirements, while non-governmental organizations have cautioned that "Voluntary initiatives should not be proposed and adopted as substitutes for regulation".[173]

Some commentators have suggested that the debate between voluntary measures and mandatory measures is largely "futile", noting that while both approaches have advantages and drawbacks, they are not mutually exclusive, and voluntary initiatives may evolve into legal requirements. Thus, both mandatory and voluntary initiatives may play a "complementary role in promoting CSR".[174]

This approach of supporting voluntary measures with mandatory requirements has been supported by NGOs such as CORE and Save the Children, which have stated "specific regulatory actions can, and should, *strengthen* voluntary CSR commitments".[175] Further, in some cases mandatory initiatives have attracted widespread corporate support. An example of this may be seen in the "*Bali Communiqué*" which was supported by a large number of international businesses prior to the United Nations Climate Change Conference in 2007.[176] The *Communiqué* called for an "ambitious" and "legally-binding" agreement, arguing that it was necessary to promote investment in low carbon technologies. This observation suggests that the debate between voluntary and mandatory CSR measures need not always be painted as a war between corporate interests and social needs.

10.5 THE BILL C-300 PROPOSAL

10.5.1 Introduction to Bill C-300

Canada's new legislative initiative regarding CSR was the Bill C-300 Proposal. Bill C-300[177] (the "Bill") was a private members bill that was intended to promote environmental best practices and international human rights standards in regards to mining, oil or gas activities[178] of Canadian corporations who are receiving support from the Government of Canada to operate

---

[173] Proposal for an Act amending the Danish Financial Statements Act (Report on social responsibility for large businesses) October 8, 2008.

[174] M. Kerr, R. Janda & C. Pitts, *Corporate Social Responsibility - A Legal Analysis* (Markham, ON: LexisNexis Canada, 2009) at 103.

[175] The Corporate Responsibility Coalition and Save the Children U.K., D. Doane & A. Holder, "Why Corporate Social Responsibility is failing children" (2007) at 7.

[176] M. Kerr, R. Janda & C. Pitts, *Corporate Social Responsibility - A Legal Analysis* (Markham, ON: LexisNexis Canada, 2009) at 100.

[177] *Corporate Accountability of Mining, Oil and Gas Corporations in Developing Countries Act*, 2nd Sess., 40th Parl., 2009.

[178] C-300 defines "mining, oil or gas activities" as "the exploration and drilling for, and the production, conservation, processing or transportation of, mineral resources, oil or gas in the territory of a developing country or on the high seas where such activities are controlled directly or indirectly by a Canadian corporation".

in developing countries.[179] Introduced and promoted by John McKay, M.P. from Scarborough East (Liberal), the private members Bill was innovative yet politically controversial.

The Bill provided the Minister of Foreign Affairs and Minister of International Trade (the "Ministers") the ability to issue guidelines in respect to corporate accountability standards in mining, oil or gas activities for corporations receiving support from the Government of Canada to operate in developing countries.[180] The Bill proposed to implement a complaint reporting process for any suspected mining, oil or gas activities which may have violated any environmental best practices and international human rights standards. After a complaint was issued, the Ministers may choose to investigate the merits of the claim. If an investigation is conducted, the Ministers were then required to disclose the results to the public in the *Canada Gazette*, and if necessary, impose other penalties and/or sanctions, which may include the removal of federal funding, provided in other statutes related to mining, oil and gas activities, such as the *Export Development Act, Department of Foreign Affairs and International Trade Act, Canada Pension Plan Investment Board Act* and the *Special Economic Measures Act.*[181]

The mechanisms provided in the Bill authorized the Ministers to receive complaints of any Canadian companies engaged in mining, oil or gas activities from any Canadian citizen or permanent resident, including any resident or citizen of a developing country where such activities are occurring. The complaint was required to be in writing and identify the relevant provisions of the guidelines which had not been complied with as well as any reasonable grounds supporting the belief that a contravention occurred.

If the Minister receiving the complaint determined it was frivolous, vexatious or made in bad faith, they could decline to investigate the matter. However, in the event the Minister receiving the complaint decides to conduct an examination, section 4(4) of the Bill allowed the Minister to consider information from the corporation or the public, including evidence from witnesses outside of Canada. In addition, the Ministers were able to examine a matter on their own initiative if they have reason to believe that a corporation engaged in mining, oil or gas activities has contravened a guideline set out in section 5 of the Bill.

Whether the complaint was frivolous or not, the Ministers were required to publish the results of their determination, including the reasons, of any investigation conducted within 8 months after the complaint had been received. If the Ministers found that a corporation acted inconsistently with one of the guidelines, they were required to notify the President of Export

---

[179] C-300 defines "developing countries" as "countries and territories named in the list of countries and territories eligible for Canadian development assistance established by the Minister of International Cooperation".

[180] Guidelines are specified under section 5 of the Bill.

[181] To provide the Ministers with such authority, the Bill further proposed to amend relevant provisions in these Acts.

Development Canada and the Chairperson of the Canada Pension Plan Investment Board.

Furthermore, the Ministers were required to notify the Governor in Council should they determine that any inconsistency of the guidelines set out in section 5 of the Bill has, or will, give rise to grave breach of international peace and security or international human rights within section 4 of the *Special Economic Measures Act.*[182]

Section 5 of the Bill set out how the Minister was to construct the guidelines. It reads as follows:

5. (1) Within 12 months of the coming into force of this Act, the Ministers shall issue guidelines that articulate corporate accountability standards for mining, oil or gas activities.

(2) The guidelines shall incorporate:

(a)   the IFC's[183] *Policy on Social & Environmental Sustainability, Guidance Notes to those standards, and Environmental, Health and Safety General Guidelines*;

(b)   the *Voluntary Principles on Security and Human Rights*;

(c)   human rights provisions that ensure corporations operate in a manner that is consistent with international human rights standards; and

(d)   any other standard consistent with international human rights standards.

(3) In carrying out their duties under subsection (1), the Minsters shall offer to consult with government departments or agencies, representatives of the mining, oil and gas industries, non-governmental organizations and other interested persons in or outside Canada as they may see fit.

(4) Guidelines issued under this section shall be made available to the public, and the Ministers shall give notice of them in the *Canada Gazette* and in any other manner that the Ministers consider appropriate.

The Minister was required to submit an annual report to both Houses of Parliament within three years of the Bill coming into force and every year thereafter. The report was required to comment on the Act's provisions and contain any recommendations for amendments.

Review of the report must be completed by a committee designated by the House of Commons and a review of that report must be submitted within 60 days. Review of the Act was to be done by a designated Committee in the House of Commons within five years of it coming into force. The Commit-

---

[182] Section 4 of the *Special Economic Measures Act*, S.C. 1992, c. 17, allows the Governor in Council, to call upon the Canadian members of an international organization to take economic measures against a foreign state where the Governor in Council is of the opinion that a grave breach of international peace and security has occurred that has or is likely to result in a serious international crisis.

[183] IFC is defined as International Finance Corporation, and is affiliated with the World Bank Group.

tee designated by the House of Commons was to also submit a report within one year of the implementation of Bill C-300.

Sections 8 to 11 proposed amendments to the following 4 statutes: the *Export Development Act, Department of Foreign Affairs and International Trade Act, Canada Pension Plan Investment Act* and the *Special Economic Measures Act.* These amendments enhance the enforcement of the Bill and read as follows:

a) *Export Development Act* is amended by adding the following after section 10.1:

10.2 (1) The Corporation *shall not enter into, continue or renew a transaction* related to mining, oil or gas activities as that term is defined in the *Corporate Accountability of Mining, Oil and Gas Corporations in Developing Countries Act,* unless such activities are consistent with the guidelines issued under section 5 of the Bill.

(2) Continued compliance with the guidelines issued under section 5 of the *Corporate Accountability of Mining, Oil and Gas Corporations in Developing Countries Act* shall be a *condition to any contract* entered into by the Corporation related to mining, oil or gas activities within the meaning of that Act. [emphasis added]

b) Section 10 of the *Department of Foreign Affairs and International Trade Act* is amended by adding the following after subsection (3):

(4) In carrying out his or her duties and functions under paragraphs 2(d) and (e) and 3(a) that relate to mining, oil or gas activities as that term is defined in the *Corporate Accountability of Mining, Oil and Gas Corporations in Developing Countries Act,* the Minister shall ensure that these activities are consistent with the guidelines issued under section 5 of that Act.

(5) For greater certainty, with the exception of ordinary consular services available to all Canadian citizens, *no undertaking made through a program developed by the Minister in the exercise of his or her powers under this section shall promote or support mining, oil or gas activities, as that term is defined in the Corporate Accountability of Mining, Oil and Gas Corporations in Developing Countries Act, that are inconsistent with the guidelines* issued under section 5 of that Act. [emphasis added]

c) Section 36 of the *Canada Pension Plan Investment Board Act* is renumbered as subsection 36(1) and is amended by adding the following:

(2) In taking into consideration the standards and procedures that a person of ordinary prudence would exercise, every investment manager who invests the assets of the Board shall take into consideration the provisions of section 5 of the *Corporate Accountability of Mining, Oil and Gas Corporations in Developing Countries Act.*

(3) *Every investment manager who invests the assets of the Board shall ensure that the assets are not invested in any corporations whose activities have been found by either Minister, as that term is defined in the Corporate Accountability of Mining, Oil and Gas Corporations in De-*

*veloping Countries Act, to be inconsistent with the guidelines referred
to in section 5 of the Corporate Accountability of Mining, Oil and Gas
Corporations in Developing Countries Act.* [emphasis added]

d)   Subsection 4(1) of the *Special Economic Measures Act* is replaced by
      the following:

*4. (1) The Governor in Council may make such orders and regulations
with respect to the restriction or prohibition of any of the activities referred to subsection (2) in relation to a foreign state*

> *(a) where the Governor in Council deems it necessary for the pur-
> pose of implementing a decision, resolution or recommendation of
> an international organization, of which Canada is a member, that
> calls on its members to take economic measures against a foreign
> state;*

> *(b) where the Governor in Council is of the opinion that a grave
> breach of international peace and security has occurred that has
> resulted, or is likely to result, in a serious international crisis; and*

> *(c) where the Governor in Council is of the opinion that grave
> breaches of human rights have occurred in the foreign state and
> continue or are likely to continue.* [Emphasis added]

*(1.1) For greater certainty, "grave breaches of human rights" means
"crime against humanity", "genocide" or "war crime" as defined in the
Crimes Against Humanity and War Crimes Act.*

10.5.2 John McKay and Bill C-300

At the time of tabling the private members Bill, John McKay was a member
of the federal Liberal Party and Her Majesty's legal opposition. Since he
first tabled the Bill on February 9, 2009, Mr. McKay has received significant
domestic and international reaction for Bill C-300. Interest groups such as
Development and Peace (Canada), Amnesty International, Mennonite Central Committee, Christian Reform, World Vision, Evangelical Fellowship,
Halifax Initiative, Make Poverty History, Mining Watch Canada, Africa
Files, The North-South Institute, Canadian Labour Congress, Ecojustice
Canada, Rights and Democracy, Social Justice Committee of Montreal, and
Canadian Network on Corporate Accountability all publicly declared their
support for the Bill. In addition, John McKay received strong political support from the Bloc Québécois as well as members of the Liberal party. As
part of his initiative to increase public support, McKay has also received
over 500,000 postcards from the Canadian public advocating the passage of
Bill C-300.[184]

On September 20, 2010, Liberal M.P. John McKay gave a speech in
the House of Commons regarding Bill C-300. During this speech, John
McKay highlighted the high level of domestic and international support of

---

[184] CPAC Bill C-300 Broadcast (October 30, 2010) online: <http://www.youtube.com/watch?v=
7kAsAfiyBBM>.

the Bill as a symbol of why Canadian mining companies operating in developing countries need stronger CSR measures. McKay spoke on the declining reputation of Canadian mining companies in developing countries, and argued that there must be a solid basis for the countless allegations made against these companies, as they range from non-compliant environmental practices, to fundamental human right violations and political corruption charges. McKay also refuted many of the criticisms against the Bill which contend that it is draconian, causes reputational damage to the Canadian mining industry, and deters companies from doing business in Canada as it gives incentives for them to move into other jurisdictions. McKay rejects these accusations and argues that the Bill is a modest initiative which provides a process for the government to investigate allegations made against mining companies operating in developing countries. As McKay argued;

> This really is a modest bill. It has run into a virtual tsunami of objections from the industry and the government. Government members may face clear and overwhelming testimony from those who have chosen to turn their backs on the poor, the helpless and the aboriginal. By voting against this bill, they embrace the status quo. If this bill does not pass, we will have failed vulnerable people and struggling democracies. We will be diminished in the eyes of the world. We will erode our credibility to speak in international fora. We will be smaller in every way.[185]

10.5.3 Support for Bill C-300

As previously mentioned, numerous special interest groups have publicly declared their support for Bill C-300. Publicly, one of the strongest advocates for the Bill was Mining Watch Canada. On a Business News Network interview, Catherine Coumans, argued that the Bill addressed the declining reputation of Canadian mining companies operating in developing countries and provides incentives for them to follow Canadian standards for CSR.[186] The argument is that Canadian taxpayers have the right to encourage mining companies, that are receiving funding from their government, to behave in a socially responsible way.

In September 2009, McGill University Faculty of Law professor, Richard Janda published a report entitled "Bill C-300: Sound and Measured Reinforcement for CSR".[187] The report states that Bill C-300 will likely provide a competitive advantage, not disadvantage, for Canadian companies operating internationally as it sets higher standards for CSR. Janda also

---

[185] House of Commons Debates, No. 066, 3rd Sess., 40th Parl., (September 20, 2010) online: <http://www.parl.gc.ca/HousePublications/Publication.aspx?Doc=66&Language=E&Mode=1&Parl=40&Pub=Hansard&Ses=3>.

[186] "Will Bill C-300 Pass?" Business News Network (October 27, 2010) online: <http://watch.bnn.ca/squeezeplay/october-2010/squeezeplay-october-27-2010/#clip366784>.

[187] Richard Janda "Bill C-300: Sound and Measured Reinforcement for CSR", A Report on the Legal and Policy Dimensions of Bill C-300 Prepared for the Canadian Network on Corporate Accountability (September 2009) online: <http://www.johnmckaymp.on.ca/images/news manager/newsfiles/bill%20c-300%20report%20-%20final.pdf>.

addresses a number of substantive legal issues raised by its critics as he succinctly writes:

> Whereas it is true that there are constraints upon the exercise of the federal trade and commerce power in regard to the regulation of a single industry, such constraints are inapplicable to Bill C-300. Rather, Bill C-300 would simply place a valid set of conditions upon existing government support to the extractive sector. The general requirement that a complaint appear to be reasonable on its face is sufficiently stringent to allow the Minister in question efficiently to screen out complaints that are frivolous and vexatious. While one of its underlying purposes is to promote the responsible conduct of Canadian mining, oil, and gas companies operating in developing countries, Bill C-300 does not apply extraterritorially. The direct effects of Bill C-300 are domestic and within federal jurisdiction ... Bill C-300 complaints mechanism is consistent with the administrative law standards of procedural fairness and natural justice. The international standards referred to in s. 5(2) of Bill C-300 are fully transparent and provide a strong basis for a regulatory framework that establishes a level playing field at the global level. There are no adverse legal implications arising from the fact that the Ministers have up to twelve months to issue the guidelines ... There is no conflict between government representatives receiving evidence from witnesses abroad and the courts' exclusive adjudicative role. Indeed, there is ample precedent for such foreign fact finding. All of the material terms contained in Bill C-300 have been given adequate definition directly in its provisions, through incorporation by reference, or in light of a construction of the bill's purpose and meaning as a whole.[188]

10.5.4 Criticisms of Bill C-300

Critics contend that the Bill is significantly flawed in its language, jurisdiction and policy perspective. Substantively, critics argue that the Bill does not contain fair procedural guidelines for mining companies operating in developing countries. In addition, the Bill did not adequately describe how the Ministers are to implement the broadened authority under C-300. Considering how severe the sanctions could potentially be, critics argued that the Bill was "draconian" since it provided vague and unclear guidelines, which are prone to being politically abused by opposing parties and industry competitors. Issues of extraterritoriality and the authority to issue sanctions, such as demanding that the Canada Pension Plan remove its investments of mining companies violating CSR guidelines are also unpractical and problematic from a jurisdictional point of view. From a policy perspective, critics were concerned how the Bill "targets" Canadian mining companies as it provides their competitors with a distinct commercial advantage in foreign markets. Some critics contend that the Bill acts as a punitive mechanism for alleged violation of CSR as one Toronto-based lawyer states,

---

[188] *Ibid.*

> In a best case scenario, the adoption of Bill C-300 will create a duplication of many aspects of CSR work already performed more competently through existing organizations. In a worst case scenario, it establishes a punitive approach to social responsibility and risks setting the mining industry back by many years in terms of its environmental sustainability, diplomatic, community and social responsibility achievements to date.[189]

Furthermore, the increased financial resources needed to implement C-300 and investigate the claims brought before the Ministers may be difficult for the government to budget. Politically, there is strong sentiment regarding the creation of a procedural process whereby competitors of Canadian mining companies can easily abuse the complaint process by reporting frivolous accusations against Canadian mining companies.[190]

10.5.5 Federal Government Corporate Social Responsibility Initiatives

The Bill C-300 private members bill also resulted in some CSR initiatives by the Conservative Government of Prime Minister Stephen Harper. The Department of Foreign Affairs and International Trade defined CSR "as the way companies integrate social, environmental, and economic concerns into their values and operations in a transparent and accountable manner". Bill C-300 was one of the by-products of wide stakeholder consultation and was aimed to be consistent with the National Roundtables on Corporate Social Responsibility (CSR) and the Canadian Extractive Sector in Developing Countries ("Roundtables").[191]

The Roundtables are a response to the 38th Parliament's Standing Committee on Foreign Affairs and International Trade report entitled, "Mining in Developing Countries — Corporate Social Responsibility".[192] An Advisory Group Report was released on March 29, 2007 and provides broad recommendations regarding how to establish and implement a CSR framework for Canadian mining, oil and gas companies operating abroad. If implemented, the CSR framework would establish standards and reporting obligations for Canadian companies and create an ombudsman office to in-

---

[189] Michael Bourassa, "Bill C-300 Threatens Canada's International Extractive Sector" (August 2009) Fasken Martineau website online: <http://www.fasken.com/en/bill_c-300_threatens_canadas_international_extractive_sector/>.

[190] The European Commission, Communication From The Commission To The European Parliament, The Council and the European Economic and Social Committee, "Implementing the Partnership for Growth and Jobs: Making Europe a Pole of Excellence on Corporate Social Responsibility" COM (2006) 136; U.K., Department of Trade and Industry, "Corporate Social Responsibility: A Government Update" (2004).

[191] Department of Foreign Affairs and International Trade, "National Roundtables on Corporate Responsibility (CSR) and the Canadian Extractive Industry in Developing Countries" (March 29, 2007) online: <http://www.mining.ca/www/media_lib/MAC_Documents/Publications/CSRENG.pdf>.

[192] Department of Foreign Affairs and International Trade, "Mining in Developing Countries – Corporate Social Responsibility" (October 2005) online: <http://www.international.gc.ca/trade-agreements-accords-commerciaux/assets/pdfs/scfait-response-en.pdf>.

vestigate and assess complaints. Enforcement mechanisms are also proposed as procedures for withholding government services to companies in cases of serious non-compliance are contained in the report. Recommendations supporting the development of tools to promote CSR practice in the extractive sector and adherence to the CSR framework are also provided.

Furthermore, as referenced in section 5 of Bill C-300, the guidelines are to be based on the International Finance Corporation's Policy on Social and Environmental Sustainability,[193] Guidance Notes to those standards, and Environmental, Health and Safety General Guidelines[194] and the Voluntary Principles on Security and Human Rights.[195]

10.5.6 Government's Final Position on Bill C-300

The Conservative Government's ultimate position on Bill C-300 is that it did not support the Bill and voted against it. The Liberal leader, Michael Ignatieff was absent from the House of Commons when the vote on Bill C-300 was taken, even though he was in the vicinity of the House of Commons that day. Mr. Ignatieff's lack of interest and lack of leadership on CSR appeared to be inconsistent with his prior career as a Harvard professor of history and international affairs. On October 27, Bill C-300 was defeated in the House of Commons 140 to 134.[196]

After the defeat of Bill C-300 the majority of the commentary surrounding the Bill was still positive as this excerpt best describes:

> The narrow defeat in the House of Commons of Bill C-300, The Responsible Mining Act, marks a significant turning point for the country. In spite of an unprecedented and sustained year-long lobbying effort by the mining industry aimed at defeating the Bill, the close vote reflects the degree to which legislators have come to understand the need to regulate the activities of Canadian mining companies operating internationally ... 'The high profile industry drive to stop Bill C-300 was fuelled by profits from global mining operations and tax payer dollars,' says Coumans. 'It was a campaign based on fear mongering and in defence of continuing impunity in weak governance zones around the world,' she adds. 'Those who fought Bill C-300 are on the wrong side of history and will not ultimately be able to stop the push

---

[193] International Finance Corporation, "International Finance Corporation's Policy on Social and Environmental Sustainability" (April 30, 2006) online: <http://www.ifc.org/ifcext/sustainability. nsf/AttachmentsByTitle/pol_SocEnvSustainability2006/$FILE/SustainabilityPolicy.pdf>.

[194] International Finance Corporation, "Environmental and Social Review Procedures Manual" (September 23, 2010) online: <http://www.ifc.org/ifcext/sustainability.nsf/AttachmentsByTitle/ pol_ESRP_Manual/$FILE/ESRP_Manual.pdf>.

[195] See online: <http://www.voluntaryprinciples.org/>.

[196] Full results of this vote can be found in House of Commons Debates, No. 088, 3rd Sess., 40th Parl., (October 27, 2010) online: <http://www.parl.gc.ca/HousePublications/Publication.aspx? Doc=88&Language=E&Mode=1&Parl=40&Pub=Hansard&Ses=3>.

to secure greater justice for those who suffer from unconscionable mining practices.[197]

10.5.7 The Future of Corporate Social Accountability

It has been observed by critics of CSR, that the stage has largely been ceded to those who advocate it.[198] Few corporate leaders would be expected to stand up and argue in public against efforts to rein in what may be seen as harmful corporate practices.[199] Thus, while there are still concerns as to the efficacy of CSR, and debate over its implementation, it appears to be positioned to remain on public and corporate agendas for some time. With this in mind, several trends for the future of CSR may be identified, including a trend towards stronger legislative measures, increased involvement by developing nations, and the coming issuance of ISO 26000, a guidance standard from the International Standards Association on social responsibility.

Voluntary initiatives have been met with increasing scepticism in regards to their ability to effectively motivate changes to corporate behaviour.[200] To remedy this, calls have been made for such voluntary measures to be supported by binding regulatory measures.[201] Such a policy appears to be widely popular with the public as well, with one survey finding that 80 per cent of the Canadian population would support the government setting social responsibility standards.[202] However, some commentators have questioned the effectiveness of such strategies, noting that the increasing globalization of both the capital and products markets may weaken the ability of legislation at the national level to effectively govern corporate behaviour.[203] As a result, it has been suggested that increasing regulation from international bodies will be necessary for CSR to effectively protect human rights.

Despite these misgivings, some tendency towards the increased use of regulation at the national level has already been observed, such as in Canada, where legislation has been introduced that would encourage the mining

---

[197] "Canada: Vote on Bill C-300 Signals Strong Momentum towards Regulation of Canadian Mining Industry Overseas", full pdf version can be found on the Africa Files website online: <http://www.africafiles.org/article.asp?ID=24518>.

[198] C. Crook, "The Good Company" in "A Survey of Corporate Responsibility" *The Economist* (January 20, 2005) 374: 8410.

[199] J. Kazanjian, "The Broadbent-Bennett Report and the Trouble with Tribbles", *Responding to Globalization* (Queen's Annual Business Law Symposium, 2002) at 16.

[200] See for example, M. Kerr, R. Janda & C. Pitts, *Corporate Social Responsibility - A Legal Analysis* (Markham, ON: LexisNexis Canada, 2009) at 33; United Nations Environment Programme (UNEP), "Voluntary Initiatives: Current Status, Lessons Learnt and Next Steps", UNEP Discussion Paper, based on the UNEP Multi-Stakeholder Workshop on Voluntary Initiatives (Paris, September 20, 2000).

[201] *Ibid.*

[202] R. Davis, "The Enron Pension Jigsaw: Assembling Accountable Corporate Governance by Fiduciaries" (2003) 36 U.B.C. L. Rev. 541-574, at para. 53.

[203] L. Strine, "Human Freedom And Two Friedmen: Musings On The Implications Of Globalization For The Effective Regulation Of Corporate Behavior" (2008) 58 U.T.L.J. 241 at 268 and 272.

industry to conform to presently non-binding initiatives such as the IFC's Policy on Social & Environmental Sustainability through the threat of losing access to government financial support for their overseas initiatives. Other countries, such as Denmark, have already adopted binding regulation, even though, as a member state of the European Union, it is encouraged by the European Commission to recall that CSR should be voluntary.[204] It remains possible that the coming years will see this trend continue, with further legislation introduced to encourage new CSR practices, or to solidify compliance with existing voluntary standards.

The developing influence of China, Brazil, Russia and India, has been noted as a possible "historic shift", in the global distribution of power and wealth.[205] As a result, the standards and policies of these nations have been identified as an emerging influence on global standards, potentially including CSR practices.

This possibility has been met with some trepidation, particularly due to the observation that while China has issued positive statements in respect of CSR, its human rights, environmental, workplace safety and public safety record remain of concern.[206] Indeed, several international corporations have been implicated in complicity in human rights abuses occurring in China.[207] It has been suggested that increased conformance to global CSR standards may emerge in China as a result of the increasing possibility that its companies may face either consumer backlash or exclusion from some SRI funds due to non-compliance.[208] Indeed, one study has stated that the best predictor of whether Chinese corporations have a CSR policy is their ranking amongst the Fortune 500.[209]

Finally, the International Standards Association ("ISO") is currently finalizing ISO 26000, a voluntary guidance document regarding social responsibility which is intended to "distil a globally relevant understanding of what Social Responsibility is and what organizations need to do to operate in a socially responsible way".[210] ISO 26000 has been released as a Draft Inter-

---

[204] Proposal for an Act amending the Danish Financial Statements Act (Report on social responsibility for large businesses) October 8, 2008; The European Commission, Communications From The Commission to The European Parliament, The Council and the European Economic and Social Committee, "Implementing the Partnership for Growth and Jobs: Making Europe a Pole of Excellence on Corporate Social Responsibility" COM (2006) 136.

[205] M. Kerr, R. Janda & C. Pitts, *Corporate Social Responsibility - A Legal Analysis* (Markham, ON: LexisNexis Canada, 2009) at 576.

[206] *Ibid.*, at 578.

[207] J. Kahn, "Yahoo helped Chinese to prosecute journalist" *The New York Times* (September 8, 2008).

[208] M. Kerr, R. Janda & C. Pitts, *Corporate Social Responsibility - A Legal Analysis* (Markham, ON: LexisNexis Canada, 2009) at 579.

[209] J.G. Ruggie, *Human Rights Policies of Chinese Companies: Results from a Survey*, Harvard University, John F. Kennedy School of Government online: <http://www.business-humanrights.org/Documents/Ruggie-China-survey-Sep-2007.pdf>.

[210] The International Organization for Standardization (ISO), Central Secretariat, "ISO and Social Responsibility" (2006) .

national Standard ("DIS"), which provides an indication as to the shape the final text will take. Comments on the draft text were collected until February 14, 2010, and the final text is expected to be published as an International Standard in late 2010.[211]

The DIS posits that CSR has seven core elements: organizational governance, human rights, labour practices, the environment, fair operating practices, consumer issues and community involvement and development, and provides detailed guidance in respect of each.[212] Additionally, the DIS provides information regarding how these principles may be put into practice within an organization, including how to identify areas of action which are relevant to the operation of the corporation, and how organizations may best exercise influence with others so as to promote social responsibility.[213]

ISO 26000 is intended to apply widely to both private and public organizations, whether they operate in the profit or non-profit sectors.[214] However, it explicitly provides that it is not intended as a management system standard.[215] As such, the ISO does not intend it to be used for certification purposes, or regulatory or contractual use. Thus, ISO 26000 may be considered a voluntary guidance document on the practice of CSR.

---

[211] The ISO, Future ISO 26000 standard on social responsibility published as Draft International Standard (September 14, 2009) online: <http://www.iso.org/iso/pressrelease.htm?refid=Ref1245>.

[212] The ISO, Draft International Standard ISO/DIS 26000, at 29.

[213] *Ibid.*, at 67-69.

[214] *Ibid.*, at vi.

[215] *Ibid.*, at 1.

INDEX